5TH EDITION

HARBRACE
COLLEGE
HANDBOOK

HARCOURT, BRACE & WORLD, INC.

New York · Burlingame

To the Instructor

The *Harbrace College Handbook* is both a guide for the individual writer and a text for use in class. It presents its subject matter in a readily usable form, and thus lightens the instructor's task of reading student papers.

Numbers. The book contains only thirty-five major sections, or numbers, referring to the principles of effective writing. These include (as has been shown by a comprehensive examination of student writing) everything to which instructors normally refer in marking papers. But the principles less frequently needed have not been overlooked. They are subordinated logically to the thirty-five primary numbers and may be found readily by reference to the back end papers or to the detailed index. If an instructor wishes to have any of these subordinate principles conveniently before his students, he can have them added in the blanks provided on the chart inside the front cover. Some college students may need Sections 1-18 only for review or for occasional reference.

Symbols. Instead of the simplified list of numbers, the instructor may, if he prefers, use the corresponding symbols. Most of these symbols are well known to English teachers; they are entered on both front and back charts.

General Plan. The sections on **Sentence Sense (1)** and **Grammatical Terms (35)** are general sections. The former may be used, whenever needed, as an introduction to the other sections; the latter should be used throughout as a glossary of terms. For corrections of specific errors, students will normally be referred to Sections **2-34.** Many instructors may wish to begin with Section **32, Planning and Writing the Whole Composition.** Emphasis on good subject matter and clarity of organization will help the student keep in mind the primary objectives of his writing. Otherwise the correction of the many errors in grammar, mechanics, punctuation, and spelling may lead some students to consider these secondary matters of more importance than clarity of thought.

Drill Materials. Exercises are provided both for the major sections and for many subsections. Many of these exercises consist of lively paragraphs instead of conventional lists of unrelated sentences. Many other exercises are of a positive type, in which the student is asked not to correct errors but to give reasons why sentences are correct, to drill orally so that correct forms will sound right, or to compose good sentences to illustrate the principle being studied. Some classes may need very little of the drill materials; others may need all of them, or even additional exercises such as those in the *Harbrace College Workbook,* Form 5 (keyed to the *Harbrace College Handbook,* Fifth Edition).

Recent Language Study. Practical teachers of English composition welcome the new knowledge of grammar that has come from the active linguistic scholarship of the last few decades. Perhaps the most important contribution of this scholarship to English composition has been the emphasis on the grammatical principles that really apply to— and function in—our English language. Any English handbook such as this owes a great debt to all scholars, past and present, who have increased our understanding of the language. The authors of this handbook have endeavored to adapt from recent studies whatever has seemed most useful for the teaching of composition—after first trying out everything in their own freshman English classrooms.

Acknowledgments. Among the many individuals who have generously offered suggestions for making this handbook more usable, the authors wish especially to thank Professors William O. S. Sutherland, Jr. (Texas), Edward Lueders (Long Beach State), Phyllis H. Kernberger (Pierce), Bud T. Cochran, James B. Fisher, and Harry J. Rougier (Dayton), Marcella Frank (New York University), Ernest S. Clifton, Arthur Sampley, Eva Joy Sampley, Olma Boaz, and other members of the English Staff (North Texas State), and Bain Tate Stewart and others on the Freshman Staff (Tennessee). For important contributions to Section 33 (**Library Paper**), the authors are grateful to Miss Eleanor Goehring, of the Library Staff (Tennessee), and to Miss Ruth Alane Gresky (Tennessee). To Mr. Roy F. Montgomery is owed continuing appreciation for his help with the exercises.

To the Student

Contemporary Usage; Authority.   This Fifth Edition of the *Harbrace College Handbook* attempts to describe the usual practice of good contemporary writers, and to state that practice as simply as possible. The "rules" in boldface are to be interpreted as descriptions derived from usage, and they have authority only to the extent that they describe usage. In the illustrations throughout the book, the labels WRONG and RIGHT indicate, first, what is usually avoided and, second, what might be expected in standard written English. In your reading you should observe the practice of good writers so that you may eventually gain the confidence that comes from first-hand knowledge of what good writing is.

Numbers or Symbols.   A number or a symbol written in the margin of your paper indicates a need for correction or improvement and calls for revision. If a number is used, turn directly to the corresponding number in color at the top of the page in the handbook. If a symbol is used, first consult the alphabetical list of symbols inside the front cover to find the number to which you should turn.

Ordinary References.   The ordinary reference will be to the number or symbol in color standing at the head of one of the thirty-five sections of the handbook. The statement in large boldface at the beginning of each section covers the section as a whole. One of the statements in smaller boldface within the section will usually be needed to solve your problem. Study the section to which you have been referred—the whole of the section if necessary—and master the specific part of the section that explains your difficulty.

Specific References.   Whenever your instructor wishes to refer you to a specific part of a section, he will add the appropriate letter to the number or symbol.

EXAMPLES   **2c** (*or* **frag-c**), **18b** (*or* **sp-b**), **28d** (*or* **ref-d**).

General References.   At times your instructor may give you a very general reference from which you are to determine and correct your error. For example, the symbol **gr** will refer you to the whole division on GRAMMAR, including Sections **1–7**; the symbol **m** to the division on MECHANICS, including Sections **8–11**; the symbol **p** to the division on PUNCTUATION, Sections **12–17**; and so forth. An obvious error may be called to your attention by the symbol x, and general awkwardness by the symbol **k.**

Patterns and Diagrams.   To supplement the explanations, sentence patterns and simple diagrams are frequently used. The diagrams are often limited to parts of sentences —in order to concentrate your attention on the immediate problem.

Additional Help.   Some of the principles treated in English handbooks can be mastered only by students who understand the fundamentals of the sentence. A well-developed "sentence sense" is especially helpful in the mastery of Sections **2 (Sentence Fragment), 3 (Comma Splice), 5 (Case), 6 (Agreement), 12 (The Comma), 14 (The Semicolon), 21 (Wordiness), 23 (Unity), 24 (Subordination), 25 (Coherence), 26 (Parallelism), and 30 (Variety).** If you have difficulty in understanding these sections, you should first master the fundamentals of the sentence treated in Section **1 (Sentence Sense),** and then turn again to the principle immediately involved. If you fail to understand any grammatical term used in the handbook, consult the alphabetical list in Section **35** (**Grammatical Terms**).

Correction and Revision. After you have mastered the principle underlying the correction of each error called to your attention, you should make careful revision of your paper in the manner recommended by your instructor. One method of revision is explained and illustrated in Section **8** (**Manuscript Form and Revision**), pages 91–96. To prove that you have found the specific principle needed for the revision, your instructor may ask you to write the appropriate letter (**a, b, c,** etc.) after the number or symbol he has supplied. An *ex* written by the instructor after a number or symbol calls for the writing out of the appropriate exercise.

Contents

GRAMMAR

MECHANICS

PUNCTUATION

SPELLING

DICTION

30 Variety   314

LARGER ELEMENTS

31 The Paragraph   320

HARBRACE COLLEGE HANDBOOK 5TH EDITION

HARBRACE COLLEGE HANDBOOK 5TH EDITION

GRAMMAR

Sentence Sense

1

Master the essentials of the sentence as an aid to clear thinking, effective writing, and intelligent reading.

Acquiring sentence sense means developing the ability to recognize what *makes* a sentence. This sentence sense, or understanding of the structure (the basic patterns) of the sentence, is the key to good writing and reading. It is prerequisite to the intelligent use of this handbook, especially of Sections **2** (Sentence Fragment), **3** (Comma Splice), **5** (Case), **6** (Agreement), **12** (The Comma), **14** (The Semicolon), **21** (Wordiness), **23** (Unity), **24** (Subordination), **25** (Coherence), **26** (Parallelism), and **30** (Variety).

1a
Learn to recognize verbs.

The verb is the heart of the sentence: "He *ran* fast." "You *are* late." Without a verb no group of words is grammatically a sentence: "after a while," "no advice from anyone," "all waiting for the signal," "hoping to go to the fair." (See Section **2**.) A verb is often defined as a word (or a group of words) that expresses action, indicates a state of being, or asserts something. A verb changes its form to show time (*use, used; sing, sang*) and to indicate, in the present tense, a singular subject in the third person (*they use, he uses; I ask, he asks*). (See Section **7**.) Another important characteristic of the verb is that it can end in *-ing* (*is having, was acting, should be studying*). Such form changes are called inflection. (See Section **35**.)

A verb is used (1) in making a statement, (2) in asking a question, or (3) in giving a command.

> The tornado then *touched* the ground.
> *Is* a devilfish dangerous?
> *Read* one of Hardy's novels.

The verb may consist of one word (as in the three sentences above) or a group of words. The group, often referred to as a verb phrase (or cluster), comprises the verb together with the auxiliary words. Words commonly used as auxiliaries are *has, have, had, am, is, are, was, were, be, been, do, does, did, used to, may, might, must, have to, has to, had to, shall, will, am (is, are, etc.) going to, am (is, are, etc.) about to, would, should, ought to, can,* and *could*.

> Joe *did take* a course in supervised rest.
> Joe *will be taking* a course in supervised rest.
> Joe *should have been taking* a course in supervised rest.
> Joe *is going to take* (*will take*) a course in supervised rest.

The words that make up a verb phrase are often separated.

> A gentleman *may*, of course, *become* angry at times.
> He *does* not often *show* his anger.

A verb may be combined with the adverb *not*, or with a contraction of *not*.

> He *can*not *go*.   It *is*n't cold.
> He *can*'t *go*.   He *does*n't *know*.

The student who can find the verb (or verb phrase) and can separate it from other elements has gone a long way toward acquiring sentence sense.

▶ EXERCISE 1   For each blank in the following sentences supply an appropriate verb (or verb phrase). Then compose five sentences of your own and underline each verb (or verb phrase).

1. When I _____ a senior in high school, I _____ a big red hot rod that _____ _____ only nine miles on a gallon of ethyl gasoline.   2. Of course, Ed Fuller, who _____ at the service station near my home, _____ always happy when I _____ in and _____, "_____ her up with ethyl."   3. Every time I _____ gasoline, Ed quickly _____ everything under the hood and _____ all the car windows.   4. I always _____ prompt and smiling service.   5. Smiling _____ easy for him then.

6. No longer, however, _____ Ed _____ forward to give me quick service, for I _____ now _____ a tiny car that _____ fully thirty miles on a gallon.   7. Sometimes, after I _____ _____ into the station, I _____ a full two minutes before the gloomy Ed _____ me.   8. He usually _____ heavily and _____, "I _____ you _____ a tank of regular?"   9. After I _____ _____ yes, he slowly _____ the tank.   10. He _____ not even _____ under the hood unless I _____ him to do so.   11. When I _____ him only two or three dollars, he _____ as sad as Miniver Cheevy; apparently Ed _____ for the "good old days," when I _____ a gas-guzzling jalopy.

▶ EXERCISE 2   First add various auxiliaries (see the list on page 2) to the following; then use each verb phrase in a sentence. Underline each verb phrase.

1. think	3. seemed	5. been	7. organize
2. slept	4. sat	6. pacify	8. endanger

9. stiffen   13. falsify   17. participated
10. conclude   14. remarked   18. widen
11. withdrawing   15. readjust   19. occurred
12. enlarge   16. jeopardizing   20. operating

▶ EXERCISE 3   Underline the fifteen verbs and seven verb phrases in the following sentences.

1. Jim angrily called himself a fool, as he had been doing all the way through the woods.   2. Why had he listened to Fred's mad idea?   3. What were ghosts and family legends to him, in this year of grace and nuclear fission?   4. He had mysteries enough of his own, of a highly complex electronic sort, which would occupy him through the rest of a lifetime.   5. But now he was plodding along here, like the Mississippi schoolboy that he had been a dozen years before; this ghost chase in the middle of the night was preposterous.   6. It was an outrage to everything he stood for; it was lunacy.   7. It was—he swallowed the truth like a bitter pill—frightful!   8. The legend and the ghost had been a horror to him as a child; and they were a horror still.   9. As he stood at the edge of the weed-choked, briar-tangled slope, on the top of which the decayed mansion waited evilly, he felt almost sick.   10. The safe, sure things of every day had become distant, childish fantasies.   11. This grotesque night and whatever, ghoulish and monstrous, inhabited it were clammily and horribly real.

1b
Learn to recognize subjects and objects of verbs.

Every grammatically complete sentence has a verb and its subject, or at least these are implied.[1] In the following

---

[1] See **le** below. For a discussion of incomplete sentences, which do not bulk large in written English, see pages 34–35. In this book the word *sentence* will refer to the grammatically complete sentence.

sentences the subjects are in **boldface** and the verbs are in *italics*.

The **ship** *sank*.
[**You**] *Walk* carefully.
Some **men** on farms *work* long hours during the summer.

The subject and words associated with it ("Some **men** on farms") are called the *complete subject;* the verb and the words associated with it ("*work* long hours during the summer") are called the *complete predicate*. The subject of a sentence that asks a question (an interrogative sentence) is more readily located when the sentence is recast in the form of a statement.

Has the **last** of the deserters *surrendered?*
The **last** of the deserters *has surrendered*.

Many sentences require objects of the verb to complete their meaning. In the following sentences the objects are in SMALL CAPITALS.

Frank *has met* HELEN.
I *laid* the PLIERS on that shelf.
One **man** in the crowd *raised* his VOICE in protest.

A good way to recognize subjects and objects is to observe meaning. In order to find the subject, simply ask, in connection with the verb, "Who or what?"

The **actor,** after a long flight from South America, happily *greets* the REPORTERS at the Miami airport. [*Who* or *what* greets? The *actor* greets.][2]

Ordinarily an object receives, or is in some way affected

---

[2] It is sometimes helpful to make a diagram, or to form a mental picture, of the subject and its verb, thus:

$$\text{actor} \mid \textit{greets}$$

Any student who can bring the subject and verb together in this way should have little trouble in making the two "agree" (see Section 6); for example, **actor** *greets*, **actors** *greet*.

by, the action of the verb. To find the object, ask, in connection with the subject and verb, "Whom or what?" For example, in the sentence about the actor, "The actor greets *whom?*" *Reporters,* the answer, is the direct object.

Some verbs (such as *give, offer, bring, take, lend, send, buy,* and *sell*) may have both an indirect object and a direct object. To find the indirect object, ask, "*To whom* or *for whom* is something done?"

> **Dad** *gave* HARRY a BOAT. [Dad gave a boat (direct object) *to whom? Harry* is the indirect object.]

Another way to recognize subjects and objects is to observe their form. A noun or a pronoun (a word used in place of a noun) is the most frequently used subject or object of the verb. Forms of pronouns (*I, you, he,* etc.) are easy to recognize; see the list on page 53. Most nouns (words used to name persons, places, things, ideas, or actions) change their form to indicate number (*movement, movements; city, cities; woman, women*) and the possessive case (*John's* car, the *boys'* dogs, the *men's* job). Such suffixes as *-ance, -ation, -ence, -ment, -ness,* and *-ship* frequently indicate that a word is a noun: *appearance, determination, reference, atonement, boldness, hardship.* The articles *a, an,* and *the* are sometimes called "noun indicators" or "noun determiners" because they regularly point to a following noun: "a *chair,*" "an *activity,*" "the last *race.*"

A third way to recognize subjects and objects is to become thoroughly aware of the meaningfulness of English word order, normally SUBJECT—VERB—OBJECT. As you study carefully the following commonly used sentence patterns,[3] observe the importance of word order (especially in Pattern 2) in determining meaning. If a diagram helps you to form a mental picture of a sentence, also study the diagrams.

---

[3] For patterns with subject complements, see **1c** and **5f**.

1. SUBJECT—VERB.
   Henry slept.

   Henry | slept

2. SUBJECT—VERB—OBJECT.
   The boy hit the ball.

   boy | hit | ball

   The ball hit the boy.

   ball | hit | boy

3. SUBJECT—VERB—INDIRECT OBJECT—DIRECT OBJECT.
   She fried me an egg.

   She | fried | egg
   \ me

4. (Subject)—VERB—OBJECT.
   (You) Help me.

   (You) | Help | me

5. *There*[4]—VERB—SUBJECT.
   There are no objections.

   There

   objections | are

6. AUXILIARY—SUBJECT—VERB—OBJECT?
   Is he taking a vacation?

   he | Is taking | vacation

   For some variations of these patterns, see **30b**.

   Note: Subjects, verbs, and objects may be compound.

   EXAMPLES

   Mary and Jane played.

   Mary
   Jane | played

   Mary played and sang.

   played
   Mary
   sang

   Mary played baseball and tennis.

   baseball
   Mary | played
   tennis

   [4] The introductory word *there* is called an expletive. It is never the subject.

▶ EXERCISE 4   In the following sentences, point out (and diagram, if so requested) the twelve verbs, the nine subjects, and the nine objects, direct and indirect.

1. On New Year's Eve, I joined the happy throng at Times Square.   2. Between eleven and twelve o'clock, the noisy mob celebrated the death of the old year. 3. Many people leaned against boarded-up store windows, milled in the streets, or blew ear-splitting horns.   4. Others formed snake lines and whipped their way through the crowd.   5. A few fighting ragamuffins gave the police trouble.   6. Confetti filled the air.   7. Airplanes roared overhead.   8. Subways thundered.   9. Television cameras flashed the spectacular hubbub across the nation.

▶ EXERCISE 5   Write twenty brief sentences according to these patterns:

1. SUBJECT—VERB. (four sentences)
2. SUBJECT—VERB—OBJECT. (four sentences)
3. SUBJECT—VERB—INDIRECT OBJECT—DIRECT OBJECT. (three sentences)
4. (Subject)—VERB—OBJECT. (two sentences)
5. *There*—VERB—SUBJECT. (three sentences)
6. AUXILIARY—SUBJECT—VERB—OBJECT? (four sentences)

1c

Learn to recognize all the parts of speech.

Words are usually grouped into eight classes or "parts of speech": *verbs, nouns, pronouns, adjectives, adverbs, prepositions, conjunctions,* and *interjections.* Verbs, nouns, adjectives, and adverbs are sometimes called *vocabulary words* because they make up more than ninety-nine percent of all words listed in the dictionary. But pronouns, prepositions, and conjunctions—though small in number—

are important because they are used over and over in our speaking and writing. Prepositions and conjunctions, often called *function words,* connect and relate vocabulary words and pronouns. Of the eight word classes, only three—prepositions, conjunctions, and interjections—do not change their form to indicate meaning.

For a summary of the form changes of verbs, nouns, pronouns, adjectives, and adverbs, see Section **35,** under **Inflection.** Also see Section **35** for the definitions of the eight parts of speech.

Parts of speech	Uses in the Sentence	Examples
1. VERBS	Indicators of action or state of being (often link subjects and complements)	Dad *had eaten.* She *was* angry. Jane *is* a waitress.
2. NOUNS	Subjects, objects, complements	*Ed* will pay the *men* for the *work.*
3. PRONOUNS	Substitutes for nouns	*He* will pay *them* for *it.*
4. ADJECTIVES	Modifiers of nouns and noun substitutes	*tall* man *That* one is *new.*
5. ADVERBS	Modifiers of verbs, adjectives, adverbs, or whole clauses	acted *wisely,* a *very* tall man, *almost never* sang
6. PREPOSITIONS	Words used before nouns and noun substitutes to relate them to other words in the sentence	food *for* thought, an island *in* the middle *of* the lake, praised *by* him

Parts of speech	Uses in the Sentence	Examples
7. CONJUNCTIONS	Connectives	you *and* I, win *or* lose, old *but* agile Come *if* you can.
8. INTERJECTIONS	Expressions of emotion (unrelated grammatically to the rest of the sentence)	*Alas! Whew! Oh,* pardon me.

Classifying Words as Parts of Speech

The dictionary shows the word class (often the several word classes) in which a given word may be used, but the actual classification of any word is dependent upon its use in the sentence. Notice how the classification of *round* varies in accordance with its use in the following sentences:

The second *round* was tiring. [Noun]
Any *round* table will do. [Adjective]
Some drivers *round* corners too rapidly. [Verb]
The sound goes *round* and *round*. [Adverb]
He lives *round* the corner. [Preposition]

Adjectives and **adverbs** are usually placed in the sentence near the words they modify, and in diagrams they are attached to these words.[5] In the following sentence the adjectives are in boldface and the adverbs in italics.

The *exceedingly* **tall** man walked *very rapidly*.

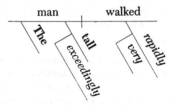

[5] For the different forms of adjectives and adverbs, see Section 4.

A predicate adjective helps to complete the meaning of a linking verb (*am, is, are, was, were, be, been, taste, smell,* etc.) and modifies the subject. See also **4b**.

SUBJECT—LINKING VERB—PREDICATE ADJECTIVE.

The man is old.   man | is \ old

Some common **prepositions** are *across, after, as, at, because of, before, between, by, for, from, in, in front of, in regard to, like, of, on, over, through, to, together with, under, until, up, with.* In the following sentence the prepositions are in italics. (See **1d** for the position of prepositions in diagrams.)

The poems *by* Burns express *with* great force his love *of* liberty.

A preposition always has an object, a noun or a noun substitute. In the sentence above, *Burns, force,* and *liberty* are objects of prepositions. The preposition with its object (and any modifiers) is called a prepositional phrase. See **1d**. The preposition may follow, rather than precede, the noun or noun substitute, and be placed at the end of the sentence. At times a sentence is most idiomatic or emphatic with the preposition at the end.

UNNATURAL   *For* what are you waiting?
NATURAL   What are you waiting *for?*
NATURAL   We live *by* faith.
NATURAL (*and more emphatic*)   Faith is what we live *by.*

Note: Words like *up, off, on, out, in, over* may be used as prepositions, as adverbs, or as parts of verb-adverb combinations (verb equivalents).

Prepositions	Adverbs	Verb-adverb combinations
up the ladder	Look *up.*	*Look up* (Find) George.
a mile *off* shore	He marched *off.*	I *put off* (delayed) the work.

Conjunctions fall into two classes: (1) the co-ordinating conjunctions (*and, but, or, nor, for,* and sometimes *so* and *yet*), used to connect words or phrases, or clauses that are of equal rank; and (2) the subordinating conjunctions (such as *after, because, if, since, till, when, where, while*), used to connect subordinate clauses with main clauses. In diagrams, conjunctions are usually placed on broken lines drawn between parts connected by the conjunctions.

When the weather permitted, boys *and* girls played on the lawn *and* walks *and* even in the street.

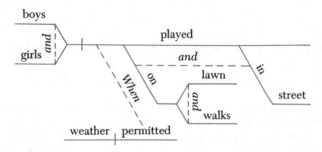

An **interjection** is followed by an exclamation point when the emotion expressed is strong, otherwise by a comma. In diagrams the interjection is set off by itself to indicate its grammatical independence of the rest of the sentence.

Oh, I can hardly believe it.

Oh	[Interjection]
I can believe	[Subject + predicate]

▶ EXERCISE 6   As you fill in the blanks below with appropriate parts of speech to make logical sentences, note how word order, inflectional endings, and function words determine your choices. Above each word you add, write its part of speech.

1. The _____ have _____ed a _____.
2. _____ were _____ing in the _____.

3. _____ly the _____ are not _____.
4. A very _____ _____ may _____.
5. _____ of the _____ on the _____ looked _____.
6. Did _____ and _____ _____ their _____?
7. A _____ boy was _____ing _____ly on the _____.
8. Either _____ or _____ ought to _____ the _____.
9. _____ _____ not _____ a _____ or a _____.
10. During the _____ _____, _____ _____ed for _____.

1d

Learn to recognize phrases and subordinate clauses.

Phrases

A phrase is a group of related words, without subject and predicate, used as a noun substitute (called a *noun phrase*) or a modifier (called an *adjective phrase* or an *adverb phrase*). A phrase is formed with (1) a preposition —and therefore called a *prepositional phrase,* (2) a participle—and called a *participial phrase,* (3) a gerund—and called a *gerund phrase,* or (4) an infinitive—and called an *infinitive phrase.*

A **prepositional phrase** consists of a preposition and its object, along with any modifiers: *in the lake, for a beautiful lady, by studying.* Prepositional phrases often come in groups, thus:

|The boy | *with the dog* ‖ *on a leash* |lives| *on the farm* ‖ *near the mill.* |

[Arrows show modification. (See **1d(2)**).]

Verbals. Participles, gerunds, and infinitives are derived from verbs and are therefore called *verbals.* (See also

Section 35.) They are much like verbs in that they have
different tenses, can take subjects and objects, and can be
modified by adverbs. But they are not verbs, for they cannot serve as the heart of a sentence: they cannot make a
statement, ask a question, or give a command. Compare
the following:

The boy *ate* an apple. Did he *eat* it? *Eat!*
  [Verbs in complete sentences]
The boy *eating* the apple . . .
  [Participle (present)—an adjective modifying *boy*]
Eating an apple, the boy . . .
  [Participle (present)—an adjective modifying *boy*]
The apple *eaten* by the boy . . .
  [Participle (past)—an adjective modifying *apple*]
Eating an apple is good for the health.
  [A gerund serving as a noun]
To eat an apple . . . [Infinitive—in a sentence fragment. All
  verbals are, by themselves, only fragments of sentences.]

Note that the gerund *eating*, like the present participle
eating, ends in *-ing* and that the two are to be distinguished
only by their use in the sentence: the participle is the
adjective and the gerund is the noun.

A **verbal phrase** consists of a verbal and its related words.

The boy *eating the apple* is my brother.
  [Participial phrase]
Riding a horse is good exercise.
  [Gerund phrase]
To swim in the ocean is fun.
  [Infinitive phrase]

(1) **Phrases used as nouns**

Gerund phrases are always used as nouns. Infinitive
phrases are often used as nouns (though they may also
function as modifiers).[6]

---

[6] Occasionally a prepositional phrase is used as a noun: "*After supper*
will be too late." [The prepositional phrase is the subject.]

NOUNS	PHRASES USED AS NOUNS

This *decision* is important.

Choosing a major is important.
[Gerund phrase—subject]

She likes the *job*.

She likes *to do the work.*
[Infinitive phrase—object]

(2) **Phrases used as modifiers**

Prepositional phrases nearly always function as adjectives or adverbs. Infinitive phrases are also used as adjectives or adverbs. Participial phrases are always used as adjectives.

ADJECTIVES	PHRASES USED AS ADJECTIVES
a *significant* discovery	a discovery *of significance* [Prepositional phrase]
Appropriate language is important.	Language *to suit the occasion* is important. [Infinitive phrase]
a *destructive* storm	a storm *causing much destruction* [Participial phrase]

ADVERBS	PHRASES USED AS ADVERBS
Drive *carefully.*	Drive *with care.* [Prepositional phrase]
Certainly Frank lacks confidence.	*To be sure,* Frank lacks confidence. [Infinitive phrase]

The examples on page 15 show how phrases function in the same way as single-word modifiers. Remember, however, that phrases are not merely substitutes for single words. Many times phrases express more than can be packed into a single word.

EXAMPLES   The gas gauge fluttered *from empty to full.*
He telephoned his wife *to tell her of his arrival.*
Walking down Third Avenue, I noticed many new buildings.

In diagrams, phrase modifiers are attached to the words modified.

Momentarily forgetting the rules, a player *on the bench* ran *onto the field to tackle an opponent.*

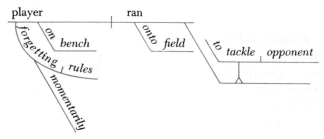

▶ EXERCISE 7   Change each italicized adjective or adverb below into a natural-sounding prepositional phrase.

1. The *west* wind is cold.
2. I built the *front* porch.
3. Fido ate the *fish* bait.
4. It is an *English* custom.
5. Make a *right* turn.
6. Go *now.*
7. I wrote *hastily.*
8. You may sit *here.*
9. Work *diligently.*
10. I agreed *reluctantly.*

▶ EXERCISE 8   Bracket and classify (as an adjective or an adverb) each of the twenty-four prepositional phrases in the following paragraphs.

1. Wasn't it St. Augustine who said that he knew the meaning of time until the moment someone asked him to

define the word?   2. Through the ages, wise men have presented to posterity numerous and diverse concepts of time.   3. In Ecclesiastes is the famous "To everything there is a season, and a time to every purpose."   4. Boileau has written, "Time flies and draws us with it."   5. And Shakespeare has said, "Time's the king of men."   6. Not one of these quotations about time, however, provides an adequate definition for thinkers like St. Augustine.

7. Such a definition was no problem for Carlyle, who frankly admitted that time is a great mystery.   8. In *Heroes and Hero-Worship,* he wrote, in effect, that the word cannot be defined.   9. With one sweeping statement, Carlyle vividly depicted the attributes of time and its relationship to humanity.   10. He observed: "The illimitable, silent, never-resting thing called Time" rolls and rushes on "like an all-embracing ocean tide, on which we and all the Universe swim like exhalations, like apparitions which *are,* and then *are not:* this is forever very literally a miracle."

▶ EXERCISE 9   In the following sentences point out the participial, gerund, and infinitive phrases and show how each is used as an adjective, an adverb, or a noun. (If you prefer, do this exercise by making a simple diagram for each verbal.)

1. Eddie and Cliff had nearly everything they needed to build their diving float.   2. They had spent the whole morning in rolling the eight oil drums from Cliff's back yard down to Eddie's.   3. Now the problem was to find some lumber.   4. Eddie, ransacking his brain, finally thought of a supply.   5. Mr. Kelly had torn down an old barn last fall to build a garage.   6. Going to the lake yesterday, Eddie had seen the leftover boards, still piled there and overgrown with weeds.   7. But getting them now, before the Donovan boys found them too, was the important thing.   8. "Get on your feet, boy, and stop

wasting our time."   9. Cliff, nudged into movement by a front bicycle wheel, obediently got up.   10. Away they wheeled, pedaling as if the devil himself were after or the Donovans ahead of them.   11. It would be hard to say which might be worse.   12. Coming up to the site, the boys were happy to find the boards safe underneath the weeds.

Subordinate Clauses

A clause is a group of words which contains both a verb and its subject. Unlike a *main clause* (which can stand alone as a sentence because it is grammatically complete —see le), a *subordinate clause* functions as a noun, an adjective, or an adverb and is therefore only part of a sentence. Subordinating conjunctions (such as *after, although, as, because, before, if, since, until, when, while*) and relative pronouns (such as *who, which, that*) are called "subordinate clause markers" because they introduce subordinate clauses and make them dependent.

SENTENCE   The money was stolen.

SUBORDINATE CLAUSES   *after* the money was stolen
because the money was stolen
[the money] *which* was stolen

(3) **Subordinate clauses used as nouns**

NOUNS	NOUN CLAUSES
The newspaper *accounts* may be false.	*What the newspapers say* may be false. [Subject]

accounts | may be \ false

newspapers | say | What
/\ may be \ false

| I do not remember his *name*. | I do not remember *what his name is.* [Object] |
| Give the tools to *Paul*. | Give the tools to *whoever can use them.* [Object of the preposition *to*] |

▶ EXERCISE 10 Bracket the noun clauses in the following sentences and explain the use of each clause.

1. The repairman said that he would have to take the typewriter into the shop. 2. What it needed most of all was to be junked. 3. But he remembered that his customer had a sentimental fondness for this old machine. 4. And he had long ago learned that a battered, used-up piece of machinery could be to some people what politics, wife, or religion was to others. 5. What one man loved, other men had to pretend to respect. 6. The repairman wondered whether that saying was in the Bible. 7. He thought that it might well be.

▶ EXERCISE 11 Compose five sentences containing noun clauses.

(4) Subordinate clauses used as modifiers

Two types of subordinate clauses, the adjective clause and the adverb clause, are used as modifiers.

ADJECTIVE	ADJECTIVE CLAUSE
The *corner* lot needs mowing.	The lot *that is on the corner* needs mowing.

ADVERB	ADVERB CLAUSE
The work stops *then*.	The work stops *when it rains*.

Adjective clauses: Any clause that modifies a noun or a noun substitute is an adjective clause. Adjective clauses, which nearly always follow the words modified, are most frequently introduced by a relative pronoun, which often is the subject or object in the subordinate clause.

A man *who knows the truth* is fortunate. [The relative pronoun *who* is the subject of *knows* in the adjective clause.]
He is a man *whom I have always admired.* [The relative pronoun *whom* is the object of *have admired.*]

Other words (for example, conjunctions and adverbs) may introduce adjective clauses: "a time *when all things went well for him,*" "the reason *why I changed my mind.*"

Note: If not used as a subject, the word introducing an adjective or a noun clause may sometimes be omitted. (See also **22a.**)

> He is a man [*whom* or *that*] I have always admired.
> I know [*that*] she is right.

▶ EXERCISE 12   Bracket the five adjective clauses in the following sentences.

1. William was not at the corner where he usually took the bus. 2. The bus driver, who knew all his regular passengers, commented about it to one of those getting on. 3. The passenger remembered something that William had said one day about beginning his vacation in the middle of the week. 4. That sounded reasonable to the driver, who after all had a schedule to maintain. 5. Edging the big bus back into the traffic that was streaming by, he mentally put William on his "absent with leave" list for the next two weeks.

▶ EXERCISE 13   Compose five sentences containing adjective clauses and bracket the clauses.

Adverb clauses: Any clause that modifies a word (or word group) other than a noun or noun substitute is an adverb clause. An adverb clause may modify a verb, an adjective, an adverb, or even a whole clause.

An adverb clause often precedes or follows the main clause:

ADVERB CLAUSE, MAIN CLAUSE.

> When Bill decided to leave, everyone expressed regret. [An adverb clause in this position is usually followed by a comma. See **12b.**]

MAIN CLAUSE   ADVERB CLAUSE.

Everyone expressed regret when Bill decided to leave. [An adverb clause in this position is usually not set off by a comma. See **12b**.]

Adverb clauses may also appear within the main clause:

I can, *if you wish*, help you paint the woodwork. [A parenthetical adverb clause set off by commas. See **12d**.]

The position of the adverb clause depends on its relative importance in the sentence. See **29a-b.**

▶ EXERCISE 14   Bracket the eleven adverb clauses in the following paragraph.

1. While Mr. Baker was shaving, he thought of the day ahead.   2. He always began his day's work before he arrived at the office.   3. After he got on the train, he nearly always started planning his day.   4. Sometimes he began before the train arrived if it was a minute or two late.   5. But this morning, as he was shaving the tender place under his chin, details of the day's work clicked through his mind.   6. Since he had first been made head accountant, he couldn't remember having brought the job home with him.   7. Whenever anything was not the usual routine with him, he naturally wondered.   8. Suddenly he remembered; while he was rinsing his razor under the hot water, he smiled cheerfully.   9. Today, unless the state auditors broke a long habit, they would show up. 10. And because this time he had worked extra carefully to have the books ready for them, he could look forward happily to their coming.

▶ EXERCISE 15   Compose ten sentences containing adverb clauses, using ten different subordinating conjunctions. Bracket each adverb clause and underline each subordinating conjunction.

1e
Learn to recognize main clauses and the various types of sentences.

As we have already noted in **1d**, a main clause, like a subordinate clause, contains both a verb and its subject; but it is not used as a noun or a modifier, and it can stand alone. When it is combined with another clause, it is called a *main* clause. When it stands by itself, it is called a *sentence.*

A sentence is a unit of expression that can stand alone grammatically, though it may require other sentences to complete its meaning. It is followed in speaking by a full stop and in writing by a period, a question mark, or an exclamation point.

> He refused the offer. [Statement—followed by a period]
> Refuse the offer. [Command—followed by a period]
> Did he refuse the offer? [Question—followed by a question mark]
> How absurd the offer! [Exclamation—followed by an exclamation point]

Although a grammatically complete sentence has both a verb and its subject, sometimes one of these is implied. In a command like "Refuse the offer" the subject is implied: "*You* refuse." In an exclamation like "How absurd the offer!" the verb is implied: "offer *is.*"

Sentences are classified, according to the number and kind of clauses they contain, as (1) simple, (2) compound, (3) complex, or (4) compound-complex.

A **simple sentence** is a sentence made up of one main clause.

EXAMPLE   The work stops.

A **compound sentence** is a sentence made up of two (or more) main clauses.

EXAMPLE   The work stops, but the tools are kept in readiness.

Except when joined by one of the co-ordinating conjunctions (*and, but, or, nor, for*), main clauses are separated by a semicolon. See Section **14**.

The work stops; however, tools are kept ready.
The work stops; tools are kept ready.

A **complex sentence** is a sentence made up of one main clause and at least one subordinate clause.

EXAMPLE   The work stops when it rains.

A **compound-complex sentence** is a sentence made up of two (or more) main clauses and at least one subordinate clause.

EXAMPLE   The work stops when it rains, but the tools are kept in readiness.

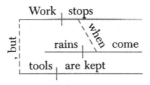

▶ EXERCISE 16   Classify each of the following sentences (selected from the *New Yorker*) as (1) simple, (2) compound, (3) complex, or (4) compound-complex. Be prepared to justify your classification by analysis of the sentence.

1. Our mother, a former high-school valedictorian, used to powder her speech with didactic couplets applicable to the life of the young.
2. In so erratic a fantasy, torment and disaster appear to arise not from the necessary order of things but merely from the whim of the dramatist, and death itself is shown to have no significance beyond the momentary inconvenience it causes the hero.
3. His women, as a group, are aggressive, and inclined to speak up instead of just speaking.
4. Time and again we are led through one or another of Conrad's works, detail by detail, to reach the startling

conclusion that what Conrad put into the story is still there and that the story means what he said it meant.

5. Once, the stone floor of the portico must have rung with the sound of iron wheels and shod hoofs; now it is silent and the doors of the stables are shut.

6. It was hard to believe that he was beholden to anyone, and easy to feel that at that moment this proud, vain, pudgy, irascible, and noisy tyrant was—by some demonic energy generated within himself—holding humanity for ransom.

7. The harvests are scanty, for the clay sheds the rain, and, with no trees to hold it, the water rushes to the valley, carrying seeds with it and carving great, gray, gutterlike channels.

8. As part of our program to promote clean and efficient business methods, we spent many years developing a copying paper that would eliminate the need for carbons.

9. His face faintly suggested mumps, and he once tipped the theatre-ticket girl in the lobby of the Hotel New Yorker three cents for getting him four tickets to a show that was sold out for a month in advance.

10. The crowd moved through the two anterooms into the Great Hall, where, from their portraits on the wall, mayors, presidents, and justices looked down with the complacent rosiness of those who have dined and died.

▶ EXERCISE 17   Compose ten sentences and classify each sentence as (1) simple, (2) complex, (3) compound, or (4) compound-complex. Write at least two sentences of each type.

▶ EXERCISE 18   Analyze the following sentences (selected from *Fortune*) according to instructions given for Exercise 16.

1. The sponsors say this marvelous new device can be improved.
2. It will be a machine with thick eyeglasses that generates its own energy by pacing the floor and lubricates itself by biting its fingernails.
3. The first inkling of what impended was an earthquake.
4. The green sea of sugar cane rolled violently under the repeated shocks, then seemed to surge forward upon the doomed village of Kapoho, engulfing it in leafy billows.
5. In trying to comprehend the phenomenon of life in all its diversity, fecundity, and grandeur, science meets its highest challenge.
6. A buyer at an auction may get so caught up in the momentum of the game that he will unwittingly top his own high bid.
7. Taylor came up with several styles, and later he added dogs' coats that matched women's and children's coats.
8. The dealer has difficulty only in replacing what he has already sold.
9. He spends much time corresponding with his clients who may wish to sell, and every day he reads the obituary columns.
10. A revolution in military technology—the shift to missiles—has just about put an end to the development and production of manned military aircraft.
11. The talent for self-examination is another intangible asset.
12. Like his perfumes, he is a volatile essence in a small, stylish package.
13. As the motorist emerges from the Holland Tunnel, Jersey City proudly puts its worst foot forward.
14. The tourists themselves are a vital part of Hawaii's $1.2-billion economy; visitors plunked down over $100 million last year, and are expected to be spending nearly six times that much by 1970.

15. A dealer may spend many hours of anguished deliberation before he sets a final price on a particular item, but once the price is set he is firm.

16. A notion just then gaining currency was that microorganisms like bacteria and molds, far from being simple, actually possessed chemical powers in some ways surpassing those of fruit flies, mice, or even men.

17. In the meantime, American businessmen can only envy the protective device nature permitted a small Caribbean fish to develop.

18. Its eyes have two pupils so that when it is feeding on the surface, it can watch all at once what's going on in the air and under the water.

19. There is nothing particularly sententious to say about this city street, except that it is lacking in the amenities.

20. Looking backward through an autumn haze of imperfect memory, he catches seductive glimpses of a world that never was, a world that nonetheless he wants desperately to return.

▶ EXERCISE 19   Compose ten varied sentences and analyze them as directed by the instructor.

▶ EXERCISE 20   Analyze the following sentences of the Gettysburg Address as directed by the instructor.

1. Fourscore and seven years ago our fathers brought forth on this continent a new nation, conceived in liberty, and dedicated to the proposition that all men are created equal.

2. Now we are engaged in a great civil war, testing whether that nation, or any nation so conceived and so dedicated, can long endure.

3. We are met on a great battlefield of that war.

4. We have come to dedicate a portion of that field as a final resting place for those who here gave their lives that that nation might live.

5. It is altogether fitting and proper that we should do this.
6. But in a larger sense we cannot dedicate, we cannot consecrate, we cannot hallow this ground.
7. The brave men, living and dead, who struggled here, have consecrated it far above our power to add or detract.
8. The world will little note, nor long remember, what we say here; but it can never forget what they did here.
9. It is for us, the living, rather to be dedicated here to the unfinished work which they who fought here have thus far so nobly advanced.
10. It is rather for us to be here dedicated to the great task remaining before us, that from these honored dead we take increased devotion to that cause for which they gave the last full measure of devotion; that we here highly resolve that these dead shall not have died in vain; that this nation, under God, shall have a new birth of freedom, and that government of the people, by the people, for the people shall not perish from the earth.

Sentence Fragment

2

Do not carelessly write a sentence fragment —a phrase or a subordinate clause—as if it were a complete sentence.

Caution: Can you distinguish between phrases and clauses, and between main and subordinate clauses? Until you can do so, you are likely to write careless sentence fragments. You may need to master the fundamentals of the sentence treated in Section 1, **Sentence Sense,** before you can understand Section 2.

A sentence fragment—a phrase or a subordinate clause —should not be set off as if it were a complete sentence. The fragment should be either (1) included in the preceding or following sentence—that is, attached to the main clause—or (2) rewritten to form a sentence by itself. (See also Section 24.)

WRONG   He registered for the summer session. Hoping thus to graduate ahead of his class. [We have here one sentence and one fragment, a participial phrase.]

RIGHT   He registered for the summer session, hoping thus to graduate ahead of his class. [Participial phrase included in the sentence]

RIGHT   He registered for the summer session. By this means he hoped to graduate ahead of his class. [Participial phrase made into a sentence]

WRONG   He registered for the summer session. Because he hoped thus to graduate ahead of his class. [We have here one sentence and one fragment, a subordinate clause.]

RIGHT He registered for the summer session because he hoped thus to graduate ahead of his class. [Subordinate clause included in the sentence]

RIGHT By registering for the summer session, he hoped to graduate ahead of his class.

RIGHT He registered for the summer session. By this means he hoped to graduate ahead of his class. [Subordinate clause made into a sentence]

TESTS FOR SENTENCE COMPLETENESS

A sentence fragment may be obvious to the student who will read it aloud in context. If he reads the fragment properly, he will find that either it is not preceded by a full stop or else it is not followed by one. That is, the fragment belongs with the preceding sentence or with the following one.

Sentence completeness may also be tested (1) by searching for the verb and its subject and (2) by determining whether this verb and subject are introduced by a subordinating conjunction or relative pronoun. If the supposed sentence does not have a verb and its subject, it may be identified at once as a phrase. *Hoping thus to graduate ahead of his class,* for example, has no verb. *Hoping* is a participle and *to graduate* is an infinitive, but there is no verb. Even when both verb and subject are present, they may be introduced by a subordinating conjunction or relative pronoun and thus constitute a subordinate clause. *Because he hoped to graduate ahead of his class* has the verb *hoped* and the subject *he.* But since these words are introduced by the subordinating conjunction *because,* the group of words is a subordinate clause—still a sentence fragment.

Make a diagram, or at least form a mental picture, of the core of each sentence: its subject + its verb. Then if you find that subject and verb are not introduced by a subordinating conjunction or relative pronoun such as *because, since, if, when, who,* or *which,* you may be reasonably sure that the sentence is grammatically complete.

He registered for the summer session.

$$\text{He} \mid \text{registered} \qquad \text{[Subject—verb]}$$

The diagram shows subject and verb, and there is no subordinating conjunction or relative pronoun: the sentence is complete.

▶ EXERCISE 1   Find the seven fragments in the following paragraphs. Revise each fragment by attaching it logically to a main clause or by rewriting the fragment so that it will stand by itself as a sentence.

1. As a weather watcher, I am often amused by official forecasts.   2. Or, rather, by occasional prophecies made by weather men who seldom bother to glance out the window.   3. For example, one day last spring when heavy rain and large hail lashed the city.   4. I promptly telephoned the weather bureau.   5. To ask about the possibility of a tornado.   6. A confident voice replied glibly, "Oh, don't worry about a tornado; we're not even in an alert area."

7. Relieved, I turned on the radio, found a chair near a window, and watched the angry clouds.   8. Amazingly enough, I soon saw a swirling funnel emerge from a black cloud and reach for the ground.   9. Just north of the city, about five miles away.   10. Of course, I immediately notified the weather bureau.

11. A short time later.   12. An important message interrupted the jazz on the radio: "The weather bureau has issued a warning that a tornado may strike north of here."   13. I smiled as I repeated the words "may strike."   14. Knowing that the official prophets were vigilant.   15. As they busily observed falling barometers and erratic wind gauges instead of paying attention to the turbulent weather itself.

2a

Do not carelessly write a phrase (participial, prepositional, or infinitive) as a complete sentence.

WRONG   I made little progress. *Finally giving up all my efforts.* [Participial phrase]

RIGHT   I made so little progress that I finally gave up all my efforts. [Fragment included in the sentence]

RIGHT   I made little progress. Finally I gave up all my efforts. [Fragment made into a sentence]

WRONG   Soon I began to work for the company. *First in the rock pit and later on the highway.* [Prepositional phrases]

RIGHT   Soon I began to work for the company, first in the rock pit and later on the highway. [Fragment included in the sentence]

WRONG   He will have an opportunity to visit his home town. *And to talk with many of his old friends.* [Infinitive phrase]

RIGHT   He will have an opportunity to visit his home town and to talk with many of his old friends. [Fragment included in the sentence]

▶ EXERCISE 2   Eliminate each fragment below by including it in a sentence or by making it into a sentence.

1. We had a wonderful time at the lake. Swimming near the dock and fishing on the barge.
2. I spray the shrubbery twice a year. Once in the late spring and again in the early fall.
3. The pampered Dennis finally left home. Earnestly seeking to become an individual in his own right.
4. He was once a beautiful child. With curly black hair and bright blue eyes.
5. I want to make high grades. To succeed not only as an athlete but also as a scholar.
6. In high school I was a "discipline problem." In more ways than one.
7. My grandmother is a delightful conversationalist.

Often speaking of the "days of her youth," during what she calls the "Renaissance period."

8. I think that it is wise to ignore his sarcasm. Or to make a quick exit.

9. Squinting her eyes, the gossip leaned forward. To whisper this question in my ear: "Have you seen that mangy little thug she dates?"

10. Bill smiled self-consciously. Like a politician posing before a television camera.

2b

Do not carelessly write a subordinate clause as a complete sentence.

WRONG   A railway control board should be constructed with care. *Because from this board trains are moved through a system of tracks and switches.* [Subordinate clause]

RIGHT   A railway control board should be constructed with care because from this board trains are moved through a system of tracks and switches. [Fragment included in the sentence]

WRONG   I had some definite ideas about college. *Although I had never before been on a college campus.* [Subordinate clause]

RIGHT   I had some definite ideas about college although I had never before been on a college campus. [Fragment included in the sentence]

WRONG   I am now reading Hoover's *Masters of Deceit. Which is an exposé of the strategy of modern Communists.* [Subordinate clause]

RIGHT   I am now reading Hoover's *Masters of Deceit,* which is an exposé of the strategy of modern Communists. [Fragment included in the sentence]

RIGHT   I am now reading Hoover's *Masters of Deceit.* This is an exposé of the strategy of modern Communists. [Fragment made into a sentence]

▶ EXERCISE 3   Some of the following word groups are fragments, and some are sentences. Write *F* after each fragment; write *S* after each sentence.

1. As soon as he started imitating my favorite comedian by doing the rhumba with a lamp shade on his head.
2. And the sheriff believed that he could handle the prisoner easily enough alone.
3. In fact, that is my pride, my joy, and my dependable money-maker.
4. Which is more than I can say for the last agent we had here.
5. This was the nightmare that haunted her, the dread of the inevitable surrender.
6. But this isn't an ordinary herd of black Anguses.
7. Although I know, of course, that this is an entirely different situation.
8. When several of the guests asked for second helpings.
9. As a rule, it takes all night for the paint to harden.
10. As if he knew everything and we were all ignoramuses.

2c

Do not carelessly write as a complete sentence any other fragment, such as an appositive (noun or noun substitute) or a member of a compound predicate.

WRONG	My father was born in Cartersville. *A little country town where everyone knows everyone else.* [Appositive modified by a subordinate clause]
RIGHT	My father was born in Cartersville, a little country town where everyone knows everyone else.
WRONG	William was elected president of his class. *And was made a member of the National Honor Society.* [Detached member of a compound predicate]
RIGHT	William was elected president of his class and was made a member of the National Honor Society.

▶ EXERCISE 4   Attach each fragment below to the preceding sentence or make the fragment into an independent sentence.

1. Fred received an invitation to my wedding. And acknowledged it by sending me a sympathy card.
2. You should work when you are young and enthusiastic. And should leave dreams to old men.
3. I am often told to do things I do not like. Such as getting out of bed.
4. The hydraulic lift raises the plows out of the ground. And lowers them again.
5. I had a feeling that some sinister spirit of evil brooded over the place. A feeling that I could not analyze.

Note: At times a sentence without an expressed subject or verb, or both, may be clear because omitted words can be readily supplied by the reader. Such elliptical expressions occur in commands, in exclamations, and in questions and answers, especially in dialogue. But these expressions are not real fragments since the completion is unmistakably implied.

COMMANDS   Come nearer. [You come nearer.]
            Please enter. [You will please enter.]

EXCLAMATIONS   Too bad! [That is too bad!]
                What a pity! [What a pity it is!]

QUESTIONS AND ANSWERS
    Why did he go? Because his friends were going. [He went because his friends were going.]
    Will you play with me? A lot? [Will you play with me a lot?]
    Perhaps. [Perhaps I will.]

Real fragments are sometimes used intentionally by professional writers, especially in fiction. In the following passages, the intentional fragments are in italics.

He wasn't a gorilla. *Just the cutest little baboon.* And the garbage wasn't garbage. It was ice cream. *A genuine strawberry and fish-guts sundae.*   —ALDOUS HUXLEY

Too soon there would be overpopulation, overcrowding, and slum conditions. *Which is a horrid thought, for one who loves an island for its insulation.* —D. H. LAWRENCE

Such fragments are employed consciously, for rhetorical effect, by experienced writers but are not common in expository writing emphasized in college. Students are usually advised to learn the fundamentals of English composition and the accepted style of expository writing before permitting themselves the liberties taken by experienced craftsmen.

▶ EXERCISE 5   Identify each fragment; determine whether it falls under the rule for **2a**, **2b**, or **2c**; then make the appropriate correction. Write *C* after each numbered item which contains no fragment.

1. I knew that he was asking for trouble. As soon as I heard of his buying that motorcycle.
2. He let me believe that I had first chance at the job. But without definitely committing himself.
3. He was still angry with me. His eyes glaring fiercely.
4. He killed three ducks with one shot. Against the law of averages but possible.
5. She dressed exactly like the Hollywood starlets. Since she wanted to become one of them herself.
6. To watch Dempsey in the ring was to watch a perfectly engineered machine operated with exact precision.
7. To anyone who knew him in 1840, it would have seemed ridiculous beyond belief. To predict that one day this rawboned frontier lawyer would be President of the United States.
8. The festival beginning on the twentieth of June and continuing through the month of July.
9. Early in life he decided upon a simple philosophy. From which grew all his subsequent opinions.
10. Doc Potter is exactly what you said he would be. A thoroughly profane and entertaining old reprobate.

▶ EXERCISE 6   Attach each fragment below to an existing sentence or make it into an independent sentence.

1. Very late in *The Merry Wives of Windsor*, Shakespeare introduces an incident which is altogether extraneous to either of the plot lines in the play. 2. And which advances the action in no way whatsoever. 3. Bardolph in a very brief scene with the Host announces that "the Germans" desire three of the Host's horses. 4. So that they may go to meet "the Duke," who is to be at court on the next day. 5. The Host seems to know so little of these Germans that he must ask if they speak English. 6. A highly improbable ignorance on his part, for in his next lines he states that they have been already a week at his tavern. 7. But he lets them have the horses. 8. Insisting, however, that they must pay for them. 9. Two scenes later Bardolph returns to the tavern with the report that the villainous Germans have handled him roughly on the road. 10. Thrown him into a puddle, and run off with the horses. 11. Immediately on his heels, in come first Sir Hugh and then Dr. Caius. 12. With rumors confirming Bardolph's assurance of the evil character of the Germans. 13. So that the Host is at last alarmed. 14. He is convinced now that the Germans have indeed cozened him of a week's board bill. 15. And stolen his horses in the bargain.

[See other exercises on sentence fragments at the end of Section 3.]

Comma Splice
and Fused Sentence

3

Do not carelessly link two main clauses with only a comma between them (comma splice), or, worse, without any punctuation (fused sentence).

COMMA SPLICE   The current was swift, he could not swim to shore. [Two main clauses linked only by a comma]

FUSED SENTENCE   The current was swift he could not swim to shore. [Omission of all punctuation makes an error even worse than the comma splice.]

If you cannot recognize main clauses and distinguish them from subordinate clauses, study Section 1, **Sentence Sense**, as you apply the following instructions to your writing.

3a

Correct either comma splices or fused sentences by one of the following methods:

(1) **By subordinating one of the main clauses—usually the best method. (See also Section 24.)**

WRONG   The current was swift, he could not swim to shore.

RIGHT   Since the current was swift, he could not swim to shore. [First main clause changed to a subordinate clause]

PATTERN   SUBORDINATE CLAUSE, MAIN CLAUSE.

RIGHT The current was so swift that he could not swim to shore. [With the second main clause changed to a subordinate clause, the pattern is reversed and no comma is needed.]

RIGHT Because of the swift current he could not swim to shore. [First main clause changed to a prepositional phrase]

RIGHT The swiftness of the current prevented his swimming to shore. [The two main clauses changed to one simple sentence]

(2) By making each main clause into a sentence.

WRONG Hiking is great fun you should try it. [Fused sentence]

RIGHT Hiking is great fun. You should try it. [Each main clause made into a sentence]

RIGHT The current was swift. He could not swim to shore.

PATTERN SENTENCE. SENTENCE.

(3) By joining the main clauses with a semicolon.

WRONG Hiking is great fun, you should try it. [Comma splice]

RIGHT Hiking is great fun; you should try it.

RIGHT The current was swift; he could not swim to shore.

PATTERN MAIN CLAUSE ; MAIN CLAUSE.

(4) By joining the main clauses with a comma + a co-ordinating conjunction.

WRONG I thought about the problem, I found the solution. [Comma splice]

RIGHT I thought about the problem, and I found the solution. [Main clauses joined by a comma + *and*, one of the co-ordinating conjunctions]

PATTERN
MAIN CLAUSE ,*and* (or *but, or, nor, for*) MAIN CLAUSE.

Some exceptions: Short co-ordinate clauses in series, parallel in form and unified in thought, may be separated by commas.

RIGHT I came, I saw, I conquered.

ALSO RIGHT I came; I saw; I conquered.

The comma is also used to separate a statement from an echo question.

You can come, can't you? [Statement echoed by question]

Main clauses separated only by commas are fairly common in some informal types of writing. Occasionally examples are found in more formal writing, chiefly when there is a balance or contrast between the clauses.

But this was better, this was much more satisfying.
—ALDOUS HUXLEY

The English of those days did not paint broadly, they filled in with deft touches. —BONAMY DOBRÉE

They were unprepared, their people were divided and demoralized. —WALTER LIPPMANN

But the immature writer is much more likely to produce an ordinary comma splice than an effective sentence of this sort. He will do well to make sure that main clauses in his sentences are separated (1) by a comma + a coordinate conjunction or (2) by a semicolon.

3b

Caution: Do not let a conjunctive adverb, a transitional phrase, or a divided quotation trick you into making a comma splice. (See also 14a.)

Conjunctive adverbs (such as *accordingly, also, anyhow, besides, consequently, furthermore, hence, henceforth, however, indeed, instead, likewise, moreover, meanwhile, nevertheless, otherwise, still, then, therefore, thus*) and **transitional phrases** (such as *for example, in fact, on the contrary, on the other hand, that is*) connecting main clauses are always preceded by a semicolon.

EXAMPLES

I don't like ice cream; however, I eat it sometimes at parties.
I don't like ice cream; therefore I seldom eat it.
I seldom eat ice cream; in fact, I do not like it.

On the other hand, co-ordinating conjunctions (*and, but, or, nor, for*) connecting main clauses are usually preceded by a comma.

EXAMPLE   I don't like ice cream, but I eat it sometimes at parties.

Note this difference: the co-ordinating conjunction is restricted to its position *between* the main clauses; the conjunctive adverb (or the transitional phrase) may come between the main clauses or at various places within the clause following the semicolon.

EXAMPLES

I don't like ice cream; I eat it, however, sometimes at parties.
I don't like ice cream; I eat it sometimes, however, at parties.
I don't like ice cream; at parties, however, I sometimes eat it.

Divided quotations

WRONG   "Your answer is wrong," he said, "correct it."
RIGHT   "Your answer is wrong," he said. "Correct it."

WRONG   "What are you looking for?" she asked, "may I help you?"
RIGHT   "What are you looking for?" she asked. "May I help you?"

EXERCISES ON BUILDING SENTENCES
AND OBSERVING SENTENCE PATTERNS
(TO AVOID THE COMMA SPLICE)

▶ EXERCISE 1   Write two sentences to illustrate each construction specified below.

1. Main clause; main clause.
2. Main clause, *coordinating conjunction* main clause.
3. Main clause; *conjunctive adverb* (,) main clause.
4. Sentence. Sentence beginning with a conjunctive adverb.
5. Main clause; *transitional phrase,* main clause.
6. Sentence. Sentence beginning with a transitional phrase.
7. Sentence. Sentence interrupted by a transitional phrase or a conjunctive adverb.

▶ EXERCISE 2   All of the following sentences (selected from *Harper's Magazine*) are correctly punctuated. Identify the pattern or construction of each sentence.

1. The other day a police car shot past me at about 150 miles an hour, and I did not even crunch my toes.
2. Most significant is the rapid increase in tax cheating in all income groups; this always bespeaks wide resistance to the tax level.
3. The plan was unanimously approved. Moreover, it worked.
4. But policemen are scarce in the country districts; besides, the Moustheni Explorers planned to work at night.
5. Among other things he has put out a salty critique, enumerating with pertinent cartoons and pungent examples "Ten Common Pitfalls." In one section, for example, Kahn addresses himself to the danger of trying to prepare for opposite extremes.
6. Some call his theory nonsense; others think it has revolutionary significance.
7. Some will admire it greatly, and some will detest it.
8. Winter is reluctantly loosening its grip on this land; storm after storm alternates with brief periods of thaw.
9. In the gardens of Hyderabad House the lilac bushes dripped softly; water trickled through the channels of rockeries and overflowed the normally arid bowls of the fountains.
10. He may haggle fiercely over details, but he also has a magnificent detachment and an almost saintly freedom from any sense of grievance toward his detractors.

EXERCISES ON RECOGNITION AND REVISION
OF THE COMMA SPLICE

▶ EXERCISE 3   Determine which of the following sentences contain comma splices. (As an aid to your analysis, you may wish to bracket each subordinate clause and to under-line the subject and verb of each main clause.) Write *C* after each sentence that needs no revision. Correct each comma splice in the most appropriate way.

1. There used to be alligators in that lake, I remember seeing them when I was a boy.
2. "This is the way you do it," he explained, "you step on the clutch and the brake and press the starter."
3. We were lucky in our choice of a day for the trip, though it had been raining at bedtime, the weather cleared during the night.
4. There was no coffee, no bacon, no bread, and the milk had begun to sour, therefore my breakfast consisted of marmalade and four limp crackers.
5. Walt calls that place of his a "farm," but "weed patch" would describe it better, wouldn't it?
6. Typhus used to kill far more soldiers than warfare itself did, however, this disease is little heard of now.
7. Washington Irving was one of the first American writers to exploit local legends, by writing "Rip Van Winkle," he helped to start America's folklore tradition.
8. To earn money by baby-sitting, a co-ed must know the rudiments of domestic science, for example, she should know how to warm a bottle and burp the baby.
9. If Jay's batting eye had been a little better, for example, he would have been the best baseball player in the league.
10. On top of the hill is a windmill, after you pass that, you will see the town in the valley below.

▶ EXERCISE 4   Revise each comma splice (or fused sentence) by some method of subordination. Write *C* after any sentence that needs no revision.

1. Frantically I wound and jerked the starting cord a tow of gravel barges was bearing directly down upon me.

2. Sheila has her mind made up, nothing you can say will change it.
3. We have enough bricks we can build a barbecue pit.
4. I spoke of the Rufus Kane matter to Chief Kelly, he recalled the case quite clearly.
5. The plaster hardens rapidly it should not be mixed in large quantities.
6. When you come to a red brick church across from a filling station, turn left and go exactly one block.
7. There is a roadside market on the Maryville highway you can buy all the berries you want there.
8. At farrowing, her pigs weighed slightly over three pounds apiece, this is a little above average weight.
9. We do not plan to come back in the fall, therefore we are giving up our apartment.
10. One man was digging at the bottom of the well, the other stayed at the top to haul up the loose dirt.

▶ EXERCISE 5 Revise each comma splice (or fused sentence) by the method that seems most appropriate. Be ready to explain and justify the method used. Write C after any sentence that needs no revision. (You may find it helpful to analyze the sentences as directed in Exercise 3.)

1. Let me know at least a week before you expect to be here, I will need that long to get your cabin ready.
2. You must first preheat your oven then you put your rolls in to bake.
3. The winters here are quite mild, however I cannot say the same for the summers.
4. I could have sworn I had an extra pair of shoelaces in this drawer, I surely can't find them now.
5. I have never been able to understand why there is no traffic light on this corner.
6. "Don't unsaddle him," George called from the doorway, "I'll want to ride down after the mail in a minute or two."

7. The Santa Gertrudis is an American breed of cattle, it was developed to combine the heat-resistance of the Brahma with the meat-producing qualities of the Shorthorn.

8. In 1728 William Byrd was a member of a party of surveyors, they were charged with the task of determining the proper boundary between Virginia and North Carolina.

9. The bay was far too rough to venture upon, therefore we decided to walk around by land.

10. The Red Cross opened its blood bank to the survivors, as a result, many lives were saved.

EXERCISES ON THE SENTENCE FRAGMENT AND COMMA SPLICE

▶ EXERCISE 6   Test the following for sentence fragments and comma splices (or fused sentences) and make appropriate corrections. Write *C* after any numbered item that needs no revision.

1. The teacher's friendliness impressed me. Nothing like that having been expected.

2. Just to stand up in the face of life's problems. That takes courage.

3. A few hundred feet out in the lake, drifting away in the offshore wind, was a derelict canoe.

4. Edgar Allan Poe attended West Point there he was not a success.

5. Dine at the Campus Cookery. Where the beans taste like caviar.

6. Hour after hour Coast Guard boats methodically zigzagged over the area, sweeping the water with searchlights.

7. Strange-sounding names and faraway places. Travel brings you to them.

8. Some students claim that Walt Whitman is the best American poet, their opinion of his works, however,

is far too favorable, according to the admirers of Lowell, Longfellow, Whittier, and Emily Dickinson.

9. Some of the most beautiful scenery in Canada is in the Maritime Provinces. The forests, the rivers, and the sea in combination.

10. But the peasants remember many periods of inflation, and they therefore prefer to keep their produce rather than exchange it for paper currency.

▶ EXERCISE 7 Correct each fragment and comma splice in the following paragraph by the method that seems most suitable. Be ready to explain and justify the method used. Write C after each sentence that needs no revision.

1. When Boyd and Nancy were preparing to move to Pennsylvania. 2. Nancy asked me if I knew anybody who would want a cigar box full of cat bones. 3. These were the dismantled parts of a cat skeleton. 4. Which she had used when teaching a science course in the local school. 5. I told her that I would be delighted to have them. 6. Feeling quite sure that the day would come when I should find them useful. 7. In this way one former cat, retired from teaching, found a home with me, then I went on my vacation, and while I was away, my landlady decided to refinish the floor of my room. 8. I suppose I should count it among my blessings. 9. That I wasn't around to hear what she had to say about the miscellaneous gear I have accumulated during my residence there. 10. But she was very kind about it all. 11. And had nothing to say when I came back. 12. Except that she hoped I liked the new floor. 13. The floor was quite elegant, her rearrangement of my goods and chattels is a puzzle that I haven't yet altogether untangled. 14. I am still finding, in all sorts of odd places, things that I had long ago forgotten. 15. But search as I will, I cannot find those cat bones, I wish I had the nerve to ask what she did with them.

Adjectives and Adverbs

4

Distinguish between adjectives and adverbs and use the appropriate forms.

Adjectives and adverbs are modifiers. That is, they make clearer and more specific the meaning of other words in the sentence. Adjectives modify nouns; adverbs modify verbs, adjectives, other adverbs, or whole clauses. In the following sentences the adjectives are in **boldface** and the adverbs are in *italics*.

Boys like toys. [No modifiers]

Young boys *usually* like **colored** toys.

Very **young** boys *almost always* like *brightly* **colored** toys.

Unquestionably, boys like toys. [*Unquestionably* modifies the whole clause, *boys like toys.*]

FORMS OF ADJECTIVES AND ADVERBS

Most adjectives and adverbs have distinct forms which must be used with care. The dictionary shows, for example, that the form *beautiful* is used only as an adjective and *beautifully* only as an adverb: The **beautiful** woman sang *beautifully.* In this sentence *beautiful* is the required form as modifier of the noun *woman,* and *beautifully* is the required form as modifier of the verb *sang.*

Although the *-ly* ending is the usual sign for the adverb, a few words ending in *-ly* are adjectives. As a rule, the *-ly* makes adjectives out of nouns (*man* becomes *manly*) and adverbs out of adjectives (*bashful* becomes *bashfully*). A few other words ending in *-ly* (such as *only, early, cowardly*) may be either adjectives or adverbs, and the same is true for a considerable number of common words not ending in *-ly* (such as *far, fast, late, little, near, right, straight, well*).

ADJECTIVES	ADVERBS
He came on a **late** train.	He came *late*.
I have **little** energy.	He was a *little* ambitious.
The **early** bird gets the worm.	He rose *early* to go to work.

A good dictionary shows the appropriate form for adjective or adverb, but only the use to which the word is put in the sentence determines whether the adjective or the adverb form is required.

▶ EXERCISE 1   Compose sentences to illustrate each of the following words (1) as an adjective and (2) as an adverb: *only, far, near, right, straight.*

▶ EXERCISE 2   In the following sentences identify each italicized word as an adjective or an adverb and explain why it is appropriately used.

1. We took a *leisurely* drive. We drove *leisurely*.
2. He is *sure* of victory. He will *surely* win.
3. The Boy Scouts did *good* work. The Boy Scouts did the work *well*.
4. The silence in the catacombs was *awful*. It was *awfully* silent in the catacombs.
5. I feel *bad* after failing that test. I failed that test *badly*.
6. He expressed *real* gratitude. He was *really* grateful.

4a

Use the adverb form for modifiers of verbs, adjectives, and other adverbs.

(1) Modifiers of verbs

WRONG   His clothes fit him *perfect*. [The adjective *perfect* misused to modify the verb *fit*]

RIGHT   His clothes fit him *perfectly*.

WRONG   He ran *good* for the first half mile. [The adjective *good* misused to modify the verb *ran*]

RIGHT   He ran *well* for the first half mile.

(2) Modifiers of adjectives

WRONG   The farmer has a *reasonable* secure future. [The adjective *reasonable* misused to modify the adjective *secure*]

RIGHT   The farmer has a *reasonably* secure future.

WRONG   The plane was a *special* built fighter.

RIGHT   The plane was a *specially* built fighter.

COLLOQUIAL[1]   *Most* all men

STANDARD   *Almost* all men [*Almost* is the regular adverb.]

COLLOQUIAL (OR DIALECTAL)   It's *real* hot.

STANDARD   It's *really* (or *very*) hot.

(3) Modifiers of adverbs

COLLOQUIAL   She was *most* always late.

STANDARD   She was *almost* always late.

4b

Use the adjective form after linking verbs.

LINKING VERBS   *Is, was, were, am, are,* etc., *seems, becomes* (and their equivalents) and the verbs pertaining to the senses (*feel, look, smell, sound, taste*).

PATTERN   SUBJECT—LINKING VERB—ADJECTIVE.

[1] For the distinction between colloquial and standard usage see Section 19.

In the following sentences each italicized adjective modifies the subject.

The man is *old*. [*Old* man]
Still water runs (*or* is) *deep*. [*Deep* water]
The dog acts (*or* seems) *intelligent*. [*Intelligent* dog]
The tree grew (*or* became) *tall*. [*Tall* tree]
James returned (*or* was) *tired*. [*Tired* James]
The woman looked *angry*. [An *angry* woman]

Apparent exception: The modifier should be an adverb when it refers to the action of the verb. In that case the verb is not used as a linking verb.

PATTERN   SUBJECT—VERB—ADVERB.

The blind beggar felt *cautiously* along the wall. [The adverb *cautiously* qualifies the verb *felt*.]
The woman looked *angrily* at him. [The adverb *angrily* qualifies the verb *looked*.]

Note: A modifier following a verb and its direct object is an adjective when it refers to the object rather than to the action of the verb.

PATTERN   SUBJECT—VERB—OBJECT—ADJECTIVE.

The man dug the hole *deep*. [*Deep* is an adjective: *deep* hole.]
The boy held the rope *tight*. [*Tight* rope]

▶ EXERCISE 3   Write five sentences to illustrate this pattern:

SUBJECT—LINKING VERB—PREDICATE ADJECTIVE.

4c

Use the appropriate forms for the comparative and the superlative.

In general the shorter adjectives (and a few adverbs) form the comparative degree by adding *-er* and the superlative by adding *-est;* the longer adjectives and most adverbs form the comparative by the use of *more* (*less*) and the superlative by the use of *most* (*least*). Some adjectives, such as *good* and *bad*, and some adverbs, such as *well* and *badly*, have an irregular comparison. But these are among our common words and are seldom confused.

	Positive	*Comparative*	*Superlative*
ADJECTIVES	warm	warmer	warmest
	exhausted	more exhausted	most exhausted
	good	better	best
	bad	worse	worst
ADVERBS	warmly	more warmly	most warmly
	well	better	best
	badly	worse	worst

(1) **Use the comparative degree for two persons or things.**

Was Monday or Tuesday *warmer?*
James was the *taller* of the two boys. [The superlative is occasionally used in such sentences, especially in informal speaking and writing.]

(2) **Use the superlative degree for three or more persons or things.**

Today is the *warmest* day of the year.
William was the *tallest* of the three boys.

4d

Avoid any awkward or ambiguous use of a noun form as an adjective.

Although many noun forms (*boat* race, *show* business, *opera* tickets, etc.) are used effectively as adjectives, especially when appropriate adjectives are not available, such forms should be avoided when they are either awkward or ambiguous.

AWKWARD	The man sometimes forgets his *gentleman* habits.
BETTER	The man sometimes forgets his *gentlemanly* habits. [The regular adjective form substituted]

AMBIGUOUS IN WRITING   The *head doctor* spoke.
CLEAR   The doctor in charge of the operation spoke.
CLEAR   The psychiatrist spoke.

▶ EXERCISE 4   In the following sentences choose the standard form of the modifier within parentheses. Justify your choice by a simple diagram or by analysis of the sentence. If necessary, use your dictionary to distinguish between formal and colloquial usage.

1. If you study (consistent, consistently) and (regular, regularly), you should overcome (most, almost) any handicap.
2. The wind blew (fierce, fiercely), and the snow fell (continuous, continuously) all the long night.
3. The next few weeks passed very (rapid, rapidly).
4. I am afraid that the good woman is (some, somewhat) confused.
5. Dave is (uncommon, uncommonly) light on his feet for such a (heavy, heavily) built man.
6. It was a (fair, fairly), warm day in April.
7. It was a (fair, fairly) warm day in April.
8. Mr. Porter was so excited that he could not play his part (good, well).
9. I want someone who can do the work (prompt and efficient, promptly and efficiently) and still behave (courteous, courteously) toward the customers.
10. Do you realize how (bad, badly) your mother will feel if you do not work (steady, steadily) or (serious, seriously) enough?

▶ EXERCISE 5   Revise the following sentences to provide the proper adjectives or adverbs in accordance with standard English usage. Write *C* after each sentence that needs no revision.

1. William, the oldest of the two brothers, always got along good with his studies.

2. Timmy felt sleepily under his pillow to see if the tooth was still there.
3. If you didn't snore so noisy, you wouldn't keep waking yourself up.
4. A good hog has short legs and a reasonable wide body.
5. The author pictures the scene so vivid that the reader is eager to know what happens next.
6. If you want to catch him, you had better be quick about it.
7. We felt sure we had acted quick enough.
8. The boys played good last Saturday and won the game very easy.
9. I have tried both brands, and I still cannot decide which I like best.
10. Henry, I do wish you would not stop so sudden.

▶ EXERCISE 6   Using standard English, compose sentences containing the constructions specified below.

1. *fast* used as an adjective
2. *fast* used as an adverb
3. *surely* used as a modifier of a verb
4. a predicate adjective after *looked*
5. an adverb modifying *looked*
6. an adjective following and modifying a direct object
7. an adverb following a direct object and modifying the verb
8. the superlative form of *bad*
9. the comparative form of *good*
10. a clear, effective noun form used as an adjective

Case

5
Use the proper case form to show the function of pronouns or nouns in sentences.

The case of a pronoun is the form it takes to show its function in the sentence as subject of a verb (subjective or nominative case), possessor (possessive case), or object of a verb, verbal, or preposition (objective case). Nouns and some indefinite pronouns (*anyone, someone, everyone,* etc.) have a distinctive case form only for the possessive (the *boy's* book, the *boys'* mother; see 15a), but six of our common pronouns have distinctive forms in all three cases and must be used with care.

Subjective:	I	we	he, she	they	who
Possessive:	my	our	his, her	their	whose
	(mine)	(ours)	(hers)	(theirs)	
Objective:	me	us	him, her	them	whom

Note: The personal pronouns *it* and *you* change form only to indicate the possessive—*its, your, (yours)*.

5a
Take special care with pronouns in apposition and in compound constructions.

(1) Appositives

An appositive takes the same case as the noun or pronoun with which it is in apposition.

WRONG	We—John and *me*—are responsible for the damage.
RIGHT	We—John and *I*—are responsible for the damage. [*I* takes the subjective case with *we* since the two pronouns are in apposition.]
WRONG	The damage was caused by us—John and *I*.
RIGHT	The damage was caused by us—John and *me*. [*Me* in the objective case, the same as *us*]
WRONG	Let's you and *I* go together.
RIGHT	Let's you and *me* go together. Let us—you and *me*—go together. [*Me* and *us* in the same case]
WRONG	Two boys—John and *me*—represented our class.
RIGHT	Two boys—John and *I*—represented our class. [*I* must be in the subjective case since it is in apposition with the subject *boys*.]
RIGHT	Our class was represented by two boys, John and *me*. [*Me* in the objective case since it is in apposition with *boys*, object of the preposition *by*.]

Note: Do not let an appositive following a pronoun trick you into making a mistake with case.

EXAMPLES	*We* boys often study together. [*We* is the subject of *study*: We *study*. No one would write Us *study*.]
	He would not let *us* girls do any of the hard work. [Since *us* is the subject of the infinitive (*to*) *do*, it takes the objective case. See **5e**.]

(2) Compound constructions

WRONG	My brother and *me* share expenses.
RIGHT	My brother and *I* share expenses. [*I* is a subject of the verb *share*.]
WRONG	Everyone but Hazel and *she* signed the petition.
RIGHT	Everyone but Hazel and *her* signed the petition. [Her is an object of the preposition *but*.]
WRONG	Last summer my father hired Tom and *I*.
RIGHT	Last summer my father hired Tom and *me*. [*Me* is an object of the verb *hired*.]

Caution: In formal writing *myself* is usually avoided as a substitute for *I* or *me*. See **19i**.

▶ EXERCISE 1 Compose brief sentences correctly using five of the following compound elements as appositives and five as subjects or objects.

1. Bill and he
2. Bill and him
3. you or I
4. you or me
5. her sister and her
6. her sister and she
7. Ann and she
8. her and Ann
9. they or we
10. them or us

5b

Determine the case of each pronoun by its use in its own clause.

(1) Pronoun as subject of a clause.

The subject of a clause always takes the subjective case, even when the whole clause is the object of a verb or a preposition.

WRONG He will employ *whomever* is willing to work.
RIGHT He will employ *whoever* is willing to work. [*Whoever* is the subject of *is willing*. The whole clause *whoever is willing to work* is the object of *will employ*.]

WRONG He has respect for *whomever* is in power.
RIGHT He has respect for *whoever* is in power. [The complete clause *whoever is in power*, not merely the pronoun *whoever*, is the object of the preposition *for*.]

(2) Pronoun followed by a parenthetical *I think*, *he says*, etc.

Such parenthetical expressions as *I think*, *he says*, *we know* often cause the subjective *who* (*whoever*, *whosoever*) to be incorrectly changed to *whom* (*whomever*, *whomsoever*).

WRONG   Henry is a person *whom* I think will prove worthy of every trust.

RIGHT   Henry is a person *who* I think will prove worthy of every trust. [*Who* is the subject of *will prove*.]

$$\frac{who \ \ \ will \ prove}{}$$

WRONG   Jones is a man *whom* we know is dependable.

RIGHT   Jones is a man *who* we know is dependable.

(3) Pronoun following *than* or *as*.

A pronoun following *than* or *as* takes the subjective or objective case according to whether the pronoun is subject or object of an implied verb.

EXAMPLES   He is older than *I* [am].

He is as wise as *they* [are].

He likes you better than *I* [like you].

He likes you as much as *I* [like you].

He likes you better than [he likes] *me*.

He likes you as much as [he likes] *me*.

5c

In formal writing use *whom* for all objects.

EXAMPLE   For whom did you vote? [Good usage, formal or informal, always requires the objective *whom* when it immediately follows a preposition.]

Informal English tends to avoid the use of the objective *whom* unless it comes immediately after a preposition.

FORMAL   *Whom* did you vote for?

INFORMAL   Who did you vote for? [*Who* may be used in an informal situation to begin any question.]

RIGHT   The artist *whom* she loved has gone away. [*Whom* is the object of the verb *loved*.]

RIGHT   The artist she loved has gone away. [*Whom* is avoided.]

▶ EXERCISE 2 First, underline each subordinate clause below and determine the use of the relative pronoun in its own clause; then choose the correct pronoun within the parentheses.

1. (Who, Whom) will be his opponent is not yet known.
2. (Who, Whom) he will fight is not yet known.
3. He will fight (whoever, whomever) the officials choose.
4. He will fight (whoever, whomever) wins today's boxing match.
5. Lefty Larson is the man (who, whom) I think will win.
6. Mildred, (who, whom) is a good cook, wants to borrow your recipe.
7. Mildred, (who, whom) you know, wants to ride with you to church.
8. Frank, (who, whom) you know is a poor dancer, prefers to go skating.
9. I will vote for (whoever, whomever) I think will make the best president.
10. Is that the blonde (who, whom) you were telling me about?

5d

A pronoun immediately before the gerund (verbal noun) is usually in the possessive case.

EXAMPLES *His* leaving the farm was a surprise.
Mother approved of *my (our, his, her, your, their)* going to the fair.

Note: Since the gerund (verbal noun) and the present participle (verbal adjective) both end in *-ing*, they are sometimes difficult to distinguish. See **Verbals**, Section **35**. When the emphasis is on the noun or pronoun preceding the verbal, the verbal may be interpreted as a participle modifying the noun or pronoun. Then the noun or pronoun is not used in the possessive case.

PARTICIPLE (VERBAL ADJECTIVE)	GERUND (VERBAL NOUN)
We caught *John* running away.	*John's* running away was unexpected.
We could not think of *him* acting the part.	*His* acting was surprisingly good.

5e

Use the objective case for subject, object, or complement of an infinitive.

EXAMPLES He asked *me* to help *him*. [*Me* is the subject and *him* is the object of the infinitive *to help. Me to help him* is the object of the verb *asked.*]

We expected *him* to be *her*. [*Him* is the subject and *her* is the complement of the infinitive *to be.*]

Note: In formal writing the complement of the infinitive *to be* is in the subjective case when the infinitive *to be* has no subject.

I would like to be *he.*

5f

Use the subjective case for the complement of the verb *be.*

PATTERN SUBJECT—LINKING VERB *BE*—COMPLEMENT.

That	may be	*he (she).*
It	was	*he (she, they).*
It	is	*I.*

Note: Informal usage accepts *It is me (It's me).*

▶ EXERCISE 3 Give the reason why each italicized noun or pronoun below is correct by pointing out its function. If any sentence sounds wrong to you, read it aloud several times so that you will become accustomed to saying and hearing correct case forms.

1. Just between you and *me*, both her sister and *she* are in love with the same man.
2. The losers, you and *he*, deserve this booby prize.
3. It is Doris and *she whom* he blames.
4. He blames Doris and *her*, not you and *me*.
5. *Jack's* teasing did not annoy Tom or *me*.
6. Since Marian eats a great deal more than *I*, I do not weigh as much as *she*.
7. Let's you and *me* send an invitation to Kate and *him*.
8. The professor asked *us* students to write a composition about bores *whom* we know.
9. He introduced me to Ruth and *her*, *who* I think are his sisters.
10. *We* boys always co-operate with our coach, *whom* we respect and *who* respects us.

▶ EXERCISE 4   Choose the correct pronoun within parentheses below; give a reason for each choice.

1. Bob and (I, me), (who, whom) usually swim near the beach, encountered serious trouble last week when (he, him) and (I, me) decided to swim out far beyond the breakers. 2. For a while, splashing about in the deep water was great fun for (we, us) swimmers. 3. Soon, however, when a rip tide took Bob and (I, me) by surprise, our laughter quickly changed to screams. 4. For what seemed like eternity, Bob and (I, me) futilely struggled to free ourselves from the opposing currents. 5. Of course, we kept screaming for help, though there was no one (who, whom) we thought could hear us—no one else so foolish as (we, us), (who, whom) would dare go beyond the breakers.

6. Suddenly, out of nowhere, there appeared a skinny little man (who, whom) it seemed would never have the strength to save either Bob or (I, me). 7. Yet, without a word, this scrawny creature swam out to Bob and (I, me), knocked me unconscious, and saved my life. 8. Without

assistance from either the man or (I, me), Bob eventually saved himself by drifting with the churning currents instead of fighting them.

9. On the beach a curious crowd gathered around Bob and (I, me), but the man (who, whom) had saved my life was nowhere to be found.   10. And never again did Bob or (I, me) see the tiny swimmer (who, whom), like an apparition, had vanished as quickly and as strangely as he had appeared.

▶ EXERCISE 5   Find and correct all case errors in the following sentences. Write C after each sentence that needs no revision.

1. He can play a trumpet as well as me.
2. It was she who paid the bill.
3. Helen objected to me encouraging him to join the fraternity.
4. Us girls should do the cooking.
5. Between you and I, I wouldn't trust Joey Piper's dead body in a lead coffin.
6. Let's all—Walter, Luke, you, and I—give her a surprise birthday party.
7. I enjoy reading satire as much as he.
8. Whom do you think is the best pitcher in the league?
9. That must be either her brother or she at the door now.
10. Sheriff Comstock, to who I had introduced myself, had on his desk the records of three men who he believed were capable of committing a burglary such as that in East Dover Heights.

Agreement

6

Make a verb agree in number with its subject; make a pronoun agree in number with its antecedent.[1]

If you find it difficult to distinguish verbs and relate them to their subjects, you may need to review 1a and 1b.

Singular subjects require singular verbs; plural subjects require plural verbs. Pronouns agree with their antecedents (the words to which they refer) in the same way. Note that in the subject the -s ending is the sign of the plural, that in the verb it is the sign of the third person singular.

EXAMPLES   The *engine runs* smoothly. [Singular subject—singular verb]

The *engines run* smoothly. [Plural subject—plural verb]

The *woman* washes *her* clothes. [Singular antecedent—singular pronoun]

The *women* wash *their* clothes. [Plural antecedent—plural pronoun]

Make a diagram, or at least form a mental picture, of each subject and its verb

$$\left(\frac{engine \mid runs}{\qquad} \qquad \frac{engines \mid run}{\qquad} \right)$$

and of each antecedent and its pronoun (*woman* ← *her*, *women* ← *their*). This practice will make it easy to avoid errors in agreement.

---

[1] For other kinds of agreement see Section 27.

6a

Make a verb agree in number with its subject.

(1) Do not be misled (a) by nouns or pronouns intervening between the subject and the verb or (b) by subjects and verbs with endings difficult to pronounce.

WRONG   The *recurrence* of like sounds *help* to stir the emotions.

RIGHT   The *recurrence* of like sounds *helps* to stir the emotions.

WRONG   His *interest were* many and varied. These *risk seem* unnecessary. The *scientist ask* pertinent questions. The *Communist are* . . . .

RIGHT   His *interests were* . . . . These *risks seem* . . . . The *scientist asks* . . . . The *scientists ask* . . . . The *Communists are* . . . .

The number of the subject is not changed by the addition of parenthetical expressions introduced by such words as *with, together with, as well as, no less than, including, accompanied by.*

> *John,* together with James and William, *was drafted* into the Army.
>
> *Thomas,* like his two brothers, *was* often in debt.

(2) Subjects joined by *and* are usually plural.

> A hammer and a saw *are* useful tools.
>
> Mary, Jane, and I *were* tired after our morning's work.

Exceptions: A compound subject referring to a single person, or to two or more things considered as a unit, is singular.

> My best friend and adviser *has gone.* [A single individual was both friend and adviser.]
>
> The tumult and the shouting *dies.*—KIPLING. [Two nouns considered a single entity]

Each or *every* preceding singular subjects joined by *and* calls for a singular verb.

Each boy and each girl *is* to work independently.
Every boy and girl *has been urged* to attend the play.

(3) Singular subjects joined by *or, nor, either . . . or, neither . . . nor* usually take a singular verb.

Neither the boy nor the girl *is* to blame for the accident.
Either the man or his wife *knows* the exact truth of the matter.

When the meaning is felt to be plural, informal English occasionally uses the plural verb: "Neither she nor I *were* dancing, for we felt tired."

If one subject is singular and one plural, the verb usually agrees with the nearer.

PERMISSIBLE Neither teacher nor pupils *are* in the building.
PERMISSIBLE Neither pupils nor teacher *is* in the building.

PERMISSIBLE Either you or I *am* mistaken.
BETTER Either you *are* mistaken or I *am*.

(4) When the subject follows the verb (as in sentences beginning with *there is, there are*) special care is needed to determine the subject and to make sure that it agrees with the verb.

According to the rules, there *are* to be at least three *contestants* for each prize.

contestants	*are*

There *are* many possible *candidates*.
There *is* only one good *candidate*.

Before a compound subject the first member of which is singular, a singular verb is sometimes used: "In the basement there *is* a restaurant, which serves delicious food, and a poolroom and two barber shops."

Note: The expletive *it* is always followed by a singular verb: "It *is* the *woman* who suffers." "It *is* the *women* who suffer."

(5) A relative pronoun used as a subject takes a plural or singular verb to accord with its antecedent.

> *Boys* who *work* . . . A *boy* who *works* . . .
> Mary is among the *students* who *have done* honor to the college. [*Students* is the antecedent of *who*.]
> Mary is the only *one* of our students who *has achieved* national recognition. [*One*, not *students*, is the antecedent of *who*. The sentence means, "Of all our students Mary is the only *one* who *has achieved* national recognition."]

(6) The indefinite pronouns *each, either, neither, another, anyone, anybody, anything, someone, somebody, something, one, everyone, everybody, everything, nobody, nothing* regularly take singular verbs.

> Each *takes* his turn at rowing.
> Neither *likes* the friends of the other.
> Someone *is* likely to hear the signal.
> Everyone *has* his prejudices.
> Nobody *cares* to listen to worries.

None is plural or singular, depending upon the other words in the sentence or in the immediately surrounding sentences (the context) which condition its meaning.

> None *are* so blind as those who will not see.
> None *is* so blind as he who will not see.

(*Any, all, more, most* and *some* are used with plural or singular verbs in much the same way as *none*.)

(7) Collective nouns (and numbers denoting fixed quantity) usually take singular verbs because the group or quantity is usually regarded as a unit.

> The whole family *is* concerned. [The common use: *family* regarded as a unit]
> The family *have gone* about their several duties. [Less common: individuals of the family regarded separately]

A thousand bushels *is* a good yield. [A unit]
A thousand bushels *were crated.* [Individual bushels]

The number in the class *was* small. [*The number* is regularly taken as a unit.]
A number of the class *were* sick. [*A number* refers to individuals.]

The data *is* sound. [A unit]
The data *have been* carefully *collected.* [Individual items]

(8) **A verb agrees with its subject, not with its predicate noun.**

RIGHT   His chief support *is* his brother and sister.
RIGHT   His brother and sister *are* his chief support.

But such sentences are often better recast so as to avoid the disagreement in number between subject and predicate noun.

BETTER   His support came chiefly from his brother and sister.

(9) **Nouns plural in form but singular in meaning usually take singular verbs. In all doubtful cases a good dictionary should be consulted.**

Regularly singular: acoustics, aesthetics, civics, economics, genetics, linguistics, mathematics, measles, mumps, news, physics, semantics

Regularly plural: environs, trousers

Some nouns ending in *-ics* (such as *athletics, acoustics,* and *statistics*) are considered singular when referring to an organized body of knowledge and plural when referring to activities, qualities, or individual facts.

Athletics [various games] *provide* good recreation.
Athletics [activity in games] *builds* strong muscles.

Acoustics *is* an interesting study.
The acoustics of the hall *are* good.

Statistics *is* a science.
The statistics *were* easily *assembled.*

(10) A title of a single work or a word spoken of as a word, even when plural in form, takes a singular verb.

> *Twice-Told Tales was written* by Hawthorne.
> The New York *Times has* a wide circulation.
> *They is* a pronoun.

▶ EXERCISE 1   Read the following correct sentences aloud, stressing the italicized words. If any sentence sounds wrong to you, read it aloud as many times as necessary for the verb form to sound right.

1. After the lecture, *everybody* in the group *is* invited to meet the speaker.
2. The *farmer,* as well as his sons, *grows* wheat.
3. *Each* of those lawyers *has* won many suits.
4. One of the *men who were* fishing on the pier caught a stingaree.
5. He was the *only one* in the group *who was* bored.
6. A *dictionary* and a *thesaurus are* lying on my desk.
7. Doyle's "*The Five Orange Pips*" *is* a fascinating story.
8. There *are* a few *cookies* and potato *chips* left.
9. Here *come* the *clowns!*
10. Every *one* of the *boys who belong* to the organization *is* planning to help build and decorate the float.

▶ EXERCISE 2   Choose the correct form of the verb within parentheses in each of the following sentences.

1. Neither of those boys (have, has) taken the qualifying examination.
2. There (are, is) still several problems to be solved.
3. The books on that shelf (are, is) dusty.
4. Every magazine in those racks (are, is) at least six months old.
5. Each of the lawyers (seem, seems) ambitious and capable.
6. The cat or her kittens (are, is) to blame for turning over the Christmas tree.

7. (Do, Does) either of you know how to play bridge?
8. Everyone in the stands (were, was) unusually quiet.
9. The millionaire, along with his wife and three sons, often (travel, travels) abroad.
10. Down (go, goes) the red handkerchiefs! Several of the players (were, was) offside.

▶ EXERCISE 3   In the following sentences, find each verb and relate it to its subject. Then revise each sentence to secure agreement of subject and verb. Justify every change. Write C after each sentence that needs no revision.

1. Neither of you appreciates my sense of humor.
2. Do either of you know where to go if the alarm should sound?
3. This book, a collection of recent articles published by the editor and others, give you a comprehensive view of a many-sided question.
4. There come to my mind now three men who might have qualified, but none of the three was given the chance.
5. Everybody one met in the streets that summer were excitedly talking about Essex's homecoming.
6. The significance of words are taught by simply breaking them up into suffixes, prefixes, and roots.
7. A majority of delinquent children are from broken homes.
8. A simple majority is sufficient to elect a candidate to office.
9. Application exercises for each chapter enables the student to practice the principles which the various chapters set forth.
10. His aging parents and the provision he might make for them were his one principal concern.

▶ EXERCISE 4   Rewrite the following *correct* sentences as directed. Change verbs to secure agreement and make any additional changes required for good sentence sense

1. Certain portions of our collection are kept in an underground, air-conditioned vault and are never placed on exhibit. [Insert *One* before *Certain*.]   2. Each piece in the exhibit has to be carefully dusted and polished once a day and then put back in place. [Change *Each piece* to *The pieces*.]   3. I might mention that this particular specimen has a distinguished place in history. [Change *this* to *these*.]   4. Our staff takes great pride in the efficient cataloging system which we have developed here. [Insert *members* after *staff*.]   5. In this room is my assistant, who is cataloging a newly arrived shipment. [Change *assistant* to *assistants*.]   6. One of our research parties has just returned from the field and is to be meeting with the directors during the remainder of the week. [Change *One* to *Two*.]   7. A detachment of four men has been left behind to maintain a permanent camp at the excavation site. [Omit *A detachment of*.]   8. Eaton Murray, the leader of the expedition and an especially capable man, is among the four. [Insert *John Wade* after *and*.]   9. Neither of the others is known to us here. [Change *is known* to *are unknown*.]   10. Both, however, were selected for particular abilities which they have shown. [Change *they* to *he*.]

6b

Make a pronoun agree in number with its antecedent.

A singular antecedent (one which would take a singular verb) is referred to by a singular pronoun; a plural antecedent (one which would take a plural verb) is referred to by a plural pronoun.

(1) In standard[2] English use a singular pronoun to refer to such antecedents as *man, woman, person, one, anyone, anybody, someone, somebody, everyone, everybody,*

[2] See pages 198–99 for the distinction between standard and colloquial English.

each, kind, sort, either, neither, no one, nobody. See also **6a(6)**.

WRONG   An outstanding trait of primitive *man* was *their* belief in superstitions.

RIGHT   An outstanding trait of primitive *man* was *his* belief in superstitions.

COLLOQUIAL   Each of the sons had planned to follow *their* father's occupation.

STANDARD   Each of the sons had planned to follow *his* father's occupation.

COLLOQUIAL   Everybody stood on *their* chairs.

STANDARD   Everybody stood on *his* chair.

Note: Avoid illogical sentences that may result from strict adherence to this rule.

ILLOGICAL   Since every one of the patients seemed discouraged, I told a joke to cheer *him* up.

LOGICAL   Since all the patients seemed discouraged, I told a joke to cheer *them* up.

(2) Two or more antecedents joined by *and* are referred to by a plural pronoun; two or more singular antecedents joined by *or* or *nor* are referred to by a singular pronoun. If one of two antecedents joined by *or* is singular and one plural, the pronoun usually agrees with the nearer. See also **6a(2),(3)**.

RIGHT   *Henry and James* have completed *their* work.

RIGHT   Neither *Henry nor James* has completed *his* work.

WRONG   When a *boy or girl* enters college, *they* find it different from high school.

RIGHT BUT CLUMSY   When a *boy or girl* enters college, *he or she* finds it different from high school.

BETTER   When *boys and girls* enter college, *they* find it different from high school.

RIGHT   Neither the *master* nor the *servants* were aware of *their* danger. [The plural *servants* is the nearer antecedent.]

RIGHT   Neither the *servants* nor the *master* was aware of *his* danger. [If the danger is to the master rather than the servants, the subjects can be reversed.]

(3) **Collective nouns are referred to by singular or plural pronouns depending on whether the collective noun is considered singular or plural. See also 6a(7).**

Special care should be taken to avoid making a collective noun *both* singular and plural within the same sentence.

WRONG   If the board of directors *controls* the company, *they* may vote themselves bonuses. [*Board* is first singular with *controls*, then plural with *they*.]

RIGHT   If the board of directors *control* the company, *they* may vote themselves bonuses. [Made plural throughout as demanded by the last half of the sentence]

RIGHT   If the board of directors *controls* the company, *it* may vote itself a bonus. [Last half of the sentence changed to agree with the first]

▶ EXERCISE 5   Compose brief sentences using each antecedent and pronoun listed below.

EXAMPLE   type ← its
           That *type* of battery soon loses *its* power.

1. everybody ← he   6. committee ← its
2. neither ← she   7. none ← those
3. each ← his   8. none ← he
4. a person ← him   9. boy or his sisters ← they
5. committee ← they   10. girls or their brother ← he

▶ EXERCISE 6   Write *C* after each correct sentence below. If a sentence contains a pronoun that does not agree with its antecedent in number, eliminate the error by substituting a correct pronoun form.

1. According to G. B. Shaw, a woman delights in wounding a man's ego, though a man takes most pleasure in gratifying hers.

2. An author like Shaw, however, seldom captures the whole truth with their generalizations.
3. A generalization is frequently only partially true, though a person may quote it and think they wholly believe it.
4. For example, nearly everyone, to express their appreciation, has said with great conviction, "A friend in need is a friend indeed."
5. At the same time, probably no one will deny that far too often a successful man avoids the very shoulders that they have climbed upon or despises the hands that once fed them.
6. Each of these quotations present two facets of truth, not the whole truth: (1) "As a rule man is a fool." (2) "What a piece of work is a man! how noble in reason!"
7. That these quotations are contradictory anyone in their right mind can see.
8. Though contradictory, each of the quotations may be true if they are applied to specific persons in particular circumstances.
9. A great satirist like Swift or Mark Twain in their works may often depict man as a fool.
10. Yet every reader who thinks for himself knows that the satirist—by pointing out man's foibles and follies—strives to reform man by showing him the value of making good use of his reason for lofty purposes.

▶ EXERCISE 7   In the following sentences select the pronoun in parentheses that agrees with its antecedent in accordance with standard English usage. Note also any pronouns that would be acceptable in conversation or familiar writing but not in formal writing.

1. The foreman unlocked the shed and everybody went in and got (his, their) tools.   2. Each man, and Charlie too, left (his, their) lunch pail inside.   3. Roy and Dave

were tearing out concrete forms, and (he, each, they) took a section apiece and went to work.   4. One or another would yell for help to clear away the salvage lumber (he was, they were) tearing out.   5. The helpers were supposed to pile the lumber outside the foundation, where Andy was cleaning (it, them) up and stacking (it, them) for re-use.   6. Every few minutes someone would call out for the water boy to bring (him, them) a drink.   7. The crew was small, but (its, their) thirst was large.   8. Charlie, the water boy, had all he could do to keep (it, them) satisfied. 9. "If anybody here ever drank water when (he was, they were) off the job," he grumbled, "I'd be proud to shake (him, them) by the hand."   10. But nobody volunteered (his, their) hand to be shaken.   11. Every minute, instead, somebody new would be yelling for water, and Charlie would trudge off toward (him, them).   12. It was either Roy or Dave who was whooping for (his, their) ninetieth drink when the noon whistle blew.   13. Nobody was so ready to stop where (he was, they were) as Charlie. 14. "Whoever wants a drink knows where (he, they) can get it," he let it be known, and emptied his bucket out on the ground.

▶ EXERCISE 8   In Exercise 7 make each change as directed below and then complete the sentence so as to secure agreement of pronoun with its antecedent. In Sentence 1, change *everybody* to *the workmen*. In 4, change *One or another* to *Both*. In 9, change *anybody here* to *these men*. In 11, change *somebody new* to *two or three more*.

Tense

Mood; *Shall* and *Will*

7

Use the appropriate form of the verb.

Appropriate Tense Form (Principal Parts)

7a

Use the appropriate tense form.

Tense, from the Latin word meaning "time," refers to changes in the form of the verb—as we shall see below—to indicate the time of the action. But tense and time do not always agree. The present tense, for example, is by no means limited to action in the present time. It may be used also to recall vividly the events of the past, as in the **historical present,** or to refer to future action: "I leave for Chicago tomorrow morning." English verbs have six tenses.

1. PRESENT—present action: "He *sees* me now"; customary action: "He *sees* me daily"; and other uses such as: "Napoleon *opens* the campaign brilliantly" [historical present, used instead of the past tense]; "I *start* my vacation a week from Friday" [used instead of the future tense]; "Some early philosophers knew that the earth *is* round" [**timeless truth,** expressed in the present even when the main verb is in the past].

2. PAST—past action not extending to the present: "He *saw* me at the game yesterday."

3. FUTURE—action at some time after the present: "He *will see* me next month in New York." The future is frequently expressed by the phrase *is going to:* "He *is going to see* me next month in New York."

4. PRESENT PERFECT—past action extending to the present: "He *has seen* me many times."

5. PAST PERFECT—past action completed before some indicated time in the past: "My friend *had seen* me before the game started." "I *had* already *decided* to talk with him before I left the house." [Sometimes put in the simple past tense: "My friend *saw* me before the game started." But note that "I *decided* to talk with him before I left the house" would be a change of meaning.]

6. FUTURE PERFECT—action to be completed before some indicated time in the future: "He *will have seen* me again before my departure tomorrow." [Commonly put in the simple future tense: "He *will see* me again before my departure tomorrow." The future perfect tense is seldom used.]

These six tenses are built on three forms, called **principal parts:** (1) the present stem (infinitive)—*see, use,* (2) the past tense—*saw, used,* and (3) the past participle—*seen, used.* Most English verbs, like *use,* are **regular;** that is, they form both the past tense (*used*) and the past participle (*used*) by adding *-d* or *-ed* to the present stem (*use*). Other verbs, like *see,* are **irregular** because they change the present stem (*see*) to form the past tense (*saw*) and the past participle (*seen*). It will be noted in the conjugation on the following pages that the present stem is the basis for both present and future tenses; the past, for the past tense alone; and the past participle, for the present perfect, past perfect, and future perfect tenses.

CONJUGATION OF THE VERB *TO SEE*
(Principal Parts: *see, saw, seen*)

	Active Voice		*Passive Voice*	
	Singular	Plural	Singular	Plural

INDICATIVE MOOD[1]

PRESENT TENSE

	Singular	Plural	Singular	Plural
1.	I see	we see	I am seen	we are seen
2.	you see	you see	you are seen	you are seen
3.	he (she, it) sees	they see	he (she, it) is seen	they are seen

PAST TENSE

1.	I saw	we saw	I was seen	we were seen
2.	you saw	you saw	you were seen	you were seen
3.	he saw	they saw	he was seen	they were seen

FUTURE TENSE

1.	I shall see	we shall see	I shall be seen	we shall be seen
2.	you will see	you will see	you will be seen	you will be seen
3.	he will see	they will see	he will be seen	they will be seen

PRESENT PERFECT TENSE

1.	I have seen	we have seen	I have been seen	we have been seen
2.	you have seen	you have seen	you have been seen	you have been seen
3.	he has seen	they have seen	he has been seen	they have been seen

PAST PERFECT TENSE

1.	I had seen	we had seen	I had been seen	we had been seen
2.	you had seen	you had seen	you had been seen	you had been seen
3.	he had seen	they had seen	he had been seen	they had been seen

FUTURE PERFECT TENSE (seldom used)

1.	I shall have seen	we shall have seen	I shall have been seen	we shall have been seen
2.	you will have seen	you will have seen	you will have been seen	you will have been seen
3.	he will have seen	they will have seen	he will have been seen	they will have been seen

[1] Such terms as *mood, indicative, subjunctive,* and *voice* are explained in Section 35, Grammatical Terms.

Active Voice	Passive Voice

SUBJUNCTIVE MOOD

PRESENT TENSE

Singular: if I, you, he see	if I, you, he be seen
Plural: if we, you, they see	if we, you, they be seen

PAST TENSE

Singular: if I, you, he saw	if I, you, he were seen
Plural: if we, you, they saw	if we, you, they were seen

PRESENT PERFECT TENSE

Singular: if I, you, he have seen	if I, you, he have been seen
Plural: if we, you, they have seen	if we, you, they have been seen

PAST PERFECT TENSE

(Same as the Indicative)

IMPERATIVE MOOD

PRESENT TENSE

see	be seen

INFINITIVES

PRESENT TENSE

to see	to be seen

PRESENT PERFECT TENSE

to have seen	to have been seen

PARTICIPLES

PRESENT TENSE

seeing	being seen

PAST TENSE

seen	been seen

PRESENT PERFECT TENSE

having seen	having been seen

GERUNDS

PRESENT TENSE

seeing	being seen

PRESENT PERFECT TENSE

having seen	having been seen

In addition to the simple verb forms illustrated on the preceding page, English uses a progressive form to show action in progress and a "do" form for (1) emphatic statements, (2) questions, or (3) negations.

SIMPLE FORM   I see, he sees; I saw, he saw; I am seen.
PROGRESSIVE FORM   I am seeing, he is seeing; I was seeing, he was seeing; I am being seen.
"DO" FORM   (1) I do see, he does see; I did see, he did see.
      (2) Does he see her? Did he see her?
      (3) He does not see her. He did not see her.

Note: For other auxiliaries not mentioned above see 1a, page 2.

▶ EXERCISE 1   Some verbs are frequently confused because of similarity in spelling or meaning. Master the principal parts of the following verbs. Then compose sentences (three to illustrate each verb) in which each verb is correctly used (1) in the past tense, (2) in the present perfect tense, and (3) in the present tense (progressive form, using the present participle).

Present stem (infinitive)	Past tense	Past participle	Present participle
lie (to recline)	lay	lain	lying
lay (to cause to lie)	laid	laid	laying
sit (to be seated)	sat	sat	sitting
set (to place or put)	set	set	setting

WRONG   He *layed* (or *laid*) down on the bed. [Past tense of the intransitive verb *lie* needed]
RIGHT   He *lay* down on the bed.

Note: For definition of *transitive* and *intransitive* see Section **35.**

WRONG   He *lay* the book on the table. [Past tense of the transitive verb *lay* needed]
RIGHT   He *laid* the book on the table.
RIGHT   The book is *lying* (not *laying*) on the table.

WRONG   He *set* in the chair. [Past tense of the intransitive verb *sit* needed]

RIGHT   He *sat* in the chair.

RIGHT   He *set* the bucket on the table. [Transitive]

RIGHT   The man is *sitting* (not *setting*) in the chair.

The writer usually knows the tense needed to express his ideas. He can determine the correct form of this tense by consulting his dictionary for the principal parts of the verb. In the dictionary every irregular verb is listed by its infinitive or present stem—for example, *see.* Then follow the past tense (*saw*), the past participle (*seen*), and the present participle (*seeing*). *See, saw,* and *seen* are the principal parts from which the writer can readily derive the proper form for any of the six tenses. For regular verbs (such as *use*) the past tense and the past participle, when not given, are understood to be formed by adding *-d* or *-ed.*

WRONG   The boy *seen* where the bullet had entered. [Past tense needed; the dictionary gives *saw* as the correct form.]

RIGHT   The boy *saw* where the bullet had entered.

WRONG   I *use* to live in the country. [Past tense needed]

RIGHT   I *used* to live in the country.

▶ EXERCISE 2   Make your own SPECIAL LIST OF PRINCIPAL PARTS of verbs which you need to study and review. Include from the following list any verbs whose principal parts are not thoroughly familiar to you, and add all verbs that you have used incorrectly in your writing. Master your SPECIAL LIST and compose sentences to illustrate the correct use of each principal part.

Present stem	Past tense	Past participle
begin	began	begun
bite	bit	bitten
blow	blew	blown
break	broke	broken
bring	brought	brought
burst	burst	burst
catch	caught	caught

Present stem	*Past tense*	*Past participle*
choose	chose	chosen
come	came	come
dive	dived, dove	dived
do	did	done
drag	dragged	dragged
draw	drew	drawn
drink	drank	drunk
eat	ate	eaten
fall	fell	fallen
fly	flew	flown
freeze	froze	frozen
get	got	got, gotten
give	gave	given
go	went	gone
grow	grew	grown
hang (execute)	hanged	hanged
hang (suspend)	hung	hung
know	knew	known
lead	led	led
lose	lost	lost
raise	raised	raised
ride	rode	ridden
ring	rang, rung	rung
rise	rose	risen
run	ran	run
shrink	shrank, shrunk	shrunk
sing	sang, sung	sung
sink	sank, sunk	sunk
speak	spoke	spoken
spring	sprang, sprung	sprung
steal	stole	stolen
swim	swam	swum
swing	swung	swung
take	took	taken
tear	tore	torn
throw	threw	thrown
wear	wore	worn
weave	wove	woven
write	wrote	written

Logical Tense Form (Sequence)

7b

Make a verb in a subordinate clause, an infinitive, or a participle agree logically (naturally) with the verb in the main clause.

(1) Verbs in subordinate clauses

RIGHT   The audience *rises* as the speaker *enters*. [The present *enters* follows the present *rises*.]

RIGHT   The audience *rose* as the speaker *entered*. [The past *entered* follows the past *rose*.]

RIGHT   I *have ceased* worrying because I *have heard* no more rumors. [The present perfect follows the present perfect.]

RIGHT   I *believed* (or *had believed*) that the letter *had* (not *has*) *been lost*. [The past perfect in the subordinate clause follows the past or past perfect in the main clause.]

RIGHT   I *believe* (or *will believe, have believed*) that the letter *has* (not *had*) *been lost*. [The present perfect in the subordinate clause follows present, future, or present perfect in the main clause.]

RIGHT   You *will find* that he *will have done* well. [The future perfect in the subordinate clause is used only with the future in the main clause.]

POOR   I *hoped* that I *could have gone*.

BETTER   I *hoped* that I *could go*. [In the past time indicated by *hoped* I was still anticipating going.]

POOR   When I *was* at camp four weeks, I *received* word that my father *had died*.

BETTER   When I *had been* at camp four weeks, I *received* word that my father *had died*. [The past perfect *had been* or *had died* indicates a time prior to that of the main verb *received*.]

POOR   If Bill *attended* classes regularly, he *could have passed* the final examination.

BETTER   If Bill *had attended* classes regularly, he *could have passed* the final examination.

(2) Infinitives

Use the present infinitive to express action contemporaneous with, or later than, that of the governing verb; use the perfect infinitive for action prior to that of the governing verb.

> I was happy *to find* (not *to have found*) you at home.
> [Present infinitive—the finding and the happiness were contemporaneous.]
> I hoped *to go* (not *to have gone*). I hope *to go*. [Present infinitives. At the time indicated by the verbs I was still hoping *to go*, not *to have gone*.]
> I am happy *to have helped* him. [Perfect infinitive—the helping prior to the happiness]
> I should like *to have lived* in Shakespeare's time. [Perfect infinitive—expressing time prior to that of the governing verb. Simpler: I wish I had lived in Shakespeare's time.]
> I should have liked *to live* (not *to have lived*) in Shakespeare's time. [Present infinitive—for time contemporaneous with that of the governing verb]

(3) Participles

Use the present participle to express action contemporaneous with that of the governing verb; use the perfect participle for action prior to that of the governing verb.

> *Walking* along the streets, he met many old friends. [The walking and the meeting were contemporaneous.]
> *Having walked* all the way home, he found himself tired. [The walking was prior to the finding.]

Caution: Do not confuse gerunds and participles. See Section **35, Verbals.**

> After *walking* home he found himself tired. [Gerund]
> *Having walked* (not *After having walked*) home, he found himself tired. [Participle. *After* would be redundant.]

Subjunctive Mood

7c

Use the subjunctive mood in the few types of expressions in which it is still regularly used.

Distinctive forms for the subjunctive occur only in the third person singular of the present tense (*I demand that he* **see** *a physician* instead of the indicative *he sees a physician*) and in the verb *to be* as indicated by boldface below.

Present indicative		*Present subjunctive*	
I am	we are	if I **be**	if we **be**
you are	you are	if you **be**	if you **be**
he is	they are	if he (she, it) **be**	if they **be**

Past indicative		*Past subjunctive*	
I was	we were	if I **were**	if we were
you were	you were	if you were	if you were
he was	they were	if he (she, it) **were**	if they were

Although the subjunctive mood has been largely displaced by the indicative, it is still regularly used (1) in *that* clauses of motions, resolutions, recommendations, orders, or demands and (2) in a few idiomatic expressions.

EXAMPLES   I move that the report *be* approved.
Resolved, that dues for the coming year *be* doubled.
I recommend (order, demand) that the prisoner *be* released.
I demand (request, insist) that the messenger *go* alone.
If need *be; suffice* it to say; *come* what may; etc. [Fixed subjunctive in idiomatic expressions]

Many writers prefer the subjunctive in contrary-to-fact conditions and in expressions of doubts, wishes, or regrets.

STANDARD   If the apple *were* ripe, it would be delicious. [Subjunctive]
INFORMAL   If the apple *was* ripe, it would be delicious. [Indicative]
RIGHT   If the apple *is* ripe, I will eat it. [The indicative is regularly used in conditions not contrary to fact.]

STANDARD	The man looks as if he *were* sick. [Subjunctive]
INFORMAL	The man looks as if he *was* sick. [Indicative]
STANDARD	I wish that he *were* here. [Subjunctive]
INFORMAL	I wish that he *was* here. [Indicative]

▶ EXERCISE 3   Choose the proper form for the subjunctive mood in the parentheses below.

1. We insist that he (be, is) punished.
2. I wish that James (was, were) here.
3. We have talked of a trip to Madrid as though it (was, were) impossible.
4. Present-day problems demand that we (be, are) ready for any emergency.
5. "A good idea," one of the members said, "but I propose that the suggestion (be, is) tabled for the present."
6. If there (was, were) time, I could finish my report.
7. "If this (be, is) treason, make the most of it."
8. I demand that he (make, makes) an explanation.
9. I wish he (was, were) present to explain his continued neglect of his duties.
10. If he (was, were) here, he might explain everything to our full satisfaction.

▶ EXERCISE 4   Compose five sentences in which the subjunctive is required. Compose three other sentences in which either the subjunctive or the indicative may be used, giving the indicative (informal) form in parentheses.

Shifts in Tense or Mood

7d

Avoid needless shifts in tense or mood.[2]

| WRONG | He *came* to the river and *pays* a man to ferry him across. [Inconsistent use of tenses within one sentence] |
| RIGHT | He *came* to the river and *paid* a man to ferry him across. |

[2] See also Section 27, Shifts in Point of View.

INCONSISTENT   It is necessary to restrain an occasional foolhardy park visitor lest a mother bear *mistake* his friendly intentions and *supposes* him a menace to her cubs. [Mood shifts improperly from subjunctive to indicative within the compound predicate.] But females with cubs *were* only one of the dangers. [A correct enough sentence if standing alone, but here inconsistent with present tense of preceding one, and therefore misleading] One *has* to remember that all bears *were* wild animals and not domesticated pets. [Inconsistent and misleading shift of tense from present in main clause to past in subordinate clause] Though a bear *may* seem altogether peaceable and harmless, he *might* not remain peaceable and he is never harmless. [Tense shifts improperly from present in introductory clause to past in main clause.] It *is* therefore an important part of the park ranger's duty *to watch* the tourists, and above all *don't* let anybody try to feed the bears. [Inconsistent. Mood shifts needlessly from indicative to imperative.]

IMPROVED   It is necessary to restrain an occasional foolhardy park visitor lest a mother bear *mistake* his friendly intentions and *suppose* him a menace to her cubs. But females with cubs *are* only one of the dangers. One *has* to remember that all bears *are* wild animals and not domesticated pets. Though a bear *may* seem altogether peaceable and harmless, he *may* not remain peaceable and he is never harmless. It *is* therefore an important part of the park ranger's duty *to watch* the tourists and above all not *to let* anybody try to feed the bears.

▶ EXERCISE 5   In the following passage correct all errors and inconsistencies in tense and mood and any other errors in verb usage. Write *C* after any sentence which is satisfactory as it stands.

1. Across the Thames from Shakespeare's London lay the area known as the Bankside, probably as rough and unsavory a neighborhood as ever laid across the river from any city.   2. And yet it was to such a place that Shakespeare and his company had to have gone to build their new theater.   3. For the Puritan government of the City had set up all sorts of prohibitions against theatrical

entertainment within the city walls.   4. When it became necessary, therefore, for the Company to have moved their playhouse from its old location north of the city, they obtain a lease to a tract on the Bankside.   5. Other theatrical companies had went there before them, and it seemed reasonable to have supposed that Shakespeare and his partners would prosper in the new location. 6. Apparently the Puritans of the City had no law against anyone's moving cartloads of lumber through the public streets.   7. There is no record that the Company met with difficulty while the timbers of the dismantled playhouse are being hauled to the new site.   8. One difficulty the partners had foresaw and forestalled, and that is the effort that their old landlord might make to have stopped their removing the building.   9. Lest his presence complicate their task and would perhaps defeat its working altogether, they waited until he had gone out of town. 10. And when he came back, his lot was bare; the building's timbers were all in stacks on the far side of the river; and the theater is waiting only to be put together.   11. It is a matter of general knowledge that on the Bankside Shakespeare continued his successful career as a showman and went on to enjoy even greater prosperity after he had made the move than before.

Shall and Will

7e

Observe such distinctions as exist between *shall* (*should*) and *will* (*would*).

(1) Use *should* in all persons to express an obligation (in the sense "ought to") or a condition.

I (You, He, We, They) *should* (i.e., *ought to*) help the needy.
If I (you, he, we, they) *should* resign, the program would not be continued.

(2) Use *would* in all persons to express a wish or a customary action.

> *Would* that I (you, he, we, they) had received the message!
> I (You, He, We, They) *would* spend hours by the seashore during the summer months.

Shall is generally used for the first person in asking questions (*Shall* I enter?), and it is often used in all persons for special emphasis. Except for these uses of *shall*, and for the use of *should* to express an obligation or condition, informal English tends to use *will* and *would* in all persons.

Note: Some careful writers distinguish between *shall* and *will:*

(a) By using *shall* in the first person and *will* in the second and third to express the simple future or expectation (I *shall* plan to stay; he *will* probably stay).

(b) By using *will* in the first person and *shall* in the second and third to express determination, threat, command, prophecy, promise, or willingness (I *will* stay; you and he *shall* stay).

(c) By using in a question the same form expected in the answer (*Will* he be allowed to go? Expected answer: He *will*).

▶ EXERCISE 6   Select the form in parentheses that is consistent with contemporary usage. Justify your choice.

1. To save time we (should, would) fly to the coast.
2. No totalitarian tyrant (will, shall) treat us with contempt.
3. (Will, Shall) I expect you at eight?
4. Very often during those years we (should, would) go to the country for relaxation.
5. At school we learn what we (should, would) do throughout life.

▶ EXERCISE 7   Compose five sentences to illustrate the chief distinctions in the use of *shall*, *should*, and *would*. Explain the meaning of each sentence.

▶ EXERCISE 8 Write *C* after any of the following sentences that needs no revision for tense, mood, or *shall* and *will* (*should* and *would*). Revise every other sentence after classifying it according to the error invloved: (a) tense—principal parts, (b) sequence of tenses, (c) mood, (d) shift in tense or mood, (e) *shall* and *will* (*should* and *would*).

1. Start the engine and then you should release the brake.
2. If you set up too late, you may wish to lay in bed till noon next day.
3. If Mary enrolled in the class at the beginning, she could have made good grades.
4. It has been said that a rolling stone gathers no moss.
5. A stone laying in one position for a long time may gather moss.
6. The members recommended that all delinquents are fined.
7. It was reported that there use to be very few delinquents.
8. As soon as the boy entered the room, he sat down at the desk and begins to write rapidly.
9. Can there be any question about the correctness of the estimate?
10. Until I received your letter, I was hoping to have had a visit from you.
11. When the runner began the last lap, he seen that he had no chance to win the race.
12. We attend religious services to learn how we would conduct ourselves toward our fellows.
13. Follow the main road for a mile; then you need to take the next road on the left.
14. If need is, we can all stay together.
15. After having entered the room, he sat down quietly at the table.
16. The beggar could not deny that he had stole the purse.
17. I should have liked to have been with the team on the trip to New Orleans.

MECHANICS

Manuscript Form and Revision; Syllabication

8

Put your manuscript in acceptable form. Make revisions with care.

8a

Use the proper materials.

(1) **Paper.**   Unless you are given other instructions, use standard theme paper, size 8½ by 11 inches, with lines about half an inch apart, and write only on the ruled side of the paper. (The usual notebook paper, even if it is the standard size, should not be used because the narrow spaces between lines make for hard reading and allow insufficient space for corrections.) For type-written manuscripts use the unruled side of theme paper; or, if you prefer, regular weight typewriter paper (not onion skin), size 8½ by 11 inches.

(2) **Ink.**   Use black or blue-black ink.

(3) **Typewriter.**   Unless otherwise instructed, submit type-written papers only if you do your own typewriting. Use a black ribbon and make sure that the type is clean.

8b

Arrange your writing in clear and orderly fashion on the page. Divide a word at the end of a line only between syllables.

(1) **Margins.** Leave sufficient margins—about an inch and a half at the left and top, an inch at the right and bottom—to prevent a crowded appearance. The ruled lines on theme paper indicate the proper margins at the left and top.

(2) **Indention.** Indent the first lines of paragraphs uniformly, about an inch in longhand and five spaces in typewritten copy.

(3) **Paging.** Use Arabic numerals—without parentheses or period—in the upper right-hand corner to mark all pages after the first.

(4) **The Title.** *Do not put quotation marks around the title or underline it* (unless it is a quotation or the title of a book), and use no period after the title. Center the title on the page about an inch and a half from the top or on the first ruled line. Leave the next line blank and begin the first paragraph on the third line. In this way the title will stand off from the text. Capitalize the first word of the title and all succeeding words except articles and short conjunctions and prepositions.

(5) **Poetry.** Quoted lines of poetry should be arranged and indented as in the original. (See also 16a.)

(6) **Punctuation.** Never begin a line with a comma, a colon, a semicolon, or a terminal mark of punctuation; never end a line with opening quotation marks, bracket, or parenthesis.

(7) **Endorsement.** Papers are endorsed in the way prescribed by the instructor to facilitate handling. Usually papers carry the name of the student and the course, the date, and the number of the assignment.

(8) **Word Division at End of Line.** The writer will seldom need to divide words, especially short ones, if he leaves a reasonably wide right-hand margin. The reader will object less to an uneven margin than to a number of broken words.

WRONG   ignit-ion, sentin-el [Words not divided between syllables. Whenever you are uncertain about the proper syllabication of a word, consult a good dictionary.]

RIGHT   ig-nition (*or* igni-tion), sen-tinel (*or* senti-nel)

RIGHT   can-ning, com-mit-ting [Double consonants are usually divided except when they come at the end of a simple word: kill-ing.]

WRONG   enjoy-ed, gleam-ed, watch-ed, remember-ed [Never confuse the reader by setting off an *-ed* pronounced as part of the preceding syllable.]

WRONG   e-nough, a-gainst, e-vade (The saving of space is not sufficient to justify the break. Begin the word on the next line.]

WRONG   man-y, show-y, dyspepsi-a [The final letter can be written as readily as the hyphen, and the single letter should not be carried over to the beginning of the next line.]

WRONG   fire-eat-er, mass-pro-duced, Pre-Raphael-ite

RIGHT   fire-eater, mass-produced, Pre-Raphaelite [Divide hyphenated words only where the hyphen comes in the regular spelling.]

▶ EXERCISE 1   With the aid of your dictionary write out the following words by syllables, grouping (1) those that may properly be divided at the end of a line, and (2) those that may not be divided:

affection	levy	through	veiled
against	looked	tolerate	walked
alone	nature	transient	weary
combed	omit	treaty	willing
decadent	rainy	troller	willow
erase	thirsty	trolley	wily
immense	thought	vary	windy

8c
Write legibly, so that your writing may be read easily and accurately.

(1) Spacing for Legibility.   Adequate space between lines and between the words in the line is essential to easy reading. In typewritten copy use double space between lines. Single-spaced copy is difficult for the instructor to read and even more difficult for the student to revise. Leave one space after a comma or semicolon, one or two after a colon, and two or three after a period, a question mark, or an exclamation point. In longhand make each word a distinct unit: join all the letters of a word and leave adequate space in the line before beginning the next word.

(2) Shaping for Legibility.   Shape each letter distinctly. Avoid flourishes. Many pages of manuscript, though artistic and attractive to the eye, are almost illegible. Dot the *i*, not some other letter nearby. Cross the *t*, not the adjoining *h* or some other letter. Make dots and periods real dots, not small circles. Let all capitals stand out distinctly as capitals and keep all small letters down to the average of other small letters. Remember that you will not be present to tell the reader which letters you intend for capitals, which for small letters.

8d
Revise the manuscript with care.[1]

(1) Revising the Paper Before Submitting It to the Instructor. If time permits, the writer should put the paper aside

---

[1] For marks used in correcting proofs for the printer see *Webster's New Collegiate Dictionary*, "Preparation of Copy for the Press," or *The American College Dictionary*, Text Edition, "Preparation of Copy for the Typesetter or Publisher" in the "Guide to Usage."

for a day or more after completing his first draft. Then he will be able to read the paper more objectively, to see what parts need to be expanded, what to be excised. After he has revised his paper, he should make a completely new copy to submit to the instructor. If slight revisions are needed in this final copy or if the student is writing in class, the paper may be handed in—after corrections have been made—without re-writing. The changes should be made as follows:

(a) Draw one line horizontally through any word to be deleted. Do not put it in parentheses or make an unsightly erasure.

(b) In case of a short addition of one line or less, place a caret ($_\wedge$) in the line where the addition comes and write just above the caret the word or words to be added.

CHECK LIST FOR REVISION

1. Have I stated my central idea clearly, and have I developed it adequately in effective paragraphs? (See Sections **31-32**.)
2. Is the paper correct in
    (a) manuscript form? (See Section **8**.)
    (b) grammar and mechanics? (See Sections **1-7, 9-11**.)
    (c) punctuation? (See Sections **12-17**.)
    (d) spelling? (See Section **18**.)
3. Is the diction standard, exact, concise? (See Sections **19-22**.)
4. Are the sentences as effective as possible? (See Sections **23-30**.)
5. What do my answers to the foregoing questions show my chief difficulties to be? (Review intensively the sections of this book which deal with your defects. Later, after the paper has been read and returned by the instructor, observe the same procedure for additional defects noted by your instructor.)

(2) **Revising the Paper after the Instructor Has Criticized It.**
The best way to learn the mechanics of writing is by
correcting one's own errors. Corrections made by
another are of comparatively little value. Therefore
the instructor points out the errors but *allows the
student to make the actual revision for himself.*

The instructor usually indicates a necessary correction by a number or a symbol from the handbook
marked in the margin of the paper opposite the error.
For example, if he finds a fragmentary sentence, he
will write either the number **2** or the symbol **frag.**
The student should then find in the text the specific
part (**a**, **b**, or **c**) of Section **2** that deals with his error,
correct the error in red (or as the instructor directs),
and write the appropriate letter after the instructor's
number or symbol in the margin. (See the example
paragraph marked by the instructor and then corrected
by the student on pages 94–95.)

The comma. After the number **12** in the margin the
student should take special care to supply the appropriate letter (**a**, **b**, **c**, or **d**) to show why the comma is
needed. The act of inserting a comma teaches little;
understanding why it is required in a particular situation is a definite step toward mastery of the comma.

The following pages reproduce a paragraph from a
student paper and show, on the first page, the instructor's markings (for grammar and other details) and,
on the second page, the same paragraph after it has
been corrected by the student. These corrections
should be in a different color to make them stand out
distinctly from the original paragraph and the markings of the instructor.

Give special attention to the instructor's comments
on content and organization, which are even more
important than details of grammar and mechanics.

Marked by the Instructor—with Numbers

3   Making photographs for newspapers is hard work,

12   it is not the romantic carefree adventure glorified

       in motion pictures and fiction books. For every

18   great moment recorded by the stareing eye of the

       camera, there are twenty routine assignments that

28   must be handled in the same efficient manner. He

       must often overcome great hardships. The work con-

24   tinues for long hours. It must meet the deadline.

       At times he is called upon to risk his own life to

2   secure a picture. To the newspaper photographer,

       getting his picture being the most important thing.

Marked by the Instructor—with Symbols

cs   Making photographs for newspapers is hard work,

?/   it is not the romantic carefree adventure glorified

       in motion pictures and fiction books. For every

sp   great moment recorded by the stareing eye of the

       camera, there are twenty routine assignments that

ref   must be handled in the same efficient manner. He

       must often overcome great hardships. The work con-

sub   tinues for long hours. It must meet the deadline.

       At times he is called upon to risk his own life to

       secure a picture. To the newspaper photographer,

frag   getting his picture being the most important thing.

Corrected by the Student

3 *a*   Making photographs for newspapers is hard work,/;

12 *c* it is not the romantic,carefree adventure glorified

in motion pictures and fiction books. For every

18 *d* great moment recorded by the ~~stareing~~ *staring* eye of the

camera, there are twenty routine assignments that

28 *c* must be handled in the same efficient manner. ~~He~~ *The*
newspaper photographer must often overcome great
~~must often overcome great hardships. The work con-~~
hardships and work long hours to meet the deadline.

24 *a* ~~tinues for long hours. It must meet the deadline.~~

At times he is called upon to risk his own life to

2 *a* secure a picture. To the newspaper photographer,

getting his picture ~~being~~ *is* the most important thing.

Corrected by the Student

cs-a   Making photographs for newspapers is hard work,/;

9/c it is not the romantic,carefree adventure glorified

in motion pictures and fiction books. For every

sp-d great moment recorded by the ~~stareing~~ *staring* eye of the

camera, there are twenty routine assignments that

ref-c must be handled in the same efficient manner. ~~He~~ *The*
newspaper photographer must often overcome great
~~must often overcome great hardships. The work con-~~
hardships and work long hours to meet the deadline.

sub-a ~~tinues for long hours. It must meet the deadline.~~

At times he is called upon to risk his own life to

frag-a secure a picture. To the newspaper photographer,

getting his picture ~~being~~ *is* the most important thing.

8e

Keep a record to check the improvement in your writing.

A clear record on a single sheet of paper will show at a glance the progress you are making from paper to paper. As you write each paper, try to avoid mistakes already pointed out. Master the correct spelling of each word you have misspelled. *Be sure that you have made every correction and have considered every comment on your last paper before you write the next.* If you follow this plan consistently throughout the year, your writing will show marked improvement.

One simple but useful way to record your errors is to write them down in the order in which they occur in each paper, grouping them in columns according to the seven major divisions of the handbook as illustrated below. In the spaces for Paper Number 1 are recorded the errors from the student paragraph on the preceding page. In the spelling column appears the correct spelling of the misspelled word, and in other columns the section number with the letter to indicate the specific error made. You may wish to add on your record sheet other columns for date, grade, and instructor's comments.

RECORD OF ERRORS

Paper No.	Grammar 1-7	Mechanics 8-11	Punctuation 12-17	Words Misspelled 18	Diction 19-22	Effectiveness 23-30	Larger Elements 31-34
1	3 b 2 a			staring		28 c 24 a	
2							

Capitals

9

Capitalize words in accordance with general usage. Avoid unnecessary capitals.

9a
Capitalize proper names and, generally, derivatives of proper names and abbreviations of them.[1]

Capitalization of individual words may be checked in a good dictionary, such as *The American College Dictionary* or *Webster's New World Dictionary* (in the main vocabulary) or *Webster's New Collegiate Dictionary* (in the main vocabulary as well as in the special sections "Biographical Names," "Pronouncing Gazetteer," and "Abbreviations"). If a word is regularly capitalized, it will be printed with a capital letter in the dictionary entry.

Proper Names—and Derivatives of Proper Names

1. SPECIFIC PERSONS, MEMBERS OF NATIONAL, POLITICAL, RACIAL, REGIONAL, AND RELIGIOUS GROUPS: Miss Helen Evans, Milton, Miltonic, James T. Watson, Jr.; American, German; Republican, Democrat, Communist;

---

[1] For a more detailed discussion of capitalization of words and abbreviations see the *Style Manual* of the United States Government Printing Office, 1953, pp. 17–50, or *A Manual of Style*, the University of Chicago Press, 1949, pp. 23–45.

Caucasian, Negro, Indian; Texan, Southerner; Baptist, Roman Catholic, Methodist; Christ, Christian

2. GEOGRAPHICAL ITEMS: Atlantic Ocean, America, American, the Southwest, Ohio, Travis County, Oklahoma City, Lake Erie, Mississippi River, Long Island, Mount McKinley, Mammoth Cave, Smoky Mountain National Park, the West, Western, France, French

3. ORGANIZATIONS, INSTITUTIONS: American Medical Association, Phi Beta Kappa, the Newman Club, First Presbyterian Church, the Senate, the United Nations, the Standard Oil Company, Columbia University, Taft High School

4. SPECIFIC STREETS, BUILDINGS, SHIPS, AIRCRAFT, SPACE VEHICLES, TRAINS, AWARDS, TRADE-MARK NAMES: Twenty-first Street, Mercantile Building, the Alamo, *Old Ironsides*, Discoverer XIV, the *Texas Special*, the Medal of Honor, a Winchester, Fritos

5. HISTORICAL PERIODS, EVENTS, DOCUMENTS, MEMORIALS: the Middle Ages, the Revolution, World War II, the Declaration of Independence, the Atlantic Charter, the Statue of Liberty, the Tomb of the Unknown Soldier

6. CALENDAR ITEMS, SPECIAL EVENTS: Friday, June, Easter, Labor Day, Kentucky Derby, Lent, the Summer Olympics

7. PERSONIFICATIONS:

> Can Honor's voice provoke the silent dust,
> Or Flattery soothe the dull cold ear of Death?　　—GRAY

8. WORDS PERTAINING TO THE DEITY AND HOLY SCRIPTURES: God the Father, the Lord, the Saviour, the Trinity, the Almighty, the Creator, Christ and His followers, the Bible, the Old Testament

Note: Proper names and their derivatives sometimes lose significance as names of particulars and thus become common names of a general class and are no longer capitalized. For example, *quixotic* is derived from *Don Quixote; malapropism, Mrs. Malaprop; quizling, Major Vidkun Quisling.*

Caution: Some words may be used correctly as either common or as proper names: "the *God* of Moses," "a *god* of the pagans"; "a *democratic* system," "the *Democratic* party." When in doubt about capitalization, consult a recent dictionary.

Abbreviations

In general, abbreviations are capitalized or not according to the capitalization of the word abbreviated: *Y.M.C.A., FBI, m.p.h.* One important exception is *No.* for *number.* (See also Section **11.**)

9b

Capitalize titles preceding the name, or other words used as an essential part of a proper name.

EXAMPLES   Mr. Brown, Judge White, King George, Aunt Mary

(1) Titles immediately following the name, or used alone as a substitute for the name, are capitalized only to indicate pre-eminence or high distinction: John F. Kennedy, President of the United States; the President of the United States; the President. On the other hand, ordinary titles are usually not capitalized: William Smith, president of the First National Bank; the president of the bank.

(2) Words denoting family relationship (*father, mother, brother, aunt, cousin*) are generally capitalized when used as titles or alone in place of the name, but not when preceded by a possessive: Brother William; Sister Mary;[2] Mary, my sister; my brother; my sister; a trip with Father;

---

[2] This rule also applies to names of members of religious orders.

a trip with my father; a letter from Mother; a letter from my mother.

(3) Such words as *college, high school, club, lake, river, park, building, street, pike, county, railroad,* and *society* are (except in newspapers) usually capitalized when they are an essential part of a proper name, but not when used alone as a substitute for the name: Knox College, the college; Central High School, the high school; Madison Street, the street; the Pennsylvania Railroad, the railroad.

▶ EXERCISE 1 Supply capitals wherever needed in the following sentences. Be prepared to give a reason for the use of each capital.

1. In america, candidates for president frequently make promises to minority groups—such as southern democrats, negroes, farmers, laborers, westerners, and alaskans—because, if united, the minorities can determine the outcome of an election.

2. During the easter vacation, after window shopping on fifth avenue and seeing the sights on broadway, I went to bedloe island, climbed up into the crown of the statue of liberty, and took pictures of new york harbor.

3. Senator redwine, a republican, spoke on our campus and strongly advocated prohibition in hunt county.

4. We invited judge green to meet uncle henry at the cosmos club to make plans for the annual community chest drive.

5. Before the end of the summer, perhaps during july, the president of the united states will take a vacation in florida.

6. The pacific ocean was discovered in 1513 by a spaniard named balboa.

7. Many americans in the northwest are of polish or scandinavian descent.

8. The battle of new orleans, which made general jackson

famous, took place *after* the signing of the peace treaty at ghent.

9. The minister stressed not only the importance of obeying god's laws as set forth in the bible but also the need for trusting in his infinite mercy.

10. The west offers grand sights for tourists: the carlsbad caverns, the grand canyon, yellowstone national park —not to mention the attractions of hollywood, las vegas, and salt lake city.

11. Many new englanders go south for part of the winter, but usually they are back in the north before easter.

9c

In titles of books, plays, student papers, etc., capitalize the first word and all succeeding words except articles (*a, an, the*) and short conjunctions or prepositions.

EXAMPLES   *Crime and Punishment, To Have and to Hold, Midnight on the Desert, The Man Without a Country* [A conjunction or preposition of five or more letters (*without*) is usually capitalized.]

9d

Capitalize the pronoun *I* and the interjection *O* (but not *oh* except when it begins a sentence).

EXAMPLE   If *I* forget thee, *O* Jerusalem, let my right hand forget her cunning.   —PSALMS

9e

Capitalize the first word of every sentence (including quoted sentences and direct questions)

EXAMPLES   He said, "The work is almost finished."
He said that the work was "almost finished." [A fragmentary quotation does not begin with a capital.]

Capitals after the colon. After the colon, quoted sentences regularly begin with a capital; other sentences may begin with either a capital or a small letter.

9f

Avoid unnecessary capitals.

Many students err in using too many rather than too few capitals. If you have a tendency to overuse capitals, you should study the five principles treated above (**9a, b, c, d, e**) and use a capital letter only when you can justify it. You should also carefully study the following rules and examples.

(1) Such words as *freshman, sophomore, college, high school, club, society, city, lake, river, park, building, street, highway, county,* and *railroad* are not capitalized unless they are essential parts of proper names.

> a freshman in college, large city, tall building

(2) Mere direction is not capitalized.

> turning south, flying north, eastern breezes

(3) Names of the seasons are usually not capitalized.

> winter, spring, summer, autumn

(4) Course names are usually not capitalized unless derived from a proper name or followed by a number.

> mathematics, history, home economics, chemistry

(5) Words denoting family relationship preceded by a possessive and ordinary titles following a name are usually not capitalized.

> my father; Mary, his cousin; William Smith, the president of First State Bank; Mr. Miller, manager.

SUMMARY

1. a junior or a senior	the Junior-Senior Banquet
2. a college, in high school	Boston College, Cisco High School
3. each club, the society	French Club, Royal Society
4. wide lake, in the river	Lake Erie, Keuka Lake, Ohio River
5. a building, the library	Mercantile Building, Wren Library
6. busy street, new highway	on Pacific Street, Highway 67
7. each city in the county	Kansas City, Knox County
8. to the east, an eastern voyage	in the East, an Eastern rite, an Easterner
9. winter, spring, summer	December, May, August
10. language, history	English, History 2
11. my uncle, his father	Uncle Tom, an argument with Father
12. president of the First National Bank	President of the United States

▶ EXERCISE 2 Supply capitals wherever needed in the following paragraphs. Be prepared to give the reason for the use of each capital.

1. Laying aside gilbert highet's *the art of teaching,* helen, my roommate, sighed and mumbled, "this book doesn't solve my problems as a student teacher at elmwood elementary school."
2. "Since mother is a teacher," I responded, "and often tells me about her discipline problems, maybe I can help you out.   3. Now that my english assignment is finished, I've got plenty of time to listen to your troubles."
4. "I'm so discouraged," moaned helen, "because my pupils are either stupid or hard of hearing.   5. For instance, after teaching vowels and consonants for days, I

gave a test friday.   6. One child put this title on his paper: 'what i know about valves and constants.'"

7. "oh," I laughed, "my mother has a big collection of similar boners made by her students at madison high school."

8. Too absorbed in serious thought to be cheered by a pollyanna roommate, helen continued, "I wish I could read a book called *how to win students and influence parents.* 9. Maybe its advice would help me on days like last monday, when beverly atkins whimpered for hours. 10. Desperate, I asked dr. jones, principal of elmwood, what to do; he suggested the threat of spanking, which served only to make beverly cry even louder.

11. "On the telephone early tuesday morning, beverly's mother gave me what she called 'the perfect solution to the problem.' 12. She advised, 'just spank a child sitting near my beverly, who'll then get scared and stop crying.'"

▶ EXERCISE 3   Write brief sentences correctly using each of the following: (1) *freshman,* (2) *Freshman,* (3) *college,* (4) *College,* (5) *south,* (6) *South,* (7) *avenue,* (8) *Avenue,* (9) *algebra,* (10) *Algebra,* (11) *theater,* (12) *Theater.*

▶ EXERCISE 4   Copy the following, using capitals wherever needed.

1. voters in the south
2. south of new york city
3. chemistry and french
4. a river in tennessee
5. the tennessee river
6. winter in the rockies
7. fearing a revolution
8. the american revolution
9. on labor day
10. a few indians and aliens
11. the texas company
12. a company in texas
13. my mother's father
14. an oriental custom
15. deserted islands
16. the philippine islands
17. an american citizen
18. a misinformed freshman
19. "the man without a
    country"
20. the god of the christians

Italics

10

Italicize (underline) titles of publications, foreign words, names of ships, titles of works of art, and words spoken of as words. Use italics sparingly for emphasis.

In longhand or typewritten papers, italics are indicated by underlining. The printer sets all underlined words in italic type.

TYPEWRITTEN
In David Copperfield Dickens writes of his own boyhood.
PRINTED
In *David Copperfield* Dickens writes of his own boyhood.

10a

Titles of separate publications—such as books, bulletins, magazines, newspapers, musical productions—are italicized (underlined) when mentioned in writing.

EXAMPLES   Many people still enjoy Mark Twain's *Roughing It*.
            [Note that the author's name is not italicized.]
            We read *The Comedy of Errors*, which is based on the
            Menaechmi of Plautus. [An initial *a, an,* or *the* is
            capitalized and italicized only when it belongs to
            the title.]
            Mozart's *Don Giovanni;* Beethoven's *Fifth Symphony*
            He pored over *Time,* the *Atlantic Monthly,* the *Satur-
            day Evening Post,* and the *New York Times* (or:
            New York *Times*). [Italics are not commonly used

for articles standing first in the titles of periodicals, and sometimes not used for the name of the city in the titles of newspapers.]

Occasionally quotation marks are used instead of italics for titles of separate publications. The usual practice, however, reserves quotation marks for short stories, short poems, one-act plays, articles from periodicals, and subdivisions of books. See **16b.**

David Copperfield opens with a chapter entitled "I Am Born."

Exception: Neither italics nor quotation marks are used in references to the Bible and its parts.

The first part of the Bible, the Old Testament, begins with Genesis.

▶ EXERCISE 1   Underscore all words below that should be italicized.

1. While waiting in the dentist's office, I thumbed through an old issue of Sports Illustrated and scanned an article entitled "Girls on the Go-Go-Go."
2. My father reads the editorials in the San Francisco Chronicle and the comic strips in the Chicago Sun-Times.
3. A performance of Verdi's opera La Traviata was reviewed in the New York Herald Tribune.
4. Huxley's Brave New World differs greatly from Plato's Republic and More's Utopia.
5. Ivanhoe is a character in the novel Ivanhoe.

10b

Foreign words and phrases not yet Anglicized are usually italicized (underlined).

Such words are indicated in *Webster's New Collegiate Dictionary* by parallel bars (∥), and in *Webster's New*

World Dictionary by a double dagger (‡), immediately before the words; in *The American College Dictionary,* by the italicized name of the language immediately after the words.

EXAMPLES   If I ever heard a *faux pas,* Ann's remark was one.
Mexico is sometimes called the land of *mañana.*
We heartily wish him *bon voyage.*

▶ EXERCISE 2   With the aid of your dictionary list and underline five foreign words or phrases that are generally written in italics. List five other foreign words or phrases (such as "apropos," "bona fide," "ex officio") that no longer require italics.

10c

Names of ships, trains, and aircraft and titles of motion pictures and works of art are italicized (underlined).

EXAMPLES   The *Queen Mary* and the *Princess Elizabeth* sailed from New York.
Rodin's *The Thinker* stands in one of the Parisian gardens.
On Halloween I enjoy seeing motion pictures like *The Walking Dead.*

10d

Words, letters, or figures spoken of as such or used as illustrations are usually italicized (underlined).

EXAMPLES   The article *the* has lost much of its demonstrative force.
In England *elevators* are called *lifts.* [Sometimes quotation marks ("the," "elevator," "lifts") are used instead of italics. See **16c.**]
The final *e* in *stone* is silent.
The first *3* and the final *0* of the serial number are barely legible.

10e

As a rule do not use italics (underlining) to give special emphasis to a word or a group of words. Do not underline the title of your own paper.

Frequent use of italics for emphasis defeats its own purpose and becomes merely an annoyance to the reader. This use of italics has been largely abandoned by good contemporary writers. Emphasis on a given word or phrase is usually best secured by careful arrangement of the sentence. See Section **29**.

A title is not italicized when it stands at the head of a book or an article. Accordingly, a student should not italicize (underline) the title standing at the head of his own paper (unless the title happens to be also the title of a book). See also **8b(4)**.

▶ EXERCISE 3   Underscore all words below that should be italicized.

1. My handwriting is difficult to read because each o looks like an a and each 9 resembles a 7.
2. In the early 1920's, Rudolph Valentino starred as "the great lover" in The Sheik.
3. To Let was completed in September, 1920, before Galsworthy sailed from Liverpool on the Empress of France to spend the winter in America.
4. Galsworthy's novels have been reviewed in such periodicals as Harper's Magazine and the Saturday Review and such newspapers as the New York Herald Tribune.
5. According to Greenough and Kittredge, in their book entitled Words and Their Ways in English Speech, "it is more natural for us to say divide (from L. divido) than cleave (from A.S. cleofan)."
6. A Manual of Style, published by the University of Chicago Press, recommends that such Latin words or

abbreviations as *vide, idem, ibid.,* and *op. cit.* be italicized when used in literary references.

7. In the *Spirit of St. Louis,* Charles A. Lindbergh made the first solo nonstop transatlantic flight from New York to Paris.

8. The original of Benjamin West's *Penn's Treaty with the Indians* is in the Pennsylvania Academy of Fine Arts in Philadelphia.

9. Each time Ernest has an attack of hay fever, his five-year-old brother yells in mock sympathy "Gesundheit!"

10. There are two acceptable ways to spell such words as *judgment, catalogue,* and *gruesome.*

11. Stevenson is said to have revised the first chapter of *Treasure Island* no fewer than thirty-seven times.

12. Michelangelo's *Battle of the Centaurs* and his *Madonna of the Steps* are among the world's finest sculptures.

▶ EXERCISE 4 Copy the following passage, underscoring all words that should be italicized.

1. I was returning home on the *America* when I happened to see a copy of Euripides' *Medea.* 2. The play was of course in translation, by Murray, I believe; it was reprinted in Riley's *Great Plays of Greece and Rome.* 3. I admire *Medea* the play and Medea the woman. 4. Both of them have a quality of *atrocitas* which our contemporary primitivism misses. 5. Characters in modern plays are neurotic; Medea was sublimely and savagely mad.

Abbreviations and Numbers

11

In ordinary writing avoid abbreviations (with a few well-known exceptions), and write out numbers that can be expressed in one or two words.

Abbreviations

11a

In ordinary writing spell out all titles except *Mr., Messrs., Mrs., Mmes., Dr.,* and *St.* (*saint*, not *street*). Spell out even these titles when not followed by proper names.

WRONG   The Dr. made his report to the Maj.

RIGHT   The doctor (*or* Dr. Smith) made his report to the major (*or* to Major Brown).

Note: *Hon.* and *Rev.* may be used before the surname when it is preceded by the Christian name or initials, never before the surname alone.

WRONG   Hon. Smith, Rev. Jones

RIGHT   Hon. George Smith, Hon. G. E. Smith, Rev. Thomas Jones, Rev. T. E. Jones

RIGHT   (more formal) The Honorable George Edward Smith, the Reverend Thomas Everett Jones, the Reverend Mr. Jones

For forms of address in writing or speaking to officials and other dignitaries of church and state see *Webster's New World Dictionary,* "Forms of Address."

11b

In ordinary writing spell out names of states, countries, months, days of the week, and units of measurement.

WRONG He left Ia. on the last Sun. in Jul.
RIGHT He left Iowa on the last Sunday in July.

WRONG On Oct. 15 James arrived in Mex.
RIGHT On October 15 James arrived in Mexico.

WRONG Only five ft. tall, Susan weighs about a hundred lbs.
RIGHT Only five feet tall, Susan weighs about a hundred pounds.

11c

In ordinary writing spell out *Street, Road, Park, Company,* and similar words used as part of a proper name.

EXAMPLE The procession moved down Lee Street between Central Park and the neon signs of the Ford Motor Company.

Note: Avoid the use of *&* (for *and*) and such abbreviations as *Bros.* or *Inc.* except in copying official titles: A & P; Goldsmith Bros.; Best & Co., Inc.; Doubleday & Company, Inc.

11d

In ordinary writing spell out the words *volume, chapter,* and *page* and the names of subjects.

WRONG The notes on chem. are taken from ch. 9, p. 46.
RIGHT The notes on chemistry are taken from chapter 9, page 46.

11e

In ordinary writing spell out Christian names.

WRONG Jas. Smith, Geo. White
RIGHT James Smith, George White

Permissible abbreviations: In addition to the abbreviations mentioned in **11a,** the following are permissible and usually desirable.

1. *After proper names:* Jr., Sr., Esq., and degrees such as D.D., LL.D., M.A., M.D.

   Mr. Sam Jones, Sr.; Sam Jones, Jr.; Thomas Jones, M.D.

2. *With dates or numerals:* A.D., B.C., A.M., P.M. (*or* a.m., p.m.), No., $

   RIGHT   In 450 B.C.; at 9:30 A.M.; in room No. 6; for $365

   WRONG   Early this A.M. he asked the No. of your room. [The abbreviations are correct only with the numerals.]

   RIGHT   Early this morning he asked the number of your room.

3. *For names of organizations and government agencies usually referred to by their initials:* DAR, GOP, RFC, TVA, WAC, SEC

4. *In general use, but often spelled out in formal writing as indicated in parentheses:* i.e. (*that is*), e.g. (*for example*), viz. (*namely*), cf. (*compare*), etc. (*and so forth*), vs. (*versus*)

Note: Use *etc.* sparingly. Never write *and etc.* The abbreviation comes from *et cetera,* of which *et* means *and.*

Special exceptions: Many abbreviations are desirable in footnotes, in tabulations, and in certain types of technical writing. In such special writing the student should follow the practice of the better publications in the field. If he has any doubt regarding the spelling or capitalization of any abbreviation, he should consult a good dictionary such as *Webster's New Collegiate Dictionary* (in a special section, "Abbreviations") or *The American College Dictionary* or *Webster's New World Dictionary* (in the main vocabulary).

► EXERCISE 1   Decide which form in each of the following items is appropriate in ordinary writing, and check the letter (*a* or *b*) of the correct form. If both forms are permissible, check both *a* and *b*.

1. a. in the U. S.
   b. in the United States
2. a. Rev. H. E. McGill
   b. The Reverend H. E. McGill
3. a. on Hickory St.
   b. on Hickory Street
4. a. etc.
   b. and etc.
5. a. FBI
   b. Federal Bureau of Investigation

6. a. on August 15
   b. on Aug. 15
7. a. for Jr.
   b. for John Evans, Jr.
8. a. e.g.
   b. for example
9. a. at 6:15 A.M.
   b. early in the A.M.
10. a. in Bangor, Me.
    b. in Bangor, Maine

Numbers

11f

Although usage varies, writers tend to spell out numbers that require only one or two words; they regularly use figures for other numbers.

EXAMPLES   after twenty years; only thirty-four dollars; more than four million votes
after 124 years; only $34.15; exactly 4,568,305 votes [Note the commas used to separate millions, thousands, hundreds.]

Special usage regarding numbers:

1. *Use figures for dates.*

   May 1, 1961; 1 May 1961; July 12, 1763

The letters *st, nd, rd, th* should not be added to the day of the month when the year follows; they need not be added even when the year is omitted.

   May 1, July 2

When the year is omitted, the day of the month may be written out.

> May first, July second

Ordinal numbers to designate the day of the month may be written out or expressed in figures. The year is never written out except in very formal social announcements or invitations.

> He came on the fifth (*or* 5th) of May.

2. *Use figures for street numbers, for pages and divisions of a book, for decimals and percentages, and for the hour of the day when used with* A.M. *or* P.M.

> 26 Main Avenue, 460 Fourth Street
> The quotation is from page 80.
> The bar is .63 of an inch thick.
> She gets 10 per cent of the profits.
> He arrived at 4:30 P.M.

3. *Be consistent in spelling out or using figures. Normally use figures for a series of numbers.*

> The garden plot was 125 feet long and 50 feet wide and contained an asparagus bed 12 feet square.
> He earned $60 weekly, spent $15 for room rent, $17.50 for board, $12 for incidentals, and saved $15.50.

4. *Normally spell out any numeral at the beginning of a sentence. If necessary, recast the sentence.*

> WRONG   25 boys made the trip.
> RIGHT   Twenty-five boys made the trip.
>
> WRONG   993 freshmen entered the college last year.
> RIGHT   Last year 993 freshmen entered the college.

5. *The practice of repeating in parentheses a number that is spelled out (now generally reserved for legal and commercial writing) should be used correctly if at all.*

> I enclose twenty (20) dollars.   I enclose twenty dollars ($20).

► EXERCISE 2   Correct all errors in the use of numbers in the following sentences. Write *C* after each sentence that needs no correction.

1. The Thanksgiving holidays begin at one p.m.
2. On June 27th, 1959, Hawaiians voted 18 to 1 for statehood.
3. 500 freshmen are expected at the bonfire tonight.
4. On September 15 I wrote a check for $35.40.
5. On the fifteenth of September I wrote a check for thirty-five dollars.
6. Lex enjoyed the nineteen sixty Olympics.
7. At the age of 14 I spent 12 days hunting and fishing with a group of Boy Scouts in the Ozarks.
8. The reception, to be held at 27 Jackson Street, will begin about 8 o'clock.
9. 18,000 fans watched the Eagles win their 7th victory of the season.
10. The Tigers gained only 251 yards on the ground and 35 in the air.

► EXERCISE 3   Correct all errors in the use of abbreviations and numbers in the following sentences.

1. My father moved to Cal. about 10 years ago.
2. He is now living at sixty-five Sandusky St. in Frisco.
3. Geo. Washington, our first Pres., was born in seventeen hundred and thirty-two.
4. When he was 20 years old, he inherited Mt. Vernon from his half bro.
5. He assumed command of the Continental armies in Cambridge, Mass., on Jul. 3, 1775.
6. 125 men were stationed in the mts. to serve as guides.
7. These one hundred and twenty-five men have been in service for nearly 5 years.
8. Our class in math. did not meet last Wed.
9. Do you know the No. of the prof's office?
10. Rev. Williams will preach next Sun.

PUNCTUATION

The Comma

12

Use the comma where it is demanded by the structure of the sentence.

The many different uses of the comma may be grouped under a very few principles and mastered with comparative ease by anyone who understands the structure of the sentence.[1] These principles, which cover the normal practice of the best contemporary writers, are adequate for the needs of the average college student. He may note that skilled writers sometimes employ the comma in unusual ways to express delicate shades of meaning. Such variations can safely be made by the writer who has first learned to apply the following major principles:

Use commas

a. To separate main clauses joined by *and, but, or, nor,* or *for.*

[1] **Caution:** Mastery of the comma is almost impossible for anyone who does not understand the structure of the sentence. If a student cannot readily distinguish main clauses, subordinate clauses, and the various kinds of phrases, he should study Section **1, Sentence Sense,** before trying to use this section. (Mastery of Section **12** will help to eliminate one of the two most common errors in the average student paper.)

b. To separate an introductory adverb clause (or a long phrase) from the main clause.

c. To separate items in a series (and co-ordinate adjectives modifying the same noun).

d. To set off nonrestrictive and other parenthetical elements.

Main Clauses

12a

Main clauses joined by one of the co-ordinating conjunctions (*and, but, or, nor, for*)[2] are separated by a comma.

PATTERN MAIN CLAUSE $,\begin{cases} \text{and} \\ \text{but} \\ \text{or} \\ \text{nor} \\ \text{for} \end{cases}$ MAIN CLAUSE.

EXAMPLES

We were sitting before the fire in the big room at Twin Farms, and Lewis had rudely retired behind a newspaper.
—DOROTHY THOMPSON

The Army fired a missile the other day and hit a target nine thousand miles away, but we've put very little time or money into launching our best missile—our ideas.   —E. B. WHITE

Justice stands upon Power, or there is no justice.
—WILLIAM S. WHITE

The peoples of the Sahara have never been united, nor have they even considered uniting in any common cause.
—JAMES R. NEWMAN

Note: A comma precedes a co-ordinating conjunction joining the main clauses of a compound-complex sentence

---

[2] *Yet* is occasionally used as a co-ordinating conjunction equivalent to *but.* Informal writing frequently uses *so* as a co-ordinating conjunction, but careful writers usually avoid the *so*-sentence by subordinating one of the clauses.

(which has at least two main clauses and one subordinate clause).

EXAMPLE   I was glad to agree, for I feel that showing live animals arouses people's interest in their local fauna and its preservation.   —GERALD DURRELL

Caution: Do not confuse the compound sentence (two main clauses) with the simple sentence (one main clause) containing a compound predicate.

The ranchmen from the valley in the foothills rode in on saddles decorated with silver, and their sons demonstrated their skill with unbroken horses.   —JOHN STEINBECK

ranchmen _|rode , and sons _|demonstrated

The ranchmen rode with their families into the little town and encouraged their sons to demonstrate their skill with unbroken horses.

ranchmen _|rode and encouraged   [No comma before *and*]

At times the comma is used to set off what seems to be merely the second part of a compound predicate, or even a phrase. Closer examination usually discloses, however, that the material following the comma is actually a regular main clause with some words "understood"; the use of the comma emphasizes the distinction between the principal ideas in the sentence. Note the following sentences, in which the implied matter is inserted in brackets:

There is no other way for the world's living standards to be raised to anything like our level, and [there is] no other way to link or merge the economies of the free nations.   —FORTUNE

The number of high school graduates has been increasing since 1890 about thirteen times as fast as the population, and the number of college graduates [has been increasing] six times as fast.   —THE ATLANTIC MONTHLY

Exceptions to 12a:

1. *Omission of the comma:*

When the main clauses are short, the comma is frequently omitted before *and* or *or*, less frequently before *but*. Before *for* the comma is needed to prevent confusion with the preposition *for*. (In colloquial style, especially in narrative writing, the comma is frequently omitted even when the clauses are longer.)

The next night the wind shifted and the thaw began.
—RACHEL L. CARSON

2. *Use of the semicolon instead of the comma:*

Sometimes the co-ordinating conjunction is preceded by a semicolon instead of the usual comma, especially when the main clauses have internal punctuation or reveal a striking contrast. See also 14a.

It was childish, of course; for any disturbance, any sudden intruding noise, would make the creatures stop.
—ALDOUS HUXLEY

▶ EXERCISE 1   In each of the following sentences find the main clauses. Then explain why the main clauses should be (1) separated by a comma, (2) separated by a semicolon, or (3) left without any punctuation.

1. In college a smug freshman receives a kind of shock treatment for professors often use surprising facts to pry open complacent or closed minds.   2. For example, a history professor may consider William Wirt a greater hero than Patrick Henry or an English teacher may say that a double negative like "don't have no money" does not really make the meaning of a sentence positive. 3. A freshman should not become rebellious nor should he be unduly alarmed when new information threatens old, cherished opinions.   4. An intelligent student may question surprising facts but he never doubts the value of

opening his mind to new ideas.   5. Moreover, he expects to be confused, at least part of the time, in the college classroom for he, like John Ciardi, the poet, knows that a person who is not confused probably has not yet asked the right questions.

6. The governor announced that the water supply was dangerously low and proclaimed a state of civil emergency. 7. The days passed and the drought grew steadily worse. 8. The state fire marshal ordered all parks closed but forest fires broke out in spite of all precautions.   9. City-dwellers watched their gardens shrivel and die and industrial workers were laid off as electric-power output failed. 10. But perhaps the worst afflicted were the farmers for there was no hope of saving their crops and even their livestock had to be sold on a glutted market or else left to die in the fields.

▶ EXERCISE 2   Write eight sentences to illustrate Rule **12a** and two sentences to illustrate the exceptions to the rule. Be sure to use all five co-ordinating conjunctions. If necessary, refer to the pattern and examples on page 117.

Introductory Clauses and Phrases

, 2b

An adverb clause (or a long phrase) preceding the main clause is usually followed by a comma.

Introductory clauses:

PATTERN   ADVERB CLAUSE**,** MAIN CLAUSE.

EXAMPLES

Whenever I tried to put chains on a tire**,** the car would maliciously wrap them around a rear axle.   —JAMES THURBER

If any college man will work intelligently**,** I guarantee his success.   —HARDIN CRAIG

Introductory phrases:

EXAMPLES

> *In two years of acting in cowboy films,* W. S. Hart earned
> $900,000.   —H. A. OVERSTREET

> *At the critical moments in this sad history,* there have been
> men worth listening to who warned the people against their
> mistakes.   —WALTER LIPPMANN

Introductory phrases containing a gerund, a participle,
or an infinitive, even though short, must often be followed
by a comma to prevent misreading.

> *Before leaving,* the soldiers demolished the fort.
> *Because of his effort to escape,* his punishment was increased.

Short introductory prepositional phrases, except when
they are distinctly parenthetical (as in such transitional
phrases as *in fact, on the other hand, for example*), are
seldom followed by commas.

> *At ninety* she was still active.
> *During the night* he heard many noises.
> *In fact,* I hope to leave tomorrow. [Transitional phrase]
> *For example,* most boys enjoy fishing.

Many writers omit the comma after short introductory
clauses, and sometimes after longer ones, when the omission does not make for difficult reading. In the following
sentences the commas may be used or omitted at the
option of the writer:

> If we leave(,) he will be offended.
> When *he* comes to the end of the lane(,) *he* should turn to the
> left. [When the subject of the introductory clause is repeated
> in the main clause, the comma is usually unnecessary.]

Note: When the adverb clause *follows* the main clause,
the comma is usually omitted.

PATTERN   MAIN CLAUSE   ADVERB CLAUSE.

EXAMPLE   I waited there until he returned.

Such adverb clauses, however, are set off by a comma if they are parenthetical or loosely connected with the rest of the sentence, especially if the subordinating conjunction seems equivalent to a co-ordinating conjunction (or if a distinct pause is required in the reading).

> Henry is now in good health, although he has been an invalid most of his life. [*Although* is equivalent to *but*.]

> With children and young people his magic never fails, whether he is doing bottle tricks for three-year-olds or counseling teen-agers about courses or careers.   —ALICE KIMBALL SMITH

▶ EXERCISE 3   In each of the following sentences find the main clause and identify the preceding element as a subordinate clause or a phrase. Then determine whether to use or omit a comma after the introductory element. Justify your decision.

1. In order to pay his way through college George worked at night in an iron foundry.   2. During this time he became acquainted with all the company's operations. 3. At the end of four years' observation of George's work the foundry owner offered George a position as manager. 4. Although George had planned to attend medical school and enter his father's profession he found now that the kind of work he had been doing had a far greater appeal for him. 5. In fact he accepted the offer without hesitation.

Items in Series

12c

Words, phrases, or clauses in a series (and co-ordinate adjectives modifying the same noun) are separated by commas.

(1)   Words, phrases, or clauses in a series

> The room is *bright, clean, quiet*. [Form *a, b, c*]
> The room is *bright, clean,* and *quiet*. [Form *a, b,* and *c*]

The room is *bright* and *clean* and *quiet*. [Form *a* and *b* and *c*. Commas are omitted when *and* is used throughout the series.]

He walked *up the steps, across the porch,* and *through the doorway*. [Phrases in a series]

We protested *that the engine used too much oil, that the brakes were worn out,* and *that the tires were dangerous*. [Subordinate clauses in a series]

We rang the bell, we knocked on the door, but *no one answered*. [Main clauses in a series]

The final comma is often omitted, especially by newspapers, when the series takes the form *a, b,* and *c*. But students are usually advised to follow the practice of the more conservative books and periodicals in using the comma throughout the series, if only because the comma is sometimes needed to prevent confusion.

CONFUSING   The natives ate beans, onions, rice and honey. [Was the rice and honey a mixture?]

CLEAR   The natives ate beans, onions, rice, and honey; *or* The natives ate beans, onions, and rice and honey.

(2) Co-ordinate adjectives

a *clean, quiet* room; a *bright, clean, quiet* room; a *keen, watchful* man. [*Clean* and *quiet* are co-ordinate—that is, of equal grammatical rank—and modify the same noun, *room*.]

a *clean* and *quiet* room; a *bright* and *clean* and *quiet* room; a *keen* and *watchful* man. [The adjectives are co-ordinate, as shown by the easy substitution of *and* for the comma.]

a *deep, malevolent* satisfaction.   —ALDOUS HUXLEY

Note: The comma is omitted before an adjective which is thought of as part of a noun.

a quiet dining room [*Dining room* has the force of a single noun, like *bedroom*. *Quiet* and *dining* are not co-ordinate; instead, *quiet* modifies *dining room*.]

several postage stamps; beautiful blue eyes; an active school board; ambitious young men

WAYS TO RECOGNIZE ADJECTIVES
THAT ARE NOT CO-ORDINATE

1. The insertion of *and* between the adjectives distorts the meaning: "a quiet and dining room."
2. Often the word order of the adjectives cannot sensibly be reversed: "postage several stamps."
3. Having the force of a single noun, the adjective-noun combination is pronounced as a unit: compare the pronunciation of "ambitious young men" and "young, ambitious men."

▶ EXERCISE 4   In the following sentences distinguish each series and each group of co-ordinate adjectives, inserting commas where needed. Justify each comma used.

1. Do you remember Pete Moore and that old battered lunch pail he used to carry?   2. He would go past our house every morning wait on the corner for his ride hand his lunch pail up to one of the men on the truck climb up himself and go rolling away.   3. Year after year—spring summer fall and winter—Pete and his lunch pail would wait on that corner.   4. And every year they both got a little older a little more battered a little nearer used up. 5. My brothers my sisters and I used to make bets about which would wear out first.   6. Then one awful day we heard the blast at the plant saw the sky black with smoke and watched the streets fill with frightened hurrying people.   7. That day was the end of old Pete of his battered lunch pail and of the jokes we made about him.

▶ EXERCISE 5   Using necessary commas, supply co-ordinate adjectives to modify each of the following.

EXAMPLE   old maid—an arrogant, aggressive old maid

1. office boy	5. salad dressing
2. oil painting	6. motion picture
3. stock market	7. crab grass
4. best man	8. mountain lion

Parenthetical Elements

Nonrestrictive clauses (or phrases) and other parenthetical elements ("interrupters") are set off by commas. Restrictive clauses (or phrases) are not set off.

To *set off* means to put a comma after a parenthetical element at the beginning of a sentence, before a parenthetical element at the end, and both before and after one within a sentence.

Caution: When two commas are needed to set off a parenthetical element within the sentence, as in the third and sixth sentences below, the omission of one of the two commas is usually more objectionable than the omission of both.

EXAMPLES *My friends,* we have no alternative.
We have no alternative, *my friends.*
We have, *my friends,* no alternative.

He said, "The story has been told."
"The story has been told," *he said.*
"The story," *he said,* "has been told."

(1) Nonrestrictive clauses and phrases are set off by commas. Restrictive clauses and phrases are not set off.

Adjective clauses introduced by *who* or *which* are nonrestrictive (set off by commas) when they merely add information about a word already identified. Such clauses are parenthetical; they are not essential to the meaning of the main clause and may be omitted.

Henry Smith, *who is lazy,* will lose his job.
Florence, *which he visited next,* was then torn by rival factions.

Adjective clauses introduced by *who, which,* or *that* are restrictive (not set off by commas) when they are needed for identification of the word they modify. Such clauses

limit or restrict the meaning of the sentence and cannot
be omitted.

> A boy *who is lazy* deserves to lose his job.
> The city *that he visited next* was Florence.

Your voice can help you distinguish between restrictive
and nonrestrictive modifiers. As you read the following
sentences aloud, note that you neither pause nor lower the
pitch of your voice for the italicized (restrictive) passages.

RESTRICTIVE   A mother *who does not love her children* is unnatural.
RESTRICTIVE   The girl *sitting near the window* laughed at me.

When reading aloud the sentences below, you naturally
"set off" the italicized nonrestrictive modifiers (1) by
using definite pauses and (2) by lowering the pitch of your
voice. (Note also that a nonrestrictive modifier can be
omitted without changing the meaning of the clause in
which it appears.)

NONRESTRICTIVE   My mother, *who loves her children,* is an ideal
    parent.
NONRESTRICTIVE   Martha Thompson, *sitting near the window,*
    often teases me.

Carefully study the meaning of the sentences below.
Also read each one aloud, and let your voice help you
distinguish between restrictive and nonrestrictive clauses
and phrases.

NONRESTRICTIVE CLAUSE   Our newest boat, *which is painted red
    and white,* has sprung a leak. [The *which* clause, adding
    information about a boat already identified, is parenthetical.
    It is not essential to the main clause, *Our newest boat has
    sprung a leak.*]
NONRESTRICTIVE PHRASE   Our newest boat, *painted red and white,*
    has sprung a leak.
RESTRICTIVE CLAUSE (NO COMMAS)   A boat *that leaks* is of little use.
    [The clause *that leaks* is essential to the meaning of the main
    clause.]
RESTRICTIVE PHRASE (NO COMMAS)   A boat *with a leak* is of little use.

NONRESTRICTIVE CLAUSE   My new car, *which is parked across the street,* is ready. [Clause adding information about a car already identified]

NONRESTRICTIVE PHRASE   My new car, *parked across the street,* is ready.

RESTRICTIVE CLAUSE (NO COMMAS)   The car *which is parked across the street* is ready. [Clause essential to the identification]

RESTRICTIVE PHRASE (NO COMMAS)   The car *parked across the street* is ready.

Sometimes a clause (or phrase) may be either restrictive or nonrestrictive; the writer signifies his meaning by the proper use of the comma.

NONRESTRICTIVE   He spent hours caring for the Indian guides, who were sick with malaria. [He cared for all the Indian guides. All of them were sick with malaria.]

RESTRICTIVE (NO COMMA)   He spent hours caring for the Indian guides who were sick with malaria. [Some of the Indian guides were sick with malaria. He cared for the sick ones.]

▶ EXERCISE 6   In the following sentences determine whether each clause (or phrase) is restrictive or nonrestrictive. Set off only the nonrestrictive clauses (or phrases).

1. The James Lee who owns the bank is a grandson of the one who founded it.
2. James Lee who owns this bank and five others is one of the wealthiest men in the state.
3. The coach called out to Higgins who got up from the bench and trotted over to him.
4. The coach who chewed on cigars but never lighted them threw one away and reached for another.
5. Anyone who saw him could tell that something was troubling him
6. All banks which fail to report will be closed
7. All banks failing to report will be closed.
8. Henry betrayed the man who had helped him build his fortune.

9. James White who had helped Henry build his fortune died yesterday.
10. My father hoping that I would remain at home offered me a share in his business.

▶ EXERCISE 7 Compose and punctuate five sentences containing nonrestrictive clauses or phrases. Compose five sentences containing restrictive clauses or phrases and underline the restrictive elements.

(2) Nonrestrictive appositives, contrasted elements, geographical names, and items in dates and addresses are set off by commas.

Note that most appositives may be readily expanded into nonrestrictive clauses. In other words, the principle underlying the use of commas to set off nonrestrictive clauses also applies here; see pages 125–27.

APPOSITIVES AND CONTRASTED ELEMENTS

Jesse, *the caretaker*, is a good fellow. [The appositive *caretaker* is equivalent to the nonrestrictive clause *who is the caretaker*.]

Sandburg, *the biographer of Lincoln*, was awarded the Pulitzer Prize. [The appositive is equivalent to the nonrestrictive clause *who is the biographer of Lincoln*.]

My companions were James White, *Esq.*, William Smith, *M.D.*, and Rufus L. Black, *Ph.D.* [Abbreviated titles after a name are treated as appositives.]

The cook, *not the caretaker*, will assist you. [The contrasted element is a sort of negative appositive.]

Our failures, *not our successes*, will be remembered.

Trade comes with peace, *not with war*.

Appositives are usually nonrestrictive (parenthetical), merely adding information about a person or thing already identified. Such appositives are set off by commas. But when an appositive is restrictive, commas are usually omitted.

The poet Sandburg has written a biography. [*Sandburg* restricts the meaning, telling what poet has written a biography.]

His son James is sick. [*James,* not his son *William*]

William the Conqueror invaded England in 1066. [An appositive that is part of a title is restrictive.]

The word *malapropism* is derived from Sheridan's *The Rivals.*

Do you refer to Samuel Butler the poet or to Samuel Butler the novelist?

▶ EXERCISE 8　Use commas to set off contrasted elements and nonrestrictive appositives in the following paragraph. Underline restrictive appositives.

1. Years ago I read *The Marks of an Educated Man* an interesting book by Albert Wiggam. 2. According to Wiggam, one outstanding characteristic of the educated man is that he "links himself with a great cause" one that requires selfless service. 3. Certainly many famous men whether scientists or artists or philosophers have dedicated their lives to the cause of serving others. 4. For example, Louis Pasteur the famous French chemist devoted his life to the study of medicine to benefit mankind. 5. And the artist Michelangelo served humanity by creating numerous works of lasting beauty. 6. Francis of Assisi a saint of the twelfth century was also devoted to a great cause. 7. His life was the mirror of his creed a reflection of his ardent love for others. 8. Among twentieth-century philosophers is Albert Schweitzer a well-known missionary and physician. 9. Schweitzer a person who works for both peace and brotherhood is like Pasteur, Michelangelo, and St. Francis because he has linked himself with a great cause not with transitory, selfish aims. 10. I think that the author Wiggam should use the adjective *great* not *educated* to describe the man who devotes himself to a noble cause.

▶ EXERCISE 9　Compose ten sentences to illustrate the punctuation of appositives and contrasted elements.

GEOGRAPHICAL NAMES,
ITEMS IN DATES AND ADDRESSES

Pasadena, California, is the site of the Rose Bowl. [*California* may be thought of as equivalent to the nonrestrictive clause *which is in California.*]

My friends live near the Charles River at 24 Radcliff Road, Waban 68, Massachusetts. [Postal zone numbers are not separated by a comma from the name of the city.]

Tuesday, May 2, 1961, in Chicago; 2 May 1961; May, 1961, in Boston *or* May 1961 in Boston. [Commas are often omitted when the day of the month is not given, or when the day of the month precedes rather than follows the month. Students are usually advised not to follow the less conservative practice of dropping the comma after the year, as in "May 2, 1961 in Chicago."]

▶ EXERCISE 10   Copy the following sentences, inserting commas where they are needed.

1. Their son was born on Friday June 18 1954 at Baptist Hospital Knoxville Tennessee.

2. Manuscripts should be mailed to the Managing Editor 109 Parrington Hall University of Washington Seattle 5 Washington.

3. He was inducted into the army at Fort Oglethorpe Georgia on 30 September 1942.

4. William Congreve was born in Bardsey England on January 24 1670.

5. The accident occurred in De Soto Parish Louisiana on Monday January 1 1962.

6. Please send all communications to 750 Third Avenue New York 17 New York.

7. Pearl Harbor Hawaii was bombed on December 7 1941.

(3) Parenthetical words, phrases, or clauses (inserted expressions), words in direct address (vocatives), absolute phrases, and mild interjections are set off by commas.

PARENTHETICAL EXPRESSIONS

As a matter of fact, the term "parenthetical" is correctly applied to everything discussed under **12d;** but the term is more commonly applied to such expressions as *on the other hand, in the first place, in fact, to tell the truth, however, that is, for example, I hope, I report, he says.* The term would apply equally well to expressions inserted in dialogue: *he said, he observed, he protested,* etc.

You will, *then,* accept our offer?
To tell the truth, we anticipated bad luck.
The work is, *on the whole,* very satisfactory.
"We believe," *he replied,* "that you are correct."
We believe, *however,* that you should go. [When *however* means "nevertheless," it is usually set off by commas. But when *however* means "no matter how," it is not parenthetical and is therefore not set off by commas: "The trip will be hard *however* you go.]

Some parenthetical expressions causing little if any pause in reading are frequently not set off by commas: *also, too, indeed, perhaps, at least, likewise,* etc. The writer must use his judgment.

I am *also* of that opinion.
He is *perhaps* the best swimmer on the team.
Your efforts will *of course* be appreciated; *or,* Your efforts will, *of course,* be appreciated.

DIRECT ADDRESS

Come here, *Mary,* and help us.
I refuse, *sir,* to believe the report.
This, *my friends,* is the whole truth.

ABSOLUTE PHRASES[3]

Everything being in readiness, we departed promptly.
He ran swiftly, *the dog in front of him,* and plunged into the forest.
I fear the encounter, *his temper being what it is.*

[3]See Section **35,** Grammatical Terms.

MILD INTERJECTIONS

Well, let him try if he insists.
Ah, that is my idea of a good meal.

[Strong interjections call for the exclamation point. See **17c.**]

12e

Note: **Occasionally a comma, though not called for by any of the major principles already discussed, may be needed to prevent misreading.**

Use **12e** sparingly to justify your commas. In a general sense, nearly all commas are used to prevent misreading or to make reading easier. Your mastery of the comma will come through the application of the more specific major principles (**a, b, c, d**) to the structure of your sentences.

CONFUSING	Inside the room was gaily decorated. [*Inside* may be at first mistaken for the preposition.]
CLEAR	Inside, the room was gaily decorated. [*Inside* is clearly an adverb.]
CONFUSING	After all the conquest of malaria is a fascinating story.
CLEAR	After all, the conquest of malaria is a fascinating story.

▶ EXERCISE 11   All commas in the following passage are correctly used. Justify each comma by referring to Rule **12a** (main clauses joined by a co-ordinating conjunction), Rule **12b** (introductory adverb clause or long phrase), Rule **12c** (a series or co-ordinate adjectives), or Rule **12d** (parenthetical elements).

1. In the cold months there are few visitors, for northern Minnesota is not a winter playground.   2. And yet the intrepid traveler would be well rewarded by the natural beauty surrounding him.   3. The skies and the undulating

fields merge as one; unreality assails the mind and the eye. 4. The sun swings in a low arc, and at sunrise and sunset it is not hard to imagine what the world may be like in many distant aeons when ice and snow envelop the earth, while the sun, cooled to the ruddy glow of bitter-sweet, lingeringly touches the clouds with warm colors of apricot, tangerine, lavender, and rose.

5. Night skies may be indescribably clear. 6. The stars are sharp and brilliant, pricking perception; the northern constellations diagramed with utmost clarity upon the blackest of skies. 7. There is no illusion here that they are hung like lanterns just beyond reach. 8. The vast distances of space are as clear to see as the barbed points of light.

9. When the aurora borealis sweeps in to dominate the night, it elicits a quite different and emotional reaction, not unlike the surging, impressive sight itself. 10. If the luminous, pulsing scarves of light were tangible streamers, certainly it would be possible to become entangled in and absorbed into the celestial kaleidoscope.

—FRANCES GILLIS[4]

► EXERCISE 12   Insert commas where needed in the following sentences (selected and adapted from the *New Yorker*). Be prepared to justify each comma used.

1. He was in truth slightly bowlegged but he concealed the flaw by standing with one knee bent.
2. What living American has had a mountain a bird a fish a spider a lizard and a louse named after him?
3. A teacup balanced on a chair tumbled to the floor and immediately our attention turned to poltergeists.
4. A black cloud crossed the city flashed two or three fierce bolts rumbled halfheartedly and passed on.
5. When Miss Meltzer reminded Feder that there existed

[4] From "Winter North of the Mississippi" by Frances Gillis, reprinted from the *Atlantic Monthly*, March, 1961. By permission of the author.

neither sufficiently powerful lamps nor properly designed fixtures for the project he said "Of course they don't exist Meltzer. We're going to create them."

6. He dies of pneumonia shortly afterward but returns as a robust ghost to steal the overcoats off the backs of half the citizens in the city triumphantly righting one wrong with a dozen wrongs.

7. Although histoplasmosis is now established as a disease of nearly universal distribution it appears to be most prevalent in the United States.

8. Still something had to be done and Mother and Aunt Berta not being inventive decided to do what all the world was doing.

9. For a week suspended in air we had given thought to becoming engaged—I more than she perhaps for she was engaged already.

10. Clara collapsed into laughter gasping her two hands thrust to her face in a spasm.

11. Two girls one of them with pert buckteeth and eyes as black as vest buttons the other with white skin and flesh-colored hair like an underdeveloped photograph of a redhead came and sat on my right.

12. After officials have measured the jump the result is flashed on the bulletin board but that isn't as satisfactory as seeing the high-jump bar tremble and then stay up or fall.

Superfluous Commas

13

Do not use superfluous commas.

If you tend to use unnecessary commas, consider every comma you are tempted to use and omit it unless you can justify it by one of the principles in Section **12**.

Another way to avoid unnecessary commas is to observe the following rules:

13a

Do not use a comma to separate the subject from its verb, the verb from its object, or an adjective from its noun.

WRONG   Rain at frequent intervals, is productive of mosquitoes.
           [Needless separation of subject and verb]
RIGHT   Rain at frequent intervals is productive of mosquitoes.

Note, however, that a comma before the verb sometimes makes for clarity when the subject is heavily modified.

Rain coming at frequent intervals and in sufficient amounts to fill the ponds, the cisterns, and the many small containers near the house, is productive of mosquitoes.

In the following sentences the encircled commas should be omitted:

He learned at an early age⊙ the necessity of economizing. [Needless separation of verb and object]
The book says⊙ that members of the crew deserted. [Indirect discourse: needless separation of verb and object]
He was a bad, deceitful, unruly⊙ boy. [Incorrect separation of adjective and its noun]

13b

Do not use a comma to separate two words or two phrases joined by a co-ordinating conjunction.

In the following sentences the encircled commas should be omitted:

The poem has nobility of sentiment⊙ and dignity of style.
The players work together⊙ and gain a victory. [Compound predicate: *and* joins two verbs.]
He had decided to work⊙ and to save his money. [*And* joins two infinitive phrases.]

13c

Do not use commas to set off words or short phrases (especially introductory ones) that are not parenthetical or that are very slightly so.

In the following sentences the encircled commas should be omitted:

On last Monday⊙ I went to a baseball game.
Maybe⊙ he had a better reason for leaving.
The center passes the ball⊙ through his legs⊙ to a man in the backfield.
In our age⊙ it is easy to talk⊙ by wire⊙ to any continent.

13d

Do not use commas to set off restrictive (necessary) clauses, restrictive phrases, or restrictive appositives.

In the following sentences the encircled commas should be omitted:

A man⊙ *who hopes to succeed*⊙ must work hard. [Restrictive clause]

A man⊙ *disinclined to work*⊙ cannot succeed. [Restrictive phrase]

That man⊙ *Jones*⊙ will outwit his opponents. [Restrictive appositive]

13e
Do not put a comma before the first item of a series, after the last item of a series, or after a conjunction.

In the following sentences the encircled commas should be omitted:

I enjoy the study of⊙ history, geography, and geology. [Needless comma before the first item of a series. A colon here would also be needless since there is no formal introduction. See **17d.**]

History, geography, and geology⊙ are interesting subjects.

I enjoy these subjects, but⊙ for others I have less appreciation.

Field work is required in a few sciences, such as⊙ botany and geology.

▶ EXERCISE 1 Draw a circle around each comma in the following sentences that would usually be omitted in good contemporary writing. Be prepared to justify each comma that you allow to stand.

1. I gave the note to Helen, and George asked her to read it aloud.
2. I gave the note to Helen, and asked her to read it aloud.
3. Any teacher, who is enthusiastic, deserves a lively class.
4. Professor Brown, who is enthusiastic, has a lively class.
5. One of the debaters, had apparently read Castell's *College Logic.*
6. My brother, one of the debaters, had never heard of the poet, Sandburg.

7. I like to celebrate Christmas quietly, but, my family prefers parties, and fireworks.

8. An old proverb states, that love and a cough are difficult to hide.

9. Remembering a line, from Pascal, I replied, "Noble deeds that are concealed are most esteemed."

10. During the half, we drank coffee, and talked about the close, exciting, football game, especially crucial plays, such as, the pass interference, the untimely fumbles, and the surprising, field goal.

▶ EXERCISE 2   In the following sentences (adapted from Thoreau) draw a circle around each superfluous comma and be prepared to justify each needed comma.

1. We admire Chaucer, for his sturdy, English wit. 2. The easy height, he speaks from, in his "Prologue," to the *Canterbury Tales,* as if he were equal to any of the company there assembled, is as good as any particular excellence in it.   3. But, though it is full of good sense, and humanity, it is not transcendent poetry.   4. For picturesque descriptions, of persons, it is, perhaps, without a parallel in English poetry.   5. Yet, it is, essentially, humorous, as the loftiest genius never is.   6. Humor, however broad and genial, takes a narrower view than enthusiasm.   7. To his own finer vein, he added all the common wit, and wisdom, of his time, and everywhere in his works, his remarkable knowledge of the world, and nice perception of character, his rare, common sense, and proverbial wisdom, are apparent. . . .

8. The lover learns at last, that there is no person quite transparent and trustworthy, but every one has a devil in him, that is capable of any crime, in the long run.   9. Yet, as an oriental philosopher has said, "Although friendship between good men, is interrupted, their principles remain unaltered.   10. The stalk of the lotus, may be broken, and the fibers remain connected."

The Semicolon

14

Use the semicolon (a) between two main clauses not joined by *and, but, or, nor,* or *for* and (b) between co-ordinate elements containing commas. (Use the semicolon only between parts of equal rank.)

Your understanding of this section will depend upon your ability to distinguish clauses and phrases, main clauses and subordinate clauses. You may need to review Section 1, **Sentence Sense,** especially 1d and 1e, before studying Section 14.

14a

Use the semicolon between two main clauses not joined by one of the co-ordinating conjunctions (*and, but, or, nor, for*).

PATTERN MAIN CLAUSE ; MAIN CLAUSE. [Compound sentence]

EXAMPLES

We didn't abolish truth; even we couldn't do that.
                                                    —WILLIAM FAULKNER

Essentially the form of art is an imitation of reality; it holds the mirror up to nature.   —WILL DURANT

I had great anxiety and no means of relieving it; I had vehement convictions and small power to give effect to them.
                                                    —WINSTON CHURCHILL

Note: The semicolon also separates main clauses not joined by a co-ordinating conjunction in compound-complex sentences.

EXAMPLE

No society can survive if everything changes but its institutions; no society can stay sane if no one is to innovate except the technologists.   —BARBARA WARD

[Main clause subordinate clause; main clause subordinate clause.]

Conjunctive adverbs (e.g., *accordingly, also, anyhow, besides, consequently, furthermore, hence, however, indeed, instead, likewise, moreover, nevertheless, still, then, therefore, thus*) and such transitional phrases as *for example, in fact, in other words, on the contrary, on the other hand,* and *that is* are not grammatically equivalent to co-ordinating conjunctions. See **3b.** Therefore, use a semicolon before these conjunctive adverbs and transitional phrases when they connect main clauses.

PATTERN

CONJUNCTIVE ADVERB

MAIN CLAUSE ;   *or*   MAIN CLAUSE

TRANSITIONAL PHRASE ,

EXAMPLES

Kon-Tiki, on his original voyage across the sea, had no asphalt or hermetically sealed tins; nevertheless he had no serious food problems.   —THOR HEYERDAHL

The organism gets a chance to function according to its own laws; in other words, it gets a chance to realize such good as it is capable of.   —ALDOUS HUXLEY

A comma usually follows a transitional phrase such as *in other words* but not a conjunctive adverb such as *nevertheless* unless it is distinctly parenthetical.

Caution: Do not overwork the semicolon. Often compound sentences are better revised according to the principles of subordination. See Section **24.**

Exception to 14a: Co-ordinating conjunctions between main clauses are often preceded by a semicolon (instead of the usual comma) if the clauses have internal punctuation or reveal a striking contrast. See also **12a**.

EXAMPLE

American education may be sometimes slapdash and fantastic, with its short-story and saxophone courses, its strange fraternities and sororities, its musical-comedy co-ed atmosphere, its heavily solemn games departments; but at least it has never departed from the fine medieval tradition of the poor scholar. —J. B. PRIESTLEY

14b

The semicolon is used to separate a series of equal elements which themselves contain commas.

This use of the semicolon makes for clarity, showing the reader at a glance the main divisions, which would be more difficult to distinguish if only commas were used throughout the sentence.

EXAMPLES

I came to this conclusion after talking in Moscow last spring with three kinds of people concerned: foreign diplomats, students, and correspondents; the new Rector of Friendship University; and the harried Afro-Asian students themselves. —PRISCILLA JOHNSON

The challenge of facing a large audience, expectant but unaroused; the laughter that greets a sally at the outset, then the stillness as the power of imagery and ideas takes hold; the response that flows, audibly or inaudibly, from the audience to the speaker; the fresh extemporizing without which a lecture is dead; the tension and timing as the talk nears the hour; and the unexpected conclusion—this is what every professional speaker comes to know. —EDWARD WEEKS

14c

Caution: **Do not use the semicolon between parts of unequal rank, such as a clause and a phrase or a main clause and a subordinate clause.**

WRONG   A bitter wind swept the dead leaves along the street; casting them high in the air and against the buildings. [Main clause; phrase]

RIGHT   A bitter wind swept the dead leaves along the street, casting them high in the air and against the buildings.

WRONG   I hope to spend my vacation in Canada; where I enjoy the fishing. [Main clause; subordinate clause]

RIGHT   I hope to spend my vacation in Canada, where I enjoy the fishing.

Note: At times a semicolon is apparently used between parts of unequal rank. However, closer examination usually reveals that the semicolon is in reality a mark of co-ordination: following the semicolon is a group of words which, with "understood" words carried over from the preceding clause, constitutes a main clause.

EXAMPLES

Popularization is one thing; dedicated music-making [is] another.
—HARPER'S MAGAZINE

The theory applied equally well to Mrs. Kerr's case; perhaps [the theory applied] even better since it also confirmed the deep-rooted public conviction that no woman really knows what a car is for.   —IBID.

▶ EXERCISE 1   In the following sentences (selected from the *Atlantic Monthly*), all semicolons are used correctly. Be prepared to give the reason for the use of each semicolon.

1. The narrow windows and the steeply sloping roof oppressed me; I wished to turn away and go back.
2. Even stillness is a positive factor; it is to motion what silence is to sound.
3. We are not as careful or cherishing of our artists as

Europeans; nevertheless, what with television, movies, and shows, it is possible for outstanding dancers to make a living, while choreographers, directors, and dancing actors can make fortunes.

4. The rhymes are filled with fun and good humor; the music, arranged by Cecil Sharp, is a fine accompaniment; but the superb part of the book is the hilarious array of pictures in rainbow colors.

5. Beyond this are the three objectives of the American space program: "to understand the nature of the control exerted by the sun over events on the earth; to learn the nature and origin of the universe, including the solar system; and to search for the origin of life and its presence outside the earth."

6. Everybody was confused; no one knew what to do.

7. "As a historian," wrote De Voto, "I have interested myself in the growth among the American people of the feeling that they were properly a single nation between two oceans; in the development of what I have called the continental mind."

8. Treitschke confirmed him in his belief in blood and iron; Nietzsche in his veneration for the Aryan "blond beast," the superman who would conquer and decimate the subject races.

9. It is beyond possibility to mention all the outstanding books; however, some of the highlights are suggested in the chronological list that follows.

10. It was an inland country, with the forlorn look of all unloved things; winter in this part of the South is a moribund coma, not the Northern death sleep with the sure promise of resurrection.

▶ EXERCISE 2   In the following sentences on the next page insert semicolons where they are needed. Do not allow a semicolon to stand between parts of unequal rank. Write *C* after each sentence that needs no revision.

1. Although I did my best to explain why I had failed; my parents scolded me for failing the history test.
2. Mac goes around in par now, he has trimmed several strokes off his game since we played together last.
3. I hear it said by the people hereabouts that the old mansion is haunted, in fact, there are some who swear that it is.
4. Hank had dismantled his motor; intending to give it a complete overhaul for the following week's races.
5. He is fairly even-tempered most of the time, and you should have no difficulty getting along with him but whatever you do, don't ever let him get you into a political argument.
6. He lamented that he had no suggestions to offer, however, he spent the next forty minutes offering them.
7. It's all right for you to be here, I crashed this party myself.
8. I went to the address you gave me; if your brother lives there, he lives upstairs over a vacant lot.
9. In our unit at that time there were Lieutenant Holmes, who was a criminologist by profession and a university lecturer on penology, Captain Sturm, in peacetime a U.S. Steel executive, two old majors, previously retired and now still writing their memoirs, and Lieutenant Colonel Beale, a Mississippi cotton planter.
10. If you expect me to be here in time, or even to get back at all; you had better send somebody to help me.

▶ EXERCISE 3   From your reading, copy any five sentences in which the semicolon is properly used. Explain the reason for each semicolon.

▶ EXERCISE 4   Compose five sentences to illustrate the proper use of the semicolon.

[*See also the general exercises immediately following; also the general exercises following Section 17.*]

GENERAL EXERCISES ON THE COMMA
AND THE SEMICOLON

▶ EXERCISE 5   Commas are used correctly in the following sentences. Explain each comma by writing above it the appropriate letter from Section 12: **a, b, c,** or **d.**

1. After crossing the river we built no more fires, for we were now in hostile Indian country.
2. Having nothing very important to do, I simply did nothing at all.
3. If he says he'll be there, he'll be there.
4. The smith straightened up, the horse's hoof still between his knees, and then he bent back to his work.
5. Although there are a few adjustments yet to be made, the main part of the work is finished, and the next few days should see it completed altogether.
6. The panting, tormented bull lowered his head for another charge.
7. The kit contains cement, balsa, paper, and instructions for assembly.
8. You will, I suppose, be back tomorrow.
9. The old opera house, which has stood unused for years, will finally be torn down.
10. It was a long, hot, tiresome trip, and I was sorry that I had promised to go.

▶ EXERCISE 6   Explain each comma and each semicolon used in Section 1, Exercise 18, by referring to Rule **12a, b, c,** or **d** or to Rule **14a** or **b.**

▶ EXERCISE 7   Explain each comma and each semicolon used in Section 3, Exercise 2.

▶ EXERCISE 8   Insert all necessary commas and semicolons in the following sentences. Above each mark of punctuation write the appropriate rule number.

1. If I were in your position however I would be extremely cautious about believing what I heard.
2. Taking everything into consideration I believe that Robinson should have a better season this year than ever before however you understand that this is only an opinion and that I reserve the right to amend it after I have seen him work out a few times.
3. After we wash the dishes we must wash the towels.
4. Two or three scrawny mangy-looking hounds lay sprawled in the shade of the cabin.
5. While Frank was unpacking the cooking gear and Gene was chopping firewood I began to put up our shelter.
6. Phil meanwhile had gone down to the lake to try to get a few bass for our supper.
7. After perhaps an hour or so of waiting they may go away but don't expect them to go far and don't think they aren't still watching.
8. Bales of cotton hogsheads of sugar and salted meats barrels of flour and cases and crates of goods of every kind imaginable crowded the busy landing as far up and down the river as the eye could reach.
9. In complete disregard of the machine-gun bullets which were nipping through the grass tops all around us Jerry wriggled on his belly all the way out to where I was put a tourniquet on my leg and then began dragging me back to the shelter of the ditch.
10. If I am expected to arrive by eleven o'clock someone should volunteer to wake me up otherwise I shall probably sleep until noon.

The Apostrophe

15

Use the apostrophe to indicate the possessive case (except for personal pronouns), to mark omissions, and to form the plurals of letters and figures.

15a

Do not carelessly omit the apostrophe in the possessive case of nouns and indefinite pronouns.

The apostrophe indicates a relationship that may be otherwise expressed by the substitution of an *of* phrase or a similar modifier.

EXAMPLES   The girls' mother (the mother of the girls); Ted's dog (the dog owned by Ted); tomorrow's assignment (the assignment for tomorrow); no one's fault (the fault of no one); everybody's friend (the friend of everybody)

(1)   If the ending (either singular or plural) is not in an *s* or *z* sound, add the apostrophe and *s*.

EXAMPLES

The man's hat; the boy's shoes; a dollar's worth; today's problems [Singular]

The men's hats; the women's dresses; the children's playground [Plural]

One's hat; another's coat; someone's shirt; anybody's room [Indefinite pronouns—singular]

(2) **If the plural ends in an s or z sound, add only the apostrophe.**

EXAMPLES   Ladies' hats (hats for ladies); boys' shoes (shoes for boys); the Joneses' boys (the boys of the Joneses); three dollars' worth; Farmers' (or Farmers) Co-operative Society [The names of organizations frequently omit the apostrophe. Cf. Teachers College.]

(3) **If the singular ends in an s or z sound, add the apostrophe and s for words of one syllable. Add only the apostrophe for words of more than one syllable unless you expect the pronunciation of the second s or z sound.**

EXAMPLES   James's book; Moses' law; Xerxes' army; Hortense's coat

(4) **Compounds or nouns in joint possession show the possessive in the last word only. But if there is individual (or separate) possession, each noun takes the possessive form.**

EXAMPLES
   My brother-in-law's house; my brothers-in-law's houses; someone else's hat
   Helen and Mary's piano [Joint ownership]
   Helen's and Mary's clothes [Individual ownership]

▶ EXERCISE 1   Copy the following, inserting apostrophes to indicate the possessive case:

1. the girls (*sing.*) coat
2. the girls (*pl.*) coats
3. a months pay
4. two months pay
5. everybodys business
6. everyone elses clothes
7. the childs mother
8. the childrens mother
9. babys toys
10. babies toys

▶ EXERCISE 2   Rewrite the following as possessives with the apostrophe:

1. the home of my neighbor
2. homes of my neighbors
3. a book for a boy
4. books for boys

5. the car of my sister
6. the cars of my sisters
7. the ideas of a woman
8. the ideas of women
9. the boat of Robert and Jim

10. the boats of Robert and Jim (individual possession)
11. the hat of the lady
12. the hats of the ladies

15b

Do not use the apostrophe with the pronouns _his, hers, its, ours, yours, theirs, whose_ or with plural nouns not in the possessive case.

WRONG _hi's_ son (an error no one would make); _it's_ nest (fully as wrong as _hi's—it's_ means _it is_); a friend of _yours'_ and _their's; who's_ mistake (_who's_ means _who is_); _who'se_ mistake

RIGHT _his_ son; _its_ nest; a friend of _yours_ and _theirs; whose_ mistake

WRONG He makes _hat's_ for _ladies'._
RIGHT He makes _hats_ for _ladies._

15c

Use an apostrophe to mark omissions in contracted words or numerals.

EXAMPLES Can't; didn't; he's (he is); it's (it is); you're; o'clock (of the clock); the class of '55 (1955)

Caution: Place the apostrophe exactly where the omission occurs: isn't, haven't [_not_ is'nt, have'nt].

15d

Use the apostrophe and s to form the plural of letters, figures, symbols, and words referred to as words.

EXAMPLES Congreve seldom crossed his _t's_, his _7's_ looked like _9's_, and his _and's_ were usually _&'s_.

Note: This apostrophe is sometimes omitted when there is no danger of ambiguity: the 1930's, or the 1930s; two *B*'s and three *C*'s, or two *B*s and three *C*s.

▶ EXERCISE 3 Write brief sentences correctly using (a) the possessive singular, (b) the plural, and (c) the possessive plural of each of the following words.

> EXAMPLE 1. *student*
> > a. A student's attitude is important.
> > b. Several students dropped the course.
> > c. The students' parents were invited.

1. woman	5. lawyer	9. brother-in-law
2. father	6. jockey	10. genius
3. other	7. sailor	11. army
4. family	8. goose	12. Brooks

▶ EXERCISE 4 Copy the following sentences, inserting necessary apostrophes and omitting needless or faulty ones. Underline each possessive once and each contraction twice.

1. Who's going to do the dishes? Who's turn is it?
2. The choice is our's to make, not your's.
3. Shes writing copy for a new program on one of the local station's.
4. On Thursday's the childrens' department does'nt open.
5. That boys one of the worlds' worst; whats he doing now?
6. Its a ladys' world despite the saying's to the contrary.
7. *Ifs, buts,* and *maybes* wont satisfy a young swains ardent proposal.
8. They have'nt said the property is theirs'.
9. I did'nt go to sleep until after two oclock.
10. Its a mans right to see that he gets his dollars worth.
11. Theyre not coming to see Freds' new house.
12. The books format is it's best feature.

Quotation Marks (and Quotations)

16

Use quotation marks to set off all direct quotations, some titles, and words used in a special sense. Place other marks of punctuation in proper relation to quotation marks.

Quotations usually consist of (1) passages borrowed from the written work of others or (2) the direct speech of individuals, especially in conversation (dialogue).

Caution: Be careful not to omit or misplace the second set of quotation marks: the first set, marking the beginning of the part quoted, must be followed by another set to mark the end. Do not place the verb of saying within quotation marks.

WRONG "I have no intention of staying, he replied. [Second set of quotation marks omitted]

WRONG "I have no intention of staying, he replied." [Second set of quotation marks misplaced]

RIGHT "I have no intention of staying," he replied.

WRONG "I do not object, he said, to the tenor of the report." [*He said* not excluded from quotation marks]

RIGHT "I do not object," he said, "to the tenor of the report." [Two parts are quoted. Each must be enclosed, leaving *he said* outside of the quotation marks.]

16a

Use double quotation marks to enclose direct (but not indirect) quotations; for a quotation within a quotation, use single marks.

RIGHT He said, "I have no intention of staying." [Direct quotation—the exact words spoken]

RIGHT He said that he had "no intention of staying." [Direct quotation of a fragment of the speech]

WRONG He said "that he had not intended to stay." [Indirect quotation—should not be enclosed in quotation marks]

RIGHT He said that he had not intended to stay.

RIGHT "It took courage," the speaker said, "for a man to affirm in those days: 'I endorse every word of Patrick Henry's sentiment, "Give me liberty or give me death!"'" —WILLIAM LEWIN
[Note that a quotation within a quotation is enclosed by single quotation marks; one within that, by double marks.]

(1) **Long quotations (not dialogue).** Quoted passages of ten or more lines[1] are usually set off from the other matter, without quotation marks, by means of smaller type. In typewritten papers such quoted passages are single-spaced (except in copy for the printer) and indented.[2]

(2) **Poetry.** A single line of poetry or less is usually handled like other short quotations, run in with the text and enclosed in quotation marks. Longer passages should be set off from the text, indented, and quoted line by line without quotation marks.

[1] Recommended by "The MLA Style Sheet," Revised Edition, 1959, p. 8, reprinted from *Publications of the Modern Language Association of America.*

[2] When quotation marks—instead of the usual smaller type or indention—are used for a passage of two or more paragraphs, the quotation marks come before each paragraph and at the end of the last; they do not come at the end of intermediate paragraphs.

(3) **Dialogue (conversation).** Written dialogue represents the directly quoted speech of two or more persons talking together. Standard practice is to write each person's speech, no matter how short, as a separate paragraph. Verbs of saying, as well as closely related bits of narrative, are included in the paragraph along with the speech.

> "You remember Kate Stoddard, Mother?" Georgia asked. "This is Kate to pay us a little visit."
>
> Mrs. Stanton rocked and closed her eyes. "What's everybody shouting for?" she asked.
>
> "Sit down, Kate," Georgia said.
>
> Mrs. Stoddard pulled a chair close to Mrs. Stanton. "Well, I will, but I can't stay. I came for a reason."
>
> "We paid our yearly dues," Georgia said.
>
> "I don't know what makes you say that," Mrs. Stoddard said. "I don't think you've ever known me to solicit *personally*. I came about quite another matter. I wanted you to look at this." She fished in her bag and brought out the diary, which she held out rather grudgingly to Georgia. "Be careful of it! It's quite old!" —SALLY BENSON[3]

In the last paragraph, note that although a narrative passage interrupts the dialogue, the speaker is Mrs. Stoddard throughout.

(4) **Punctuation of dialogue.** Note that such expressions as "he said," when introducing a *short* speech, are usually followed by a comma; that they are set off by commas when interpolated (see **12d(3)**); that they are preceded by a comma when added at the end of a speech (unless the speech is a question or an exclamation, when the question mark or the exclamation point replaces the comma). Such expressions as "he said" before *longer* speeches are usually followed by a colon (see **17d(1)**).

---

[3] From "Spirit of '76" by Sally Benson. Originally published in *The New Yorker*, December 25, 1954.

▶ EXERCISE 1   Compose five sentences to illustrate the proper use of double and single quotation marks.

16b

Use quotation marks for minor titles (short stories, one-act plays, short poems, songs, articles from magazines) and for subdivisions of books.

EXAMPLES

The January, 1961, issue of *Holiday* contains a lively article entitled "The Antic Arts."

In this book are numerous short poems and stories, such as "The Raven" and "The Fall of the House of Usher."

Last summer I read "L'Allegro," a short lyric, and parts of *Paradise Lost.*

Stevenson's *Treasure Island* is divided into six parts, the last of which, called "Captain Silver," opens with a chapter entitled "In the Enemy's Camp."

Note: Quotation marks are sometimes used to enclose titles of books, magazines, and newspapers, but italics are usually preferred. See **10a.**

▶ EXERCISE 2   Compose five sentences showing use of quotation marks with minor titles and subdivisions of books.

16c

Words used in a special sense are sometimes enclosed in quotation marks.

EXAMPLES

The printer must see that quotation marks are "cleared"— that is, kept within the margins.

"Sympathy" means "to suffer with." [Also right: *Sympathy means to suffer with; Sympathy* means "to suffer with." See also **10d.**]

16d

Do not overuse quotation marks.

Do not use quotation marks to enclose titles of themes or to mark bits of humor. In general do not enclose in quotation marks common nicknames, technical terms, and trite or well-known expressions. Instead of placing slang and colloquialisms inside quotation marks, use formal English. Above all, do not use quotation marks for emphasis.

NEEDLESS PUNCTUATION   "Old Hickory" was wrought up over the loss of his friend.

BETTER   Old Hickory was wrought up over the loss of his friend.

INAPPROPRIATE IN FORMAL WRITING   He must have been "nuts." The tiny pink telephone is "as cute as a bug's ear."

APPROPRIATE   He must have been insane. The tiny pink telephone is an attractive novelty.

16e

In using marks of punctuation with quoted words, phrases, or sentences, follow the arbitrary printers' rules by placing:

(1) The period and the comma always within the quotation marks.

(2) The colon and the semicolon always outside the quotation marks.

(3) The dash, the question mark, and the exclamation point within the quotation marks when they apply to the quoted matter only; outside when they refer to the whole sentence.

"I will go," he insisted. "I am needed." [Comma and period always inside quotation marks]

He spoke of his "old log house"; he might have called it a mansion. [Semicolon (and colon) always outside quotation marks]

He asked, "When did you arrive?" [Here the question mark applies only to the part of the sentence within quotation marks.]

What is the meaning of "the open door"? [Here the question mark applies to the whole sentence.]

The captain shouted, "Halt!" [Here the exclamation point applies only to the quotation.]

Save us from his "mercy"! [Here the exclamation point applies to the whole sentence.]

▶ EXERCISE 3   Add correctly placed quotation marks where needed in the following sentences.

1. Surely, I replied facetiously, you know the difference between prose and poetry.
2. Dan asked, Did you accept Beverly's invitation?
3. Have you read the short poem To an Athlete Dying Young?
4. One angry spectator yelled, That blockhead!
5. Who is the author of the line A spark disturbs our clod?
6. Thomas Gray did write 'Tis folly to be wise; however, he qualified the statement with Where ignorance is bliss.
7. How he enjoyed reading the short story, The Luck of Roaring Camp!
8. Only one main character appears in Poe's short story The Tell-Tale Heart: the mad murderer.
9. Was it Knox or a Hebrew writer who asked Why is man, mere earth and ashes, proud?
10. The lip of truth shall be established forever, states an ancient proverb, but a lying tongue is but for a moment.

▶ EXERCISE 4   After you have studied 16a(3), giving special attention to the punctuation of the dialogue on page 153, and have reviewed Rule 16e, write a short, original dialogue of approximately two hundred words. Place all quotation marks properly.

▶ EXERCISE 5 Insert quotation marks where they are needed in the following sentences.

1. Campus fads come and go, I commented to Carl as we sat down to lunch in the cafeteria. But, as far as your friend Helen is concerned, this current fad of acting like Mrs. Malaprop will probably never die.

2. Be patient with Helen! Carl snapped as he unrolled his napkin and sorted his silverware. I actually like Helen's bad jokes. Her word play—

3. Please pass the salt, I interrupted.

4. Ignoring my frown, Carl continued, I'll grant you that Helen's puns are usually as old and as clever as the joke ending with Squawbury Shortcake; but here she comes. Let's change the subject pronto.

5. Clearing my throat pretentiously, I took his advice and said, Perhaps your parents should buy a perambulator.

6. A perambulator! Helen happily took up my cue as she plopped down in the chair near Carl. My parents bought me an eight-cup perambulator for my birthday. Just plug it in, and coffee is ready in four minutes!

7. Aren't you thinking of a percolator? I asked her in mock seriousness. An electric percolator heats quickly.

8. Yeah, Helen replied, winking at Carl. It's the same thing as an incubator.

9. You don't mean incubator! I barked sharply and then added a bit of my own nonsense: You mean incinerator. After a moment of silence, I yawned and said, Incinerator bombs are really fiery weapons. They cause much perturbation.

10. This time Helen had no ready answer. Admitting defeat at her own ridiculous word game, she grinned and announced, Repartee like this is for immature freshmen who like the Malaprop fad—not for me.

. /

The Period
and Other Marks

17

Use the period, the question mark, the exclamation point, the dash, the colon, parentheses, and brackets in accordance with standard usage.

The Period (.)

17a

Use the period after declarative and mildly imperative sentences, after indirect questions, and after most abbreviations. Use the ellipsis mark (three spaced periods) to indicate omissions from quoted passages.

(1) Use the period to mark the end of a declarative sentence, a mildly imperative sentence, or an indirect question.

DECLARATIVE   They changed the rules.

MILDLY IMPERATIVE   Change the rules. Let's change the troublesome rules.

INDIRECT QUESTION   He asked whether the rules had been changed.

(2) Use periods to follow most abbreviations.

EXAMPLES   Mr., Mrs., Dr., Jr., M.D., etc., i.e., e.g., A.D., B.C., A.M., P.M., C.O.D., R.S.V.P., P.S.

Frequently current usage omits periods after many abbreviations, especially of organizations and national or international agencies.

EXAMPLES TV, CBS, CIO, ROTC, VA, FBI, USN, FHA, TVA, CARE, UN

If you have any doubt about the punctuation of a given abbreviation, consult a good dictionary such as *Webster's New Collegiate Dictionary* (in a special section, "Abbreviations") or *The American College Dictionary* or *Webster's New World Dictionary* (in the main vocabulary).

Caution: Do not use periods to indicate that such words as *I've, can't, 2nd, 15th,* and *gym* are contractions or abbreviations.

(3) Use the ellipsis mark (three spaced periods) to indicate an omission of one or more words within a quoted passage.

EXAMPLES

No man is an island . . . every man is a piece of the continent, a part of the main. ———JOHN DONNE

. . . to be honest, as this world goes, is to be one man picked out of ten thousand. ———SHAKESPEARE

If the omission ends with a period, use four spaced periods (one to mark the end of the sentence and three to show the omission).

EXAMPLES

Poetry lifts the veil from the hidden beauty of the world. . . . ———SHELLEY

A foolish consistency is the hobgoblin of little minds. . . . With consistency a great soul simply has nothing to do. ———EMERSON

The fundamental justification for poetry on the stage . . . lies in the play itself, in the illusion the play undertakes to create. . . . ———ARCHIBALD MACLEISH

The Question Mark (?)

17b

Use the question mark to follow direct (but not indirect) questions.

EXAMPLES

Who started the riot?

Did he ask who started the riot? [The sentence as a whole is a direct question despite the indirect question at the end.]

"Who started the riot?" he asked.

He asked, "Who started the riot?"

You started the riot? [Question in the form of a declarative sentence]

You told me—did I hear you correctly?—that you started the riot. [Interpolated question]

Did you hear him say, "What right have you to ask about the riot?" [Double direct question followed by a single question mark]

Did he plan the riot, employ assistants, and give the signal to begin?

Did he plan the riot? employ assistants? give the signal to begin? [Question marks used between the parts of the series cause full stops and throw emphasis on each part.]

Caution: Do not use the question mark to indicate the end of an indirect question. See also **17a(1)**.

EXAMPLES   He asked who started the riot. To ask why the riot started is unnecessary. I want to know what the cause of the riot was. How foolish it is to ask what caused the riot!

OTHER USES OF THE QUESTION MARK

A question mark (within parentheses) is used to express the writer's uncertainty as to the correctness of the preceding word, figure, or date: "Chaucer was born in 1340(?) and died in 1400." But the question mark is not a desirable means of expressing the author's wit or sarcasm.

QUESTIONABLE   This kind (?) proposal caused Gulliver to take refuge in nearby Blefuscu. [Omit the question mark. If the context does not make the irony clear, either revise your sentence or give up your attempt to strike an ironic note.]

Courtesy questions common to business letters may be followed by question marks but are usually followed by periods: "Will you (= Please) write me again if I can be of further service."

Caution: Do not use a comma or a period after a question mark.

WRONG   "Are you ready?," he asked.
RIGHT   "Are you ready?" he asked.

The Exclamation Point (!)

17c

Use the exclamation point after an emphatic interjection and after a phrase, clause, or sentence to express a high degree of surprise, incredulity, or other strong emotion.

EXAMPLES
What! I cannot believe it! How beautiful! [*What* and *how* often begin exclamations.]
Oh! You have finally come! (*Or:* Oh, you have finally come!)
March! Halt! Get out of this house! [Sharp commands—vigorous imperatives]

Forbid it, Almighty God! I know not what course others may take, but as for me, give me liberty, or give me death!
—PATRICK HENRY

Caution 1: Avoid overuse of the exclamation point. Use a comma after mild interjections, and end mildly exclamatory sentences with a period.

Well, you are to be congratulated.
Alas, I cannot go.

Caution 2: Do not use a comma or a period after the exclamation point.

WRONG   "Halt!," cried the corporal.
RIGHT   "Halt!" cried the corporal.

▶ EXERCISE 1   Illustrate the chief uses of the period, the question mark, and the exclamation point by composing and correctly punctuating brief sentences as directed below.

EXAMPLE   *a declarative sentence containing a quoted direct question*
          "Is Fred a ventriloquist?" she asked.

1. a declarative sentence containing a quoted exclamation
2. a direct question
3. an indirect question
4. a double direct question
5. a declarative sentence containing an interpolated question
6. a vigorous imperative
7. a mild imperative
8. a direct question having the form of a declaration
9. an ellipsis at the beginning of a quoted sentence
10. an ellipsis at the end of a quoted sentence

▶ EXERCISE 2   Correctly punctuate the following sentences by supplying needed periods, question marks, and exclamation points. Be prepared to give a reason for each mark you add. (*In this exercise* place all end marks that appear together with quotation marks *inside* the quotation marks; see **16c**.)

1. Frank asked me why I did not take Ellen to the dance
2. Frank asked, "Why didn't you take Ellen to the dance"
3. Did Frank ask you why I did not take Ellen to the dance
4. "What will you sell that wreck for" Mr Lacy asked

5. Stumbling toward the telephone, I wondered who could be calling me after 11:30 PM
6. The joker on the other end of the line chirped softly, "Honey, how many hours each week do you watch TV"
7. After a short silence the voice asked me what channel I was watching then
8. What a surprise that was
9. On April 15th I arrived in Washington, DC
10. Members of the YMCA smiled when the speaker was introduced; his name was Dr A J Byrd

The Colon (**:**)

17d

Use the colon after a formal introductory statement to direct attention to what is to follow. Avoid needless colons.

The colon and the semicolon, notwithstanding the similarity of the names, differ greatly in use. The semicolon (see Section 14) is a strong *separator* almost equal to a period, and is used only between equal parts. The colon after a statement or a main clause is a formal *introducer*, calling attention to something that is to follow. The colon usually means *as follows*.

(1) The colon may direct attention to an appositive (or a series of appositives) at the end of a sentence, to a formal list or explanation, or to a long quotation.

EXAMPLES

All her thoughts were centered on one objective: marriage. [A dash or a comma, which might be used instead of the colon, would be less formal.]

We may divide poems into three classes: narrative, lyric, and dramatic. [A dash might be used instead of the colon; because of the series a comma would be confusing.]

At any rate, this much can be said: The Council is not the vital organ it is supposed to be.   —THE ATLANTIC MONTHLY

Competition in the steel industry is described by one of the Corporation's competitors as follows: "Your ability to win when competition for business gets tough comes in the entire setup of your operation, the quality of your management, . . and so on. You have to play a judgment game. This is no 2-cent poker."   —FORTUNE

(2) **The colon may separate two main clauses when the second clause explains or amplifies the first.**

EXAMPLES

The scientific value of even the most recent contributions to this literature, however, is seriously qualified: The sole witness to the dream is the dreamer himself.   —SCIENTIFIC AMERICAN

By that time epidemic was becoming pandemic: the virus raced through the tropics in June and by August had blanketed the southern hemisphere.   —HOLIDAY

Note: After the colon a quoted sentence regularly begins with a capital, but other sentences (as the examples above show) may begin with either a capital or a small letter.

(3) **The colon may direct attention to a business letter following the salutation, to the verse following the Biblical chapter, or to the minute following the hour.**

EXAMPLES   Dear Sir:
            Matthew 6:10; 9:30 A.M.

(4) **Avoid needless colons.**

When there is no formal introduction or summarizing word, the colon is usually a needless interruption of the sentence.

NEEDLESS   All her thoughts were centered on: marriage.
BETTER   All her thoughts were centered on marriage.

NEEDLESS	Three kinds of poems are: narratives, lyrics, and dramas. [Awkward separation of verb and its complement]
BETTER	Three kinds of poems are narratives, lyrics, and dramas.

▶ EXERCISE 3   Punctuate the following sentences by adding appropriate colons or semicolons. When deciding whether a colon or a semicolon should separate two main clauses, use the colon only when the second main clause explains or amplifies the first. Write *C* after any sentence that needs no change.

1. Within two hours we had a strange variety of weather rain, hail, sleet, snow.
2. Promptly at 815 P.M. the minister began his sermon by quoting John 2021.
3. Two questions well worth asking yourself every day are these What must I do? Have I done it?
4. The conference had only one purpose agreement upon a suitable topic for a research paper.
5. Professor Boaz smiled a quick greeting I sat down and tried to look like an intelligent sophomore.
6. My roommate has a simple formula for looking like a sophomore Act depressed.
7. At first I merely looked gloomy later, however. I had good reason to feel depressed.
8. Professor Boaz started suggesting fantastic subjects "Causes of the Korean War," "An Analysis of the 1961 Recession," "Early Poetry of W. B. Yeats."
9. I then dared to mention that the only interests I have are cars, sports, and girls.
10. At the end of the conference I acted like the freshman that I am ironically enough, it was the professor who looked as depressed as an intelligent sophomore.
11. I offered to contribute everything I had brought with me two apples, an orange, and a banana.

The Dash (—)

17e

Use the dash[1] to mark a sudden break in thought, to set off a summary, or to set off a parenthetical element that is very abrupt or that has commas within it.

PUNCTUATION OF PARENTHETICAL MATTER

Dashes, parentheses, commas—all are used to set off parenthetical matter. Dashes set off parenthetical elements sharply and therefore tend to emphasize them:

> Rifle cartridges and shotgun shells — measured by today's prices — were cheap in 1905.   —DAVID L. COHN

Parentheses tend to minimize the importance of the parts thus set off:

> Rifle cartridges and shotgun shells (measured by today's prices) were cheap in 1905.

Commas are the mildest, most commonly used separators and tend to leave the parts more closely connected with the sentence. Dashes and parentheses should be used sparingly, only when commas will not serve equally well. (For the use of the comma to set off parenthetical matter, see **12d**; for the use of parentheses, see **17f**.)

(1)   Use the dash to mark a sudden break in thought.

EXAMPLES
> "It is hard to explain — " he said, and paused as they composed themselves.   —LIONEL TRILLING

> Can I — I mean, where do you get a saw like that?
>   —GERALD WARNER BRACE

> In fact, she was always right — in a way.   —J. F. POWERS

[1] On the typewriter the dash is made by two hyphens without spacing before or after.

(2) Use the dash to set off a brief summary or appositive.

EXAMPLES

The German borrowings are also homely and everyday—
weiners, pretzels, hunk, and dunk.   —BERGEN EVANS

The long neck, the small head, the knickers whose cuffs were
worn down near his ankles—all these points, often observed
by caricaturists, were visible in the flesh.   —JOHN UPDIKE

(3) Use dashes to set off a parenthetical element that is
very abrupt or that has commas within it.

EXAMPLES

A telltale suggestion of relief—or was it gratitude?—bright-
ened their eyes.   —JOHN MASON BROWN

He stood up—small, frail, and tense—staring toward things in
his homeland.   —NORA WALN

I was mediocre at drill, certainly—that is, until my senior year.
     —JAMES THURBER

Caution: The dash should be used carefully in formal
writing. It is more in keeping with an informal style, but
even there it becomes ineffective when overused.

Parentheses ( )

17f

**Use parentheses (1) to enclose figures, as in this rule, and
(2) to set off parenthetical, supplementary, or illustrative
matter.**

EXAMPLES

Dashes are used (1) to mark breaks, (2) to set off summaries,
and (3) to set off parenthetical elements. [Parentheses enclose
figures used to enumerate items.]

Mr. Brown's horses (the best, no doubt, in the whole state)
were exhibited at the fair. [Dashes would be used if the
writer wished to emphasize the parenthetical matter.]

It is strange (as one reviews all the memories of that good friend and master) to think that there is now a new generation beginning at Haverford that will never know his spell.

—CHRISTOPHER MORLEY

When the sentence demands other marks of punctuation with the parenthetical matter, these marks are placed after the second parenthesis. The comma is never used before the first parenthesis. If a whole sentence beginning with a capital is in parentheses, the period or other terminal mark is placed inside the second parenthesis. A parenthetical statement not beginning with a capital is not followed by a period within the parentheses.

Brackets [ ]

17g

Use brackets to set off editorial corrections or interpolations in quoted matter.

EXAMPLES

At the office he found a note from the janitor: "Last night i [sic] found the door unlocked." [A bracketed sic (meaning thus) tells the reader that the error appears in the original— is not merely a misprint.]

Every man who loved our vanished friend [Professor Gummere] must know with what realization of shamed incapacity one lays down the tributary pen. —CHRISTOPHER MORLEY

▶ EXERCISE 4   Correctly punctuate each of the following sentences by supplying commas, dashes, parentheses, or brackets. Be prepared to justify all marks you add, especially those you choose to set off parenthetical matter.

1. Gordon Gibbs or is it his twin brother? plays left tackle.
2. Joseph who is Gordon's brother is a guard on the second string.

3. "Dearest" his voice broke; he could say no more.
4. This organization needs more of everything more money, brains, initiative.
5. Some of my courses for example, French and biology demand a great deal of work outside the classroom.
6. A penalty clipping cost the Steers fifteen yards.
7. This ridiculous sentence appeared in the school paper: "Because of a personal fool *sic* the Cougars failed to cross the goal line during the last seconds of the game."
8. The word *Zipper* a trade-mark like Kodak is now used frequently without the initial capital as a common name.
9. Rugged hills, rich valleys, beautiful lakes these things impress the tourist in Connecticut.
10. Our course embraced these projects: 1 the close reading of *Hamlet,* 2 the writing of critiques on various aspects of this tragedy, and 3 the formation of a tentative theory of tragedy.

► EXERCISE 5 Punctuate the following sentences (selected and adapted from the *Atlantic Monthly*) by supplying appropriate end marks, commas, colons, dashes, and parentheses. Do not use unnecessary punctuation. Be prepared to justify each mark you add, especially when you have a choice of correct marks (e.g., commas, dashes, or parentheses).

1. At another college the student is asked What is this thing called love What do college girls want in a man
2. "Do they still have good food at the Automat" he asked
3. "Oh I know" Granny exclaimed "Let me think about it"
4. "I know" I said "But that's not the real bed what happened to it"
5. For forty-eight years 1888–1936 he taught at Harvard
6. I tell you again What is alive and young and throbbing with historic current in America is musical theatre

7. Louise had then she has it still something near to genius for making improbable persons, places, and situations sound attractive

8. *Good and* can mean *very* "I am good and mad" and "a hot cup of coffee" means that the coffee not the cup is to be hot

9. At last she had become what she had always wished to be a professional dancer

10. All of a sudden I was leaning my racket against the net I had lost the second set too and was drying my shaking hand on the white towel as the crowd stirred slightly

11. At last Marvin stood up, uneasily. "You you think we'd better take him to the vet"

12. There are three essential qualities for vulture country a rich supply of unburied corpses, high mountains, a strong sun

13. They failed forgivably! to see the less happy results of their enthusiasm

14. A significant little adage which circulates in Michigan athletic circles says in effect that there are three aspects of college life at Michigan intellectual, social, and athletic but that the student has time for only two

15. Women sit in their corner discussing items out of their exclusively feminine world children, servants, gardens, gossip

16. An older law was operating at the box office if you try to please everybody, you don't please anybody

17. As one man put it "Rose Bowl, Sugar Bowl, Orange Bowl all are gravy bowls"

18. Industrialization of Red China with German machines and German technology what a prize

19. We are told and we believe women more than men that to win love but more imperatively to retain love we must be beautiful

20. There is a democratic process the box office that determines the success and eminence of an artist

SPELLING

Spelling

18

Spell every word according to established usage as shown by a good dictionary.[1]

When one of your misspelled words is pointed out, do not guess at the correct spelling or ask a friend. Consult the dictionary for the correct spelling and write it down in your INDIVIDUAL SPELLING LIST. By keeping a list of all the words you misspell throughout your first college year, and by analyzing and mastering these words as they are called to your attention, you can make steady improvement in your spelling. You may wish to keep your spelling list alphabetically in a small notebook with a separate page for each letter, and to include all words looked up because of uncertainty concerning spelling.

The college student cannot count upon much class time devoted to spelling. Correct spelling is his individual responsibility. By following the program outlined in this section, he can improve his spelling tremendously. *Ignorance of the correct spelling of ordinary words is now, and*

[1] Careful study of Section 18 will help to eliminate one of the two most common errors in the average student paper.

will probably continue to be, the one universally accepted sign of the uneducated man.

In order to fix the correct spelling of the word in your memory, use the following:

THE EYE Look carefully at the word (1) as it appears in the dictionary and (2) as you write it *correctly* in your spelling list. Photograph the word with your eye so that you may visualize it later.

THE EAR Pronounce the word aloud several times, clearly and distinctly, in accordance with the phonetic spelling in the dictionary. Note any difference between the pronunciation and the spelling. Careful pronunciation and an awareness of the difference, if any, between spelling and pronunciation help in the spelling of many words.

THE HAND After you are sure of the correct picture and the correct pronunciation, write the word several times—at least once by syllables carefully pronounced. See the correct picture of the word and listen to your pronunciation of it as you write it down. Writing out the word is definitely helpful to many persons as the final step in fixing the correct spelling in the memory.

18a

Do not allow mispronunciation to cause misspelling.

▶ EXERCISE 1 In the four lists below determine which words you tend to mispronounce—and to misspell.

(1) Careless omission

Pronounce this first list distinctly, making it a point *not to omit* the sound represented by the italicized letters.

accident*a*lly	gove*r*nment	recognize
a*r*ctic	lib*r*ary	represen*ta*tive
can*d*idate	liter*a*ture	su*r*prise
environ*m*ent	occasion*a*lly	us*u*ally
every*b*ody	prob*a*bly	vet*e*ran
gen*e*rally	quan*t*ity	visu*a*lize

(2) Careless addition

Pronounce this second list distinctly, making it a point *not to add* any syllable or letter.

athlete	entrance	lightning
disastrous	grievous	mischievous
drowned	height	remembrance
elm	hindrance	umbrella

(3) Careless change

Pronounce this third list distinctly, making it a point *not to change* letters, particularly letters in italics.

accum*u*late	intro*d*uce	parti*c*ular
accurate	opt*i*mistic	then (*not* than)

(4) Careless transpositions of letters

Pronounce this fourth list distinctly, making it a point *not to transpose* italicized letters.

cava*lr*y	irre*lev*ant	p*r*efer
child*r*en	pe*rh*aps	prescription
hund*r*ed	pe*rs*piration	preserve

Add to your INDIVIDUAL SPELLING LIST any of the words in the four lists that you have a tendency to misspell.

18b

Distinguish between words of similar sound and spelling, and use the spelling demanded by the meaning.

▶ EXERCISE 2 Study the following list, perhaps ten word groups at a time, to improve your ability to select the word needed to express your meaning. With the aid of your dictionary compose a sentence to illustrate the correct use of each word. Add to your INDIVIDUAL SPELLING LIST any word that you tend to misspell.

accent, ascent, assent
accept, except
advice, advise
affect, effect
all ready, already
all together, altogether
allusive, elusive, illusive
altar, alter
berth, birth
born, borne

capital, capitol
choose, chose
cite, sight, site
coarse, course
complement, compliment
conscience, conscious
council, counsel, consul
decent, descent, dissent
desert, dessert
device, devise

dual, duel
dyeing, dying
fair, fare
formally, formerly
forth, fourth
freshman, freshmen
hear, here
holy, wholly
instance, instants
irrelevant, irreverent

its, it's
know, no
later, latter
lead, led
lessen, lesson
lose, loose
moral, morale
of, off
passed, past
peace, piece

personal, personnel
plain, plane
precede, proceed
presence, presents
principal, principle
prophecy, prophesy
quiet, quite
respectfully, respectively
right, rite, wright, write
sense, since

shone, shown
stationary, stationery
statue, stature, statute
there, their, they're
threw, through
to, too, two
weak, week
weather, whether
whose, who's
your, you're

18c

Distinguish between the prefix and the root.

The root is the base to which prefix or suffix is added. Take care not to double the last letter of the prefix (as in *disappear*) when it is different from the first letter of the root or to drop the last letter of the prefix when the root begins with the same letter (as in *immortal* and *un-necessary*).

dis- (prefix)	+ appear (root)	= disappear
grand-	+ daughter	= granddaughter
im-	+ mortal	= immortal
un-	+ necessary	= unnecessary

18d

Apply the rules for spelling in adding suffixes.

[For more detailed rules consult the section entitled "Orthography" in *Webster's New International Dictionary*, Second Edition, or *Webster's New Collegiate Dictionary;* or "Spelling" in *Webster's Third New International Dictionary.*]

(1) **Drop the final e before a suffix beginning with a vowel but not before a suffix beginning with a consonant.**

Drop the final *e* before a suffix beginning with a vowel.

bride	+ -al	= bridal
combine	+ -ation	= combination
come	+ -ing	= coming
fame	+ -ous	= famous
plume	+ -age	= plumage
precede	+ -ence	= precedence
prime	+ -ary	= primary

Retain the final *e* before a suffix beginning with a consonant.

care	+ -ful	= careful
care	+ -less	= careless
entire	+ -ly	= entirely
place	+ -ment	= placement
rude	+ -ness	= rudeness
stale	+ -mate	= stalemate
state	+ -craft	= statecraft
sure	+ -ty	= surety

Some Exceptions: *due, duly; awe, awful; hoe, hoeing; singe, singeing.* After *c* or *g* the final *e* is retained before suffixes beginning with *a* or *o: notice, noticeable; courage, courageous.*

▶ EXERCISE 3   Explain in each case why the final *e* should be dropped or retained.

1. confine	+ -ing		6. love	+ -ly
2. confine	+ -ment		7. peruse	+ -al
3. arrange	+ -ing		8. like	+ -ness
4. arrange	+ -ment		9. like	+ -ing
5. love	+ -ing		10. like	+ -ly

(2) **Double a final single consonant before a suffix beginning with a vowel (a) if the consonant ends a word of one syllable or an accented syllable and (b) if the consonant is preceded by a single vowel. Otherwise, do not double the consonant.**

drop, dropping [In a word of one syllable preceded by a single vowel. But preceded by a double vowel: *droop, drooping.*]

admit, admitted [In accented syllable, preceded by a single vowel. But in unaccented syllable: *benefit, benefited.*]

▶ EXERCISE 4   Note the importance of the last rule in forming the present participle and the past tense of verbs. Example: *regret, regretting, regretted.* Supply the present participle for each of the following verbs, justifying the spelling by the rule: *appear, compel, differ, happen, occur, plan, profit, remit, scoop, ship.*

(3) **Except before a suffix beginning with *i*, final *y* is usually changed to *i*.**

defy	+ -ance	= defiance	
happy	+ -ness	= happiness	
mercy	+ -ful	= merciful	
modify	+ -er	= modifier	
modify	+ -ing	= modifying	[Not changed before *i*]

Note: Verbs ending in *y* preceded by a vowel do not change the *y* to form the third person singular of the present tense or the past participle: *array, arrays, arrayed.* Exceptions: *lay, laid; pay, paid; say, said.*

▶ EXERCISE 5   Explain why the final *y* has, or has not, been retained before the suffixes of the following words: *alloys, craftiness, employed, employs, fanciful, fancying, studied, studying, volleys, volleying.*

(4)   Form the plural by adding *s* to the singular, but by adding *es* if the plural makes an extra syllable.

> boy, boys; cap, caps
> bush, bushes; match, matches [The plural makes an extra syllable.]

Exceptions:

a. If the noun ends in *y* preceded by a consonant, change the *y* to *i* and add *es: sky, skies; comedy, comedies.* But after a vowel the *y* is retained and only *s* is added: *joy, joys.*

b. If the noun ends in *fe*, change the *fe* to *ve* and add *s: knife, knives.*

c. If the noun ends in *o* preceded by a vowel, add *s: radio, radios.*

d. For plurals of compound words such as *father-in-law* usually add the *-s* to the chief word, not the modifier: *fathers-in-law, maids of honor.*

For other plurals formed irregularly, consult your dictionary.

Note: Add *'s* to form the plurals of letters, signs, and figures. See also **15d.**

▶ EXERCISE 6   Supply plural forms for words listed below. If words are not covered by the rules given under **18d,** consult your dictionary.

cup	army	foot	passer-by
wife	cameo	son-in-law	room
box	marsh	valley	leaf
child	ox	alumnus	goose
key	sheep	radius	mouse

18e

Apply the rules for spelling to avoid confusion of *ei* and *ie*.

When the sound is *ee*, write *ie* (except after *c*, in which case write *ei*).

		(after *c*)
chief	pierce	ceiling
field	relief	conceit
grief	wield	deceive
niece	yield	perceive

When the sound is other than *ee*, usually write *ei*.

eight	heir	sleigh
foreign	neighbor	weigh
height	reign	vein
deign	feign	stein

Exceptions: Fiery, financier, leisure, seize, species, weird.

▶ EXERCISE 7   Write out the following words, filling out the blanks with *ei* or *ie*. Justify your choice for each word.

| bes—ge | dec—t | fr—ght | r—gned | s—ve |
| conc—ve | f—nd | pr—st | s—ne | th—f |

Hyphenated Words

18f

Hyphenate words chiefly to express a unit idea or to avoid ambiguity. (For division of words at the end of a line, see 8b.)

A hyphenated word may be either two words still in the process of becoming one word or a new coinage made by the writer to fit the occasion. In the former case a recent dictionary will assist in determining current usage. Many words now written as one were originally separate words and later hyphenated in the transitional stage. For example, *post man* first became *post-man* and then *postman*. More recently *basket ball* has passed through the transitional *basket-ball* to *basketball*. The use of the hyphen in compounding is in such a state of flux that authorities often disagree. Some of the more generally accepted uses are listed below.

(1) **The hyphen may be used to join two or more words serving as a single adjective before a noun.**

[The dictionary ordinarily cannot help with this use of the hyphen. The writer joins recognized words to coin a new unit idea to fit the occasion.]

A know-it-all expression, a bluish-green dress

But the hyphen is omitted when the first word of the compound is an adverb ending in *-ly* or when the words follow the noun.

A slightly elevated walk, a gently sloping terrace
His expression suggested that he knew it all.
The dress was a bluish green.

(2) **The hyphen is used with compound numbers from twenty-one to ninety-nine.**

twenty-two, forty-five, ninety-eight

(3) **The hyphen is used to avoid ambiguity or an awkward union of letters or syllables between prefix or suffix and root.**

His re-creation of the setting was perfect. [*but* Fishing is good recreation.]
He re-covered the leaky roof. [*but* He recovered his health.]

Micro-organism, re-enter, semi-independent, shell-like, thrill-less, sub-subcommittee.

(4) **The hyphen is used with the prefixes ex-, self-, all-, and the suffix -elect.**

ex-governor, self-made, all-American, mayor-elect

EXERCISES ON SPELLING

The general list of words most frequently misspelled is made up of 654 (651 + *it's, too, two*) common words that everyone needs in his business and social life. The list is drawn, by kind permission of Dean Thomas Clark Pollock, from his study of 31,375 misspellings in the written work of college students.[2] In the list as given below the words *its, it's* and *to, too, two* are treated as word groups; all other words are listed individually, usually omitting any word that is spelled the same as a part of a longer word. For example, the list includes *definitely* but not *definite, existence* but not *exist, performance* but not *perform.* Each of the first hundred words in the general list below was misspelled more than forty-three times (or more than an *average* of forty-three times in the case of words grouped in Dean Pollock's report).

▶ EXERCISE 8   With the aid of your dictionary study the words in the general list in small units (perhaps fifty words at a time) until you feel sure (1) of the meaning and (2) of the spelling of each word. Then without the aid of your dictionary test yourself by writing sentences in which each word is correctly used and spelled. Add to your IN-DIVIDUAL SPELLING LIST each word that you tend to misspell.

[2] See Thomas Clark Pollock, "Spelling Report," *College English,* XVI (November, 1954), 102–09; and Thomas Clark Pollock and William D. Baker, *The University Spelling Book,* Prentice-Hall, Inc., New York, 1955, pp. 6–12.

GENERAL SPELLING LIST

1. *The Hundred Words Most Frequently Misspelled*[3]

1. accommodate
2. achievement
3. acquire
4. all right
5. among
6. apparent
7. argument
8. arguing
9. belief*
10. believe*
11. beneficial
12. benefited
13. category
14. coming
15. comparative
16. conscious
17. controversy
18. controversial
19. definitely
20. definition
21. define
22. describe
23. description
24. disastrous
25. effect
26. embarrass
27. environment
28. exaggerate
29. existence*
30. existent*
31. experience
32. explanation
33. fascinate
34. height

35. interest
36. its (it's)
37. led
38. lose
39. losing
40. marriage
41. mere
42. necessary
43. occasion*
44. occurred
45. occurring
46. occurrence
47. opinion
48. opportunity
49. paid
50. particular

51. performance
52. personal
53. personnel
54. possession
55. possible
56. practical
57. precede*
58. prejudice
59. prepare
60. prevalent
61. principal
62. principle
63. privilege*
64. probably
65. proceed
66. procedure
67. professor

68. profession
69. prominent
70. pursue
71. quiet
72. receive*
73. receiving*
74. recommend
75. referring*
76. repetition
77. rhythm
78. sense
79. separate*
80. separation*
81. shining
82. similar*
83. studying
84. succeed
85. succession
86. surprise
87. technique
88. than
89. then
90. their*
91. there*
92. they're*
93. thorough
94. to* (too,* two*)
95. transferred
96. unnecessary
97. villain
98. woman
99. write
100. writing

[3] An asterisk indicates the most frequently misspelled words among the first hundred. The most troublesome letters for all 654 words are indicated by italics.

II. The Next 551 Words Most Frequently Misspelled

101. absence
102. abundance
103. abundant
104. academic
105. academically
106. academy
107. acceptable
108. acceptance
109. accepting
110. accessible
111. accidental
112. accidentally
113. acclaim
114. accompanied
115. accompanies
116. accompaniment
117. accompanying
118. accomplish
119. accuracy
120. accurate
121. accurately
122. accuser
123. accuses
124. accusing
125. accustom
126. acquaintance
127. across
128. actuality
129. actually
130. adequately
131. admission
132. admittance
133. adolescence
134. adolescent
135. advantageous
136. advertisement
137. advertiser
138. advertising
139. advice

140. advise
141. affect
142. afraid
143. against
144. aggravate
145. aggressive
146. alleviate
147. allotted
148. allotment
149. allowed
150. allows

151. already
152. altar
153. all together
154. altogether
155. amateur
156. amount
157. analysis
158. analyze
159. and
160. another
161. annually
162. anticipated
163. apologetically
164. apologized
165. apology
166. apparatus
167. appearance
168. applies
169. applying
170. appreciate
171. appreciation
172. approaches
173. appropriate
174. approximate
175. area
176. arise
177. arising

178. arouse
179. arousing
180. arrangement
181. article
182. atheist
183. athlete
184. athletic
185. attack
186. attempts
187. attendance
188. attendant
189. attended
190. attitude
191. audience
192. authoritative
193. authority
194. available
195. bargain
196. basically
197. basis
198. beauteous
199. beautified
200. beautiful

201. beauty
202. become
203. becoming
204. before
205. began
206. beginner
207. beginning
208. behavior
209. bigger
210. biggest
211. boundary
212. breath
213. breathe
214. brilliance
215. brilliant

216. Britain
217. Britannica
218. burial
219. buried
220. bury
221. business
222. busy
223. calendar
224. capitalism
225. career
226. careful
227. careless
228. carried
229. carrier
230. carries
231. carrying
232. cemetery
233. certainly
234. challenge
235. changeable
236. changing
237. characteristic
238. characterized
239. chief
240. children
241. Christian
242. Christianity
243. choice
244. choose
245. chose
246. cigarette
247. cite
248. clothes
249. commercial
250. commission

251. committee
252. communist
253. companies
254. compatible

255. competition
256. competitive
257. competitor
258. completely
259. concede
260. conceivable
261. conceive
262. concentrate
263. concern
264. condemn
265. confuse
266. confusion
267. connotation
268. connote
269. conscience
270. conscientious
271. consequently
272. considerably
273. consistency
274. consistent
275. contemporary
276. continuous(ly)
277. controlled
278. controlling
279. convenience
280. convenient
281. correlate
282. council
283. counselor
284. countries
285. create
286. criticism
287. criticize
288. cruelly
289. cruelty
290. curiosity
291. curious
292. curriculum
293. dealt
294. deceive

295. decided
296. decision
297. dependent
298. desirability
299. desire
300. despair

301. destruction
302. detriment
303. devastating
304. device
305. difference
306. different
307. difficult
308. dilemma
309. diligence
310. dining
311. disappoint
312. disciple
313. discipline
314. discrimination
315. discussion
316. disease
317. disgusted
318. disillusioned
319. dissatisfied
320. divide
321. divine
322. doesn't
323. dominant
324. dropped
325. due
326. during
327. eager
328. easily
329. efficiency
330. efficient
331. eighth
332. eliminate
333. emperor

334. emphasize
335. encourage
336. endeavor
337. enjoy
338. enough
339. enterprise
340. entertain
341. entertainment
342. entirely
343. entrance
344. equipment
345. equipped
346. escapade
347. escape
348. especially
349. etc.
350. everything

351. evidently
352. excellence
353. excellent
354. except
355. excitable
356. exercise
357. expense
358. experiment
359. extremely
360. fallacy
361. familiar
362. families
363. fantasies
364. fantasy
365. fashions
366. favorite
367. fictitious
368. field
369. finally
370. financially
371. financier
372. foreigners

373. forty
374. forward
375. fourth
376. friendliness
377. fulfill
378. fundamentally
379. further
380. gaiety
381. generally
382. genius
383. government
384. governor
385. grammar
386. grammatically
387. group
388. guaranteed
389. guidance
390. guiding
391. handled
392. happened
393. happiness
394. hear
395. here
396. heroes
397. heroic
398. heroine
399. hindrance
400. hopeless

401. hoping
402. hospitalization
403. huge
404. humorist
405. humorous
406. hundred
407. hunger
408. hungrily
409. hungry
410. hypocrisy
411. hypocrite

412. ideally
413. ignorance
414. ignorant
415. imaginary
416. imagination
417. imagine
418. immediately
419. immense
420. importance
421. incidentally
422. increase
423. indefinite
424. independence
425. independent
426. indispensable
427. individually
428. industries
429. inevitable
430. influence
431. influential
432. ingenious
433. ingredient
434. initiative
435. intellect
436. intelligence
437. intelligent
438. interference
439. interpretation
440. interrupt
441. involve
442. irrelevant
443. irresistible
444. irritable
445. jealousy
446. knowledge
447. laboratory
448. laborer
449. laboriously
450. laid

451. later
452. leisurely
453. lengthening
454. license
455. likelihood
456. likely
457. likeness
458. listener
459. literary
460. literature
461. liveliest
462. livelihood
463. liveliness
464. lives
465. loneliness
466. lonely
467. loose
468. loss
469. luxury
470. magazine
471. magnificence
472. magnificent
473. maintenance
474. management
475. maneuver
476. manner
477. manufacturers
478. material
479. mathematics
480. matter
481. maybe
482. meant
483. mechanics
484. medical
485. medicine
486. medieval
487. melancholy
488. methods
489. miniature
490. minutes

491. mischief
492. moral
493. morale
494. morally
495. mysterious
496. narrative
497. naturally
498. Negroes
499. ninety
500. noble

501. noticeable
502. noticing
503. numerous
504. obstacle
505. off
506. omit
507. operate
508. oppose
509. opponent
510. opposite
511. optimism
512. organization
513. original
514. pamphlets
515. parallel
516. parliament
517. paralyzed
518. passed
519. past
520. peace
521. peculiar
522. perceive
523. permanent
524. permit
525. persistent
526. persuade
527. pertain
528. phase
529. phenomenon

530. philosophy
531. physical
532. piece
533. planned
534. plausible
535. playwright
536. pleasant
537. politician
538. political
539. practice
540. predominant
541. preferred
542. presence
543. prestige
544. primitive
545. prisoners
546. propaganda
547. propagate
548. prophecy
549. psychoanalysis
550. psychology

551. psychopathic
552. psychosomatic
553. quantity
554. really
555. realize
556. rebel
557. recognize
558. regard
559. relative
560. relieve
561. religion
562. remember
563. reminisce
564. represent
565. resources
566. response
567. revealed
568. ridicule

569. ridiculous
570. roommate
571. sacrifice
572. safety
573. satire
574. satisfied
575. satisfy
576. scene
577. schedule
578. seize
579. sentence
580. sergeant
581. several
582. shepherd
583. significance
584. simile
585. simple
586. simply
587. since
588. sincerely
589. sociology
590. sophomore
591. source
592. speaking
593. speech
594. sponsor
595. stabilization
596. stepped

597. stories
598. story
599. straight
600. strength

601. stretch
602. strict
603. stubborn
604. substantial
605. subtle
606. sufficient
607. summary
608. summed
609. suppose
610. suppress
611. surrounding
612. susceptible
613. suspense
614. swimming
615. symbol
616. synonymous
617. temperament
618. tendency
619. themselves
620. theories
621. theory
622. therefore
623. those

624. thought
625. together
626. tomorrow
627. tragedy
628. tremendous
629. tried
630. tries
631. tyranny
632. undoubtedly
633. unusually
634. useful
635. useless
636. using
637. vacuum
638. valuable
639. varies
640. various
641. view
642. vengeance
643. warrant
644. weather
645. weird
646. where
647. whether
648. whole
649. whose
650. yield
651. you're

▶ EXERCISE 9   Analyze your INDIVIDUAL SPELLING LIST to
learn why you misspell words and how you can most
readily improve your spelling.

Spelling is an individual matter. No two persons make
exactly the same errors in spelling. Therefore it is important that you compile and master your INDIVIDUAL SPELL-
ING LIST. Once you analyze this list to determine why
you misspell words, you can concentrate on the part of
Section 18 (a, b, c, d, e, or f) that treats your difficulty.

When each misspelled word is first called to your attention, consult your dictionary and copy down the correct spelling as directed at the opening of Section 18. Then write out the word by syllables, underline the trouble spot, and indicate why you misspelled the word, by using the letter **a** (omission, addition, change, or transposition), **b** (confusion of words similar in sound), **c** (failure to distinguish prefix from root), **d** (error in adding suffix), **e** (confusion of *ei* and *ie*), **f** (error in hyphenation), or **g** (any other reason for misspelling).

EXAMPLES

Word (correctly spelled)	Word (spelled by syllables)—with trouble spots underlined	Reason for error
1. candidate	can di date	a (letter omitted)
2. athlete	ath lete	a (letter added)
3. prejudice	prej u dice	a (letter changed)
4. marriage	mar riage	a (letters transposed)
5. among	a mong	b (confused with *young*)
6. its	its	b (confused with *it's*)
7. misspell	mis spell	c (prefix not distinguished)
8. bridal	brid al	d (drop final *e* before vowel)
9. careful	care ful	d (retain final *e* before consonant)
10. duly	du ly	d (exception to the rule)
11. occurred	oc curred	d (before a vowel double final single consonant after a single vowel in accented syllable)
12. merciful	mer ci ful	d (change final *y* to i except before *i*)
13. believe	be lieve	e (*ie* when the sound is *ee*)
14. receive	re ceive	e (*ei* when the sound is *ee* after *c*)
15. forty-five	for ty-five	f (hyphen with compound number)

DICTION

Good Use—Glossary

19

When in doubt about the meaning of a word, consult a good dictionary. Select the word most appropriate to the occasion. In standard writing employ only words in general and approved use.

Words are the coinage of thought, the medium by which men exchange ideas. To possess a large and varied vocabulary is to possess intellectual wealth. This wealth is not the private property of the few, but a common fund from which anyone may draw as much as he needs. The treasury of language is a good dictionary. And like wealth, the mere accumulation of a vocabulary is nothing; the care and good sense with which it is used is everything.

19a

Use only a good dictionary, and be sure to use it intelligently.

A good dictionary of the English language is based upon the scientific examination of the writing and speaking habits of the English-speaking world; it records the origin, development, and changing use of words. Any dictionary is reliable only to the extent that it is based on usage. There can be no perfect dictionary, as Dr. Johnson recognized long ago. Among the full or unabridged dictionaries, the following are especially useful:

Webster's New International Dictionary. Second Edition, Springfield, Massachusetts: G. & C. Merriam Company (1934).

Webster's Third New International Dictionary. Springfield, Massachusetts: G. & C. Merriam Company (1961).

New Standard Dictionary. New York: Funk & Wagnalls Company (1947, 1952).

Century Dictionary and Cyclopedia. 12 vols. New York: The Century Company [c1911].

New Century Dictionary. 2 vols. New York: D. Appleton-Century Company (1948, 1959).

A *New English Dictionary on Historical Principles.* 10 vols. and Supplement. Oxford: Clarendon Press, 1888–1933. (A corrected reissue in twelve volumes and one supplementary volume appeared in 1933 under the title *The Oxford English Dictionary.*)—Abbreviated *NED* or *OED.*

Most students must consult these large dictionaries in the library. But even if a student possesses a large dictionary, he will still find indispensable, for more convenient use, one of the smaller dictionaries on the college or adult level, such as the following:

American College Dictionary (1947, 1962).—*ACD*
New College Standard Dictionary (1947).
Webster's New Collegiate Dictionary (1949, 1960).—*NCD*
Webster's New World Dictionary (1953, 1962).—*NWD*

Note: Dictionaries are usually kept up to date by frequent slight revisions, sometimes with supplementary pages for new words. The last thorough revision of the dictionaries listed above is shown by the earlier dates in parentheses.

Intelligent use of a dictionary requires some knowledge

of its plan and special abbreviations as given in the introductory matter. Let us take, for example:

(1) Spelling, Pronunciation   (2) Parts of Speech, Inflected Forms

(3) Meanings

(4) Origin

Synonyms

ex·pel (ĭk spĕl′), *v.t.*, **-pelled, -pelling. 1.** to drive or force out or away; discharge or eject: *to expel air from the lungs, an invader from a country.* **2.** to cut off from membership or relations: *to expel a student from a college.* [ME *expelle(n)*, t. L: m. *expellere* drive out] **—ex·pel′·la·ble,** *adj.* **—ex·pel′ler,** *n.* **—Syn. 2.** oust, dismiss.

Reproduced from *The American College Dictionary.* Copyright 1947, © 1961 by Random House, Inc. Used by permission.

ex·pel′ (ĕks·pĕl′; ĭks-), *v. t.;* EX·PELLED′ (-pĕld′); EX·PEL′LING. [L. *expellere, expulsum,* fr. *ex* out + *pellere* to drive.] **1.** To drive or force out; to eject. **2.** To cut off from membership in or the privileges of an institution or society; as, to *expel* a student from college. **— Syn.** See EJECT. **— ex·pel′la·ble,** *adj.*

By permission. From Webster's New Collegiate Dictionary. Copyright, 1961 by G. & C. Merriam Co., Publishers of the Merriam-Webster Dictionaries.

ex·pel (ik-spel′), *v.t.* [EXPELLED (-speld′), EXPELLING], [ME. *expellen;* L. *expellere; ex-,* out + *pellere,* to thrust, drive], **1.** to drive out by force; make leave; eject. **2.** to dismiss or send away by authority; deprive of rights, membership, etc.: as, he was *expelled* from school because of misconduct. **—*SYN.* see eject.**

From *Webster's New World Dictionary of the American Language,* College Edition, © 1962 by the World Publishing Company.

(1)   **Spelling and pronunciation.** The spelling of *expel* (by syllables separated by a dot) is given first, with pronunciation indicated (within parentheses) immediately following. The sound of each letter is shown by the key to pronunciation at the bottom of the page or on one of the inside covers. The *NCD* gives two acceptable pronunciations for the first syllable; the *ACD* and the *NWD* give only one. The accent on *expel,* as shown by the mark (′), falls on the last syllable.

(2) Part of speech and inflected forms come next: *v. t.* classifies *expel* as a "verb, transitive"; the words in boldface (*ACD*) or in small capitals (*NCD* and *NWD*) give the inflected forms for the past participle and the present participle; other parts of speech formed from the base word are given in the last one or two lines of the entry.

(3) Meanings (including synonyms and antonyms). Two separate meanings of *expel* are shown after the numbers *1* and *2*. In the *NCD* and in the *NWD* such definitions are arranged in the historical order of development, thus enabling the reader to see at a glance something of the history of the word. *But he should note that the meaning which developed first, and is consequently placed first, may no longer be the most common.* For example, the *NCD* and the *NWD*, in defining *prevent*, begin with the original but obsolete meaning "to anticipate" and come later to the present meaning "to hinder." The *ACD*, which puts the most common meaning first, begins with "to hinder" and comes later to the obsolete meaning. With *expel*, as with many words, the meaning that first developed is still the most common.

The meaning is made clearer by comparing the word to other words of similar meaning (synonyms, abbreviated **Syn.**) or opposite meaning (antonyms, abbreviated **Ant.**). The *ACD* lists for *expel* the two synonyms *oust* and *dismiss;* the *NCD* and the *NWD* refer to another word, *eject*, under which a helpful special paragraph compares *expel* to *eject* and other synonyms.

For more detailed information about *expel* the student may consult one of the unabridged dictionaries in the library. In *Webster's New International Dictionary*, Second Edition, the entry for this word is more than twice as long as that in the *ACD, NCD,* or *NWD*, and includes a quotation from Spenser. In *Webster's Third New International Dictionary* the entry is nearly four times as long and gives nine quotations to illustrate the various uses of the word. *The Oxford English Dictionary*, the most detailed of all dictionaries of the English language, quotes some fifty English writers of the past five or six hundred years to show the exact meaning of *expel* at each stage of its history. The following passage (about one third of the complete entry) illustrates the method used by the *OED*.

Expel (ekspe·l), *v.* Forms: 4–5 expelle, 6–7 expell, 6– expel. [ad. L. *expell-ěre*, f. *ex-* out + *pellěre* to drive, thrust: cf. COMPEL. OF. had *espellir*, and in 15th c. *expeller*.]

1. *trans.* To drive or thrust out; to eject by force. Const. *from* (rarely *out of*) also with double obj. (by omission of *from*).

a. With obj. a person, etc.: To eject, dislodge by force from a position; to banish from, compel to quit, a place or country.

c 1489 CAXTON *Sonnes of Aymon* xx. 446 Reynawde and his brethern were thus expelled out of it [mountalban]. 1532 MORE *Confut. Tindale* Wks. 819/2 God .. expelled those heretikes and scismatikes out of heauen. 1577 tr. *Bullinger's Decades* (1592) 838 The Apostles receiued power from the Lord..that they should expell and cast them [the devils] out. 1628 HOBBES *Thucyd.* (1822) 8 The Bœotians ..expelld Arne by the Thessalians seated themselues in that Country [Bœotia]. *c* 1710 C. FIENNES *Diary* (1888) 266 Such a State takes Care..to Expel him their Dominions by proclamation. 1749 WEST tr. *Pindar's Olympic Odes* xii. 36 Sedition's Civil Broils Expell'd thee from thy native Crete. 1754 HUME *Hist. Eng.* I. xi. 229 He sent .. two knights..to expel them the convent. 1863 FR. A. KEMBLE *Resid. Georgia* 31 Bidding the elder boys..expel the poultry.

b. With a material thing as obj.: To drive out from a receptacle, etc. by mechanical force; to discharge, send off (*e.g.* a bullet from a gun, † an arrow from a bow); to drive off or dislodge (a substance) from a chemical compound, mixture, solution, etc. Also, † *To expel forth*.

1669 STURMY *Mariner's Mag.* v. xii. 80 The Shot is .. expelled with no other thing, than by the Air's exaltation. 1695 WOODWARD *Nat. Hist. Earth* III. (1723) 151 It [water] is usualy expelled forth in vast Quantities. *a* 1700 DRYDEN (J.), The virgin huntress was not slow T'expel the shaft from her contracted bow. *c* 1790 IMISON *Sch. Art* I. 74 Expelling the water into the bason. 1807 T. THOMSON *Chem.* (ed. 3) II. 394 Alcohol..absorbs about its own weight of nitrous gas, which cannot afterwards be expelled by heat. 1838 — *Chem. Org. Bodies* 168 Not capable of being expelled by a stronger base. 1860 MAURY *Phys. Geog. Sea* xi. § 512 If still more heat be applied .. the air will be entirely expelled. 1878 HUXLEY *Physiogr.* 77 The matter .. thus expelled from the powder by heat.

From the *Oxford English Dictionary* by permission of The Clarendon Press, Oxford. Copyright 1933.

(4) **Origin; development of the language.** The origin of the word—also called *derivation* or *etymology*—is shown in square brackets, as in the *ACD*: [ME *expelle*(*n*), t. L: m. *expellere* drive out]. This bracketed information means that *expel* was used in English during the Middle English (ME.) period, A.D. 1100–1500, with the spelling *expelle*(*n*); that it was taken from (t.) Latin (L.) and is a modification of (m.) the Latin word *expellere*, meaning "to drive out." The *NCD* does not give the Middle English form of *expel*, but it does break down the Latin word into the prefix *ex* "out" + the root or combining form *pellere* "to drive." Breaking up a word, when possible, into prefix, combining form, and suffix will often help, as in the case of *expel*, to get at the basic meaning of the word.

EXAMPLES

	Prefix	Combining Form	Suffix
circumvention	*circum-*, around	+ *venire*, to come	+ *-ion*, act of
dependent	*de-*, down	+ *pendere*, to hang	+ *-ent*, one who
intercede	*inter-*, between	+ *cedere*, to pass	
preference	*pre-*, before	+ *ferre*, to carry	+ *-ence*, state of
transmit	*trans-*, across	+ *mittere*, to send	

The bracketed information given by a good dictionary is especially rich in meaning when associated with the historical development of our language. English is one of the Indo-European (IE.)[1] languages, which apparently had at one time, thousands of years ago, a common vocabulary. In the recorded Indo-European languages, many of the more familiar words are remarkably alike. Our word *mother*, for example, is *mater* in Latin (L.), *mater* in

---

[1] The parenthetical abbreviations for languages here and on the next few pages are those commonly used in the bracketed derivations in dictionaries.

Greek (Gk.), and *matar* in the ancient Persian and in the Sanskrit of India. Our pronoun *me* is exactly the same in Latin, in Greek, in Persian, and in Sanskrit. Words in different languages which apparently go back to a common parent language are called *cognates*. The large numbers of these cognates make it seem probable that at one time, perhaps three thousand years before Christ, the Indo-Europeans lived in one region and spoke a common language. By the opening of the Christian era they had spread themselves over most of Europe and as far east as India. Of the eight or nine language groups into which they had developed (see the inside back cover of the *NWD* or the entry "Indo-European languages" in the *NCD*), English is chiefly concerned with the Greek (Hellenic) on the eastern Mediterranean, with the Latin (Italic) on the central and western Mediterranean, and with the Germanic in northwestern Europe, from which English is descended.

Two thousand years ago the Greek, the Latin, and the Germanic each comprised a more or less unified language group. After the fall of the Roman Empire in the fifth century, the several Latin-speaking divisions developed independently into the modern Romance languages, chief of which are Italian, French, and Spanish. Long before the fall of Rome the Germanic group was breaking up into three groups: (1) East Germanic, represented by the Goths, who were to play a large part in the last century of the Roman Empire before losing themselves in its ruins; (2) North Germanic, or Old Norse (ON.), from which we have modern Danish (Dan.) and Swedish (Swed.), Norwegian (Norw.) and Icelandic (Icel.); and (3) West Germanic, the direct ancestor of English, Dutch (D.), and German (G.).

The English language may be said to have begun about the middle of the fifth century, when the West Germanic Angles and Saxons began the conquest of what is now England and either absorbed or drove out the Celtic-speaking inhabitants. The next six or seven hundred years are known as the Old English (OE.) or Anglo-Saxon (AS.) period of the English language. The fifty or sixty thousand words then in the language were chiefly Anglo-Saxon, with a small mixture of Old Norse words as a result of the Danish (Viking) conquests of England beginning in the eighth century. But the Old Norse words were so much like the Anglo-Saxon that they cannot always be distinguished.

The transitional period—about 1100 to 1500—from Old English to Modern English is known as Middle English (ME.). Changes already under way were accelerated by the Norman Conquest beginning in 1066. The Normans or "Northmen" had settled in northern France during the Viking invasions and had adopted the Old French (OF.) in place of their native Old Norse. The Normans, coming over to England by thousands, made French the language of the King's court in London and of the ruling classes (both French and English) throughout the land, while the masses continued to speak English. Only toward the end of the fifteenth century did English become once more the common language of all classes. But the language that emerged had lost most of its Anglo-Saxon inflections and had taken on thousands of French words (derived originally from Latin). It was, however, still basically English, not French, in its structure. The marked and steady development of the language (until it was partly stabilized by printing, which began in London in 1476) is suggested by the following passages, two from Old English and two from Middle English.

Hē ǣrst gescēop	eorðan bearnum
He first created	*for earth's children*
heofon tō hrōfe,	hālig scippend.
heaven as a roof,	*holy creator.*

[From the so-called "Hymn of Cædmon." Middle of the Old English Period.]

Ēalā, hū lēas and hū unwrest is þysses middan-eardes
Alas! how false and how unstable is this midworld's

wēla. Sē þe wæs ǣrur rīce cyng and maniges landes
weal! He that was before powerful king and of many lands

hlāford, hē næfde þā ealles landes būton seofon fōt mǣl.
lord, he had not then of all land but seven foot space.
[From the *Anglo-Saxon Chronicle*, A.D. 1087. End of the Old
English Period.]

A knight ther was, and that a worthy man,
That fro the tyme that he first bigan
To ryden out, he loved chivalrye,
Trouthe and honour, fredom and curteisye.
[From Chaucer's Prologue to the *Canterbury Tales*,
about 1385.]

Thenne within two yeres king Uther felle seke of a grete
maladye. And in the meane whyle hys enemyes usurpped upon
hym, and dyd a grete bataylle upon his men, and slewe many
of his peple.
[From Sir Thomas Malory's *Morte d'Arthur*, printed 1485.]

▶ EXERCISE 1   With the aid of your dictionary select the
five words in the passage from Malory's *Morte d'Arthur*
that were taken into English—after the Norman Conquest,
of course—from the Old French. Copy both the Old
French word and the Latin source (if given). (Note that
in this passage from Malory all words of one syllable are
from Anglo-Saxon. The preposition *upon* may be a combination of two Anglo-Saxon words, *up* and *on,* but more
probably it was taken from the Old Norse during the
Danish invasions of Britain in the ninth century.)

Although Sir Thomas Malory wrote nearly five hundred
years ago, we can still read his *Morte d'Arthur* with relative
ease. William Caxton, who printed Malory's book in 1485,
observed that "our language as now used varieth far from

that which was used and spoken when I was born." The books he was printing, with millions that have followed since, have helped greatly to stabilize the language.

A striking feature of Modern English (that is, English since 1500) is its immense vocabulary. As already noted, Old English used some fifty or sixty thousand words, very largely native Anglo-Saxon; Middle English used perhaps a hundred thousand, many taken through the French from Latin and others directly from Latin; and now our unabridged dictionaries list over four times as many. To make up this tremendous word hoard, we have borrowed most heavily from the Latin, but we have drawn some words from almost every known language. English writers of the sixteenth century were especially eager to interlard their works with words from Latin authors; and as Englishmen pushed out to colonize and to trade in many parts of the globe, they brought home new words as well as goods. Modern science and technology have drawn heavily from the Greek. The result of all this borrowing is that English has become the richest, most cosmopolitan of all languages.

In the process of enlarging our vocabulary we have lost most of our original Anglo-Saxon words. But those that are left make up the most familiar, most useful part of our vocabulary. Practically all of our simple verbs, our articles, conjunctions, prepositions, and pronouns are native Anglo-Saxon; and so are many of our familiar nouns, adjectives, and adverbs. Every speaker and writer uses these native words over and over, much more frequently than the borrowed words. If every word is counted every time it is used, the percentage of native words runs very high, usually between 70 and 90 per cent. Milton's percentage was 81, Tennyson's 88, Shakespeare's about 90, and that of the King James Bible about 94. English has been enriched by its extensive borrowings without losing its individuality; it is still fundamentally the *English* language.

► EXERCISE 2   Note the origins of the words on a typical page (or on several typical pages) of your dictionary. Copy down examples of words derived from (1) Anglo-Saxon; (2) Old French or Latin through Old French; (3) Latin directly; (4) Greek through Latin; (5) Greek directly; (6) other languages.

(5) Dictionary labels—levels of usage. An unabridged English dictionary attempts to define all the words that have been used by English writers during the Modern English period. The better abridged dictionaries for adults —such as *NCD*, *NWD*, and *ACD*—list between 100,000 and 150,000 words. Most dictionaries use labels (*Colloq.*, *Slang*, *Dial.*, *Substandard*, *Obs.*, *Archaic*, *Eccl.*, *Naut.*, etc.) to show the standing or special use of a word. Any word, or any meaning of a word, that does not have one of these labels is said to be "standard"; that is, it belongs to the general vocabulary and may be used whenever appropriate to the writer's meaning and style. Labeled words, or labeled meanings of words, should be used with appropriate care as suggested below in the "Outline for Dictionary Labels" and treated further under **19 b, c, d, e, f, g, and h.**

Note that none of the three entries illustrated on page 190 gives a label before either of the two meanings for *expel.* Thus we see that the word is fully standard. But let us note the *NCD* entry for *impose*, in which three of the meanings are labeled.

im·pose′ (ĭm·pōz′), *v. t.* [F. *imposer*, fr. *im-* in + *poser* to place.] **1.** To subject (one) *to* a charge, penalty, or the like.   **2.** To lay as a charge, duty, command, etc.; hence, to levy; inflict; as, to *impose* burdens or a penalty.   **3.** *Eccl.* To lay on (the hands), as in confirmation.   **4.** *Archaic.* To place; deposit.   **5.** To pass or palm off; as, to *impose* inferior goods on a buyer.   **6.** To obtrude; as, to *impose* oneself upon others.   **7.** *Print.* To arrange in order on a table of stone or metal (**imposing stone** *or* **table**) and lock up in a chase. — *v. i.* **1.** To impress oneself or itself, esp. obnoxiously; presume; as, to *impose* upon good nature.   **2.** To practice tricks or deception; — with *on* or *upon*. — **im·pos′er** (-pōz′ẽr), *n.*

By permission. From Webster's New Collegiate Dictionary. Copyright 1949, 1951, 1953 by G. & C. Merriam Co.

For the transitive verb *impose* seven different meanings are given, of which the first, second, fifth, and sixth are unlabeled and therefore standard. The third, labeled *Eccl.,* is a technical word in ecclesiastical usage; the fourth, labeled *Archaic,* is antiquated—no longer used in ordinary writing; and the seventh, labeled *Print.,* is a technical term used in printing. Neither of the two meanings of the intransitive verb *impose* is labeled, and therefore both are standard.

OUTLINE FOR DICTIONARY LABELS

a. Standard words—not labeled by the dictionary.
(Used freely by the educated in general writing, selected to suit the purpose and style of the writer, from the very formal to the informal.)

FORMAL   He has none. It is impossible. We should consider the essentials.

INFORMAL   He hasn't any. It's impossible. Let's consider essentials.

b. Colloquialisms—labeled *Colloq.*
(Used freely by the educated in conversation and in very informal writing.)

EXAMPLES   He *hasn't got* any. It's *no go.* Let's get down to *brass tacks.*

c. Slang—labeled *Slang.*
(Used only with special care, and almost never in formal writing.)

EXAMPLES   The plan was evidently *cockeyed* (for *absurd*).
The wounded man soon *kicked the bucket* (for *died*).

d. Dialectal words (*localisms, provincialisms*)—labeled *Dial., Scot., South African,* etc.
(Generally avoided in writing because the words may be known only in a limited region.)

EXAMPLES   The rogue was brought before the *bailie* (for *bailiff*).
I lost my book *somewheres* (for *somewhere*).

e. Illiteracies (substandard expressions)—labeled *Illit.* or *Vulgar* (if included in the dictionary at all).
(Always avoided except to illustrate substandard speech in written dialogue.)

EXAMPLE   They ain't got none.

f. Obsolete and archaic words—labeled *Obs., Archaic.*
(No longer used, but retained in the dictionary to explain older writings.)

EXAMPLE   Edward was he *hight* (for *called*).

g. Technical words—labeled *Law, Med.*[2] (medicine), *Naut.* (nautical), *Phar.* (pharmacy), *Surg.* (surgery), *Zool.* (zoology), etc.
(Generally limited in use to writing or speaking for specialized groups.)

EXAMPLE   The *hyperemia* (for *increase in blood*) in the left arm is difficult to explain.

h. Poetic words—labeled *Poetic.*
(Avoided in general writing and speaking.)

EXAMPLE   The man sat *oft* (for *often*) in the moonlight.

The labeling or classification of words is often difficult, for the language is constantly changing and many words are on the borderline, as between slang and colloquial or between colloquial and standard; and it is to be expected that good dictionaries will frequently differ in classifying such words. Although classes of words (especially standard, colloquial, substandard) are commonly referred to as "levels of usage," we are not to think of one class as always higher or better than another. Actually any one of the eight classes may be the best for a given occasion. Even the substandard word is best when the writer is trying to

---

[2] The *NWD* writes "in *law,*" "in *medicine,*" etc., and thus avoids abbreviations.

illustrate the speech of the uneducated. Technical language is often best in speech and writing addressed to those in one's profession. The occasion and the purpose of the writer or speaker will determine the best words to select. The standard (unlabeled) words which make up the bulk of the English vocabulary are usually best for general writing and, along with colloquialisms, for conversation. But it should be noted that *Webster's Third New International Dictionary* has discontinued the label *Colloquial*, thus leaving to the writer's judgment the problem of avoiding many unlabeled words, or meanings of words, that would be inappropriate in the usual expository prose. Our standard words range from the very learned to the very simple and are adequate for the most dignified or the most informal style.

▶ EXERCISE 3   Classify according to the labels of your dictionary the thirty-three words beginning with *hunky*.

EXAMPLE   The thirty-three words in *Webster's New Collegiate Dictionary* preceding *hunky* (beginning with *hummingbird*) may be classified as indicated below. *Italics* indicate that a word belongs in the class in respect to one or more, but not all, of its meanings.

a. STANDARD (NOT LABELED) hummingbird, *hummock*, *humor*, humorist, humoristic, *humorous*, *hump*, humpback, humpbacked, humped, humph, humpy, humus, Hun, *hunch*, hunchback, hunchbacked, *hundred*, hundredfold, hundred-per-center, hundredth, hundredweight, hung, *Hungarian*, hunger, hungeringly, hunger strike, *hungry*, hunks
b. COLLOQUIAL   *hunch*, hunk
c. SLANG   *hump*, *Hungarian*
d. DIALECTAL   *hummock*, *hump*, hunkers
e. ILLITERATE   (None listed)
f. OBSOLETE (or ARCHAIC) *humor*, *humorous*, *hunch*, *Hungarian*, hungerly, *hungry*
g. TECHNICAL   *humor*, humoresque, *humorous*, *hundred*
h. POETIC   (None listed)

FURTHER EXERCISES ON THE USE OF THE DICTIONARY

▶ EXERCISE 4   What is the etymology of the following words?

adjective	conjunction	dialogue	monarchy
aristocracy	democracy	emperor	oligarchy

▶ EXERCISE 5   What were the first English meanings of the following words? What meanings developed later?

doom	inspiration	prevent	sanguine
gallery	knave	proper	silly

▶ EXERCISE 6   List synonyms for each of the following words. (For synonyms and antonyms you may find that your dictionary should be supplemented by a book of synonyms such as *Roget's International Thesaurus*, New York, 1936, which is available also in a pocketbook size.)

act	change	fight	see
anger	eat	go	think

▶ EXERCISE 7   List antonyms for each of the following words.

awkward	clever	gallantry	quiet
clear	fast	greed	study

▶ EXERCISE 8   Study the following pairs of words in your dictionary (in the special paragraphs, if any, that compare and contrast the pairs) and write sentences to illustrate the shades of difference in meaning.

cause—reason	help—aid	push—shove
freedom—liberty	position—situation	valid—sound

▶ EXERCISE 9   Determine the preferred American spelling of the following words: *connexion, gypsy, labour.* Which of the following words should be written separately, which should be written solid, and which should be hyphenated?

| cropeared | girlscout | heartfelt | toiletwater |
| cubbyhole | heartbroken | heartfree | vestpocket |

▶ EXERCISE 10   Determine the pronunciation for each of the following words. Which of the words change the accent to indicate a change in grammatical function?

| absent | exquisite | Montaigne | vehement |
| contest | impious | object | Viet-Nam |

▶ EXERCISE 11   Classify each of the following words as a verb (transitive or intransitive), a noun, an adjective, an adverb, a preposition, or a conjunction. Give the principal parts of each verb, the plural (or plurals) of each noun, and the comparative and superlative of each adjective or adverb. (Note that some words are used as two or more parts of speech.)

| bad | drag | often | since | stratum |
| bite | into | sheep | sing | tomato |

▶ EXERCISE 12   Which of the following words are usually capitalized? Which are capitalized only for certain meanings?

| easter | italic | platonic | spanish |
| italian | liberian | roman | stoical |

▶ EXERCISE 13   Divide the following words into syllables.

| analytic | industrious | liberty | vindictive |
| indistinguishable | laboriously | supplement | vocabulary |

▶ EXERCISE 14   Get from your dictionary specific information about each of the following. Note the source of information as (a) general vocabulary, (b) list of abbreviations, (c) gazetteer, (d) biographical list, or (e) appendix.

| Annam | Esau | Melpomene | *vive le roi* |
| Attila | Escorial | Louis Pasteur | WAC |

19b

Colloquialisms are generally avoided in standard (formal) writing.

Colloquial words or expressions (labeled *Colloq.*) are appropriate to conversation and to informal writing. For these purposes colloquialisms often give a desirable tone of informality. But colloquial expressions tend to bring a discordant note into expository or other formal types of writing.

COLLOQUIAL   The repeated *phone* calls only *aggravated* me but made my sister *plenty mad.*

STANDARD   The repeated *telephone* calls only *annoyed* me but made my sister *very angry.*

Contracted forms (*won't, I'd, he'll, hasn't*) are proper for informal writing and equally proper for all but the most extremely formal speech. In formal expository writing, such contractions are normally written out—*will not, I would* or *I should, he will, has not.*

INFORMAL   *It's* really too bad that *he's* been held up and *can't* be here for the opening.

FORMAL   *It is* unfortunate that he *has been* detained and *cannot* be here for the opening.

▶ EXERCISE 15   Consult your dictionary for *colloquial* meanings of the following words: *brass, dig, fizzle, kick, way.* For each word compose a sentence in which the word is used with a colloquial meaning. Then in each sentence substitute a standard word with the same meaning.

19c

Slang and jargon should be used sparingly if at all in standard speech and writing.

Slang, according to *The American College Dictionary,* is "language of a markedly colloquial character, regarded as below the standard of cultivated speech." Some slang words have a pungent quality: *caboodle, goon,* and *moocher* may soon join *van, sham, mob,* and *banter* as standard members of the English language. But much slang is trite and tasteless, and is used in an ineffective attempt to mask an inadequate vocabulary. Some people describe everything as "swell" or "lousy," when they really want to say *excellent, generous, satisfying, distinguished,* or *contemptible, foolish, inadequate.*

The objection to slang, then, is not based upon arbitrary *don'ts,* but upon slang's habitual alliance with lazy thinking. Slang is the sluggard's way of avoiding the search for the exact, meaningful word.

For the same reason *jargon*—language which is meaningless, or at least very confusing except to a special group—should be avoided. Almost every trade or occupation has its own jargon. A man with recent military experience might write the following jargon about his first day in college:

The mustering-in was snafu.

This sentence would be easily understood by his army friends; other readers might require a formal statement:

The registration was confused.

A particularly confusing type of jargon is found in much government writing. (See also **21a, Wordiness.**)

BUREAUCRATIC JARGON   All personnel functioning in the capacity of clerks will indicate that they have had opportunity to take due cognizance of this notice by transmitting signed acknowledgment of receipt of same.

IMPROVED   All clerks will acknowledge in writing the receipt of this notice.

COMMERCIAL JARGON   Allow us to express our appreciation of your esteemed favor.

IMPROVED   Thank you for your letter.

19d

Dialectal words should be used appropriately.

Dialectal words (also called *localisms* or *provincialisms*) should normally be avoided in speaking and writing outside the limited region where they are current. Speakers and writers may, however, safely use dialectal words known to the audience they are addressing.

DIALECT   I *reckon* he filled the *poke* with apples.
STANDARD   I *suppose* he filled the *bag* with apples.

19e

Illiteracies and improprieties should be avoided.

Illiteracies (also called *vulgarisms*) are the *substandard* expressions of uneducated people, usually not listed in the dictionary.

SUBSTANDARD   The boys *ain't* going. *They's* no use asking them.
STANDARD   The boys *are not* going. *There's* no use asking them.

An *impropriety* is a good word used with the wrong sense or function.

WRONG   I *except* your invitation. [Wrong meaning]
RIGHT   I *accept* your invitation.

QUESTIONABLE   She sang *good*. [Wrong function—adjective used
                     as adverb]
STANDARD   She sang *well*.

19f

Obsolete, archaic, or obsolescent words should be avoided.

All dictionaries list words (and meanings for words) that have long since passed out of general use. Such words as *parfit* (perfect), *ort* (fragment of food left at a meal), *yestreen* (last evening), *waxen* (to grow or become) are still found in dictionaries because these words, once the standard vocabulary of great authors, occur in our older literature and must be defined for the modern reader.

Some archaic words—like *wight, methinks,* and *quoth*—have been used for purposes of humor. Modern practice tends to label such usage as juvenile.

19g

Technical words should be used only when appropriate to the audience.

When you are writing for the general reader, avoid all unnecessary technical language. Since the ideal of the good writer is to make his thought clear to as many people as possible, he will not describe an apple tree as a *Malus pumila* or a high fever as *hyperpyrexia.* (Of course technical language, with its greater precision, is highly desirable when one is addressing an audience that can understand it.)

Sometimes, however, even though some dictionaries label words as technical expressions (*electron* and *atomic theory,* for example), the words are well enough known to justify their general use.

19h

Avoid (1) "fine writing," (2) "poetic" expressions, and (3) unpleasing combinations of sound or overuse of alliteration.

(1) **Avoid "fine writing."** "Fine writing" is the unnecessary use of ornate words and expressions. It is generally fuzzy and repetitious; it tends to emphasize words rather than ideas. A simple, direct statement like "From childhood I have looked forward to a journey" can become by

fine writing something like this: "From the halcyon days of early youth I have always anticipated with eagerness and pleasure the exciting vistas of distant climes and mysterious horizons."

(2) **Avoid "poetic" expressions.** Genuine poetry has its very proper place, and the vivid language of simile and metaphor enriches even colloquial prose. But the sham poetry of faded imagery (*eye of night* for *moon*) and inappropriate expressions like *oft, eftsoons, 'twas,* and *'neath* are misplaced in the usual prose style.

(3) **Avoid unpleasing combinations of sound or overuse of alliteration.** Good prose has rhythm, but it does not rhyme. If you write, "In foreign relations, the western nations are subject to dictation," you distract the reader's attention from your meaning. Equally offensive to the average reader is the overuse of alliteration (repetition of the same consonant sound), as in "Some people *s*hun the *s*eashore."

OTHER EXERCISES ON USAGE

▶ EXERCISE 16   In the following list put *C* after any sentence that requires no revision, even for standard writing. Write *Colloq.* for each sentence approved for informal use only. Label each violation of good usage. Then rewrite all sentences (except those marked *C*) to make them conform to standard English. You may find the **Glossary of Usage** (**19i**) helpful in determining some inappropriate usages.

1. If I had of known you was coming, I would of waited longer.
2. Everyone suspicioned the old man of stealing our apples.
3. The ad in the paper was sort of hazy.
4. The sifting snow screened our view of the highway.
5. George was not dumb, though he looked like he was.
6. The profs dished out more than we could take.

7. Has your neighbor done sold his house?
8. The boy had a keen desire to win the game.
9. You do things different from anybody I know.
10. We filled the bucket with H_2O.
11. The poor man was in a sad fix.
12. I suppose that your findings are correct.
13. "You are batty," I yelled. "Now scram!"
14. I am terribly aggravated with your doings.
15. Ten miles is all the farther that I can live away from my store.
16. Where do you live at now?
17. The general was completely sold on the private who had some spunk.
18. 'Twas a clear, cool eve, and the moon shed an effulgent glow.
19. A first-rate farmer raises heaps of farm produce.
20. I am kind of late today, for I do not feel so good.
21. He took and snatched the parcel from her hands although he knew that he hadn't ought.
22. Since Richard hopes to become a musician, he is taking piano lessons.
23. Because of the depression he lost considerable in his business.
24. Her folks live in the country ten miles outside the city limits.
25. He calculated he could win out in the election.

▶ EXERCISE 17   Rewrite the following passage in standard informal English.

1. I know, Dean, I'm over a barrel good this time. 2. You wouldn't of made all this hullabaloo if you wasn't plenty peeved. 3. So I'm on the hook. 4. Well, I won't try to put the monkey on somebody else's back—pass the buck, that is. 5. I done what the prof says I done, and I can't say as I blame him for being some aggravated over it. 6. I guess I'd be doing flips if I was him.

▶ EXERCISE 18   Rewrite the following passages of bureaucratic, legal, or academic jargon in simple standard
English.[3]

1. It is obvious from the difference in elevation with relation to the short depth of the property that the contour
   is such as to preclude any reasonable developmental
   potential for active recreation.
2. Verbal contact with Mr. Blank regarding the attached
   notification of promotion has elicited the attached
   representation intimating that he prefers to decline the
   assignment.
3. Voucherable expenditures necessary to provide adequate dental treatment required as adjunct to medical
   treatment being rendered a pay patient in in-patient
   status may be incurred as required at the expense of
   the Public Health Service.
4. I hereby give and convey to you, all and singular, my
   estate and interests, right, title, claim and advantages
   of and in said orange, together with all rind, juice,
   pulp and pits, and all rights and advantages therein.
5. I prefer an abbreviated phraseology, distinguished for
   its lucidity.
6. Realization has grown that the curriculum or the experiences of learners change and improve only as those
   who are most directly involved examine their goals,
   improve their understandings and increase their skill in
   performing the tasks necessary to reach newly defined
   goals.

[3] Quoted, by permission, from Stuart Chase's *Power of Words*, Harcourt,
Brace and Company, New York, 1953, pp. 250–53.

Glossary of Usage

Consult the following glossary to determine the standing of a word or phrase and its appropriateness to your purpose.

The glossary below can include only a few of the words likely to cause difficulty. If the word you are looking for is not included, or if you need more information about any word in the list, consult a good recent college dictionary, remembering that dictionaries do not always agree. The following list does not represent the usage of any one dictionary, but justification for each usage label can usually be found in at least two of the leading dictionaries.

Before attempting to use this list, you should read pages 198–201, 204 to make sure that you understand the distinctions between STANDARD (both *formal* and *informal*) and COLLOQUIAL (19b) and that you understand the meaning of SLANG (19c), DIALECTAL (19d), ILLITERATE or SUBSTANDARD (19e), OBSOLETE or ARCHAIC (19f), TECHNICAL (19g), and POETIC (19h). It is sometimes forgotten that words and expressions labeled *Colloquial* are appropriate to conversation and to informal types of writing.

A, an. Use *a* before a consonant sound, *an* before a vowel sound.

> EXAMPLES *a* band, *a* well, *a* yard, *a* unit (*y* sound), *a* one (*w* sound), *a* hammer, *a* history; *an* apple, *an* olive, *an* hour (silent *h* before the vowel)

Accept, except. Do not confuse. The verb *accept* means "to receive." *Except* means "to exclude."

> Mary accepted (*not* excepted) an invitation to dinner.
> They excepted (*not* accepted) Mary from the invitation.

Ad. Colloquial shortening of *advertisement*. Use the full word in formal writing.

Affect, effect. Do not confuse. *Affect* (a verb) means "to influence." "The attack affected the morale of the troops." *Effect* is both a verb and a noun. As a verb it means "to bring to pass." "The medicine effected a complete cure." As a noun *effect* means "result." "The effect of the medicine was instantaneous."

Aggravate. Means "to intensify, to increase." "Lack of water aggravated the suffering." Colloquially it means "to irritate, exasperate, provoke, annoy." "He was extremely annoyed (*not* aggravated)."

Agree to, agree with. One agrees *to* a plan but *with* a person.

Ain't. A substandard contraction for *has not, have not;* a colloquial shortening for *am not, are not, is not* generally disapproved by the educated.

Alibi. Colloquial for *excuse*. Standard English accepts the word only in its technical legal sense.

All the farther. Dialectal for *as far as*.

    STANDARD   A mile is as far as (*not* all the farther) we can go.

Allude, refer. Do not confuse. *Allude* means "to refer to indirectly." "When he mentioned dictators, we knew that he was alluding to Hitler and Mussolini." *Refer* means "to mention something specifically." "I refer you to the third act of *Hamlet*."

Allusion, illusion. Do not confuse *allusion,* "an indirect reference," with *illusion,* "an unreal image or false impression."

Alot. Always written as two words: *a lot.* **A lot** is colloquial in the sense of *many*.

Already, all ready. *Already* (one word) means "prior to some specified time, either present, past, or future." "By noon the theater was already full." *All ready* (two words) means "completely ready." "I am all ready to go."

Alright. Incorrect spelling. Use *all right*.

Also. A weak connective. *And* is a better connective. "I met Harry and Tom (*not* also Tom)."

Altogether, all together. *Altogether* (one word) means "wholly, thoroughly, in all." "The report is altogether true." *All together* (two words) means "in a group, collectively." "The packages were all together on the table."

Alumnus, alumna. *Alumnus,* a male graduate; *alumni,* two or more male graduates. *Alumna,* a female graduate; *alumnae,* two or more female graduates. *Alumni,* male and female graduates grouped together.

A.M., P.M. (also a.m., p.m.). Use only with figures. "He came at 10:00 A.M. (*not* in the A.M.) and left at 4:00 P.M." "He came in the morning and left in the afternoon (*not* in the P.M.)."

Among, between. *Among* always implies more than two. "Joseph's brethren divided the spoils among them." *Between* literally implies only two. "I divided the cake between John and Mary." But *between* is used for more than two to indicate a reciprocal relation. "A treaty was concluded between the three nations."

Amount, number. Use *amount* to refer to things in bulk or mass, *number* to refer to countable objects. "A large amount of grain; a number of watermelons."

An, a. See A, an.

And etc. Never place *and* before *etc.* The *and* is redundant since *etc.* is an abbreviation of *et* (and) + *cetera* (other things).

And which, but which. Do not thwart subordination by inserting *and* or *but* before a subordinate clause. "Law enforcement is a current problem which (*not* and which) is hard to solve." "The college needs new dormitories which (*not* but which) cannot be erected until funds are provided." But *and* or *but* may be used before *which* to join two *which* clauses. "Law enforcement is a problem which is current and which is hard to solve."

Ante-, anti-. *Ante-* means "before," as in *antebellum. Anti-* means "against," as in *anti-British.* The hyphen is used after *anti-* before capital letters and before *i,* as in *anti-imperialist.*

Anyone, everyone, someone. Distinguish from *any one, every one, some one. Anyone* (one word) means "any person, anybody." *Any one* (two words) means "any single person or thing." Similarly with *everyone, someone.*

Anyways. Dialectal for *in any case, anyway.*

STANDARD I may not get the pass I have requested, but I am planning to go anyway (*not* anyways).

Anywheres. Dialectical for *anywhere*.

Apt. See **Likely, liable, apt.**

Around. Colloquial in the sense of "about, near."

COLLOQUIAL   To come around noon; to stay around the house; to pick around ten quarts.

STANDARD   To come about noon; to stay near (*or* about) the house; to pick about ten quarts.

As. (1) Generally avoid *as* in the sense of "because." *For* or *since* is usually clearer.

VAGUE   He worked steadily as the day was cool.
SPECIFIC   He worked steadily, for the day was cool.

(2) In standard English do not use *as* in place of *that* or *whether*.

COLLOQUIAL   I feel as I should go.
STANDARD   I feel that I should go.

(3) In negative statements careful writers prefer *so . . . as* to *as . . . as*. "I am not so strong as I used to be." "He will go only so far as he is forced to go."
See also **Like, as, as if.**

As to. A vague substitute for *about*.

EXACT   She spoke to me about (*not* as to) her plans.

At. Redundant in such sentences as the following:

REDUNDANT   Where does he live at? Where are you at now?
IMPROVED   Where does he live? Where are you now?

At about. *About* is preferable.

WORDY   He arrived at about noon.
BETTER   He arrived about noon.

Awful. Colloquial in the sense of "very bad, ugly, shocking."

COLLOQUIAL   The suit was awful.
STANDARD   The suit was very ugly.

Awhile, a while. Distinguish between the adverb *awhile* and the article and noun *a while*. "Rest awhile before leaving." "Rest for a while (*not* awhile) before leaving."

Badly. Colloquial in the sense of *very much* with verbs signifying *want* or *need*.

STANDARD   She needs a new coat very much (*not* badly).

Balance. Colloquial when used for *rest* or *remainder* (except in reference to a balance at the bank).

STANDARD   We enjoyed the rest (*not* balance) of the trip.

Bank on, take stock in. Colloquial expressions for *rely on, trust in.*

Because. Do not use *because* to introduce a noun clause.

AWKWARD   Because he was sick was no excuse.
BETTER   The fact that he was sick was no excuse, *or* His sickness was no excuse.

See also **Reason is because.**

Being as, being that. Substandard for *since, because.*

Beside, besides. Do not confuse. *Beside* is a preposition meaning "by the side of." "Sit beside me." *Besides,* used chiefly as an adverb, means "in addition to." "We ate apples and other fruit besides."

Better. See **Had better, had rather, would rather.**

Between, among. See **Among, between.**

Bunch. Colloquial (or slang) for *group* (or *intimate group*) of people.

STANDARD   Tom belonged to our group (*not* bunch).

Bust, busted, bursted. Inelegant forms of the verb *burst*, which uses the same form for all its principal parts: *burst, burst, burst.*

But, only, hardly, scarcely. These words, negative in implication, should not be used with another negative.

POOR   He didn't have but one hat.
BETTER   He had but one hat; *or,* He had only one hat.

POOR   He wasn't sick only three days.
BETTER   He was sick only three days.

POOR   I don't hardly (scarcely) know.
BETTER   I hardly (scarcely) know.

But what. Colloquial for *that.*

COLLOQUIAL   He had no doubt *but what* he would succeed.
STANDARD   He had no doubt *that* he would succeed.

But which, and which. See **And which, but which.**

Calculate. Colloquial or dialectal for *think, guess, plan.*

Can, may. In formal usage *can* denotes ability and *may* denotes possibility or permission. The use of *can* to denote permission is colloquial.

COLLOQUIAL   Can I go?
FORMAL   May I go?

Can't hardly. A double negative in implication. Use *can hardly.* See **But, only, hardly, scarcely.**

Case, line. Often used in wordy expressions. Say "Jones had good intentions," *not* "In the case of Jones there were good intentions." Say "Get some fruit," *not* "Get something in the line of fruit."

Censure, criticize. See **Criticize, censure.**

Compare to, compare with. "One object is compared *with* another when set side by side with it in order to show their relative value or excellence; *to* another when it is formally represented as like it." (*NCD*)

RIGHT   He compared the book with the manuscript.
RIGHT   He compared the earth to a ball.

Complected. Dialectal or colloquial for *complexioned.*

STANDARD   He was a light-complexioned [*not* light-complected] man.
STANDARD   He was a man of light complexion.

Considerable. An adjective; colloquial as a noun; substandard as an adverb.

COLLOQUIAL   He lost considerable in the depression.
STANDARD   He lost a considerable amount of property during the depression.

SUBSTANDARD He was considerable touched by the girl's plea.
STANDARD   He was considerably touched by the girl's plea.

Contact. Frequently overused for more exact words or phrases such as *ask, consult, inform, query, talk with, telephone, write to.*

Continual, continuous. *Continual* means "occurring in steady, rapid, but not unbroken succession." "The rehearsal was hampered by continual interruptions." *Continuous* means "without cessation." "The continuous roar of the waterfall was disturbing."

Could of. Substandard corruption of *could have.*

Criticize, censure. In standard English, *criticize* means "to examine and judge as a critic," not necessarily "to censure." *Censure* means "to find fault with" or "to condemn as wrong."

Data, strata, phenomena. Plurals of *datum, stratum, phenomenon.* "These data, these strata, these phenomena, this stratum, this phenomenon." *Stratum* and *phenomenon* have alternative plurals in *s.* The singular *datum* is seldom used. The plural *data* is often construed as a collective noun taking a singular verb: "This data is new."

Deal. Colloquial or commercial term for *transaction, bargain.*

Definitely. Frequently overused as a vague intensifier.

Didn't ought. See **Had ought, hadn't ought, didn't ought.**

Differ from, differ with. Do not confuse. *Differ from* means "to stand apart because of unlikeness." "The Caucasian race differs from the Mongolian race in color, stature, and customs." *Differ with* means "to disagree." "On that point I differ with you."

Done. The past participle of the verb *to do. I do, I did, I have done. Done* is substandard for *did* or for the adverb *already.*

SUBSTANDARD	He done well.
RIGHT	He did well.
SUBSTANDARD	He has done sold the dog.
RIGHT	He has already sold the dog; *or,* He has sold the dog.

Don't. A contraction for *do not,* but not for *does not.*

WRONG	He don't smoke. [He do not smoke.]
RIGHT	He doesn't smoke. [He does not smoke.]

PROPER CONTRACTIONS
I don't, we don't, you don't, they don't. [do not]
He doesn't, she doesn't, it doesn't. [does not]

Each other, one another. Used interchangeably. Some writers prefer *each other* when referring to only two, and *one another* when referring to more than two.

Effect, affect. See **Affect, effect.**

Either, neither. Refers to one of two, not to one of more than two. "*Either* Mary or Jane will go." "*Neither* Mary nor Jane will go."

Elegant. Means *polished, fastidious, refined.* Used colloquially for *delicious, good.*

STANDARD   This food is delicious (*not* elegant).

Emigrate, immigrate. *Emigrate* means "to leave a place of abode for residence in another country." *Immigrate* means "to come for permanent residence into a country of which one is not a native."

Enthuse. Colloquial for *to make enthusiastic, to become enthusiastic.*

COLLOQUIAL   She enthuses over anything.
STANDARD   She becomes enthusiastic about anything.

Equally as good. The *as* is redundant. Say "equally good" or "as good as."

Etc. See **And etc.**

Everyone, anyone, someone. See **Anyone, everyone, someone.**

Everywheres. Dialectal for *everywhere.*

Exam. Colloquial shortening of *examination.* For formal purposes, use the full word.

Except, accept. See **Accept, except.**

Expect. Colloquial if used to mean "suppose."

COLLOQUIAL   I expect the report is true.
STANDARD   I suppose the report is true.

Farther, further. Some writers prefer *farther* to express geographic distance. "They went even farther the next day." *Further* is regularly preferred to express the meaning, "more, in addition." "Further reports came."

Faze. A verb used colloquially for *worry, disconcert.* Not related to the noun *phase,* standard English for *aspect* or *stage.*

Fellow. Colloquial for *man, sweetheart.*

Fewer, less. *Fewer* refers especially to number. "Fewer than twenty persons attended." *Less* refers especially to value, degree, or amount. "The suit costs less than the overcoat."

Fine. The adjective *fine* is much overused as a vague word of approval. Choose a more exact expression. *Fine* is colloquial or dialectal when used as an adverb meaning "well, excellently."

COLLOQUIAL	She plays the organ fine.
STANDARD	She plays the organ well.

Flunk. Colloquial for *fail*.

Folks. Colloquial for *parents, relatives, persons of one's own family*.

Former. Refers to the first named of two. Not properly used when three or more are named.

Funny. Colloquial for *strange, queer, odd*. In standard usage *funny* means "amusing."

Further, farther. See **Farther, further.**

Gentleman, lady. Generally preferable: *man, woman*. Use *gentleman, lady* when your purpose is to distinguish persons of refinement and culture from the ill-bred. Use the plural forms in addressing an audience: "Ladies and Gentlemen."

QUESTIONABLE	Lady preacher, saleslady, lady clerk, cleaning lady, ladies' colleges
BETTER	Woman preacher, saleswoman, woman clerk, cleaning woman, women's colleges

Get, got. The verb *to get* is one of the most useful words in standard English. It is common in such good idioms as *get along with* (someone), *get the better of* (someone), *get at* (information), *get up* (a dance), *get on* (a horse), or *get over* (sickness). But *get* or *got* is also used in expressions that are colloquial or slangy.

SLANG	He *got his hooks on* her estate.
STANDARD	He *got possession of* her estate.

Good. Not generally approved as an adverb.

QUESTIONABLE	He reads good. He works good.
STANDARD	He reads well. He works well; *or*, He does good work.

Gotten. Past participle of *get*, the principal parts of which are *get* (present), *got* (past), *got*, or *gotten* (past participle). In England *gotten* is now archaic, but in the United States both *got* and *gotten* are in general use.

Grand. Avoid the vague colloquial use of *grand* to mean "excellent." Select the exact word to fit the meaning.

LOOSE   We had a grand trip.

BETTER   We had a delightful (pleasant, exciting) trip.

Guy. Colloquial for *man, boy, fellow.*

Had better, had rather, would rather. Good idioms used to express advisability (with *better*) or preference (with *rather*). *Better* is a colloquial shortening of *had better.*

COLLOQUIAL   He better listen to reason.

STANDARD   He had better listen to reason.

Had of. Substandard for *had.*

SUBSTANDARD   I wish I had of gone.

STANDARD   I wish I had gone.

Had ought, hadn't ought, didn't ought. Substandard combinations.

SUBSTANDARD   He hadn't ought to have gone.

STANDARD   He ought not to have gone.

Half a, a half, a half a. Use *half a* or *a half,* but avoid the redundant *a half a.*

REDUNDANT   He worked a half a day.

STANDARD   He worked half a day.

STANDARD   He worked a half day. [Perhaps more formal and more specific]

Hanged, hung. Use *hanged* rather than *hung* when speaking of an execution.

The man was hanged (*not* hung) for murder.

Hardly. See **But, only, hardly, scarcely.**

Healthful, healthy. *Healthful* is sometimes preferred in the sense of "giving health," as in "healthful climate, healthful food." *Healthy* commonly means "having health," as in "healthy boy, healthy woman, healthy people."

Himself, myself, yourself. See **Myself, himself, yourself.**

Hisself. Substandard for *himself.*

Homey. Colloquial for *homelike, intimate.*

Honorable, Reverend. See **Reverend, Honorable.**

If, whether. Some writers prefer *whether* to *if* after such verbs as *say, learn, know, understand, doubt,* especially when followed by *or.* "I did not know whether he would ride or walk."

Illusion, allusion. See **Allusion, illusion.**

Immigrate, emigrate. See **Emigrate, immigrate.**

Imply, infer. The writer or speaker *implies;* the reader or listener *infers.* "His statement *implies* that he will resign." "From his statement I *infer* that he will resign."

In, into. Do not confuse. *In* indicates "location within." "He was in the room." *Into* indicates "motion or direction to a point within." "He came into the room."

In-, un-. See **Un-, in-.**

In back of, in behind, in between. Wordy for *back of, behind, between.*

Incredible, incredulous. *Incredible* means "too extraordinary to admit of belief." *Incredulous* means "inclined not to believe on slight evidence."

Individual, party, person. *Individual* refers to a single person, animal, or thing. *Party* refers to a group, never to a single person (except in colloquial or legal usage). *Person* is the preferred word for general reference to a human being.

> COLLOQUIAL   He is the interested party.
> STANDARD   He is the interested person.

Infer, imply. See **Imply, infer.**

Inferior than. Say *inferior to* or *worse than.*

Ingenious, ingenuous. *Ingenious* means "clever, resourceful," as "an ingenious device." *Ingenuous* means "open, frank, artless," as "ingenuous actions."

In regards to. Use either of the correct idioms, *in regard to* or *as regards.*

Inside of, outside of. The *of* is often useless. "We live inside (*not* inside of) the city." *Inside of* is colloquial for *within; outside of* is colloquial for *except, besides.*

> STANDARD   within (*not* inside of) two days; everybody except (*not* outside of) James.

Into, in. See **In, into.**

Invite. Slang when used as a noun.

> STANDARD   We have an invitation (*not* invite) to the party.

Irregardless. Substandard for *regardless.*

Its, it's. Do not confuse the possessive *its* and the contraction *it's* (= *it is*).

Just. Colloquial for *completely, simply, quite.*

COLLOQUIAL   He was just tired out.
STANDARD   He was completely tired out.

Kind, sort. Singular forms, modified by singular adjectives.

COLLOQUIAL *or* SUBSTANDARD   I like these kind (*or* sort) of shoes.
STANDARD   I like this kind (*or* sort) of shoes.

Kind of, sort of. Loosely colloquial when used as an adverb to mean "somewhat, rather, after a fashion."

COLLOQUIAL   I was kind of (sort of) tired.
STANDARD   I was somewhat tired.

COLLOQUIAL   I kind of (sort of) thought you would go.
STANDARD   I rather thought you would go.

Kind of a, sort of a. Omit the *a* in standard writing.

STANDARD   What kind of (*not* kind of a) car does he drive?
What sort of (*not* sort of a) car does he drive?

Lady, gentleman. See **Gentleman, lady.**

Later, latter. Do not confuse. *Later* is the comparative of late and means "more late." *Latter* refers to the last named of two. If more than two are named, use *last* or *last-mentioned* instead of *latter.*

Lay, lie. Do not confuse. See **7a, Exercise 1.**

Lead, led. Present tense and past tense of the verb. Do not confuse with the noun *lead* (pronounced *led*), the name of the metal.

Learn, teach. *Learn* means "to acquire knowledge"; *teach* means "to impart knowledge." "She taught (*not* learned) him his lesson."

Leave, let. Do not use *leave* for *let*. *Leave* means "to depart from"; *let* means "to permit." But "Leave (*or* Let) me alone" is a standard idiom.

SUBSTANDARD   I will not leave you go today.
STANDARD   I will not let you go today.

Less, fewer. See **Fewer, less.**

Let's us. *Let's* is the contraction of *let us.* Therefore *Let's us go* is redundant for *Let's go. Let's don't stay* is redundant for *Let's not stay.*

Lie, lay. Do not confuse. See 7a, Exercise 1.

Like, as, as if. *Like* is commonly used as a preposition and *as* or *as if* as a conjunction. *Like* is much used colloquially as a conjunction, but this use is generally avoided in standard writing.

> STANDARD He worked like a man. Do as (*not* like) I do. It looks as if (*not* like) it might rain.

Likely, liable, apt. Standard writing tends to use *likely* to express mere probability; to use *liable* to suggest, in addition, the idea of harm or responsibility. "My friends are likely to arrive tomorrow." [Mere probability] "The boy is liable to cut his foot with the ax." [Probability + the idea of harm] "The hotel will not be liable for stolen property." [Responsibility] *Apt* implies a predisposition or dexterity. "He is apt to worry." "He is an apt pupil." [Associate *apt* with *aptitude; liable* with *liability*] In colloquial usage *likely, liable,* and *apt* are interchangeable.

Line, case. See **Case, line.**

Locate. Colloquial for *settle.*

> STANDARD He settled (*not* located) in Texas.
> STANDARD He located his factory in Texas. [With object]

Lose, loose. Do not confuse. *Lose* means "to cease having." *Loose* (verb) means "to set free." *Loose* (adjective) means "free, not fastened."

Lot, lots of. Colloquial for *much, many, a great deal.*

Lovely. Avoid the vague colloquial use of *lovely* to mean "very pleasing." Select the exact word to fit the meaning.

Mad. Colloquial for *angry.*

Math. Colloquial shortening of *mathematics.* Use the full word in formal writing.

May be, maybe. Do not confuse the verb form *may be* with the adverb *maybe,* meaning "perhaps." "He may be waiting for my letter." "Maybe he will come tomorrow."

May, can. See **Can, may.**

May of. Substandard corruption of *may have.*

Mean. Colloquial for *ill-tempered, indisposed, ashamed.*

Might of. Substandard corruption of *might have.*

Mighty. Colloquial for *very.*

Moral, morale. Distinguish the adjective *moral* ("a *moral* question") from the noun *morale* ("the *morale* of the team").

Most. A colloquial shortening for the adverb *almost.*

COLLOQUIAL	The trains arrive most every hour.
STANDARD	The trains arrive almost every hour.
STANDARD	The trains are most crowded during the holidays. [*Most* is correctly used as an adverb to form the superlative.]

Must of. Substandard corruption of *must have.*

Myself, himself, yourself. Properly intensive or reflexive pronouns. "I myself will go; I will see for myself." In general *myself* is not a proper substitute for *I* or *me;* but it is substituted colloquially (1) for *I* after comparisons with *than* or *as* ("Everyone worked as well as myself") or (2) for *me* when it is the second member of a compound object ("He allowed my brother and myself to go home").

Neither, either. See **Either, neither.**

Nice. In formal writing, means "precise" or "exact." Do not overwork *nice* as a vague word of approval. Find an exact word.

VAGUE	It was a nice day.
SPECIFIC	It was a bright (mild, sunny) day.

No account, no good. Colloquial for *worthless, of no value.*

No place. Colloquial for *nowhere.*

Nowhere near. Colloquial for *not nearly.*

Nowheres. Dialectal for *nowhere.*

Number. See **Amount, number.**

O, oh. Interjections. *O* is used especially in very formal direct address, is always capitalized, and is never followed by any mark of punctuation. "O God, deliver us!" *Oh* is used to express grief, surprise, or a wish, and is followed by a comma or an exclamation point. "Oh, I hope so."

Of. See **Could of, Had of, Ought to of.**

Off of. *Of* is superfluous. "He fell off (*not* off of) the platform."

OK, O.K., okay. A colloquial expression for *correct* or *all right.*

One another, each other. See **Each other, one another.**

Only. See **But, only, hardly, scarcely.**

Other times. Use *at other times.*

Ought. See **Had ought.**

Ought to of. Substandard corruption of *ought to have.*

Out loud. Colloquial for *aloud.*

> STANDARD   He read the poem aloud (*not* out loud).

Outside of. See **Inside of, outside of.**

Party, person, individual. See **Individual, party, person.**

Per. Used especially in commercial writing. In standard English some authors use *per* only with Latin words, such as *diem, annum.*

> COMMERCIAL   His salary was four thousand dollars per year.
> STANDARD   His salary was four thousand dollars a year.

Per cent (or **percent**). Means "by the hundred." Use only after a numeral: "10 per cent, 20 per cent." In other situations *per cent* is colloquial for *percentage.* "A large percentage, a small percentage." Do not overwork *percentage* for *portion, part.*

Person, party, individual. See **Individual, party, person.**

Phase. See **Faze.**

Phenomena. Plural of *phenomenon.* See **Data, strata, phenomena.**

Phone. Colloquial shortening of *telephone.* Use the full word in formal writing.

Photo. Colloquial shortening of *photograph.* Use the full word in standard writing.

Plenty. Colloquial when used as an adverb.

> COLLOQUIAL   It is plenty good enough.
> STANDARD   It is quite good enough.

P.M., A.M. See **A.M., P.M.**

Poorly. Colloquial for *in poor health.*

Practical, practicable. *Practical* means "useful, sensible," not "theoretical." *Practicable* means "feasible, capable of being put into practice." "The sponsors are practical men, and their plans are practicable."

Prefer. Not to be followed by *than,* but by *to, before, above, rather than.*

UNIDIOMATIC   I should prefer that than anything else.
IDIOMATIC   I should prefer that to anything else

Principal, principle. Distinguish between *principal,* an adjective or noun meaning "chief" or "chief official," and the noun *principle,* meaning "fundamental truth."

Prof. Colloquial shortening of *professor.* In formal writing, use the full word.

Quite. An adverb meaning "entirely, positively." Used colloquially to mean "to a great extent, very."

COLLOQUIAL   The lake is quite near.
STANDARD   The lake is rather near.
STANDARD   His guess was quite wrong.

Quite, quiet. Do not confuse. *Quite* is an adverb meaning "entirely." *Quiet* is an adjective meaning "calm."

Quite a few, quite a bit, quite a little, quite a good deal. Colloquial for *a good many, a considerable number, a considerable amount.*

Raise, rear. Some writers prefer *rear* to *raise* in the sense of "bringing up children." "He reared (*not* raised) the boy from infancy."

Raise, rise. See **Rise, raise.**

Real. Colloquial or dialectal for *very* or *really.*

STANDARD   She was very (*not* real) brave.

Rear. See **Raise, rear.**

Reason is because. Formal English usually completes the construction *The reason is* (*was*) with a *that* clause or recasts the sentence.

COLLOQUIAL   The reason why he missed his class was because (*or* on account of) he overslept.
STANDARD   The reason why he missed his class was that he overslept.
STANDARD   He missed his class because he overslept.

Reckon. Colloquial or dialectal for *think, suppose.*

Refer. See **Allude, refer.**

Respectfully, respectively. Do not confuse. *Respectfully* means "in a manner showing respect." "Yours respectfully." *Respectively* means "each in the order given." "The President respectfully paid tribute to the Army, Navy, and Air Force, respectively."

Reverend, Honorable. To be followed by the first name, the initials, or some title of the person referred to as well as the surname. See 11e.

Right. Colloquial or dialectal as an adverb meaning "very, extremely."

> STANDARD   I am very (*not* right) glad to see you.

Right along. Colloquial for *continuously.*

> STANDARD   The clock struck continuously (*not* right along). I knew it all the time (*not* right along).

Rise, raise. Do not confuse. *Rise* is an intransitive verb. "I rise every morning." "I rose at four o'clock." "I have risen at four o'clock for many months." *Raise* is a transitive verb. "I raise vegetables." "I raised vegetables last year." "I have raised vegetables for many years."

Said. The adjective *said*, meaning "before-mentioned," should be used only in legal documents.

Same, said, such. Except in legal documents, not used as substitutes for *it, this,* or *that.*

> QUESTIONABLE   When said coat was returned, same was found to be badly torn.
> BETTER   When this coat was returned, it was found to be badly torn.

Says. Substandard for *said.*

> SUBSTANDARD   He smiled and says to her, "I am tired."
> STANDARD   He smiled and said to her, "I am tired."

Scarcely. See **But, only, hardly, scarcely.**

Seldom ever, seldom or ever. Unidiomatic expressions for *seldom if ever, hardly ever.*

Should of. Substandard corruption of *should have.*

Show. Colloquial for *play, opera, motion picture.*

Show up. Colloquial in the sense of "expose," "prove superior to."

> STANDARD   The women were superior to (*not* showed up) the men.

Sight. Colloquial for *a great deal.*

> STANDARD   "He left a great deal (*not* a sight) of money."

Sit, set. Do not confuse. See 7a, Exercise 1.

So. An overworked word. Do not overwork *so* to join co-ordinate clauses.

> COLLOQUIAL   The work had tired him, so he did not begin his journey the next day.
> STANDARD   Since the work had tired him, he did not begin his journey the next day.

In clauses denoting purpose, *so that* is usually preferred to *so.*

> QUESTIONABLE   He came early so he might see a friend.
> BETTER   He came early so that he might see a friend.

Some. Slang when used as an intensive. "He is making an excellent (*not* some) race."

Someone, anyone. See **Anyone, everyone, someone.**

Someplace. Colloquial for *somewhere.*

Somewheres. Dialectal for *somewhere.*

Sort. See **Kind, sort.**

Sort of. See **Kind of, sort of.**

Sort of a. See **Kind of a, sort of a.**

Strata. Plural of *stratum.* See **Data, strata, phenomena.**

Such. Note carefully the use of *such* in the dictionary. When *such* is followed by a relative clause, the proper relative is *as.* "I shall give such aid as I think best." When *such* is completed by a result clause, it should be followed by *that.* "There was such a rain that we could not drive." Avoid the weak and vague use of *such.* "We have had a good (*not* such a good) time."

Such, same, said. See **Same, said, such.**

Suit, suite. *Suit* may be either a verb or a noun. "*Suit* yourself in getting a *suit* of clothes. ' *Suite* is used only as a noun to refer to a group of attendants ("a prince with his *suite*") or to related rooms, etc. ("a *suite* of rooms").

Sure. Colloquial for *surely, certainly.*

STANDARD This is certainly (*not* sure) a quiet place.

Sure and. See **Try and.**

Suspicion. Dialectal when used as a verb in place of *suspect.*

DIALECTAL I did not suspicion anything.
STANDARD I did not suspect anything.

Swell. The adjective is slang for *excellent, first-rate.*

STANDARD Our last symphony concert was first-rate (*not* swell).

Take and. Dialectal or substandard.

STANDARD He knocked (*not* took and knocked) the ball over the base line.

Take stock in. See **Bank on, take stock in.**

Tasty. Colloquial for *savory* or *tasteful.*

Teach. See **Learn, teach.**

Terrible, terribly. Colloquial for *extremely bad.*

Than, then. Do not confuse the conjunction *than* ("older *than* I am") with the adverb of time *then* ("*then* and now").

That. Used colloquially as an adverb.

COLLOQUIAL I can approach only that near.
STANDARD I can approach only so near.

Their, there, they're. Do not confuse. *Their* is the pronoun ("*their* house"), *there* is the adverb ("he lives *there*"), and *they're* is the abbreviation for *they are.*

These kind, these sort. See **Kind, sort.**

This here, that there, these here, them there. Substandard expressions. Use *this, that, these, those.*

To, too, two. Distinguish the preposition *to* ("*to* the store") from the adverb *too* ("*too* cold") and the numeral *two* ("*two* apples").

Try and, sure and. Colloquial for *try to, sure to.*

STANDARD Try to (*not* and) calm yourself. Be sure to (*not* and) come early.

Ugly. Colloquial for *ill-tempered.*

    STANDARD   He was never in an ill-tempered (*not* ugly) mood

Un-, in-. Do not confuse. The prefix *un-* (from AS. *un-*, not) is used regularly with words derived from Anglo-Saxon (*undo, untie*); *in-* (from L. *in-*, not) is used with either Anglo-Saxon or Latin derivatives. (But distinguish *in-*, not, from the other Latin prefix *in-*, in or into, as in *inbreed, induct.*)

United States. When used as a noun, always *the United States*, with the article.

Used to could. Substandard or facetious for *used to be able.*

Very. Some careful writers avoid using *very* to modify a past participle that has not yet established itself as an adjective. They insert some appropriate adverb—such as *much, greatly, deeply* —between *very* and the past participle.

    QUESTIONABLE   His singing was very appreciated.
    BETTER   His singing was very greatly appreciated.

Wait on. Means *to attend, to serve.* Colloquial for *wait for.*

    STANDARD   I waited for (*not* waited on) him to begin.

Want. Cannot take a *that* clause as its object.

    SUBSTANDARD   I want that he should have a chance.
    STANDARD   I want him to have a chance.

Want in, out, down, up, off, through. Colloquial or dialectal for *want to come in* or *get in, out, down, up, off, through.*

Ways. Colloquial for *distance.*

    STANDARD   A long distance (*not* ways).

Where. Improperly used for *that.*

    POOR   I saw in the newspaper where the strike had been settled.
    BETTER   I saw in the newspaper that the strike had been settled.

Where at. Redundant.

    REDUNDANT   Where is she at?
    STANDARD   Where is she?

Which, who. Use *who* or *that* instead of *which* or *what* to refer to persons. "Mr. Jones was the man who (*not* which) helped me."

While. Do not overuse as a substitute for *and* or *but*. The conjunction *while* usually refers to time.

Who, which. See **Which, who.**

Worst way. Colloquial or dialectal for *very much.*

Would of. Substandard corruption of *would have.*

Would rather. See **Had better, had rather, would rather.**

You-all. A Southern colloquialism for *you* (plural).

You was. Substandard for *you were.*

Yourself, myself, himself. See **Myself, himself, yourself.**

Exactness

Idiom; Freshness

20

Select words that are exact, idiomatic, and fresh.

A word is exact when it expresses the precise idea or conveys the emotional suggestion intended by the writer. By this definition the measures of a right word will be the purpose of the writer, the subject he has selected, and his attitude toward his subject and his readers.

You need not have a remarkably large vocabulary to choose the right word. In fact, as shown by the example below, a professional writer often uses short, familiar words (especially nouns and action verbs) effectively.

> I saw her sitting at her desk, taking the rubber band off the roll-call cards, running it back upon the fingers of her right hand, and surveying us all separately with quick little henlike turns of her head. . . . She was forever climbing up the margins of books and crawling between their lines, hunting for the little gold of phrase, making marks with a pencil.
>
> —JAMES THURBER[1]

You, also, can make effective use of the vocabulary you have. Of course, as you gain experience in writing and reading, you will become increasingly aware of the need to add new words, both short and long, to your vocabulary. When you discover a valuable new word, make it your

[1] From "Here Lies Miss Groby" by James Thurber, reprinted from the *New Yorker*, March 21, 1942, by permission of the *New Yorker*.

own by mastering its spelling, its meaning, and its exact use.

20a

Consult a good dictionary for the exact word needed to express your idea.

(1) *Exact meaning.* Make sure that the dictionary gives the meaning you have in mind.

WRONG MEANING   Thank you for your *fulsome* praise. [Defined by the dictionary as "offensive, disgusting"]
EXACT   Thank you for your *generous* praise.

WRONG MEANING   He was too *abstemious* to admit his error. [Defined by the dictionary as "sparing in use of food and drink"]
EXACT   He was too *obstinate* to admit his error.

Caution: Do not confuse words that are similar in spelling or meaning. If necessary, review the list of similar words in Section 18, Exercise 2. See also **19i**.

WRONG   She seemed scarcely *conscience* of what she was doing.
RIGHT   She seemed scarcely *conscious* of what she was doing.

Be careful to use the right conjunction to express the exact relation between words, phrases, and clauses.

INEXACT   There were other candidates, *and* he was elected.
EXACT   There were other candidates, *but* he was elected. [*And* adds or continues; *but* contrasts.]

▶ EXERCISE 1   First, consult your dictionary in order to find the exact meaning of each word below. Then write a sentence using each word correctly.

1. contribute, attribute
2. repentance, remorse
3. explicit, implicit
4. utmost, uppermost
5. sophomore, sophomoric
6. that, where (as conjunctions)

7. fallacious, sophistical
8. accept, except
9. allusion, illusion
10. deprecate, depreciate
11. pliable, plastic
12. romp, play

(2) *Denotation and connotation.* Select the word with the denotation and connotation proper to the idea you wish to express.

The denotation of a word is what the word actually points to. (Thus *cow* stands for the milk-giving quadruped.) The connotation of a word is what the word suggests or implies. (Thus *cow*, when applied to a human being, suggests awkwardness.) Connotation includes the aura of emotion or association that surrounds some words. For example, *street, avenue, boulevard, lane, place, alley promenade, prospect* all denote much the same thing to a postman. But to various readers, and in various contexts, each word may have a special connotation. *Street* may suggest city pavements; *avenue,* a broad passageway bordered on each side by trees; *boulevard,* a broad highway; *lane,* a rustic walk; *place,* a secluded corner in a large city; *alley,* a city slum; *promenade,* a street for the display of elegance, fashion, and so forth; *prospect,* an avenue commanding a splendid view. Similarly, *highway road, route, drive, trail, concourse, path, turnpike*—all denote a passage for travel, but each word carries a variety of connotations.

A word may be right in one situation, wrong in another. *Female parent,* for instance, is a proper expression, but it would be very inappropriate to say "John wept for the death of his female parent." *Female parent* used in this sense is literally correct, but the connotation is wrong. The more appropriate word, *mother,* not only conveys the meaning denoted by *female parent;* it also conveys the reason why John wept. The first expression simply implies a biological relationship; the second is full of imaginative and emotional suggestions.

▶ EXERCISE 2   Distinguish between the denotation and the connotation of the following pairs of words. Use each appropriately in a sentence.

cabin—hut   foggy—murky   palace—mansion
dirt—soil   healthy—robust   steed—nag
fire—conflagration joy—felicity   wealth—opulence

▶ EXERCISE 3   Show why the italicized words in the following sentences, although literally correct, might be inappropriate because of their connotations.

1. Miss Kincaid's exotic costume won the admiration of everyone at the party, and even the hostess remarked several times how *outlandish* she looked.
2. For the *enlightenment* of the other ladies, Mrs. Bromley measured upon her *belly* the area of her recent operation.
3. Homer squeezed a quantity of *chlorophyllaceous extrusion* onto his toothbrush.
4. The army *scampered* home at full speed.
5. The librarian cataloged her books with *dauntless* energy.
6. We are building our new home on the rim of a most delightful little *gulch*.
7. Heifetz *tucked* his *fiddle* under his chin.

▶ EXERCISE 4   Explain the denotations and connotations of the italicized words in the following selections. Note how context in some instances intensifies the connotative power of a simple, everyday word; in other instances, it determines which of several differing connotations the word will carry. For each italicized word substitute a word of nearly the same denotation and consider its relative effectiveness in the sentence.

1. Its beauty was *paralyzing*—beyond all words, all experience, all *dream*.   —CONRAD AIKEN
2. He had a thin *vague* beard.   —MAX BEERBOHM

3. It was a chill, *rain-washed* afternoon.   —SAKI
4. He had *flaxen* hair, *weak* blue eyes, and the general demeanor of a saintly but timid *codfish*.

—P. G. WODEHOUSE

5. By *midnight*, the *peace* of *Christmas*, a special *intimate* kind of *wonder*, had *descended* upon them.

—PAUL HORGAN

6. Our schools are, in a sense, the *victims* of their own success. If they are not precisely *buried* beneath the *ruins* of their own triumph, they are *conditioned* and *committed* by their achievements.

—HENRY STEELE COMMAGER

7. A little man, dry like a chip and agile like a monkey, *clambered* up.   —CONRAD

8. A Poor *Relation* is the most *irrelevant* thing in Nature, a piece of *impertinent correspondency*, an odious *approximation*.   —LAMB

9. But in a larger sense we cannot *dedicate*, we cannot *consecrate*, we cannot *hallow* this ground. —LINCOLN

10. A *desperate twist* of the wheel, a *lurch* to first one side and then the other, and then the *stone wall* of the high-banked curve leaps at him with all the speed and *terrible malignity* of an animal of prey and in one awful, tearing, crash *bludgeons* him into *oblivion*.

—PAUL GALLICO

(3) **Concreteness. Select the specific word instead of the vague word.**

All writers must sometimes use abstract words, like *wisdom* or *integrity*, and occasionally resort to generalizations, like "Men through the ages have sought freedom from tyranny." These abstractions and generalizations are vital to communication of ideas and theories. To be effective, however, the use of abstract words must be based upon clearly understood and well-thought-out ideas. Professional writers usually have little difficulty handling abstractions. But inexperienced writers tend to bog down in numerous vague generalities; content becomes drab, lifeless, because of the scarcity of interesting, specific words. Avoid this pitfall by being as specific as you can. For example, instead of writing *went* consider the possibility of *rode, walked, trudged, slouched, hobbled, sprinted.* When you are tempted to say a *fine* young man, ask yourself whether *brave, daring, vigorous, energetic, spirited,* or *loyal* would not be more appropriate.

The test for the specific word is contained in six words —*who, what, where, when, how, why.* Notice how the following sentences are improved by asking the questions Who? What? Where? When? How? or Why? about one or more elements in the sentence.

VAGUE The Dean spoke about student life and that sort of thing. [*Who* spoke about *what?*]

SPECIFIC Dean Jones spoke about the social advantages of the student union.

VAGUE My brother is going away to have a good time. [*Where* is he going? *When* is he going? *How* will he have a good time?]

SPECIFIC Next Sunday my brother is going to Gatlinburg in the Smoky Mountains, where he plans to fish and hunt for a few weeks.

VAGUE All the columnists are commenting on the high cost of living. [*Who* are commenting? *Where* did comment appear?]

SPECIFIC In the July 12 issue of the New York *Herald Tribune,* Walter Lippmann, George Sokolsky, and Robert Ruark discussed the recent advance in food prices.

VAGUE The Army team finally advanced the ball. [*How* did they do it?]

SPECIFIC Adams, the Army quarterback, received the ball from center Jim Hawkins, retreated to his ten-yard line, and threw a pass to left-end Smith, who was tackled on the Army thirty-five-yard line.

VAGUE   I think the speech was biased. [*Why?*]
SPECIFIC   Mr. Jones began his speech with no attempt to support
his statement that the policies of Governor Lacy were
a "total denial of the American way of life."

▶ EXERCISE 5   Make a list of specific words which might
be appropriately substituted for each of the following:
(1) *move*, (2) *take*, (3) *say*, (4) *criminal*, (5) *pretty*, (6) *great*,
(7) *sad*, (8) *run*, (9) *nice*, (10) *get*.

EXAMPLE   *eat:* munch, nibble, mince, gnaw, gobble, bolt, gulp

▶ EXERCISE 6   Substitute specific or emphatic words for
general words in the sentences below.

1. The officer made a bad mistake.
2. My father looked at the report.
3. The author's criticism of Blake's work is very good.
4. The journey was made to obtain information concerning various aspects of the North American Indians.
5. It is my chief desire to like all my classes.

(4) *Vividness.* Use figurative language whenever needed to
create vividly the required imaginative or emotional
impression.

A figure of speech is the use of a word in an imaginative
rather than in a literal sense. The two chief figures of
speech are the simile and the metaphor. A *simile* is an
explicit comparison between two things of a different kind
or quality, usually introduced by *like* or *as:* "He sprang
on the foe like a lion." A *metaphor* is an implied comparison: "He was a lion in the fight." (See sentences 4, 6, 7,
and 10, in Exercise 4 above, for other examples of simile
and metaphor.)

Other figures of speech are personification, metonymy,
synecdoche, litotes, and hyperbole. To say that our college
is an alma mater (fostering mother) is to *personify* an institution. In the words of *The American College Dictionary,*

we often use "the name of one thing for that of another to which it has some logical relation" (*metonymy*), such as *scepter* for *sovereignty*. *Synecdoche*, which is similar to metonymy, puts a part for the whole or the whole for a part, as *fifty head* for *fifty cattle*. *Litotes* is the name for understatement, as in the remark, "Picasso is not a bad painter." *Hyperbole* is deliberate overstatement or fanciful exaggeration: "The waves were mountains high."

A false sense of simplicity still blinds many contemporary writers to the importance of figurative language in everyday communication. Metaphors and similes are not, as is commonly supposed, merely the ornaments of poetry and old-fashioned oratory. They are essential to certain kinds of physical description and to the expression of feelings and states of mind. When a husband slumps into his chair after a hard day's work and says to his wife, "Thank goodness I'm out of that squirrel cage!" *squirrel cage* is not an ornamental word or an elegant variation. It is a very useful, although unoriginal, metaphor. His wife might respond with another figure of speech by saying, "I played bridge at the Women's Club. It was *suffocating*." Both figures, *squirrel cage* and *suffocating*, are more effective than the conventional terms *job* and *dull*. Both terms express exactly how the man and his wife felt. The husband's work was confining and active; the wife's bridge game was unbearably dull.

Metaphor and simile are especially valuable because they are concrete and tend to point up essential relationships that cannot otherwise be communicated. (For faulty metaphors see **23c**.)

▶ EXERCISE 7   Test the exactness and force of the metaphors and similes in the following sentences by attempting to state the same ideas literally.

1. Wobbling to my feet, I shuffle forward like a suspect in a police lineup.   —ATLANTIC MONTHLY

2. Now she acted all the while as if she were playing the title rôle at a funeral. —RING LARDNER

3. Man is a wild beast, carnivorous by nature, and delighting in blood. —TAINE

4. The prince became flame to refute her. —HENRY JAMES

5. His face was like a human skull, a death's-head spouting blood. —HAZLITT

6. The soul is placed in the body like a rough diamond and must be polished or the luster of it will never appear. —DEFOE

7. Napoleon was the French Revolution on horseback.

8. O full of scorpions is my mind, dear wife.

—SHAKESPEARE

9. She was as graceful as a sow on ice.

10. We are all afraid of truth: we keep a battalion of pet prejudices and precautions ready to throw into the argument as shock troops, rather than let our fortress of Truth be stormed. —CHRISTOPHER MORLEY

20b

Use the exact idiom demanded by English usage.

Idioms are short, homely, vigorous expressions that grow up with a language and are peculiar to it. Such idioms as *for many a year, to center around,* or *to strike a bargain* cannot be analyzed or justified grammatically; and yet usage has made them the very heart of the language, suitable for either formal or informal occasions. The unabridged dictionaries treat many idiomatic phrases. See, for instance, the idioms built around *go* and listed after this word in your dictionary. (Note that an idiom—like a word—may be classified as *standard, colloquial, dialectal,* or *slang.*) Writers should be careful to use the exact phrasing for each idiom, not some unidiomatic approximation.

Unidiomatic	Idiomatic
authority about	authority on
die with	die of
equally as bad	equally bad
in accordance to	in accordance with
in search for	in search of
independent from	independent of
prior than	prior to
seldom or ever	seldom if ever, seldom or never
superior than	superior to

► EXERCISE 8   In the following sentences make the idioms conform to standard English usage. If you are not sure whether a given phrase is a standard idiom, consult a good college dictionary. Write *C* after each sentence that needs no revision.

1. Your error is equally as bad as mine.
2. The steamer collided against the tug.
3. Mother is vexed at Robert.
4. The child was born in the city Miami.
5. Robert has gone in search for a secondhand car
6. I bought my car off of the man next door.
7. We plan on going to the seashore.
8. The boy soon became independent from his family
9. The small child was unequal for the task.
10. She was oblivious to the presence of her friend.
11. I am glad the ordeal is over with.
12. I was not to be taken in by such trickery
13. Mary seldom or ever misses a class.
14. The boy fell off of the pier.
15. I was sick of a cold.

► EXERCISE 9   Consult a good college dictionary to determine what prepositions are idiomatically used with *agree, charge, compare, consist, deal, differ,* and *part.* Use each of these verbs correctly in two sentences, each with a different preposition.

▶ EXERCISE 10   In a good college dictionary study the idiomatic phrases treated under *catch, put, set, tie,* and *win.* Select three different idioms formed with each verb, and illustrate each idiom in a sentence.

20c

Select fresh expressions instead of trite, worn-out ones.

Nearly all trite expressions were once striking and effective. *A bolt from the blue, acid test,* and *social whirl* are, in themselves, effective expressions. What you may not know is that excessive use has made them trite. They are now stock phrases in the language, automatic clichés that have lost their effectiveness. Good writers do not use trite, well-known phrases when fresh, original expressions are more effective. Compare the effectiveness of the following sentences.

TRITE   *It goes without saying* that we often feel *as helpless as a baby* when we try to *hitch our wagon to a star.*

ORIGINAL   When we reach out for the stars, our limitations become grotesquely apparent.   —ARTHUR KOESTLER

TRITE (AND GENERAL) I took the collie, which was *blind in one eye and could not see out of the other,* to chase rabbits in the upper fields, but its actions showed that it *did not have enough sense to come in out of the rain.*

ORIGINAL (AND SPECIFIC) I took the one-eyed collie to chase rabbits in the upper fields, but it barked at ducks and brought me a tramp's shoe from a hedge, and lay down with its tail wagging in a rabbit hole.   —DYLAN THOMAS

To avoid trite phrases you must be aware of current usage. Catch phrases and slogans pass quickly from ephemeral popularity into the Old Words' Home. Glittering political shibboleths like *grass roots, pulse of public opinion, forgotten man, the New Frontier,* are notoriously short-lived. Commercial advertising also bestows its *kiss of death* on an honorable phrase. When a mattress company bids you *sleep in peace* or promises a *midsummer night's dream* on their *airy fairy beds,* when blankets are publicized as *soft as down* or *gentle as a baby's breath,* mark the italicized words as trite expressions, for the time being at least.

Some expressions, however, survive the wear of repeated usage. Proverbs, epithets from great writers like Shakespeare, and quotations from the Bible will probably live until the English language dies out completely.

▶ EXERCISE 11   Construct sentences which contain acceptable substitutes for ten of the hackneyed expressions listed below. In your sentences include within brackets the hackneyed expressions you replace. Be careful not to replace one hackneyed expression with another.

Some Hackneyed Expressions

1. after all is said and done
2. agree to disagree
3. all work and no play
4. better late than never
5. cold as ice
6. easier said than done
7. green with envy
8. last but not least
9. white as a sheet
10. on the ball (on the beam)
11. bitter end
12. busy as a bee
13. by leaps and bounds
14. slow but sure
15. straight from the shoulder
16. sweat of his brow
17. this day and age
18. too funny for words
19. wee small hours
20. none the worse for wear

▶ EXERCISE 12   Bring to class a list of ten hackneyed expressions.

OTHER EXERCISES ON EXACTNESS

▶ EXERCISE 13   Construct sentences to illustrate one of the exact meanings of each of the following words:

latent	universal	dense	distinguish
opinion	judgment	conclusion	enchanting
aspire	equivocal	tense	handsome
affiliation	flexible	reflection	temper

▶ EXERCISE 14   Improve the following sentences by correcting errors in idiom and by introducing words that are exact and unhackneyed.

1. I shall neither go or send an explanation.
2. In accordance to your instructions, I bought the draperies off of your friend Jim.
3. I read a story where a poor man became a millionaire.
4. The poor man was in the depths of despair.
5. William would not except the appointment.
6. John could not leave without he finished his work.
7. Frank looked very funny when I told him that he had failed.
8. He made an illusion to his former position.

▶ EXERCISE 15   The following passage from G. K. Chesterton is an excellent example of precise writing. Study the italicized expressions first with the aid of a dictionary and then in the context of the sentence and the paragraph. Substitute a synonym for each italicized word and compare its effectiveness with that of the original.

If a *prosperous* modern man, with a high hat and a frock-coat, were to solemnly *pledge* himself before all his clerks and friends to count the leaves on every third tree in Holland Walk, to hop up to the City on one leg every Thursday, to repeat the whole of Mill's *Liberty* seventy-six times, to collect three hundred dandelions in fields belonging to any one of the name of Brown, to remain for thirty-one hours holding his left ear in his right hand, to sing the names of all his aunts in order of age on the top of an omnibus, or make any such unusual undertaking, we should immediately *conclude* that the man was mad, or as it is sometimes expressed, was "an artist in life." Yet these *vows* are not more extraordinary than the vows which in the Middle Ages and in similar periods were made, not by *fanatics* merely, but by the greatest figures in civic and national civilization—by kings, judges, poets, and priests. One man swore to chain two mountains together, and the great chain hung there, it was said, for ages as a monument of that *mystical folly*. Another swore that he would find his way to Jerusalem with a patch over his eyes, and died looking for it. It is not easy to see that these two *exploits*, judged from a *strictly rational standpoint*, are any saner than the acts above suggested. A mountain is commonly a stationary and reliable object which it is not necessary to chain up at night like a dog. And it is not easy at first sight to see that a man pays a very high compliment to the Holy City by setting out for it under conditions which render it *to the last degree improbable* that he will ever get there.[2]

▶ EXERCISE 16   Follow directions for Exercise 15.

On a summer morning, in the *legendary* Russia of my boyhood, my first glance upon awakening was for the *chink* between the shutters. If it disclosed a *watery pallor*, one had better not open the shutters at all, and so be spared the sight of a sullen day sitting for its picture in a puddle. How *resentfully* one would *deduce*, from a line of dull light, the *leaden* sky, the *sodden* sand, the *gruel-like mess* of broken brown blossoms under the lilacs—and that flat, *fallow* leaf (the first casualty of the season) *pasted upon* a wet garden bench!

[2] From "A Defence of Rash Vows" by G. K. Chesterton, reprinted by permission of J. M. Dent & Sons, Ltd.

But if the chink was a long *glint* of dewy brilliancy, then I made haste to have the window yield its treasure. With one blow, the room would be *cleft* into light and shade. The foliage of birches moving in the sun had the *translucent* green tone of grapes, and in contrast to this there was the *dark velvet* of fir trees against a blue of extraordinary intensity, the like of which I rediscovered only many years later, in the *montane* zone of Colorado.[3]

▶ EXERCISE 17   Analyze one (or more) of the model paragraphs from Section 31 for choice of words.

[3] From "Butterflies" by Vladimir Nabokov, reprinted from *Speak. Memory* by permission of the *New Yorker* and the author.

Wordiness and Useless Repetition

21

Avoid wordiness. Repeat a word or phrase only when it is needed to gain force or clearness.

Wordiness is an offense against exact usage. The exact word or expression says all that is necessary (see Section 20), neither too little (see Section 22) nor too much. We say too much:

a. When we use words or phrases that add nothing to the meaning.
b. When we use an unnecessarily elaborate sentence structure.
c. When we repeat words and phrases carelessly.

21a

Omit words or phrases that add nothing to the meaning.[1]

Note how the following sentences are improved by the omission of the bracketed words.

1. [It was] in 1792 [that] the cornerstone of the White House was laid.
2. [Architect] James Hoban, the designer of the White House, was a native of Dublin.

---

[1] Bureaucratic jargon, called "gobbledygook," is often extremely wordy. See the example on page 205.

3. The [architectural] design of the White House is basically [the same as] that of the Duke of Leinster's palace in Dublin.

4. The White House is [such] an impressive building, and [so] much in the spirit of its century.

5. The [usual] consensus [of the majority] is that George Washington did not cut down the cherry tree.

6. Thomas Jefferson was more democratic [to a greater degree] than most of his contemporaries.

7. When Andrew Jackson became President of the United States, the banks were close to [the point of] bankruptcy.

8. [The reason why] we honor Lincoln [is] because he saved the Union.

9. John Adams was very different [in various ways] from his predecessors.

10. The Federalist party was soon connected [up] with the new Republican movement.

SOME WORDY PHRASES

1. As a [usual] rule
2. circulated [around]
3. co-operate [together]
4. Halloween [evening]
5. [important] essentials
6. [joint] partnership
7. where . . . [at]
8. large [in size]
9. yellow [in color]
10. eleven [in number]
11. round [in shape]
12. modern colleges [of today]
13. total effect [of all this]
14. at 10 P.M. [in the evening]

Note: Unless you are repeating intentionally for emphasis, be careful not to say the same thing twice in slightly different words.

EXAMPLE   Julia delights in giving parties[; entertaining guests is a real pleasure for her].

▶ EXERCISE 1   Strike out unnecessary words from the following sentences. Write *C* after each sentence that needs no revision.

1. In this day and time, it is difficult to find in the field of science a chemist who shows as much promise for the future as Joseph Blake shows.

2. On our list are the names of many wealthy and influential citizens.
3. The marble columns were gray in color.
4. Mr. McConn divides into three groups, or classes, the students of today who go to modern colleges.
5. It was during the Renaissance that a very large number of words, many of them terms of scholarship, were then taken from the Latin.
6. My chief aim is to make life easier for the farmer.
7. After the play was over with, we walked home together.
8. I wish to refer you back to the first page.
9. We pondered in our minds how we might descend down to the bottom of the canyon.
10. In the decade from 1950 to 1960, enrollments at universities doubled; in 1960 there were twice as many students as in 1950.

21b

If necessary, revise the structure of the sentence to avoid wordiness.

Caution: In order to understand **21b** you may need to review Section **1, Sentence Sense**, especially pages 13–21.

An idea may be expressed in a sentence, a clause, a phrase, or a word. Sometimes we waste many words in trying to make an idea clear. Note in the following series of examples how the fundamental idea (printed in italics) becomes successively sharper as the expression grows less wordy.

> *The mist hung like a veil.* It obscured the top of the mountain. [Full sentences used to express the idea]
> The mist *hung like a veil* and obscured the top of the mountain. [Part of a compound predicate]
> The mist, *which hung like a veil*, obscured the top of the mountain. [Subordinate clause]

The mist, *hanging like a veil,* obscured the top of the mountain. [Participial phrase]

The mist, *like a veil,* obscured the top of the mountain. [Prepositional phrase]

The mist *veiled* the top of the mountain. [Word]

All of these sentences are acceptable, but they are not equally effective. Although any one of them may, at times, meet the special needs of the writer, the least wordy will normally be the most effective.

Practice reducing sentences to the simplest and shortest form, as in the following examples:

WORDY Another thing is good health. It is one of our great blessings. It may be had through proper diet and exercise. Rest is also desirable. [Four simple sentences—25 words]

BETTER The great blessing of good health may be had through proper diet, exercise, and rest. [Reduced to one simple sentence—15 words]

WORDY A new addition has been built at the side of the house, and this addition has been developed into a library. [Compound sentence—21 words]

BETTER An addition, built at the side of the house, has been developed into a library. [Reduced to a simple sentence containing a participial phrase—15 words]

WORDY When the Indians made tools, they used flint and bone. [Complex sentence—10 words]

BETTER The Indians made tools of flint and bone. [Reduced to a simple sentence—8 words]

WORDY There were six men who volunteered. [Complex sentence—6 words]

BETTER Six men volunteered. [Reduced to a simple sentence—3 words]

▶ EXERCISE 2 Revise the structure of the following sentences to correct wordiness.

1. My uncle was a tall man. He had a long nose. Over his right eye he had a deep scar.

2. If any workers were disgruntled, they made their complaints to the man who was in charge as manager.
3. Personally I believe it was the Spaniards rather than the Indians who first brought horses and ponies to America.
4. The grass was like a carpet. It covered the whole lawn. The color of the grass was a deep blue.
5. When anyone wants to start a garden, it is best to begin in the early part of the spring of the year.
6. Near the center of the campus of our university a new building has been erected, and it is constructed of red brick.

21c

Avoid careless or needless repetition of a word or phrase.

Use repetition only to attain greater clearness (see **22b, 22c, 26b, 31b(3)**) or emphasis (see **29e**).

CARELESS   Since the committee has already made three general *reports*, only the *report* dealing with promotions will be *reported* on today.

BETTER   Since the committee has already made three general reports, it will submit today only its recommendations on promotions.

CARELESS   It is *impossible* to ask me to do the *impossible*.
BETTER   You cannot expect me to do the impossible.

Use a pronoun instead of needlessly repeating a noun. Several pronouns in succession, even in successive sentences, may refer to the same antecedent noun, so long as the reference remains clear.

NEEDLESS REPETITION   The upper-middlebrow consumer takes his culture seriously, as seriously as his job allows, for *the consumer* is gainfully employed. In *the consumer's* leisure hours he reads Toynbee or Osbert Sitwell's serialized memoirs. *The upper-middlebrow consumer* goes to museum openings and to the theater, and *the consumer* keeps up on the foreign films.

BETTER   The upper-middlebrow consumer takes his culture seriously, as seriously as his job allows, for he is gainfully employed. In his leisure hours he reads Toynbee or Osbert Sitwell's serialized memoirs. He goes to museum openings and to the theater and he keeps up on the foreign films.

—RUSSELL LYNES

▶ EXERCISE 3   Revise the following sentences to avoid careless repetition.

1. In 1923 Ruth batted .393, and he batted .378 the next year.
2. While driving, a good driver always takes care to obey the driving laws of the state he is driving through.
3. The practice of helping one's neighbors for the enjoyment of it is a very common practice.
4. In the last act of the play we find the explanation of the title of the play.
5. Early in the morning we set out for Jones Beach so that we could enjoy all the pleasures that that great playground affords.

▶ EXERCISE 4   Make needed revision of the following sentences to correct wordiness and useless repetition. Write C after each sentence that needs no revision.

1. The National Gallery of Art, which is in Washington, D.C., and which contains the Mellon, Kress, and Widener collections of paintings and sculpture, is one of the largest marble structures in the entire world.
2. The reason why he went to Heidelberg College was because it was located in his home town of Tiffin, in the state of Ohio.
3. I wanted to visit the Sequoia National Park last summer, but I did not have the money required for such a long trip to California.
4. The radio announcer repeatedly kept saying, "Buy Peterson's Perfect Prawns," over and over and over again.

5. There were fifty people in the hospital ward who were among those who received great benefit from the new drug.
6. The reason that the National League has won so many All-Star games from the American League recently is due largely to the fact that the National League has had the larger number of home-run hitters and long-ball hitters.
7. The Finnish people, who are intensely independent by nature, always resist any attack upon the independence of their nation.
8. I had an advantage over the other contestants because of the fact that I had just looked up the word myself in a dictionary.
9. Just when, if at all, the Vikings came to America has not been determined and is unknown to us.
10. The redevelopment of downtown Central City will be under the supervision of a committee. This committee will be bipartisan politically. The project will cost almost $50,000,000.
11. The problem of charting the 3,200 miles of the Amazon is a difficult problem indeed.
12. He found the problem of discovering the legal status of the migrant workers an almost insoluble problem.
13. Are you going to go to class tomorrow?
14. In order that a man may apply to become a citizen of the United States he must make out an application stating his intention to become a citizen.

▶ EXERCISE 5   Rewrite the following passage to eliminate wordiness and useless repetition.

1. Samuel Clemens (Mark Twain) was born in 1835 at Florida, County of Monroe, State of Missouri; but while he was still quite young, his family moved to Hannibal, a small Mississippi River town, where Samuel as a boy spent the days of his youth, and he grew up to young manhood

there.   2. In 1853 Samuel Clemens left this small Missis sippi River town of Hannibal to see something of the world.   3. In his itinerant wandering during the next four years which followed, Clemens worked at the printing trade in printing shops of various cities in the East and Middle West from the Mississippi to the Atlantic seaboard. 4. In Cincinnati, Ohio, in the year of 1857 Clemens took passage on a river steamboat bound down the river for New Orleans, Louisiana.   5. On this trip down the river Clemens met the pilot who steered the boat, named Mr. Horace Bixby, who agreed for the sum of five hundred dollars in money to teach young Clemens (Mark Twain) the art of piloting boats up and down the river.   6. One may read of Mark Twain's experience as a cub pilot apprentice in his book which he wrote about it and called *Life on the Mississippi.*

Omission of Necessary Words

22

Do not omit a word or phrase necessary to the meaning of the sentence.

Most faulty omissions in student writing may be traced to carelessness. To avoid such errors, proofread all compositions before submitting them to your instructor.

EXAMPLES   We have learned the importance ∧ using perfume. [Careless omission of the preposition *of*]

John had been there only ∧ moment ago. [Careless omission of the article *a*]

I ∧ been working at a service station on Saturdays. [Careless omission of the auxiliary verb *have*]

22a

Do not omit an article, a pronoun, a conjunction, or a preposition that is necessary to make your meaning clear.

(1) Omitted article or pronoun

RIGHT   A friend and helper stood at his side; *or,* His friend and helper stood at his side. [The friend and helper are the same person.]

RIGHT   A friend and *a* helper stood at his side; *or,* His friend and *his* helper stood at his side. [To show that the friend and the helper are different persons, the article *a* or the pronoun *his* must be repeated.]

(2) Omitted conjunction

CONFUSING They noticed the young men who made up the crew were eager to start. [*Young men* can be momentarily mistaken for the object of *noticed*.]

BETTER They noticed *that* the young men who made up the crew were eager to start.

Note: The conjunction *that* is frequently omitted as an introduction to clauses when the omission is not confusing.

EXAMPLE He said he would go.

(3) Omitted preposition

AWKWARD Mardi Gras he went to New Orleans.

BETTER *For* Mardi Gras he went to New Orleans.

Note: Some idiomatic phrases indicating time or place regularly omit the preposition.

EXAMPLES *Next summer* he will go to camp. They arrived *last week*. He will come *home*.

22b

Do not omit a necessary verb or a necessary auxiliary.

AWKWARD The play is good and the characters interesting. [Singular *is* may be used with singular *play* but not with plural *characters*.]

BETTER The play is good and the characters *are* interesting. [The correct verb is supplied for *characters*.]

AWKWARD He never has and never will be given proper recognition. [*Be* is the correct auxiliary for *will* but not for *has*.]

BETTER He never has *been* given proper recognition, and he never will be. [The correct auxiliary is supplied for *has*.]

22c

Do not omit words necessary to complete comparisons (or other constructions).

CONFUSING The equipment of a soldier is heavier than a sailor. [Did the soldier's equipment weigh more than an individual sailor?]

CLEAR The equipment of a soldier is heavier than *that* of a sailor.

CLEAR A soldier's equipment is heavier than a sailor's.

CONFUSING The scenery here is as beautiful as any other place. ["Scenery" cannot be compared with "place."]

CLEAR The scenery here is as beautiful as *it is at* any other place.

CONFUSING Mr. Carter paid me more than Jim.

CLEAR Mr. Carter paid me more than *he paid* Jim; *or* Mr. Carter paid me more than Jim *did*.

INCOMPLETE He is as old, if not older, than his cousin.

IMPROVED He is as old *as his cousin*, if not older.

Note: Incomplete comparisons are a particularly common fault in advertising copy.

INCOMPLETE This filter tip screens out 50% more harmful tar products. [What two things are being compared?]

COMPLETE This filter tip screens out 50% more harmful tar products than a tea strainer would. *Or:* This filter tip screens out 50% more harmful tar products than it does bugs and flies.

[Probably no advertiser would make either of these statements, but at least they do contain some definite information—which the incomplete comparison does not.]

INCOMPLETE You will agree that Crumpet Creek Dairy products are definitely better. [Better than what? Ditch water?]

COMPLETE You will agree that Crumpet Creek Dairy products are definitely better than ever before. *Or even:* You will agree that Crumpet Creek Dairy products are definitely better than ditch water.

INCOMPLETE   That inferior detergent is as expensive. [As expensive as what?]

COMPLETE   That inferior detergent is as expensive as a fine soap.

Note: Once a frame of reference has been established, an intelligible comparison may be made without explicit mention of the second term of the comparison.

CLEAR   It is not to be inferred that of this poetical vigor Pope had only a little, because Dryden had more [*than Pope had* is clearly understood without its being stated]; for every other writer since Milton must give place to Pope; and even of Dryden it must be said, that, if he has brighter paragraphs [*than Pope has* again is clearly enough understood], he has not better poems. . . . If the flights of Dryden . . . are higher, Pope continues longer on the wing. If of Dryden's fire the blaze is brighter, of Pope's the heat is more regular and constant.   —SAMUEL JOHNSON

Standard writing avoids such intensives as *so, such,* and *too* without the completing clause.

COLLOQUIAL   I was so tired. She had such beautiful eyes. He was not too much interested in the lecture.

STANDARD   I was so tired that I could not sleep. *Or:* I was extremely tired. She has such beautiful eyes that everyone admires them. He was not especially interested in the lecture.

▶ EXERCISE 1   Supply all words that are needed to make the meaning of the following sentences clear and unambiguous. Write *C* after each sentence that needs no revision.

1. Our new Hampton shirts last much longer.
2. Jim's wife and mother stood beside him at the trial.
3. You are as good as, if not better than, anyone else.
4. Jack's novel is excellent and his poems inspired.
5. He told of the days he had neither food nor shelter.
6. William is so different from the others.
7. The lawyer had to prove whatever the witness said was false.

8. The spillway allows the water at the dam be kept at the same level.
9. He was so manly and so brave although only six years old.
10. I protested that I could not come.
11. I helped him more than James.
12. He never has and never will enjoy fishing.
13. Will you return the winter quarter?
14. The author writes more about the Hardy country than he does about Hardy.
15. The Rocky Mountains are just as beautiful.

▶ EXERCISE 2   Follow the directions for Exercise 1.

1. If Jack is in a profession he is not trained, he will not succeed.
2. Americans usually prefer beef.
3. He owned a very smart, if not the smartest, pony I ever saw.
4. She was so excited.
5. The plains are mostly given over to cattle raising but not farming.
6. The park is very attractive and enjoyed by all the children.
7. Yesterday the pilot and captain went ashore.
8. I always have and always will live in Chicago.
9. She was not too much interested in mathematics.
10. Chifford cars are longer, faster, more economical to operate.
11. Thanksgiving I went home.
12. The club was organized my first year in college.
13. The work of the farmer requires longer hours than a plumber.
14. William was more prejudiced against Henry than James.
15. In our state the winter is as mild as Louisiana.
16. Some people like cars with gear shifts much better.

EFFECTIVE SENTENCES

Unity and
Logical Thinking

The fundamental qualities of an effective sentence are unity, coherence, emphasis, and variety. Unity and coherence help to make a sentence logical and clear. Emphasis makes it forceful. Variety lends interest. Usually every good sentence contains all these equally necessary qualities of style. But for the purpose of study we may consider each quality separately. In this section and the next we shall present some of the problems of unity.

23

Bring into the sentence only related ideas and pertinent details. Complete each thought logically.

A sentence is unified when all its parts contribute to one clear idea or impression. In such a sentence, thought and expression are one, parts unite to form a perfect whole, and we say: "Here it is. We cannot alter a clause, a phrase, or even a word without disturbing the clarity of thought or the focus of the impression." Such a sentence is like a pane of clearest glass; we look through it, unconscious of its existence. But when an idea is not clear the sentence becomes like a wall that stands between us and what the writer is trying to say.

A sentence lacks unity:

   a. When it combines unrelated ideas.
   b. When it has excessive detail.
   c. When it is mixed, obscure, or illogical.

23a

Unrelated ideas should be developed in separate sentences. (If the ideas are related, they should be expressed in such a way that the relationship is immediately clear to the reader.)

UNRELATED	Mr. Smith is my teacher and he has a large family.
IMPROVED	Mr. Smith is my teacher. He has a large family. [Ideas given equal importance]
IMPROVED	Mr. Smith, my teacher, has a large family. [Unity secured by subordination of one idea. See Section 24.]
UNRELATED	Ireland has a deep culture, but the country is out of the path of general travel. [Unity thwarted by a gap in the thought]
IMPROVED	Ireland has a deep culture, but this culture is insufficiently appreciated because the country is out of the path of general travel.

▶ EXERCISE 1   Rewrite the following sentences to point up the relationship between the ideas or to achieve unity in some other way.

1. The stocks continued to drop, and the war was not far off.
2. Lee fell back on Richmond, so that Stuart was forced to retreat.

3. Mollusks which yield pearls are widespread, and pearl fishing is carried on in many parts of the world.
4. The foreman, speaking in gruff tones and seldom smiling, wore a gray coat.
5. Birds migrate to the warmer countries in the fall and in summer get food by eating worms and insects which are a pest to the farmer.

23b

Excessive detail and clumsy, excessive subordination should not be allowed to obscure the central thought of the sentence.

Such detail, if important, should be developed in separate sentences; otherwise it should be omitted.

OVERLOADED   When I was only four years old, living in an old Colonial house, little of which remains today, I could already walk the two miles that separated the house from the railroad station.

BETTER   When I was only four years old, I could already walk the two miles between my house and the railway station. [If the writer considers other details important, he may write another sentence to include them: I was living in an old Colonial house, little of which remains today.]

OVERLOADED   In 1788, when Andrew Jackson, then a young man of twenty-one years who had been living in the Carolinas, still a virgin country, came into Tennessee, a turbulent place of unknown opportunities, to enforce the law as the new prosecuting attorney, he had the qualities in him which would make him equal to the task.

BETTER   In 1788, when Andrew Jackson came into Tennessee as the new prosecuting attorney, he had the necessary qualifications for the task.

OVERLOADED AND WORDY   I have never before known a man who was so ready to help a friend who had got into difficulties which pressed him so hard. [Avoid clumsy, overlapping sub-

ordination, the house-that-Jack-built construction: *who . . .
who*, etc.]

BETTER   I have never before known a man so ready to help a
friend in trouble.

► EXERCISE 2   Recast the following sentences to eliminate
excessive detail.

1. The boat, considered seaworthy ten years ago, but now
   in need of paint and repairs, as is so often true of things
   that should be discarded, moved out into the bay.
2. The captain asked for a volunteer, and the soldier
   picked up his pack, which weighed thirty pounds, and
   asked if he might go.
3. A course in business methods helps the young man to
   get a job in order that he may prove whether he is
   fitted for business and thus avoid postponing the test,
   as so many do, until it is too late.

Note: Length alone does not make a sentence ineffective.
Most good writers compose long sentences, sometimes of
paragraph length, without loss of unity. The use of parallel
structure, balance, rhythm, careful punctuation, well-
placed connectives can bind a sentence into perfect unity.
Observe the effective repetition (indicated by italics) in
Winston Churchill's famous sentence:

We shall go on to the end, *we shall fight* in France, *we shall
fight* on the seas and oceans, *we shall fight* with growing
confidence and growing strength in the air, *we shall defend*
our Island, whatever the cost may be, *we shall fight* on the
beaches, *we shall fight* on the landing grounds, *we shall fight*
in the fields and in the streets, *we shall fight* in the hills; *we
shall never surrender*, and even if, which I do not for a moment believe, this Island or a large part of it were subjugated
and starving, then our Empire beyond the seas, armed and
guarded by the British Fleet, *would carry on the struggle*,
until, in God's good time, the New World, with all its power

and might, steps forth to the rescue and the liberation of
the old.   —WINSTON CHURCHILL[1]

In the following sentence Henry James maintains unity
by balancing the "grand hotel" with the "small Swiss
pension." (Italics have been added.)

The shore of the lake presents an unbroken array of establish-
ments of this order, of every category, *from the "grand hotel"
of the newest fashion,* with a chalk-white front, a hundred
balconies, and a dozen flags flying from its roof, *to the small
Swiss pension of an elder day,* with its name inscribed in
German-looking lettering upon a pink or yellow wall and an
awkward summer-house in the angle of the garden.
                                            —HENRY JAMES[2]

23c

**Mixed, obscure, or illogical constructions should be
avoided.**

(1) **Do not mix figures of speech by changing too rapidly
from one to another.**

MIXED   This rebellion must be checked before it boils over.
         [Figure of spirited horse being reined in + figure of
         liquid becoming overheated]
BETTER   This rebellion must be checked before it gets out of con-
         trol (*or* runs away). [Figure of spirited horse carried
         throughout]

(2) **Do not mix constructions. Complete each construction
logically.**

MIXED   Because he was sick caused him to stay at home. [An
         adverb clause, a part of a complex sentence, is here
         mixed with the predicate of a simple sentence.]

[1] From *Their Finest Hour* by Winston Churchill. By permission of
Houghton Mifflin Company.
[2] From *Daisy Miller.*

CLEAR His sickness caused him to stay at home. [Simple sentence]

CLEAR Because he was sick he stayed at home. [Adverb clause retained; main clause added to complete the complex sentence]

Note: A definition should be expressed logically. It should tell *what* the thing defined is, not when it is or where it is.

MIXED A sonnet *is when* a poem has fourteen lines. [Avoid the *is when* or *is where* construction. A *when* clause, used as an adverb, cannot be substituted for a noun.]

LOGICAL A sonnet is a poem of fourteen lines.

MIXED To banish *is where* a person is driven out of his country. [Adverb clause misused as a noun]

LOGICAL To banish a person is to drive him out of his country.

(3) **Make each part of the sentence agree logically with the other parts.**

Often a sentence which contains no grammatical error is nevertheless absurd because of failure in logical agreement.

ILLOGICAL Many of the men were refusing to re-enlist and were returning home to their family. [It is almost impossible to suppose an army in which *many of the men* share among them only one *family*.]

LOGICAL Many of the men were refusing to re-enlist and were returning home to their families. [This is a far more likely statement of what the men were actually doing.]

ILLOGICAL George is a better player than the others are. [There is no logical basis for comparison; although George is *a player*, the others are not *a player*, but *players*.]

BETTER George is a better player than any of the others.

▶ EXERCISE 3   In each sentence select the parenthetical word or phrase which logical expression of the thought requires and give reasons for your choice.

1. (A new wing was, New wings were) added to the building in 1955 and 1961.
2. Do you men realize that your (career depends, careers depend) upon the work you are doing now?
3. Their (temperament was, temperaments were) as nearly alike as any two men's could have been.
4. Every evening this week we have had (a fire, fires) in our fireplace.
5. Besides that, we have needed an extra blanket on (each bed, the beds).
6. The Empire State Building is taller than (any, any other) building in New York.
7. The Empire State Building is taller than (any, any other) building in New Orleans.
8. Tourists are not permitted to bring their (camera, cameras) inside the area.
9. Does each of them understand the nature of (his assignment, their assignments)?
10. You children may take off your (mask, masks) now and come into the dining room for refreshments.

(4) Do not use the double negative.

SUBSTANDARD   I don't want none.
STANDARD   I don't want any.

See **19i** under "But, only, hardly, scarcely."

23d

Caution: Do not make illogical, poorly reasoned statements.

One of the most important tests of good writing is the soundness of its reasoning. You should make sure that all your sentences are well thought out and contain no slips or weaknesses in your chain of reasoning. Be especially careful to avoid the common fallacies by observing the following principles of sound thinking:

(1) Be sure your generalizations are sufficiently supported.

FAULTY   None of the children in my family drink coffee; children do not like coffee. [The writer has jumped to a conclusion without finding a sufficient number of examples or instances to support his belief—*hasty generalization.*]

FAULTY   When an automobile accident occurs in this city, the police are never on hand. [Unless the writer has himself seen or read an authoritative account of every automobile accident in the city, he cannot possibly make this assertion—*overbroad generalization.* By avoiding such words as "never" and "always," the writer can generalize more safely.]

BETTER   When an automobile accident occurs in this city, the police are rarely on hand (or *often not on hand*).

(2) Be sure your evidence is objective and relevant to your assertion.

FAULTY   Henry is an honest boy; he will make a success of anything he tries. [Obviously, Henry's honesty cannot guarantee his success at a task for which he may be intellectually unsuited. The writer's inference does not follow from the evidence—*non sequitur* (it does not follow).]

FAULTY   Donald is an atheist and a profligate; his arguments against a sales tax are worthless. [The writer here tries to discredit Donald's ideas by attacking him as a man—*argumentum ad hominem.* Donald might be a dissolute man, however, and still have excellent views on economic problems such as the sales tax.]

FAULTY   Joseph Jones, our distinguished candidate for mayor, has been endorsed by Miss Leila Lovely, Hollywood's brightest star. [This fallacy is the opposite of the previous one. The writer is using Miss Lovely's prestige as an actress to enhance the political reputation of Joseph Jones. But what are Miss Lovely's qualifications to be considered an expert on politics?]

FAULTY   Whenever Jack Doe gets a job, someone in his family falls sick. He had better give up working. [The assumption here is that an event which follows another is caused by the preceding event—the *post hoc, ergo propter hoc* fallacy (after this, therefore because of this).]

▶ EXERCISE 4   Revise the following sentences as necessary to make them unified, logical, and clear.

1. Of course the other car was at fault: the driver was a woman.
2. I am certain that all Germans like opera; I have never met one who did not like it.
3. The average farm wage for the calendar year 1910 was $21.00, including board, a small sum indeed compared with the monthly wage of $144.00 in 1959, although prices have also gone up at the same time.
4. You can't do but one thing at a time, so buckle down and consider your job of studying as better than a wage earner.
5. After the first atomic bomb was exploded, it rained for a week in my home town, and yet the scientists maintain that atomic explosions do not affect the weather!
6. There were over 96,000,000 cattle in the United States in 1959 and a total population of about 179,000,000, with almost 7,400,000 farm workers.
7. Being prompt helped win Jones a raise, so he went to the ball game, but, because the grounds were wet, caused the game to be postponed and he went home to celebrate privately.
8. Whole wheat, which is especially nourishing, is being used more and more, especially in some parts of the country, by the leading bakeries to improve the texture and food content of the bread.
9. Jim was fighting a losing battle until his father bailed him out.

10. To barter is when one exchanges one commodity for another.

11. Florida is a place where many people go for the winter.

12. The Continental Divide is a watershed extending from Mexico to Canada which is created by the Rocky Mountain range, and east of the Divide water flows to the Gulf of Mexico, while west of the Divide it flows to the Pacific Ocean.

13. The United States government owns 412,000,000 acres of land in the various states which consists of national parks and forests as well as Indian reservations and military posts which are expanded by lease during periods of national emergency.

14. I ate shrimp last night, and therefore I am sick today.

15. I always buy these razor blades because all the baseball players use them.

▶ EXERCISE 5   Use the following unified and logical sentences as models for sentences of your own. Do not imitate slavishly. Aim to reproduce the design or structure of the model sentence, not to copy the details. Especially be careful to avoid repeating expressions no longer in common use.

1. MODEL SENTENCE   The human mind is capable of being excited without the application of gross and violent stimulants.
   —WORDSWORTH

   TOPIC   The human heart
   EXAMPLE   The human heart may be moved to deepest sympathy for human suffering without giving way to excessive sentimentality.

2. MODEL SENTENCE   It is a truth universally acknowledged that a single man in possession of a good fortune must be in want of a wife.   —JANE AUSTIN
   TOPIC   A poor widow

3. MODEL SENTENCE   He who would be a courtier under a king is almost certain to be a demagogue in a democracy.

—JAMES FENIMORE COOPER

TOPIC   A thief in low and high society

4. MODEL SENTENCE   I hate to see a load of bandboxes go down the street, and I hate to see a parcel of big words without anything in them.   —HAZLITT

TOPIC   The excessive use of cosmetics

5. MODEL SENTENCE   Character to a boy is a sealed book; for him a pirate is a beard, a pair of wide trousers, and a liberal complement of pistols.   —R. L. STEVENSON

TOPIC   Frugality to a spendthrift

Subordination

(An Aid to Unity)

24

Determine the most important idea of the sentence and express it in the main clause. Put lesser ideas in subordinate clauses, phrases, or words. Use co-ordination only for ideas of equal importance.

Note: If you cannot distinguish readily between phrases and clauses, between main clauses and subordinate clauses, review Section 1, **Sentence Sense**, especially **1d**, before you study **Subordination**.

The principle of subordination is of great importance in composition, since it is one of the best means of achieving sentence unity. The ability to discriminate between the main idea and the dependent idea is also a mark of maturity. As we develop the power of expression we discard *short, choppy sentences,* or a series of *brief main clauses connected by "and,"* in favor of the more precise complex sentence in which our ideas are properly subordinated.

A child will express himself somewhat like this:

I walked down the road. I saw a bird. It was in a tree. It was singing. [Short, choppy sentences—subordination lacking]

At a slightly older age the child might say:

I walked down the road, and I saw a bird, and it was in a tree, and it was singing. [*And*-sentence—subordination lacking]

A mature writer will express in the main clause of his sentence the idea he wishes to stress and will subordinate all other ideas by reducing them to a subordinate clause, a phrase, or a word.

> As I walked down the road [subordinate clause], I saw a bird [main clause] singing [word] in a tree [phrase].

If the singing of the bird is more important than the seeing of the bird, the sentence might read:

> A bird was singing in a tree as I walked down the road.

24a

In general a related series of short, choppy sentences should be combined into longer units in which the lesser ideas are properly subordinated.

CHOPPY   This is a wreck. It was formerly the stately Industrial Exhibition Hall. It is preserved deliberately as a reminder and symbol.

BETTER   This wreck, formerly the stately Industrial Exhibition Hall, is preserved deliberately as a reminder and symbol. —ROBERT TRUMBULL[1]

CHOPPY   Thousands of buildings met the same fate. This alone is now being preserved. It marks the center of the explosion. It is being preserved as a symbol. It symbolizes our wish that there be no more Hiroshimas.

BETTER   Of the thousands of buildings that met the same fate, this alone, marking the center of the explosion, is now being preserved to symbolize our wish that there be no more Hiroshimas.[2]

CHOPPY   He stood there in his buckskin clothes. One felt in him standards and loyalties. One also felt a code. This

---

[1] "Hiroshima—Ten Years After," New York *Times Magazine*, July 31, 1955, p. 5.

[2] *Ibid.* (From a bronze plaque at the entrance of the building.)

code is not easily put into words. But this code is instantly felt when two men who live by it come together by chance.

BETTER   As he stood there in his buckskin clothes, one felt in him standards, loyalties, a code which is not easily put into words, but which is instantly felt when two men who live by it come together by chance.

—WILLA CATHER

Caution: Avoid excessive or clumsy, overlapping subordination. See **23b.**

▶ EXERCISE 1   Combine the following short sentences into longer sentences in which ideas are properly subordinated.

1. The miller was a large man.   2. He weighed well over two hundred pounds.   3. He wore a red beard. 4. It was thick and broad and was shaped like a spade. 5. On his nose grew a wart.   6. Red bristles sprouted out of the wart.   7. This miller was a quarrelsome man. 8. He was proud of his bull-like strength.   9. He missed no chance to display it.   10. He especially liked to show off by tearing down doors.   11. He would jerk them off their hinges.   12. He could also butt them to pieces with his head.   13. Sometimes there was no door convenient. 14. Then he would get attention in other ways.   15. He was a loud-mouth.   16. He always had a story ready to tell.   17. His stories were ones he had picked up in barrooms.   18. Usually they were filthy.   19. It didn't matter that decent people were nearby.   20. He would tell his story anyhow.   21. He had to make a noisy display of himself in one way or another.   22. He never ran out of ways of doing it.   23. He might not be able to find a door to wreck.   24. People sometimes wouldn't listen to his stories.   25. He played a bagpipe.   26. His behavior had its reward.   27. It kept him from being a very well-liked man.

24b

Do not write *and, so,* or *but* sentences when one idea should be subordinated to another. Use co-ordination only for ideas of equal importance. (See also 30c.)

WEAK   The weather was hot and (*or* so) I stayed at home. [Two main clauses]

BETTER   Because the weather was hot [subordinate clause] I stayed at home.

ACCEPTABLE   The offer was tempting, but I did not accept it. [Co-ordination used to stress equally the offer and the refusal]

USUALLY BETTER   Although the offer was tempting, I did not accept it. [Stress on one of the two—the refusal]

INEFFECTIVE   North Dakotans are sturdy and industrious, and they are mostly Scandinavian and German stock, and they are working during this time of no immediate crisis on a promising plan to prevent future dust bowls.

BETTER   Sturdy and industrious, mostly of Scandinavian and German stock, North Dakotans are working during this time of no immediate crisis on a promising plan to prevent future dust bowls.   —TIME

INEFFECTIVE   I had always wanted to go to college, and I had always wished to become an engineer, and so I enrolled at the Carnegie Institute of Technology.

IMPROVED   Because I had always wanted to enter college and prepare myself to become an engineer, I enrolled at the Carnegie Institute of Technology.

IMPROVED   I enrolled at the Carnegie Institute of Technology to achieve my double purpose of attending college and becoming an engineer.

▶ EXERCISE 2   Revise the following sentences to subordinate the less important ideas.

1. I was daydreaming in biology class last Wednesday, and I did not pay any attention to the assignment, and so today I failed an important examination.
2. We had just reached the bend in the road on our way

home, and we saw a truckload of Boy Scouts crowded off the highway by an oncoming car.

3. First he selected a lancet and sterilized it, and then he gave his patient a local anesthetic and lanced the infected part.

4. Father Latour was at a friend's house, and he saw two fine horses, and he induced the owner to part with them.

5. I graduated from high school, and then I worked in a bank, and so I earned enough to go to college.

6. The president of the bank walked into his office promptly at nine, and just then he saw the morning paper, and the headlines startled him.

The conjunctive adverbs *however*, *therefore*, and *consequently* are often used in transitions when subordination would be preferable. Main clauses linked by these conjunctive adverbs can usually be combined and the proper relationship indicated by a subordinating conjunction. Subordinating conjunctions express such relationships as cause (*because, since*), concession (*although*), time (*after, before, since, whenever, while, until*), place (*where*), or condition (*if, unless*).

CO-ORDINATION   I became increasingly uneasy; however, I kept my seat.

SUBORDINATION   Although I became increasingly uneasy, I kept my seat. [Subordination is usually better.]

CO-ORDINATION   Fred knows almost nothing about farming; therefore I do not expect him to enjoy much success.

SUBORDINATION   Since Fred knows almost nothing about farming, I do not expect him to enjoy much success.

▶ EXERCISE 3   Write twelve sentences to illustrate the twelve subordinating conjunctions listed above. Let each conjunction introduce a subordinate clause in which you express an idea of less importance than that in the main clause.

24c

Do not place the main thought of the sentence in a subordinate clause (or construction).

FAULTY   When we have made a good soldier out of a rookie, he has learned how to march, use his weapons, and respond to commands.

BETTER   When a rookie has learned how to march, use his weapons, and respond to commands, we have made a good soldier out of him.

FAULTY   A cow kicked over a lantern, thus causing one of the world's great fires.

BETTER   A cow caused one of the world's great fires by kicking over a lantern.

FAULTY   I was asleep when the tornado struck.

BETTER   The tornado struck when I was asleep.

▶ EXERCISE 4   Revise the following sentences as necessary to give prominence to the main ideas and to subordinate less important ones.

1. The insects eat the plant off just below the soil, stopping all growth.
2. I was at a lecture when our house burned down.
3. The gasoline tank sprang a leak, when all hope for a record flight was abandoned.
4. The room was large. There was very little furniture in it. It was a lonesome place. I decided not to stay.
5. The sun was very hot, causing the men to stop work.
6. The automobile pulled up at the station. It was just noon. The train had already discharged its passengers.
7. Mary was hurrying to the library when she lost the key to her room.
8. Mary was returning home, and she found her lost key.
9. Your letter came this morning, and I was just getting ready to write you, and so you will get a very prompt reply.

10. Henry was still in high school and his father died, and so he did not go to college.
11. Throughout all the confusion the little boy had slept, and so he was unconscious of the worry and fear of those around him.
12. Fishing is an exacting sport. One must use the right hook. The bait is also important. The weather must be propitious.
13. One day I was musing on the pleasures of being idle when the thought struck me that complete idleness is hard work.
14. One should drive a stake into the ground by each plant, and then there will be no danger of the plant's growing sideways.
15. The tiny Forest Service plane in which I was riding reached the towering Douglas firs. These are in California's Lassen National Forest. Just then the plane dipped into a steep canyon.

▶ EXERCISE 5   Revise the following passage to achieve proper subordination.

1. I was walking down the street when I found a purse containing fifty dollars.   2. It was just noon.   3. Thousands of people were on the streets.   4. I could not find the owner.   5. I went into the neighboring stores, and I inquired of the shopkeepers whether anyone had lost the money, and I approached the policeman with the same question.   6. No one could say who had lost the money, and so I thought I was the rightful owner, having found the purse myself.   7. But my father did not approve my keeping the purse.   8. He asked me to advertise it.   9. He said I might use the daily paper.   10. Next day I ran an advertisement in the paper, and now a week has passed and I have had no answers, and so I think the money is really mine.

Coherence: Misplaced Parts; Dangling Modifiers

25

Avoid needless separation of related parts of the sentence. Avoid dangling modifiers.

The meaning of an English sentence depends largely on the position of its parts. Usually these parts—especially the words, phrases, and subordinate clauses serving as modifiers—can be placed in various positions; and they should be placed to give just the emphasis or meaning desired. Note how the meaning in the following sentences changes according to the position of the modifier *only:*

She said that she loved *only* him.
[She loved no one else.]
She said that *only* she loved him.
[No one else loved him.]
She said *only* that she loved him.
[She said nothing else.]
Only she said that she loved him.
[No one else said it.]

Normally the modifier should be placed as near the word modified as idiomatic English will permit.

Note: If you cannot distinguish readily the various modifiers and the parts of the sentence discussed in this chapter, review Section 1, especially 1d, and Section 4.

Misplaced Parts

25a
Avoid needless separation of related parts of the sentence.

(1) In standard written English, adverbs such as *almost, only, just, even, hardly, nearly,* or *merely* are regularly placed immediately before the words they modify.

In spoken English, which tends to place these adverbs before the verb, ambiguity can be prevented by stressing the word to be modified.

AMBIGUOUS IN WRITING	He is *just* asking for a trifle.
CLEAR	He is asking for *just* a trifle.
COLLOQUIAL	The convict *only* killed one policeman.
FORMAL	The convict killed *only* one policeman.

▶ EXERCISE 1   Place the adverbs in the following sentences immediately before the words they modify.

1. Some contemporary poets hardly show any interest in making their poems intelligible.
2. I only bet on the horse to take third place.
3. He took the penny home and polished it almost until it looked like new.
4. The man was only willing to sell a part of the farm.
5. He even works during his vacation.

(2) **Phrases should be placed near the words they modify.**

MISPLACED	The boy says that he means to leave the country *in the first stanza.*
CLEAR	The boy says *in the first stanza* that he means to leave the country.
MISPLACED	He played a great part in the war with Mexico *as a statesman.*
CLEAR	*As a statesman* he played a great part in the war with Mexico.

MISPLACED   Heated arguments had often occurred *over tech-nicalities in the middle of a game.*

CLEAR   Heated arguments *over technicalities* had often oc-curred *in the middle of a game.*

▶ EXERCISE 2   Recast the following sentences to correct undesirable separation of related parts. Explain exactly what ambiguity each separation causes in each sentence.

1. King Arthur decided to punish those who opposed him for very good reasons.
2. Romeo received word that Juliet was dead from an-other messenger.
3. The engineering work was a thing of beauty on all the large buildings.
4. He tells how Lincoln collected fees that his clients were reluctant to pay among other things.
5. My uncle wrote that he would arrive on Friday in his last letter.

(3) Clauses, especially relative clauses, should be placed near the words they modify. (See also 28a.)

AMBIGUOUS   I placed the chair in the corner of the room *which I had recently purchased.* [The relative clause seems to modify *room.*]

CLEAR   I placed in the corner of the room the chair *which I had recently purchased; or,* In the corner of the room I placed the chair *which I had recently purchased.*

AWKWARD   I saw the horse stop at the edge of the precipice *that had raced ahead.*

CLEAR   I saw the horse *that had raced ahead* stop at the edge of the precipice.

(4) Avoid "squinting" constructions—modifiers that may refer either to a preceding or to a following word.

SQUINTING   I agreed *on the next day* to help him.
CLEAR   I agreed to help him *on the next day.*
CLEAR   *On the next day,* I agreed to help him.

SQUINTING	The tug which was whistling *noisily* chugged up the river.
CLEAR	The whistling tug chugged *noisily* up the river.
CLEAR	The tug whistled *noisily* as it chugged up the river.

(5) Avoid awkward splitting of infinitives or awkward separation of parts of verb phrases.

AWKWARD	You should now begin *to*, if you wish to succeed, *hunt* for a job.
IMPROVED	If you wish to succeed, you should now begin *to hunt* for a job. [In general avoid the "split" infinitive unless it is needed for smoothness or clarity.]
AWKWARD	There stood the wagon which we *had* early last autumn *left* by the barn.
IMPROVED	There stood the wagon which we *had left* by the barn early last autumn.

Dangling Modifiers

25b

Avoid dangling modifiers.

Dangling[1] modifiers are verbal phrases (participial, gerund, infinitive) or elliptical clauses which do not refer clearly and logically to some word in the sentence.

When these modifiers come at the beginning of a sentence, the normal English word order requires them to refer to the subject of the sentence, as in the examples below.

| PARTICIPLE | *Taking our seats,* we watched the game. [We took our seats.] |
| GERUND | *After watching the late show,* Nancy was tired. [Nancy watched the late show.] |

[1] The term "dangling" is applied especially to incoherent verbal phrases and elliptical clauses. But any misplaced word, phrase, or clause dangles in the sense that it is hanging loosely within the sentence.

INFINITIVE   *To avoid the rush traffic,* Mr. Clark left the office early. [Mr. Clark avoided the rush traffic.]

ELLIPTICAL CLAUSE   *When only a small boy,* I went with my father to Denver. [*I was* is implied in the elliptical clause.]

To correct a dangling modifier, (1) rearrange the words in the sentence to make the modifier sensibly refer to the right word, or (2) add words to make the meaning clear and logical.

(1) Avoid dangling participial phrases.

DANGLING   *Taking* our seats, the game started. [*Taking* does not refer to the subject *game,* nor to any other word in the sentence.]

IMPROVED   *Taking* (or *Having taken*) our seats, *we* watched the opening of the game. [*Taking* refers to *we,* the subject of the sentence.]

IMPROVED   *After we had taken our seats,* the game started. [Participial phrase expanded into a clause]

DANGLING   The evening passed very pleasantly, *eating* candy and *playing* the radio. [*Eating* and *playing* refer to nothing in the sentence.]

IMPROVED   *We* passed the evening very pleasantly, *eating* candy and *playing* the radio. [*Eating* and *playing* refer to to *we,* the subject of the main clause.]

(2) Avoid dangling gerund phrases.

DANGLING   By *mowing* the grass high and infrequently, your lawn can be beautiful. [*Mowing* does not refer to any word in the sentence.]

IMPROVED   By *mowing* the grass high and infrequently, *you* can have a beautiful lawn. [*Mowing* refers to *you.*]

(3) Avoid dangling infinitive phrases.

DANGLING   *To write* well, good books must be read. [The under-
           stood subject of *to write* should be the same as the
           subject of the sentence.]

IMPROVED   *To write* well, a *student* must read good books. [*To
           write* refers to *student*, the subject of the sentence.]

DANGLING   *To run* efficiently, proper oiling is needed.

IMPROVED   *To run* efficiently, the *machine* must be properly oiled.

Exceptions:

1. Participles, gerunds, and infinitives designating a
general truth rather than the action of a specific person or
thing may be used without relation to the main clause.

Taking everything into consideration, the campaign was suc-
cessful.
To sum up, we all agreed to support the major.
To judge from reports, all must be going well.

2. "Absolute" phrases, which consist of a noun or pronoun followed by a participle, are grammatically independent of the rest of the sentence and need not refer to
its subject.

The game having ended, we went home.
No one having objected, the motion was passed.

(4) Avoid dangling elliptical clauses (or phrases).

An elliptical clause—that is, a clause with an implied
subject and verb—"dangles" unless the implied subject is
the same as that of the main clause.

DANGLING   When only a small boy (*or* At the age of nine), my
           father took me with him to Denver. [*I was* is im-
           plied in the elliptical clause.]

IMPROVED   When I was only a small boy (*or* When I was nine
           years old), my father took me with him to Denver.
           [Elliptical clause expanded]

IMPROVED   When only a small boy (*or* At the age of nine), *I* went with my father to Denver. [Subject of the main clause made the same as the implied subject of the subordinate clause]

DANGLING   Prepare to make an incision in the abdomen as soon as completely anesthetized.

IMPROVED   Prepare to make an incision in the abdomen as soon as the patient is completely anesthetized.

▶ EXERCISE 3   Revise the following sentences to eliminate dangling modifiers. Write *C* after each sentence that needs no revision.

1. Anticipating no such difficulties as later developed, there was no provision in the Constitution for the admission of a new state as a slave state or as a free state.
2. After sitting there awhile, it began to snow.
3. By selecting the judges from both parties, the decisions are likely to give general satisfaction.
4. To grow good tomatoes, the vines should be supported by stakes.
5. Entering Chicago from the west, a whole network of stockyards is the first thing seen.
6. Darkness having come, we stopped for the night.
7. Once made, you must execute the decision promptly.
8. The meeting was adjourned by standing and repeating the pledge.
9. Having taken his seat, we began to question the witness.
10. Vaccination to prevent smallpox is required before entering the United States from a foreign country.

▶ EXERCISE 4   Revise the following sentences to improve coherence. Write *C* after each sentence that needs no revision.

1. He was enchanted by the roast beef, causing him to tip the waiter inordinately.

2. That statement I do not find it possible to believe at this stage of the argument.
3. We found the house with no trouble after reaching Westwood.
4. After reaching Westwood, locating the house was no trouble.
5. The reduction in price was sufficient to, by itself, restore active sales.
6. Being in a hurry to get away on our trip, our automobile was not overhauled.
7. The decision having been made, everyone was happy.
8. Having a broken arm and nose, I thought the statue was very ugly.
9. John and Robert had ridden several days without sleep in the rain.
10. While wondering about this phenomenon, the sun sank from view.
11. The slaves were unwilling to submit to his plans, thinking they could free themselves.
12. After taking only a few steps, I discovered that I had forgotten my keys.
13. You are, considering the whole affair, very fortunate.
14. The first thing a student must learn is to think for himself upon entering college.
15. Located on a mountain top, this made it an ideal place for a summer resort.
16. Henry promised when he was on his way home to stop at the library.
17. To irrigate successfully, water must flow through carefully planned ditches.
18. The Browns returned this morning from their vacation in the mountains on the bus.
19. Before taking a first trip by air, the thought of flying frightens one.
20. Keep stirring the water into the mixture until pale green.

Parallelism

(An Aid to Coherence)

26

Parallel ideas should be expressed in parallel structure.

The human mind grasps parallel ideas more readily when they are expressed in parallel form. Parallel grammatical structure is characteristic of the English sentence as a means for expressing parallel ideas. (If you do not understand the constructions used in this chapter, review Section 1, especially 1c and 1d.)

26a

For the expression of co-ordinate (equal) ideas a noun should be paralleled with a noun, an active verb with an active verb, an infinitive with an infinitive, a subordinate clause with a subordinate clause, a main clause with a main clause, and so forth.

AWKWARD Let us consider the *origin* of engineering and *how engineering has progressed.* [Noun paralleled with a subordinate clause]

BETTER Let us consider the ‖ *origin* and
         ‖ *progress* of engineering.
  [Noun paralleled with noun]

Note that sentence elements joined by co-ordinate conjunctions normally should be parallel.

AWKWARD	*Walking* and *to swim* are good exercise.
	[Gerund paralleled with infinitive]
BETTER	‖*Walking* and
	‖*swimming* are good exercise.
	[Gerund paralleled with gerund]
AWKWARD	Jane is *pretty*, with *brown hair*, and has a *graceful manner*.
BETTER	Jane is ‖*pretty*
	‖*brown-haircd*, and
	‖*graceful*.
	[Adjective paralleled with adjectives]
AWKWARD	As a young man he *had been* in Africa, *fighting* in Greece, and *following* his general to India.
	[Verb paralleled with participles]
BETTER	As a young man he ‖*had been* in Africa,
	‖*had fought* in Greece, and
	‖*had followed* his general to India.
	[Verb paralleled with verbs]
AWKWARD	He retired *respected* by his associates, *admired* by his friends, and *his employees loved him*.
	[Participles paralleled with a main clause]
BETTER	He retired ‖*respected* by his associates,
	‖*admired* by his friends, and
	‖*loved* by his employees.
	[Participle paralleled with participles]
RIGHT	The dogmas ‖ of the quiet past
	are inadequate ‖ to the stormy present.

—ABRAHAM LINCOLN

[Prepositional phrase paralleled with prepositional phrase]

RIGHT	To say ‖ *that* the character of real men cannot be completely known,
	‖ *that* their inner nature is beyond our reach,
	‖ *that* the dramatic portraiture of things is only possible to poetry,
	is to say ‖ *that* history ought not to be written.

—J. A. FROUDE

[Subordinate clause paralleled with subordinate clauses]

RIGHT   Without learning the principles of general reasoning, ‖ *they will never* be able to understand the laws of their country or grasp its history; *they will never* be fit to plan a factory or organize a business, to criticize a book or detect a fallacy, to arrange their own lives or to educate their children.

—GILBERT HIGHET

[Main clause paralleled with main clause; also, pairs of infinitive phrases in parallel structure]

▶ EXERCISE 1   Revise the following sentences to give parallel structure to co-ordinate ideas.

1. These illustrations will enable you to differentiate unintentional killing from killing with intent to kill.
2. Mr. Smith said that he would give us a quiz on Friday and for us to review the first ten chapters of our textbook.
3. The story is vivid, interesting, and one that appeals to every person.
4. His duties are cleaning up the cabins and to look after the boats.
5. She spends all her time shopping and on her studies.

26b

Whenever necessary to make the parallel clear, repeat a preposition, an article, an auxiliary verb, the sign of the infinitive, or the introductory word of a long phrase or clause. (See also 22c.)

AWKWARD   I admire Tennyson *for the ideals* in his poems but not *his style.*

IMPROVED   I admire Tennyson ‖ *for the ideals* in his poems but not *for his style.*

AWKWARD In the wreck the circus lost *a camel* and *elephant.*
IMPROVED In the wreck the circus lost ‖ *a camel* and
          ‖ *an elephant.*

OBSCURE He explained *that* the advertising campaign had been
         successful, business had increased more than fifty
         per cent, and additional capital was sorely needed.
CLEARER He explained‖ *that* the advertising campaign had
                      ‖ been successful,
                      ‖ *that* business had increased more than
                      ‖ fifty per cent, and
                      ‖ *that* additional capital was sorely
                      ‖ needed.

▶ EXERCISE 2 Copy the following sentences, inserting the
words needed to bring out the parallel structure.

1. The sentences are difficult to understand, not because
   they are long but they are obscure.
2. The child learns in nursery school to take his turn, to
   respect the rights of others, and take care of his
   materials.
3. They would lie on the battlefield for hours and sometimes days.

26c

**Correlatives (*either . . . or, neither . . . nor, both . . . and,
not only . . . but also, whether . . . or*) should be followed
by elements that are parallel in form.**

FAULTY He was not only *kind* but also *knew* when to help people
        in trouble.
        [Adjective paralleled with verb]
BETTER He was‖ *not only kind*
               ‖ *but also helpful* to people in trouble.
FAULTY I debated whether *I should give* the beggar money or *to
        offer* him food.
        [Subordinate clause paralleled with infinitive]
BETTER I debated‖ *whether to give* the beggar money
                 ‖ *or to offer* him food.

Caution: Do not use parallel structure for sentence elements not parallel in thought. Never use an awkward or unidiomatic expression for the sake of a parallel. Lack of parallel structure is preferable.

MISLEADING   Our meetings were held on Friday afternoon, on Saturday morning, and on Saturday afternoon we started home.

CLEAR   Our meetings were held on Friday afternoon and on Saturday morning. On Saturday afternoon we started home.

AWKWARD   A teacher attempts to teach something, fails to inspire the pupil, kills the desire to learn, and hammers on cold iron. [Parallel structure used for ideas that could be related more clearly and effectively by way of subordination.]

BETTER   A teacher who is attempting to teach without inspiring the pupil with a desire to learn is hammering on cold iron.   —HORACE MANN

26d

Be sure that a *who* (or *which*) clause precedes *and who* (or *and which*).

FAULTY   Inez Carter is a woman of great charm and who is popular. [A *who clause* does not precede the *and who.*]

BETTER   Inez Carter is a woman ‖ *who has great charm* and ‖ *who is popular.*

▶ EXERCISE 3   Revise the following sentences by using parallel structure to express parallel ideas. Write *C* after each sentence that needs no revision.

1. I like a detective story with exciting action and which keeps me guessing.
2. You will enjoy painting a favorite corner of the room, showing an armchair, drop-leaf table, and lamp.
3. Someone has said that Americans cannot enjoy life

without a TV set, an automobile, and a summer cottage.

4. My friend told me that the trip would be delayed but to be ready to start on Friday.

5. William is a boy with a good mind and who has the highest principles.

6. A sea lion watches carefully the action of his fellows and how they obey their trainer.

7. He was quiet and in a serious mood after the talk.

8. He took up drinking, gambling, and killed several people.

9. I did not know whether I should go to some technical school or to enter a liberal arts college.

10. The real creed of a person should be living rather than in words.

11. The secretary must attend all meetings, call the roll, and keep the minutes.

12. People fall naturally into two classes: the workers and those who like to lean on others.

▶ EXERCISE 4 Carefully observe the parallel structure in the following sentences, and be prepared to participate in a class discussion of the grammatical constructions. (If necessary, review Section 1.)

1. I believe that every right implies a responsibility; every opportunity, an obligation; every possession, a duty.
   —JOHN D. ROCKEFELLER, JR.

2. Many producers are privately convinced that they can sell more products on the basis of gimmicks, special features, impulse, and innovation than on the basis of quality. —VANCE PACKARD

3. Then he drew on the skin a sketch of the Rio Grande, the bluffs to the south, a stream with a west prong coming in from the north, and the place of buried coins. —J. FRANK DOBIE

4. Quickly the buildings get shabby—little stores selling auto parts, a junkyard crammed with rusting wreckage. The city is harsh: concrete streets, brick building walls, black steel viaducts.
   —JOHN BARTLOW MARTIN

Parallelism **291**

5. These reporters felt no urge to inform their readers about how Lincoln stood, what he did with his hands, how he moved, vocalized, or whether he emphasized or subdued any parts of the address. —CARL SANDBURG

6. Electronic brains which predict election results, lie-detectors which make you confess the truth, new drugs which make you testify to lies, radiations which produce biological monsters— all these developments of the last fifty years have created new vistas and new nightmares, which art and literature have not yet assimilated. —ARTHUR KOESTLER

▶ EXERCISE 5 Note below how Newman develops the parallel between health and general education. Underline the words which bring out the parallelism and keep a long sentence—203 words—in perfect balance. With Newman's structure as a guide, construct a shorter sentence on a subject such as "The Game of Football and the Game of Life" or "The Course of a River and the Course of Life."

Again, as health ought to precede labour of the body, and as a man in health can do what an unhealthy man cannot do, and as of this health the properties are strength, energy, agility, graceful carriage and action, manual dexterity, and endurance of fatigue, so in like manner general culture of mind is the best aid to professional and scientific study, and educated men can do what illiterate cannot; and the man who has learned to think and to reason and to compare and to discriminate and to analyze, who has refined his taste, and formed his judgment, and sharpened his mental vision, will not indeed at once be a lawyer, or a pleader, or an orator, or a statesman, or a physician, or a good landlord, or a man of business, or a soldier, or an engineer, or a chemist, or a geologist, or an antiquarian, but he will be placed in that state of intellect in which he can take up any one of the sciences or callings I have referred to, or any other for which he has a taste or special talent, with an ease, a grace, a versatility, and a success, to which another is a stranger. —JOHN HENRY NEWMAN

▶ EXERCISE 6 Indicate parallelism in Lincoln's Gettysburg Address. See Section 1, Exercise 20.

Point of View

(An Aid to Coherence)

27

Avoid needless shifts in point of view.

Sudden and illogical shifts in point of view tend to obscure the meaning and thus to cause needless difficulty in reading.

27a

Avoid needless shifts in tense. (See also **7d.**)

SHIFT The boy *closed* his book and *hurries* away to the playground. [A shift from past tense to present tense]

BETTER The boy *closed* his book and *hurried* away to the playground. [Both verbs in the past tense]

Note: When the historical present is used, as in summarizing plots of narratives, care will be needed to avoid slipping from the present tense into the past tense. *Example:* "Romeo *goes* in disguise to a Capulet feast, *falls* in love with Juliet, and *marries* (not *married*) her secretly."

27b

Avoid needless shifts in mood. (See also **7d.**)

SHIFT First *rise* to your feet and then you *should address* the chairman. [A shift from imperative to indicative mood]

BETTER First *rise* to your feet and then *address* the chairman. [Both verbs in the imperative mood]

27c

Avoid needless shifts in subject or voice.

A shift in subject often involves a shift in voice. A shift in voice nearly always involves a shift in subject.

SHIFT   James liked fishing, but hunting was also enjoyed by him. [The subject shifts from *James* to *hunting*. The voice shifts from active to passive.]

BETTER   James liked fishing, but he also enjoyed hunting. [One subject only. Both verbs active.]

SHIFT   Mary took summer courses and her leisure hours were devoted to tennis. [The subject shifts from *Mary* to *hours*. The voice shifts from active to passive.]

BETTER   Mary took summer courses and devoted her leisure hours to tennis. [One subject only. Both verbs active.]

SHIFT   Paul hurried up the mountain path and soon the laurel came into his sight. [The subject shifts from *Paul* to *laurel*.]

BETTER   Paul hurried up the mountain path and soon caught sight of the laurel. [One subject only.]

27d

Avoid needless shifts in person.

SHIFT   *We* have reached a point where *one* ought to face the possibility of a great and sudden change. [A shift from first to third person]

BETTER   *We* have reached a point where *we* ought to face the possibility of a great and sudden change.

SHIFT   *Students* will find the University Book Shop a great convenience. *You* need not leave the campus to purchase any school supplies *you* may need. [A shift from third to second person]

BETTER   *The student* will find the University Book Shop a great convenience. *He* need not leave the campus to purchase any school supplies *he* may need.

27e

Avoid needless shifts in number. (See also agreement of pronoun and antecedent, **6b.**)

SHIFT   *One* should be thoughtful of *their* neighbors. [A shift from singular *one* to plural *their*]

BETTER   *One* should be thoughtful of *one's* neighbors.

SHIFT   The United Nations *deserves* encouragement. Indeed *they deserve* much more than that. [If *United Nations* takes a singular verb (*deserves*), it must not be referred to by a plural pronoun (*they*).]

BETTER   The United Nations *deserves* encouragement. Indeed, *it deserves* much more than that.

27f

Avoid needless shifts from indirect to direct discourse.

SHIFT   My friend asked whether I knew the coach and will he be with the team. [Mixed indirect and direct discourse]

RIGHT   My friend asked whether I knew the coach and whether he would be with the team. [Indirect discourse]

RIGHT   My friend asked, "Do you know the coach? Will he be with the team?" [Direct discourse]

27g

Maintain the same tone or style throughout the sentence.

INAPPROPRIATE   Analysis of the principal obstacles to harmony in the United Nations reveals that Russia and her satellites refuse to *play ball* with the rest of the world. [A shift from formal to colloquial style. Substitute *co-operate,* or a similar word, for the italicized expression.]

INAPPROPRIATE   After distributing the grass seed evenly over the lawn, rake the ground at least twice and then *gently bedew it* with fine spray. [The italicized expression is too "poetic" in a sentence with a prosaic purpose. Substitute *water it lightly.*]

INAPPROPRIATE   It seemed to Juliet, as she gazed down from the balcony, that Romeo's face was as white as *the underside of a fish*. [The italicized expression clashes with the romantic beginning of the sentence.]

27h

Maintain a consistent perspective throughout the sentence (and also throughout the larger elements of discourse).

FAULTY PERSPECTIVE   From the top of the Washington Monument, the government offices seemed to be so many beehives, and the workers droned at their tasks behind long rows of desks. [The perspective shifts from the monument to the interior of government buildings.]

CONSISTENT PERSPECTIVE   From the top of the Washington Monument, the government buildings seemed to be so many beehives, and it was easy to imagine the workers droning at their tasks behind long rows of desks.

▶ EXERCISE 1   Correct in the following sentences all needless shifts in tense, mood, subject, voice, person, number, tone, or perspective. Explain each revision by writing the number of the appropriate rule in this chapter: a, b, c, d, e, f, g, or h. Write *C* after each sentence that needs no revision.

1. According to Helen Leath, Mr. Blake knows how to deal with annoying door-to-door salesmen; they are quickly frightened away by him.
2. Pretending to be a seller of knives, Mr. Blake waves a long butcher knife near the throat of the salesman. You can well imagine what they think.
3. When the policeman gave me a ticket for rolling past a stop sign, I ask him what the fine would be.
4. A woman stepped forward, grabs the culprit by the collar, and demands that he apologize to the child.
5. He said he had a convertible model in stock and would I like to try it out.

6. Jane likes to cook, but house cleaning is not a pleasant occupation.

7. Each person has some distinctive mannerism of their own.

8. When she saw him in the room, she thinks that she is dreaming.

9. If there is little enthusiasm among the students, we might ask, "Why they should be enthusiastic?"

10. No matter what her mother may say, she always took the opposite view.

11. It is a book everyone should read, for you can derive much good from it.

12. Gentlemen, we have finished our discussion about balancing the budget; bear with me awhile until I have said a few words about budgeting the balance.

13. The foreign ministers held their conference in Paris, and contrary to rumors, the peace pipe is passed around.

14. Pick the roses in the morning, and then they should be placed in water.

15. A vacation is enjoyed by all because it refreshes the mind and the body.

16. He told his aunt that there is someone in the room.

17. Every citizen should do his duty as they see it.

18. Aunt Jane spent her summers in Wisconsin, but Arizona is her favorite winter climate.

19. Jim wondered whether Jack had left and did he say when he would return?

20. Standing before the house, he looked sadly at the family gathered around the kitchen table.

▶ EXERCISE 2 Revise the following paragraph to avoid all needless shifts. If necessary, expand the paragraph.

1. From behind the desk the shopkeeper emerged and comes toward me. 2. He is a heavy-set man, and his brown tweed coat was badly worn. 3. An assistant gave

me a chair and leaves the room, but not before he had welcomed us and even told me where one might find lodging.   4. "First, look around in this vicinity and then you should find a comfortable place in a nearby hotel," he says.   5. I hurried out of the shop and soon the hotel comes into view.   6. Be thankful for suggestions when offered you.   7. It usually helps one.

▶ EXERCISE 3   Follow the directions for Exercise 2.

1. He was an artful old codger, it always had seemed to me.   2. He has a deceptively open face and his manner is that of a simple farmer.   3. He tried to appear humble and said that "I am opposed to all pretense."   4. Nevertheless he will let it be known that he has great influence with important people.   5. Take these impressions for what they are worth; it may help one in your dealings with this reptile.

Reference of Pronouns

(An Aid to Coherence)

28

Make a pronoun refer unmistakably and definitely to its antecedent. (For agreement of pronoun and antecedent see 6b.)

One of the principal obstacles to clear and immediate understanding is the faulty use of pronouns. *He, she, it; who, which, what; this, that; the same, such,* etc. can have meaning only if the antecedent noun is immediately obvious to the reader. Hence the writer should place all pronouns as close as possible to the antecedent. If, having done this, he finds that the reference of the pronoun is still not obvious, he should repeat the antecedent or use a synonym for it. If repetition proves awkward, he should recast his sentence.

28a

Avoid ambiguous reference. Construct the sentence in such a way that the reader can easily distinguish between two possible antecedents.

AMBIGUOUS	John told William that he had made a mistake. [Who made the mistake?]
CLEAR	John said to William, "You have made a mistake."
CLEAR	In talking to William, John admitted that he had made a mistake.

AWKWARD	The books were standing on the shelf which needed sorting. See also 25a(3).
BETTER	The books which needed sorting were standing on the shelf.

28b

Avoid remote reference—reference to an antecedent (1) too far removed from the pronoun or (2) so placed in a subordinate construction that it is not central in the mind of the reader.

Make your meaning immediately clear to the reader. Save him the annoyance of searching about for the antecedent.

REMOTE   The *lake* covers many acres. Near the shore water lilies grow in profusion, spreading out their green leaves and sending up white blossoms on slender stems. *It* is well stocked with fish. [The pronoun *it* is too far removed from the antecedent *lake.*]

IMPROVED   . . . The *lake* is well stocked with fish. [Repetition of the antecedent *lake*]

VAGUE   He sat by the little window all day and worked steadily at his translating. *It* was too small to give much light. [Temporarily confusing: antecedent of *it* not clear until reader finishes the sentence]

CLEAR   He sat by the little window all day and worked steadily at his translating. The *window* was too small to give much light. [Repetition of the noun]

OBSCURE   When *Johnson's* club was organized, *he* asked Goldsmith to become a member. [Reference to antecedent in the possessive case]

IMPROVED   When *Johnson* organized his club, *he* asked Goldsmith to become a member.

Caution: As a rule avoid pronoun reference to the title of a theme, or to a word in the title.

Title: Is Work a Curse or a Blessing?

AWKWARD   To a man that is harassed by a nagging wife and undisciplined children, *it* can be a great blessing, a welcome escape.

BETTER   To a man that is harassed by a nagging wife and undisciplined children, *work* can be a great blessing, a welcome escape.

28c

Use broad reference only with discretion.

Informal English allows much latitude in the use of antecedents that must be inferred from the context. Even standard English accepts the general idea of a clause as an antecedent when the reference is unmistakable. But students who overuse *this, that, it,* or *which* to refer to the general idea of the preceding clause or sentence may be advised, as a means of insuring greater clarity, to make each of their pronouns refer to a specific substantive.

(1) Avoid reference to the general idea of a preceding clause or sentence unless the meaning is clear and unmistakable.

VAGUE   William was absent from the first performance, which caused much comment. [*Which* has no antecedent.]

CLEAR   William's absence from the first performance caused much comment. [Pronoun eliminated]

VAGUE   The story referred to James, but Henry misapplied it to himself. This is true in real life. [*This* has no antecedent.]

CLEAR   The story referred to James, but Henry misapplied it to himself. Similar mistakes occur in real life.

(2) As a rule do not refer to a noun not expressed but merely inferred from some word.

VAGUE   My mother is a music teacher. It is a profession I know nothing about.

CLEAR   My mother is a music teacher, but the teaching of music is a profession I know nothing about.

VAGUE   He wanted his teachers to think he was above average, as he could have been if he had used it to advantage.

CLEAR   He wanted his teachers to think he was above average, as he could have been if he had used his ability to advantage.

(3) Avoid the awkward use of the indefinite *it, you,* or *they*.

AWKWARD   If a person breaks the law you may be arrested. (See also **27d.**)

COLLOQUIAL (or STANDARD)   If you break the law, you may be arrested. [Colloquial when *you* means "anyone"; standard when *you* is addressed to a specific person or persons]

STANDARD   If a person breaks the law, he may be arrested.
Or, Anyone breaking the law may be arrested.

COLLOQUIAL   When *you* cannot swim, a leaking boat tossing in deep, stormy waters frightens *you*. I admit that I am afraid.

STANDARD   Since I cannot swim, I admit that a leaking boat tossing in deep, stormy waters frightens me.

COLLOQUIAL   In France *they* could not understand William.
STANDARD   In France William could not be understood.

AWKWARD   In the book *it* says that many mushrooms are edible.
IMPROVED   The book says that many mushrooms are edible.

Note: The pronoun *it* is correctly used in such idiomatic expressions as *it seems, it is cold, it is raining, it is useless to go,* and *it is five miles to town.*

28d

Avoid the confusion arising from the repetition in the same sentence of a pronoun referring to different antecedents.

CONFUSING   Although *it* is very hot by the lake, *it* looks inviting. [The first *it* is the indefinite pronoun; the second *it* refers to *lake.*]

CLEAR   Although it is very hot by the lake, the water looks
           inviting.
CONFUSING We should have prepared for our examinations earlier.
           It is too late to do *it* now.
CLEAR   We should have prepared for our examinations earlier.
           It is too late now.

▶ EXERCISE 1   Reconstruct the following sentences as necessary to correct faults in reference. Write *C* after each
sentence that needs no revision.

1. Howard was more intelligent than the average student,
   but he did not use it properly.
2. I did not even buy a season ticket, which was very
   disloyal to my school.
3. Her ladylike qualities were reflected in the gracious-
   ness of her manner. This was apparent in her every act.
4. Package wrapping has always been my job, because
   they say that I can do it better than anyone else.
5. When building roads the Romans tried to detour
   around valleys as much as possible for fear that flood
   waters might cover them and make them useless.
6. If you are taken to the courthouse, they will fine you.
7. In the article it states that the inland sea is salt.
8. Our language is rich in connectives which express
   fine distinctions of meaning.
9. One summer while visiting my grandparents I was
   attracted by three pigeons that decided to settle in
   their barn loft.
10. If all impurities are not removed from the iron, it will
    deprive steel of its ductility and prevent it from being
    rolled into bars or drawn into wire.
11. The speaker was eloquent, but he was annoyed by
    the intense heat in the auditorium.
12. My worst fault is the inability to express myself clearly
    in the presence of other people. But this is not true
    when I am with close friends.

13. I left home and hitchhiked to Chicago. This means of travel is not satisfactory, for it requires much waiting at the side of the road.

14. When the termite eggs are hatched, they grow wings and fly about the country in swarms.

15. Mary told Ann that she would be accepted as a member of the club.

16. The story awakens your interest in radium, which continues to the end of the book.

17. Visitors should heed the notice that is on the outside of the door.

18. Mary showed Jane that she had not made a mistake.

19. It may freeze tonight and damage the pipe, and it should be protected.

20. If a driver is guilty of violating a traffic law, the cost of your car insurance goes up.

Emphasis

29

Select words and arrange the parts of the sentence to give emphasis to important ideas.

As our ideas vary in importance, so our expression should vary in stress. Short factual statements and routine description or narration cannot always be varied for emphasis without doing violence to the natural order of the English language. It would be absurd for a policeman to describe a prisoner in this fashion: "Red was his hair, blue were his eyes, and on his nose sat a great brown wart." But in most types of writing, some sentences may be rearranged to achieve emphasis without sacrificing naturalness of expression.

Emphasis may be gained through the use of concrete words and figurative language (Section **20**), through economy of language (Section **21**), and through the subordination of less important ideas (Section **24**). We may also emphasize ideas:

a. By placing important words in the important positions at the beginning and end of the sentence.
b. By changing loose sentences into periodic sentences.
c. By arranging ideas in the order of climax.
d. By using the active instead of the passive voice.
e. By repeating important words.
f. By putting words out of their usual order.
g. By using balanced construction.
h. By abruptly changing the sentence length.

29a

Gain emphasis by placing important words at the beginning or end of the sentence—especially at the end. Whenever possible tuck away in the middle of the sentence parenthetical expressions and other elements of minor importance.

WEAK   The colonel will bluntly refuse, in all probability. [The weakest part of the sentence is given the most emphatic position—the end.]

EMPHATIC   In all probability the colonel will bluntly refuse. [Strong end]

EMPHATIC   The colonel, in all probability, will bluntly refuse. [Most emphatic—strong beginning and end]

WEAK   He became an archbishop in his later years, however.

EMPHATIC   In his later years, however, he became an archbishop.

WEAK   Fallacies as gross as these may easily be detected by all men who can see an inch before them.

EMPHATIC   All men who can see an inch before them may easily detect these gross fallacies.   —DRYDEN

▶ EXERCISE 1   Gain emphasis by rearranging the parts of the following sentences.

1. He had little success, but he was a tireless worker, if we may believe the reports.
2. The old man withdrew into his cabin for some good reason we must suppose.
3. He may become an expert accountant by a study of business methods at home.
4. A trailer saves hotel expense and can be moved about from place to place readily.
5. However, he could not redeem himself, in my opinion.
6. The expedition cannot possibly fail unless we lose our enthusiasm.
7. I must know your address, in the first place.

29b

Gain emphasis by changing loose sentences into periodic sentences. (Section 29b is an extension of 29a.)

A sentence in which the main clause is either placed at the end or completed at the end is called *periodic;* one that makes a complete statement and then adds details is called *loose.* Both types of sentences are effective. The loose sentence is, and should be, the more commonly used. But the periodic sentence, by holding the reader in suspense and reserving the main idea until the end, is more emphatic. Note the difference in tone in the following sentences.

LOOSE   Practice daily if you want to become a good pianist. [A clear sentence]

PERIODIC   If you want to become a good pianist, practice daily. [More emphatic]

LOOSE   History has proved amply that mere numbers may be defeated by smaller forces who are superior in arms, organization, and morale.

PERIODIC   That mere numbers may be defeated by smaller forces who are superior in arms, organization, and morale history has amply proved.

Caution: Do not overuse the periodic sentence to the point of making your style unnatural. Variety is desirable. See Section 30.

▶ EXERCISE 2   Change the following loose sentences into periodic sentences. Note the gain in emphasis.

1. I attended his wedding, many years ago, on a beautiful June afternoon, in a little village near Cincinnati.
2. He returned to the camp when he found that he could be of no further assistance.
3. It was no concern of mine that he neglected his studies.
4. The workers were afraid to return until the dam had been repaired.

5. It never entered his mind to be dissatisfied with his dreary lodgings, to resent the purposelessness of his job, or to revolt against the complacent ignorance of his associates.

▶ EXERCISE 3   Examine typical pages from several prose writers (Swift, Newman, Conrad, or others) to determine the proportion of loose and periodic sentences.

29c

Gain emphasis by arranging ideas in the order of climax.

UNEMPHATIC   We could hear the roar of cannon, the shrieks of the wounded, and the crash of falling timbers.

EMPHATIC   We could hear the roar of cannon, the crash of falling timbers, and the shrieks of the wounded. [Climax reached in "shrieks of the wounded"]

UNEMPHATIC   We have been spurned with contempt by the throne. Our supplications have been disregarded, and our remonstrances have produced additional violence and insult. Our petitions have been slighted.

EMPHATIC   Our petitions have been slighted; our remonstrances have produced additional violence and insult; our supplications have been disregarded; and we have been spurned, with contempt, from the foot of the throne!   —PATRICK HENRY

Note: A striking arrangement of ideas in reverse order of climax, called anticlimax, is sometimes used for comic effect.

Not louder shrieks to pitying heav'n are cast,
When husbands, or when lap-dogs, breathe their last.   —POPE

▶ EXERCISE 4   Arrange the ideas of each sentence in what you consider to be the order of climax.

1. He left the city because of his rapidly failing health, lack of success in business, and the loss of his club membership.

2. His confident manner, his knowledge of men, and his friendliness made him the logical man for the office.
3. Something must be done at once. The commission is faced with a deficit.
4. Give me death or give me liberty.
5. I gathered together the souvenirs of college days: my diploma, a textbook on mathematics, my fraternity pin, and a battered book bag.

29d

Gain emphasis by using the strong active voice instead of the weak passive voice.

WEAK His grave was dug by his teeth.
STRONGER He dug his grave with his teeth.

WEAK Honey was gathered by the bee as it flitted from flower to flower.
STRONGER The bee, flitting from flower to flower, gathered honey.

Exception: If the receiver of the action is more important than the doer, the passive voice is more effective.

EMPHATIC Wheat is grown in Kansas.
EMPHATIC Any person who attempts to escape will be shot.

▶ EXERCISE 5   Substitute the active for the passive voice.

1. As the station is reached, the train is seen coming around a curve.
2. On her head was worn a beautiful green hat.
3. Paul was hesitant to enter the room, for he saw that a poster was being made by Jane.
4. No moss will be gathered by a rolling stone.
5. It was decided by the members that the meetings were to be held at their homes.
6. When the play was brought to an end, the actors were greeted with a loud burst of applause by the audience.

7. It is greatly feared by the citizens that adequate punishment will not be meted out by the jury.

29e

Gain emphasis by repeating important words.

Note the great difference between the careless repetition in **21c** and the effective repetition in the following passages. See also **31b(3)**.

EMPHATIC   ... *wet* roads, *wet* fields, *wet* housetops; not a *beautiful,* scarcely a *picturesque* object met my eyes along the whole route; yet to me, *all was beautiful, all* was more than *picturesque.*   —CHARLOTTE BRONTË

EMPHATIC   There is *no mistake;* there has been *no mistake;* and there shall be *no mistake.*   —DUKE OF WELLINGTON

[See also the quotation from Winston Churchill in **23b**.]

▶ EXERCISE 6   From your reading, copy three passages in which emphasis is gained by the repetition of an important word or phrase.

29f

Gain emphasis by putting a word or phrase out of its natural order.

EMPHATIC   *Trust her* I dare not.
EMPHATIC   *Never* did I think he would return alive.

Caution: This method of securing emphasis, if overused, will make the style distinctly artificial. And of course the order of the parts of the sentence should never be such as to make for ambiguity. (See **25a**.)

▶ EXERCISE 7   Copy from your reading and bring to class five passages in which emphasis is secured by putting a word or phrase out of natural order.

29g

Use balance to gain emphasis.

A sentence is balanced when identical or similar grammatical structure is used to express contrasted ideas. A balanced sentence uses parallel structure (see Section **26**) and emphasizes the contrast between parts of similar length and movement. Overuse of balance seems especially artificial.

UNBALANCED   It is human to err, but to forgive is divine.

BALANCED   To err is human, to forgive divine.   —POPE

BALANCED   You had better talk trifles elegantly to the most trifling woman, than coarse inelegant sense to the most solid man: you had better return a dropped fan genteelly, than give a thousands pounds awkwardly; and you had better refuse a favor gracefully, than grant it clumsily.   —CHESTERFIELD

▶ EXERCISE 8   Copy from your reading and bring to class five examples of the balanced sentence.

▶ EXERCISE 9   Copy all examples of balanced structure from Lincoln's Gettysburg Address (at the end of Section **1**, Exercise 20.)

▶ EXERCISE 10   Use balanced sentences to show the contrast between the following: Men and women, youth and age, success and failure.

29h

Abruptly change the sentence length to gain emphasis.

EXAMPLE   Across an expanse of new-turned earth stretches a new public housing project, with a playyard for the children, and at 32nd Street begins the new campus of the Illinois Institute of Technology, sleek brick-and-glass buildings surrounded by new trees and new grass. And just beyond the Institute rises a great gray hulk of brick, four stories high, topped by an ungainly smokestack, ancient and enormous, filling half the block north of 34th Street between State and Dearborn. It is the Mecca Building.   —JOHN BARTLOW MARTIN

[The last short sentence, which abruptly follows a group of longer sentences, is emphatic; the author stresses *Mecca Building* because the purpose of his essay is to describe this strange place.]

▶ EXERCISE 11   Revise the following sentences as necessary to give greater emphasis. Write *C* after each sentence that needs no revision.

1. The chairman will give his report after the meeting has been called to order.
2. The soldiers were outnumbered two to one, as you may have heard.
3. It was no fault of hers that the program was a failure.
4. Hemingway created forceful prose out of his sensitivity to the real speech of Americans.
5. The zero hour had come. Already the armies were marching.
6. On the other hand, he had done the best he could, according to his story.
7. At any time I shall be ready, no matter how late the hour is.
8. He saw much to interest him: the Statue of Liberty, the art galleries, the tall buildings, and the crowds on the street.
9. Extension courses may be taken for credit during any period of the year, and of course, at any place of residence.
10. Scouting develops a boy morally, mentally, and physically.
11. Convince her against her will I cannot.
12. The storm broke in all its fury at the close of a hot day.
13. Mr. Brown knew that he had made wrong decisions, that he should apologize, that he had made a mistake.

14. I met her in Boston, many years ago, in a shop on Tremont Street, late in the fall.
15. Around her shoulders was draped a gorgeous Spanish shawl.
16. The art of the Indians was crude, but a great deal of originality was shown by some of them.
17. Her charm, her friendliness, her generosity, and her neat appearance made her a favorite with the girls.
18. As we approached the house, lights were turned on and faces appeared at the windows.
19. Make the most of it if this be treason.
20. The car overturned when we struck a rut in the road.

▶ EXERCISE 12   By pointing to specific rules in this chapter, indicate the methods of gaining emphasis used in the following sentences.

1. When the loudspeaker announces "The Two-Fisted Killer from Ecuador," he rises on short, crooked legs, lowers his shaggy black head, aims himself and charges onto the court.
   —MARSHALL SMITH

2. Why lands sink under the sea and rise again nobody knows.
   —WOLFGANG LANGEWIESCHE

3. If a man can write a better book, preach a better sermon, or make a better mouse-trap than his neighbor, though he builds his house in the woods, the world will make a beaten path to his door.   —EMERSON

4. Gone are the people who owned these farms, their most lasting works faded like old ink, their names nothing but an echo in the land records.   —KENNETH ANDLER

5. I am very fond of the company of ladies; I like their beauty, I like their delicacy, I like their vivacity, and I like their *silence*.
   —SAMUEL JOHNSON

Variety

30

Vary the length and the structure of your sentences to make your whole composition pleasing and effective.

Comparison of the two passages in the following example will illustrate the value of variety. The sentences in these parallel passages are grammatically correct, and the diction is the same. But one passage is made up entirely of simple or compound sentences. The other passage contains a varied sentence structure which is much more effective.

Not Varied	*Varied*
I had not time to be of help. The wrestler dropped at last, and Alan leaped back to get his distance. He ran upon the others like a bull, and he roared, and he went along. They broke before him like water, and they turned, and they ran. One fell against another in their haste.	But I had not time to be of help. The wrestler dropped at last; and Alan, leaping back to get his distance, ran upon the others like a bull, roaring as he went. They broke before him like water, turning, and running, and falling one against another in their haste.

—ROBERT LOUIS STEVENSON

Except for the loose, stringy sentences in **30c**, this section deals only with *good* sentences. Throughout Section **30** you are cautioned against monotonous repetition of any one type of sentence, not because these sentences are grammatically wrong, but because they do not combine to form a pleasing and effective pattern. Even the best sentence can become boring if it follows a long series of sentences similar in design.

Note: Can you distinguish readily between main clauses and subordinate clauses, clauses and phrases, compound sentences and compound predicates? If necessary, review the fundamentals of the sentence treated in Section 1, Sentence Sense, especially 1d; then study **Variety.**

30a

Usually avoid a series of short, simple sentences. Vary the length. (See also 29h.)

CHOPPY | I settled back to my place. I recharged the three pistols. I had fired them earlier. I kept watch with both eye and ear.
IMPROVED | I settled back to my place, recharging the three pistols I had fired, and keeping watch with both eye and ear. —ROBERT LOUIS STEVENSON

30b

Avoid a long series of sentences beginning with the subject. Vary the beginning.

The best writers begin about half their sentences with the subject—far more than in any other one way.[1] But some students use this kind of beginning almost exclusively. To avoid overuse, they should vary the subject-first beginning.

Basic Sentence Patterns	*Variations*
SUBJECT—VERB	VERB—SUBJECT
The professor walked in.	In walked the professor.
A man lay beside the road.	Beside the road lay a man.

[1] In a study of sentence beginnings George Summey, Jr., *American Punctuation*, New York, 1949, pp. 166–71, finds 53 per cent with subject, 28 per cent with adverb or adverb clause, 9 per cent with co-ordinating conjunction, leaving 10 per cent for all other types of beginnings.

SUBJECT—VERB—OBJECT.	OBJECT—SUBJECT—VERB.
Henry scorned honest men.	Honest men Henry scorned.
I will not do that again.	That I will not do again.
SUBJECT—LINKING VERB —COMPLEMENT.	COMPLEMENT—SUBJECT —VERB.
Bruce was a bungler then.	A bungler Bruce was then.
We shall never feel secure.	Secure we shall never feel.

In addition to shifting the word order of basic patterns, you can vary the beginnings of sentences in the following ways:

(1) Begin with an adverb or an adverb clause.

ADVERB   *Suddenly* the professor walked in.

ADVERB CLAUSE   *Although Bruce has good manners now,* he was a bungler then.

(2) Begin with a prepositional phrase or a participial phrase.

PREPOSITIONAL PHRASE   *At that moment* the professor walked in.

PARTICIPIAL PHRASE   *Waiting patiently for help,* a man lay beside the road.

(3) Begin with a co-ordinating conjunction such as *but, and, or, nor,* or *yet.*

Effective sentences can often begin with a co-ordinating conjunction, but only when the conjunction shows the proper relation of the sentence to the preceding sentence. See 31b(4).

CO-ORDINATING CONJUNCTION   The young woman wept and wrung her hands. *But* the injured man, lying beside the road, waited patiently for help. [*But* makes a contrast.]

▶ EXERCISE 1   Compose a good sentence that begins with the subject. Then revise the sentence to vary the beginning in as many ways as you can.

▶ EXERCISE 2   Classify the beginnings of the sentences in paragraph 32, page 348, into the types designated above.

30c

Avoid the loose, stringy compound sentence. (See also 24b.)

The ineffective compound sentence may be improved:

(1) **By using a subordinate clause.**

AIMLESSLY COMPOUND   The Mississippi River is one of the longest rivers in the world, and in the springtime it often overflows its banks, and many people are endangered.

IMPROVED   The Mississippi River, which is one of the longest rivers in the world, often endangers many people during the springtime by overflowing its banks.

(2) **By using a compound predicate.**

AWKWARD   He put on his coat, and next he picked up his hat and cane, and then he hurried from the house.

BETTER   He put on his coat, picked up his hat and cane, and hurried from the house.

(3) **By using an appositive or a modifier.**

COMPOUND   The town had a population of three thousand, and a tornado struck it, and it was practically demolished.

IMPROVED   The town, with its three thousand people, was struck by a tornado and practically demolished.

COMPOUND   He was the mayor of the town, and he was a genial fellow, and he invited the four young boys into his study.

IMPROVED   The mayor of the town, a genial fellow, invited the four young boys into his study.

(4) **By using phrases.**

COMPOUND   The streets were icy and we could not drive the car.

IMPROVED   Because of the icy streets we could not drive the car.

COMPOUND   You will reach your destination tomorrow, and then you can take a long rest.

VARIED   After reaching your destination tomorrow, you can take a long rest.

30d

Vary the conventional subject-verb sequence by occasionally separating subject and verb by words or phrases.

SUBJECT—VERB   The auditorium is across from the park and it is a gift of the alumni. [A loose compound sentence]

VARIED   The auditorium, across from the park, is a gift of the alumni.

SUBJECT—VERB   The crowd sympathized with the visitors and applauded every good play. [A good sentence]

VARIED   The crowd, sympathizing with the visitors, applauded every good play.

Caution: Avoid awkward or needless separation of subject and verb.

30e

Vary the usual declarative statement with an occasional exclamation, exhortation, command, or question.

STATEMENT   We will fight to the end.

EXCLAMATION   Imagine our nation not fighting to the very end!

EXHORTATION   Let us fight, then, to the very end.

COMMAND   Fight on, fellow citizens, fight to the end.

QUESTION   Who of us will not fight to the end? [A rhetorical question usually should not be answered.]

▶ EXERCISE 3   Point out the sentence variety in the following paragraph.

1. The only house I had been the owner of before, if I except a boat, was a tent, which I used occasionally when making excursions in the summer, and this is still rolled up in my garret; but the boat, after passing from hand to hand, has gone down the stream of time. 2. With this more substantial shelter about me, I had made some

progress toward settling in the world.   3. This frame, so slightly clad, was a sort of crystallization around me, and reacted on the builder.   4. It was suggestive somewhat as a picture in outlines.   5. I did not need to go outdoors to take the air, for the atmosphere within had lost none of its freshness.   6. It was not so much within-doors as behind a door where I sat, even in the rainiest weather.   7. The *Harivansa* says, "An abode without birds is like a meat without seasoning."   8. Such was not my abode, for I found myself suddenly neighbor to the birds; not by having imprisoned one, but having caged myself near them.

—HENRY DAVID THOREAU

▶ EXERCISE 4   Follow the directions for Exercise 3.

1. It was never a pilot that started the idea that night falls.   2. A pilot knows that it does not.   3. It oozes up out of the ground, fills the hollows and low places with purple pools of shadow that spread and rise to the tops of the trees and the houses.   4. Long before the sky has darkened, the world below is swimming in night.   5. And then finally darkness begins washing up over the sky from the east, climbing over the zenith, closing down at last over the final gleams of the sunset.   6. Here and there stars begin to prick through, larger and more liquid than ever seen from the ground, and the moon, big and white, outlines the earth.   7. Below the plane, lights map the town, race along the roads, accenting but not relieving the blackness, for darkness clings to the ground.   8. Whatever light there is clings to the sky to the last.

—ALMA HEFLIN[2]

---

[2] From *Adventure Was the Compass* by Alma Heflin McCormick. By permission of the author.

LARGER ELEMENTS

The Paragraph

31

Make paragraphs unified and coherent; develop them adequately.

A paragraph is a distinct unit of thought—usually a group of related sentences, though occasionally no more than one sentence—in a written or printed composition. The form of a paragraph is easy to recognize: the first line is indented. The content of a unified paragraph deals with one central idea; every sentence contributes to this idea. Moreover, each sentence fits into a logical pattern of organization and is therefore carefully related to other sentences in the paragraph.

Below is an example of a unified, coherent, adequately developed paragraph. As you read it, observe (1) the clear statement of the controlling idea in the first sentence, (2) the development of that idea in the sentences which follow, (3) the orderly arrangement of the supporting facts, and (4) the close relationship of the sentences to the central idea and to one another. (For easy reference, each of the forty-three specimen paragraphs in this chapter is numbered.)

1   As a matter of fact, the educated man uses at least three languages. With his family and his close friends, on the ordinary, unimportant occasions of daily life, he speaks, much of the time, a monosyllabic sort of shorthand. On more important occasions and when dealing with strangers in his official or business relations, he has a more formal speech, more complete, less allusive, politely qualified, wisely reserved. In addition he has some acquaintance with the literary speech of his language. He understands this when he reads it, and often enjoys it, but he hesitates to use it. In times of emotional stress hot fragments of it may come out of him like lava, and in times of feigned emotion, as when giving a commencement address, cold, greasy gobbets of it will ooze forth.   —BERGEN EVANS[1]

The central idea of the above paragraph is "the educated man uses at least three languages." The sentences developing the central idea classify the languages and describe their uses; these points are well organized, progressing from informal speech in ordinary situations to formal speech on rare occasions. Repeated references to times and situations, the comparison of the languages, and transitional devices (such as the phrase "in addition") link the sentences within the paragraph and thus contribute to its coherence.

Since each paragraph in a composition is a distinct unit of thought, the beginning of a new paragraph is an important signal to the reader. It serves as a signpost of an approaching curve in the avenue of thought; or it warns him that he must take a new avenue of thought. It announces a new time, place, person, or thing in the course of a narrative, a different point of view in description, a new step in an exposition, or an advance in argument.

Length. Expository or argumentative paragraphs in current books and magazines are usually from 50 to 250 words in length, with the average perhaps 100 words. Paragraphs tend to run longer in books and shorter in the

[1] From "Grammar for Today" by Bergen Evans, reprinted from the *Atlantic Monthly,* March, 1960. By permission of the author.

narrow columns of newspapers. Shorter paragraphs are more frequent in narrative writing, especially dialogue, in which each speech is paragraphed separately.

Indention. The first lines of paragraphs are indented uniformly, about one inch in longhand and five spaces in typewritten copy.

31a

Give unity to the paragraph by making each sentence contribute to the central thought.

A paragraph is said to have unity when each sentence contributes to the central thought. Any sentence that fails to contribute violates the unity of the paragraph and should be omitted. The central thought is usually expressed in a *topic sentence.* In the illustrations of unified paragraphs below, the central idea, when expressed, is indicated by italics.

Although a topic sentence may come anywhere within a paragraph, the central idea of an expository paragraph is often stated in the first sentence.

2 *But it is in vocabulary that the effects of the Conquest are most obvious.* French ceased, after a hundred years or so, to be the native language of very many people in England, but it continued—and continues still—to be a zealously cultivated second language, the mirror of elegance and civilization. When one spoke English, one introduced not only French ideas and French things but also their French names. This was not only easy but socially useful. To pepper one's conversation with French expressions was to show that one was well-bred, elegant, *au courant.* The last sentence shows that the process is not yet dead. By using *au courant* instead of, say, *abreast of things,* the writer indicates that he is no dull clod who knows only English but an elegant person aware of how things are done in *le haut monde.*

—PAUL ROBERTS[2]

[2] From "A Brief History of English," reprinted from *Understanding English* by Paul Roberts. By permission of Harper & Brothers.

When the topic sentence comes at or near the beginning, the conclusion of the paragraph may not only restate the central idea—and thus repeat key words or the main point of the topic sentence—but also emphasize its significance:

3 *Father got holes in his socks even oftener than we boys did in our stockings.* He had long athletic toes, and when he lay stretched out on his sofa reading and smoking, or absorbed in talking to anyone, these toes would begin stretching and wiggling in a curious way by themselves, as though they were seizing on this chance to live a life of their own. I often stared in fascination at their leisurely twistings and turnings, when I should have been listening to Father's instructions about far different matters. Soon one and then the other slipper would fall off, always to Father's surprise, but without interrupting his talk, and a little later *his busy great toe would peer out at me through a new hole in his sock.*

—CLARENCE DAY[3]

Occasionally the central idea of a paragraph may be stated in the last sentence only, especially when the writer progresses from particulars to a generalization:

4 When we watch a person walk away from us, his image shrinks in size. But since we know for a fact that he is not shrinking, we make an unconscious correcting and "see" him as retaining his full stature. Past experience tells us what his true stature is with respect to our own. Any sane and dependable expectation of the future requires that he have the same true stature when we next encounter him. *Our perception is thus a prediction; it embraces the past and the future as well as the present.*

—WARREN J. WITTREICH[4]

[3] From *Life with Father* by Clarence Day. Reprinted by permission of the publishers, Alfred A. Knopf, Inc.
[4] From "Visual Perception and Personality" by Warren J. Wittreich, reprinted from *Scientific American*, April, 1959. By permission of the publishers.

When not expressed in a topic sentence, the central idea of a unified paragraph is distinctly implied:

5   A man in cuffless shirt-sleeves with pink armgarters, wearing a linen collar but no tie, yawned his way from Dyer's Drug Store across to the hotel. He leaned against the wall, scratched a while, sighed, and in a bored way gossiped with a man tilted back in a chair. A lumber-wagon, its long green box filled with large spools of barbed-wire fencing, creaked down the block. A Ford, in reverse, sounded as though it were shaking to pieces, then recovered and rattled away. In the Greek candy-store was the whine of a peanut-roaster, and the oily smell of nuts.

—SINCLAIR LEWIS[5]

[Topic implied: *Such were the activities in Main Street.*]

▶ EXERCISE 1   Point out, or supply, the topic sentence for paragraph 16 below and for any other paragraphs assigned by your instructor.

Caution: Do not make rambling statements that are vaguely related to your topic sentence. As you write a paragraph, hold to the main idea. For instance, if the controlling idea of a paragraph is "My roommate Bill Jones cannot keep a secret," irrelevant sentences about Bill Jones or about secrecy will disrupt the unity. Every statement should pertain to Bill Jones's inability to keep a secret.

CHECK LIST FOR REVISING A PARAGRAPH
WHICH LACKS UNITY

1. Does the paragraph have a central idea clearly stated or implied? (If not, supply a topic sentence.)
2. Does the topic shift one or more times? (If so, either develop each topic in a separate paragraph, or supply

[5] From *Main Street* by Sinclair Lewis, copyright, 1920, by Harcourt, Brace and Company, Inc.; renewed, 1948, by Sinclair Lewis. Reprinted by permission of the publishers.

a topic sentence to which each of the ideas can be made to contribute.)

3. Does every sentence contribute to the central idea? (If not, cross out each irrelevant sentence. If any sentence is related to the central idea, but not clearly so, revise it to make the relationship clear.)

REVISION OF A FAULTY PARAGRAPH

My friend Cliff is often late on important occasions because of his excessive courtesy. — *Topic sentence needed*

Everybody loves Cliff in spite of all his faults and is quick to make excuses for him. ~~I am no exception.~~ — *Omit here (develop in a separate paragraph)*

For example, on Christmas Eve, Cliff was late to a special dinner because his unusually courteous habits had delayed him on a shopping trip. At the entrance of the city's largest bargain basement, he had stood for a quarter of an hour holding doors open for last-minute shoppers. Once inside, he waited a long time, courteously standing aside so that clerks could serve others first. Cliff bought a billfold for his brother. When Cliff at last left the store, he took time out — *Omit — irrelevant*

to carry heavy packages for a woman
whose car was parked two blocks away.
When he finally arrived
~~At~~ home, his family was eating dessert. The very next week, Cliff was
late on an even more important occasion: he almost missed a business
conference with a Mr. Allison, ~~one~~
~~of the company's best customers.~~ Mr.
Allison is president of the Sutter
Steele Company. This time Cliff was
delayed because of a busy elevator.
He stood for a half hour letting
everyone else get on first. When he
finally got on, he lost even more
time because he insisted that he be
the last person off. Cliff is the
type of person who cannot sleep if a
thank-you note remains unwritten or
if he has said anything to hurt anyone's feelings. Whatever the important occasion, Cliff frequently ar-
rives late because he courteously
takes time out to put others first
and himself last.

Make reference to central idea clearer

Omit—does not clearly contribute to central idea

Omit—topic shifts

▶ EXERCISE 2 Give reasons for the lack of unity in the two faulty paragraphs below, and make specific suggestions for revisions.

1. Michigan is a hunter's paradise. Deer, quail, and other kinds of wild game abound in the piny woods of the upper peninsula. Michigan has perhaps more coast line than any other state in the Union, being practically surrounded by Lake Superior, Lake Michigan, and Lake Huron. Along the coast almost every cove affords an ideal location for vacation camps. The lakes that fashion the state into two peninsulas, the upper and the lower, abound in fish which are eagerly sought by fishermen for pleasure and profit. The rugged upper peninsula is the more picturesque. It is the mining section of the state, while the lower peninsula is famous for its manufacturing. The phenomenal development of the automobile industry during the last half-century has made Detroit one of America's largest cities.

2. At my place last night, a tornadic wind played several mischievous pranks. Whistling loudly through the weather stripping, it sprayed dirty water all over the freshly mopped kitchen floor. Next, as though chiding me for my earlier complaints about stuffy air, it created enormous drafts by breaking a half dozen window panes. The moment an announcer on television started reading a special bulletin from the weather bureau, the wind knocked down my television antenna and, just as I reached for the radio, blacked out the whole house. Later I learned that a pilot flying above the turbulent weather had reported that he had never seen such a violent thunderstorm. Traveling at ninety miles an hour, the wind leveled a two-car garage belonging to Mr. Fulton, my neighbor. The wind also turned on an outdoor water faucet, flooding my pansy bed, overturned the dog house, imprisoning my fox terrier, and dumped a stolen boat into the back yard, after ripping the motor off and breaking the oars. After that savage storm, my family and I are most grateful to be alive and uninjured.

31b

Give coherence to the paragraph by so interlinking the sentences that the thought may flow smoothly from one sentence to the next.

A paragraph is said to have coherence when the relationship between sentences is clear, when the transition from one sentence to the next is easy and natural. The reader should be able to follow the thought without difficulty. In order to secure this coherence, this easy flow of the thought from sentence to sentence, the writer should rely first of all on (1) arrangement of the sentences in a clear order, and then on the use of (2) pronouns referring to the preceding sentence, (3) repeated words or ideas, (4) transitional expressions, and (5) parallel structure.

(1) **Arrange the sentences of the paragraph in a clear, logical order.**

There are several common, logical ways to order the sentences in a paragraph; the choice of an appropriate order depends upon the writer's purpose and the nature of his material. Perhaps the simplest and most common order is "time" order.

POOR ARRANGEMENT OF SENTENCES

After the death of Saul, David ruled Israel for forty years. Once he incurred the king's anger and was driven ignominiously from court. As a shepherd lad he had lived in the hills of Judea. He had vanquished the mighty Philistine with his slingshot. The sad-faced Saul was charmed with his songs. He was the sweetest singer in all Israel.

[Confused time order]

ORDERLY SEQUENCE OF SENTENCES

6 David, the shepherd lad who lived in the hills of Judea, was the sweetest singer in all Israel. It was he who charmed the sad-faced Saul with his songs. It was he, too, who vanquished the mighty Philistine with his slingshot. Later he incurred the anger of Saul and was driven from court. But upon Saul's death David came back and ruled Israel for forty years.

[David's (1) *youth in Judea,* (2) *experiences with Saul,* and (3) *reign over Israel*]

This paragraph about David is made clearer by re-arrangement in time order. Narrative paragraphs lend themselves naturally to such arrangement, and other types of paragraphs often have a time element that makes possible and natural a chronological arrangement. For example, in explaining a process—how something is done or made—the writer can follow the process through, step by step, from beginning to end. The following paragraph uses time order in explaining a way to put a wick into a lighter.

7 Threading a new wick in a cigaret lighter can be simplified by straightening out a paper clip and pushing one end of it one-fourth of an inch into the center of the new wick. Drop nail polish or transparent cement on the spot and, before it dries, roll it gently with the fingers to smooth it. When the cement hardens, remove the old wick and wadding from the lighter, and pull the new wick into position with the wire. Replace the wadding, and snip off the end of the wick with the wire attached.

—W. H. McCLAY[6]

Sentences that have no evident time order can sometimes be arranged in "space" order, in which the paragraph moves from east to west, from west to east, from the near to the distant, from the distant to the near, from the left to the right, etc. This order is used especially for descriptive paragraphs. Note the movement from the warm, low coastal gardens to the cold, high areas in the following paragraph.

[6] From "Installing a Lighter Wick" by W. H. McClay, reprinted from *Science and Mechanics Handbook Annual,* 1961. By permission of the publishers.

8 Late winter color heralds the approach of spring in all areas of the Southwest. In mild coastal gardens, this happens gradually as spring sneaks up without much fanfare. Farther inland, bulbs and flowering trees attract more attention. And in colder areas of the mountains and high desert, the appearance of the first buds on a deciduous shrub or tree is downright exciting after winter's snow.[7]

Another good arrangement of sentences is in order of "climax," according to which the least important idea is stated first and the others in order of increasing importance, as in the following paragraph. See also **29c**.

9 An ant cannot purposefully try anything new, and any ant that accidentally did so would be murdered by his colleagues. It is the ant colony as a whole that slowly learns over the ages. In contrast, even an earthworm has enough flexibility of brain to enable it to be taught to turn toward the left or right for food. Though rats are not able to reason to any considerable degree, they can solve such problems as separating round objects from triangular ones when these have to do with health or appetite. Cats, with better brains, can be taught somewhat more, and young dogs a great deal. The higher apes can learn by insight as well as by trial and error.   —GEORGE R. HARRISON[8]

Sometimes the movement within the paragraph may be from the general to the particular, from the particular to the general, or from the familiar to the unfamiliar. A paragraph may begin with a general statement which is then supported by particular details, or, reversing the process, it may begin with a striking detail or series of details and conclude with a summarizing statement. Note the movement from the general to the particular in paragraph 10 and from particular to general in paragraph 11:

[7] From "The Earliest Color," reprinted from *Sunset,* January, 1959. By permission of the publishers.

[8] From "How the Brain Works" by G. R. Harrison, reprinted from the *Atlantic Monthly,* September, 1956. By permission of the author.

10 In the ten years we have been married, I have yet to see Maurine act deviously. Although caginess is presumed to be a prerequisite for politics, she has marched to the top of the ballot by blurting out exactly what is in her mind. When she was asked to back a bill allocating a portion of dog-racing revenues for 4-H clubs, Maurine scolded her constituents for tying a worthy cause to pari-mutuel gambling. The special interests which she has offended would terrify most politicians—utility companies, dairy farmers, the Bar-Tenders' Union, the fairs in all thirty-six Oregon counties, slot-machine operators, the Farm Bureau Federation, even the American Legion.   —RICHARD L. NEUBERGER[9]

[The first sentence states the topic: *Maurine never acts deviously.* The second sentence begins the development with a general statement about her positive action. The third sentence shows specifically how she faced up to the 4-H clubs, and the fourth lists other special interests defied in the same way.]

11 Many years ago a graduate student inconvenienced himself greatly to come a long distance to see me to ask if I could help him secure some information about the term "poll tax." He was preparing a doctor's thesis, he told me, and needed to know how long this term had been in the language, what its basic meaning was, and what other meanings it may have had in the course of its use in English. He was most surprised when I opened the *OED* to the appropriate place and showed him that all he needed to know about this term had been available within a few feet of his desk in the school where he was studying. It is not at all likely that any but the exceptional student will ever need all the information about words that the larger dictionaries afford, but it is well worth the while of every student to become acquainted with the fact that such information is available for those who at any time need to make use of it.   —MITFORD M. MATHEWS[10]

[This paragraph explains how one particular graduate student learned his lesson and then suggests the value of the lesson to all students.]

---

[9] From "My Wife Put Me in the Senate," *Harper's Magazine*, June, 1955.
[10] From "The Freshman and His Dictionary" by Mitford M. Mathews, reprinted from *College Composition and Communication*, December, 1955. By permission of the National Council of Teachers of English.

Paragraphs 6, 7, 8, 9, 10, and 11 above illustrate four of many possible types of clear sentence arrangement within the paragraph. Any order of sentences, or any combination of orders, is satisfactory so long as it makes the sequence of thought clear. Proper arrangement of the sentences is the first, the basic, step to insure good transitions from sentence to sentence. All other steps presuppose that the sentences have first been arranged in the clearest possible order.

▶ EXERCISE 3   Analyze paragraph 4 above and paragraphs 32 and 39 below to determine the order used.

(2) **Link sentences by means of pronouns referring to antecedents in preceding sentences. (See also Section 28.)**

In the following paragraphs italics are used to indicate the pronouns serving as links between sentences. Such pronouns should usually come near the beginning of the sentence if they are to be of much use in paragraph coherence.

12   There is still a good book to be written about the legend of the heroic West and the cowboy. The author would have to be a social philosopher as well as an historian. The legend has not been with us long. That West has had a very short history. *It* did not begin until the 'sixties, and *its* Homeric age was over before the century ended. *It* was created by a passing set of economic circumstances, by cheap open grazing-land in the Southwest, and good prices on the hoof in Kansas City. *It* could not survive the invention of barbed wire. Yet what a legend *it* has created!

—J. B. PRIESTLEY[11]

13   The mackerel were nervous and uneasy. *Those* on the outside of the school were aware of a heavy movement, as of some large sea creature in the water near *them*. *They* felt the

---

[11] From *Midnight on the Desert.* By permission of the author.

wash of its passage through the sea—the heavy wake of displaced water. *Some* of *them* saw above *them* a moving, silver shape. . . .
—RACHEL L. CARSON[12]

▶ EXERCISE 4   Underline the pronouns used to link sentences in paragraphs 27 and 42, or in any others assigned by your instructor. Check the antecedent (in a preceding sentence) to which each pronoun refers. Underline the pronouns used to link sentences in your last paper or in your last two papers.

(3) Link sentences by repeating words or ideas used in the preceding sentences.

Notice in the next paragraph the repetition of the key words—*liberal, radical, leftist, left; conservative, rightist, right*—and of an idea—*labels, distinction, classifications,* "*ideological* positions," "This system of classifying political *philosophies.*" Notice also that the repetition of *world* and the use of *French* and *France's* link sentences within the paragraph.

14   The *liberal-conservative labels* parallel the *left-right distinction* that grew out of the *French* Revolution. In *France's* National Assembly of 1789, the *conservatives* sat to the *right* of the speaker, and became known as *rightists,* and the *radicals* sat at the *left* and became known as *leftists.* From then on, it was commonly assumed that you could place *ideological positions* somewhere on a list ranging from the *left* to the *right.* *This system of classifying political philosophies* is attractive because it seems so tidy. But it is woefully inadequate, since it is one-dimensional, whereas the *world* is three-dimensional. The *world* today is much too complex to hold still for the *left* versus *right* and the *liberal* versus *conservative* classifications.   —BOB SENSER[13]

[12] From *Under the Sea Wind* by Rachel L. Carson. Reprinted by permission of Oxford University Press, Inc.
[13] From "Don't Get Obsessed with Labels" by Bob Senser, reprinted from *Our Sunday Visitor,* May 7, 1961. By permission of the publishers.

▶ EXERCISE 5 In paragraph 34, or in any others assigned by your instructor, underline each word or idea that is repeated in order to link the sentences within the paragraph. In your last paper underline words or ideas that are repeated as a means of linking sentences.

(4) Link sentences by using such transitional expressions as the following.

ADDITION moreover, further, furthermore, besides, and, and then, likewise, also, nor, too, again, in addition, equally important, next, first, secondly, thirdly, *etc.*, finally, last, lastly

CONTRAST but, yet, and yet, however, still, nevertheless, on the other hand, on the contrary, after all, notwithstanding, for all that, in contrast to this, at the same time, although this may be true, otherwise

COMPARISON similarly, likewise, in like manner

PURPOSE to this end, for this purpose, with this object

RESULT hence, therefore, accordingly, consequently, thus, thereupon, wherefore, as a result

TIME meanwhile, at length, immediately, soon, after a few days, in the meantime, afterward, later

PLACE here, beyond, near by, opposite to, adjacent to, on the opposite side

SUMMARY, REPETITION, EXEMPLIFICATION, INTENSIFICATION to sum up, in brief, on the whole, in sum, in short, as I have said, in other words, to be sure, as has been noted, for example, for instance, in fact, indeed, in any event

Note the transitional expressions in the following paragraph. See also paragraph 17.

15 Since the major cost of advanced education, if the student is away from home, is board and lodging, one can argue that as far as possible the expansion of public education beyond high school should be arranged locally. *Otherwise* in order to offer equal opportunities we should have to envisage using public funds to provide years of free board and room for a considerable fraction of our high school graduates. *But* there are various types of professional and vocational education which can be given at only a few centers in even a very populous state. It is literally impossible, *for example*, to give adequate instruction in clinical medicine except in cities of sufficient size to support large hospitals. *Similarly*, advanced work in the arts, sciences, and letters can be done only where adequate libraries and laboratories are at hand. It is clearly in the national interest to find all the latent talent available for the lengthy training that research careers demand. *Yet* to establish research centers at every point in the United States where general education beyond the high school is desired would be not merely uneconomical, but impossible. . .

—JAMES BRYANT CONANT[14]

▶ EXERCISE 6   In paragraph 37, or in any others assigned by your instructor, underline all transitional expressions used to link sentences within the paragraph. In your last paper underline all transitional expressions used to link sentences.

(5)   Link sentences by means of parallel structure—that is, by repetition of the sentence pattern.

Note how the following paragraph is made coherent by the parallel structure of the last four sentences.

16   In the minds and in the ideals of Americans we have untouched natural resources that need developing just as much as the material treasures still tucked away in unused patents, in undeveloped river valleys, and in the atomic nuclei. For the next war, if one is still required to iron out national vanities, we shall need not so much manpower as brain power and alertness. For the continuing fight against disease, we shall need trained technical skills and unlimited resources in laboratory equipment and service. For the advancement of knowledge generally, we need a deliberate plan to free contemplative men for quiet and respected contemplation. For the realization of "fuller and more fruitful employment and a fuller and more fruitful life" we need a National Science

[14] From "The University," reprinted from *Education in a Divided World* by James Bryant Conant. By permission of Harvard University Press.

Foundation and a country-wide awareness that governmental support for knowledge-research is henceforth basic in the national policy. —HARLOW SHAPLEY[15]

▶ EXERCISE 7   In paragraph 27, or in any others assigned by your instructor, point out instances of parallel structure used to link sentences within the paragraph. Can you find instances in your own writing?

We have observed that easy transition from sentence to sentence within the paragraph depends on clear arrangement of the sentences and then on linking these sentences by means of pronouns, repeated words or ideas, transitional expressions, and parallel structure. Usually several of these aids to coherence are found in a single paragraph. In the following paragraph the linking devices are underlined and are explained in the margins.

17   It would seem that the great virtue of <u>writing</u> is its power to arrest the swift process of thought for steady contemplation and analysis.   <u>Writing is the translation of the audible into the visual.</u>   In large measure <u>it</u> is the spatialization of thought.   Yet <u>writing</u> on papyrus and parchment fostered a very different set of <u>mental habits</u> from those we associate with print

Repetition of word

Parallel structure

Pronoun (referring to writing)

Repetition of word

Repetition of idea (process of thought)

Transitional word

[15] From "Status Quo or Pioneer," *Harper's Magazine*, October, 1945.

and books. In the first place, si-   *Transitional expression*

lent reading was unknown until the

macadamized, streamlined surfaces

of the printed page arrived to per-   *Parallel structure*

mit the swift traverse of the eye

Repetition of idea (silent reading) alone. In the second place, diffi-

culty of access of manuscripts   *Transitional expression*

impelled students to memorize so

far as possible everything they

Pronoun referring to necessary memorization read. This led to encyclopedism,

but also to having on tap in oral

discourse one's entire erudition. [16]

▶ EXERCISE 8   In paragraph 36 below, or in any other paragraphs assigned by your instructor, point out all devices used to insure easy transition from sentence to sentence.

(6) Transitions between paragraphs.

Transitions from one paragraph to the next are even more necessary than those between sentences within the paragraph. The reader takes it for granted that all sentences in one paragraph are on the same topic. But the paragraph break signals a new topic or a new phase of the preceding one, and the reader wants to know at once what the new one is to be. In the three connected paragraphs

[16] From "Sight, Sound, and Fury" by Marshall McLuhan, reprinted from *Commonweal*, April 9, 1954, the weekly journal of opinion edited by Catholic laymen. By permission of *Commonweal*.

(18, 19, and 20) below, note how each opening sentence ties in with the preceding paragraph and also indicates the direction in which the new paragraph is to go.

18 In Philadelphia, the advantage of a small car was recently illustrated in a court of law. A baffled cop had dragged before a magistrate the owners of two MGs which had both been parked in the motor space designed for a single vehicle. It was the view of the cop that this arrangement resulted in an illicit mulcting of the city at the rate of a dime an hour. The magistrate disagreed; he commended the drivers for their ingenuity.

19 Another and no less precious asset arises not so much from size as from lighter and differently distributed weight. A small car is supremely handy in icy weather. It is almost never trapped by snow or mud, and it will almost never lose traction on a slippery grade. Its skids are rare and gentle. And its driver can enjoy the soul-satisfying experience of wending his way up a steep and snowy hill at an even speed among big cars which have skidded into the gutter or which lie helplessly athwart the highway.

20 For many of the more than a million Americans who own two or more cars, these and other advantages have dictated the choice of a small car as a supplement to the basic big car. The combination of, say, a station wagon and an MG provides a nice balance between capacity and chic and provides an escape from the status of a two-car family with all the financial and social implications it involves. A small car doesn't seem to be *exactly* a car; its sheepish owner can treat it as a gadget and explain that it costs next to nothing to operate.

—LAURENCE LAFORE, R. W. LAFORE, AND R. W. LAFORE, JR.[17]

The topics of the three paragraphs may be stated thus: (18) *Ease of parking small cars was recently illustrated in Philadelphia.* (19) *The light weight of small cars is especially advantageous in icy weather.* (20) *The small car needs hardly to be considered a "second" car.* The open-

[17] From "The Small Cars: Fun on Wheels," *Harper's Magazine*, March, 1955.

ing sentence of paragraph 18 refers, by *advantage*, to the previously discussed ease of parking small cars and also leads up to the illustration to be used in the paragraph. The next paragraph begins with *another . . . asset*, showing at once that an additional advantage of small cars is to be pointed out (at the same time that *another* calls attention to the one just discussed). And *these and other advantages* in the opening sentence of paragraph 20 ties in with what has preceded while leading to what is to follow.

Sometimes a paragraph is used to make a transition. Paragraph 22 below is an example of a transitional paragraph.

21 I am overwhelmed by our material and materialistic culture—and its accomplishments. We have developed manufacturing and marketing techniques unsurpassed by any other country. The editors of *Fortune* magazine have observed, "The foreign visitor is drenched with sights and sounds and smells emanating from a man-made environment to which almost all Americans appear to give all their energies."

22 What are some of the factors that make us different from the rest of the world?

23 Our *standard of living* is considerably higher than that of any other nation. In fact, the American way of living is one in which an ever-increasing standard of living is considered our birthright. And with a high standard of living, we have not only great physical and material well-being but also an opportunity to expand our economy still further, especially in the last part of the twentieth century.

24 We devote more aggressive effort to the *advertising* and *selling* of our products than any other nation. . . .
—STEUART HENDERSON BRITT[18]

[18] By permission from *The Spenders*, by Steuart Henderson Britt. Copyright 1960. McGraw-Hill Book Company, Inc.

[Note how paragraph 22 links paragraph 21 (which stresses our difference from the rest of the world) with paragraph 23 (which discusses one factor that makes us different). The paragraphs after 23 take up and develop separately the other factors.]

▶ EXERCISE 9   Analyze for transitions between paragraphs the essay entitled "The Face in the Mirror" in Section 32, pages 377–80.

31c

Develop the paragraph adequately. Supply enough information to satisfy the reader but avoid excessively long paragraphs.

(1) Supply enough information to satisfy the reader.

Avoid inadequately developed paragraphs. A topic sentence is not in itself a paragraph. In ordinary writing a very short paragraph is sometimes used for emphasis or for transition between longer paragraphs. But a *series* of paragraphs each less than fifty words in length (except in dialogue and other special types of writing) suggests inadequate development of the thought. If such choppy paragraphs deal with the same topic, they should be combined into one or more longer paragraphs. If not, each paragraph should be given adequate development.

PARAGRAPHS THAT SHOULD BE COMBINED

The line of demarcation between capitalism and socialism is sharp and clear.

Capitalism is that form of organization in which the means of production—and by that is meant the machine and the funds required to utilize the machine—are controlled by private individuals or by privately owned organizations.

Under a socialistic regime the control of the means of production, the control of capital—for even socialists concede the need for capital—is by the group. Under capitalism the profits accrue to the private individual; under socialism, to the group.

[These three short paragraphs, read together, actually make one unified paragraph of ninety words and should be so written. Taken separately, the paragraphs are short and choppy; together they form a paragraph of average length developing a clearly stated topic sentence: *The line of demarcation between capitalism and socialism is sharp and clear.*]

PARAGRAPHS THAT SHOULD BE EXPANDED

During his first term of office President Roosevelt introduced many laws to promote national recovery. These laws covered all phases of the national life.

[The reader wants to know specifically what some of these laws were.]

Forestry work is healthful, educational, and financially rewarding. A forester, for example, soon learns how to prevent and to fight forest fires.

[The reader expects to find out about three aspects of forestry work, and the writer comments briefly on only one. How is the work healthful? What else does a forester learn? What are the financial rewards?]

The football game was much more like a movie than like real life. The most improbable things happened.

[Some of the improbable happenings should be mentioned, and the implied contrast between the movies and real life elaborated.]

Each of these short paragraphs begins with a promising topic sentence and then stops before supplying enough information to satisfy the reader. In other words, the paragraphs are not adequately developed. (For methods of paragraph development, see **31d.**)

(2) Avoid excessively long paragraphs.

In current writing, paragraphs seldom run to more than two or three hundred words, and the average is much shorter, perhaps not more than one hundred words. Whenever a writer finds that he needs more than 250 words to develop his central thought, he should, if possible, divide his material into two or more paragraphs. Let us notice, for example, how we may divide the following long paragraph, which Richard Steele wrote more than two hundred years ago when readers were less hurried than those of our generation.

25 1. When a good artist would express any remarkable character in sculpture, he endeavors to work up his figure into all the perfections his imagination can form, and to imitate not so much what is, as what may or ought to be. 2. I shall follow their example, in the idea I am going to trace out of a fine gentleman, by assembling together such qualifications as seem requisite to make the character complete. 3. In order to do this I shall premise in general, that by a fine gentleman I mean a man completely qualified as well for the service and good as for the ornament and delight of society. 4. When I consider the frame of mind peculiar to a gentleman, I suppose it graced with all the dignity and elevation of spirit that human nature is capable of. 5. To this I would have joined a clear understanding, a reason free from prejudice, a steady judgment, and an extensive knowledge. 6. When I think of the heart of a gentleman, I imagine it firm and intrepid, void of all inordinate passions, and full of tenderness, compassion, and benevolence. 7. When I view the fine gentleman with regard to his manners, methinks I see him modest without bashfulness, frank and affable without impertinence, obliging and complaisant without servility, cheerful and in good humor without noise. 8. These amiable qualities are not easily obtained; neither are there many men that have a genius to excel this way. 9. A finished gentleman is perhaps the most uncommon of all the great characters in life. 10. Besides the natural endowments with which this distinguished man is to be born, he must run through a long series of education. 11. Before he makes his appearance and shines in the world, he must be principled in religion, instructed in all the moral virtues, and led through the whole course of the polite arts and sciences. 12. He should be no stranger to courts and to camps; he must travel to open his mind, to enlarge his views, to learn the policies and interests of foreign states, as well as to fashion and polish himself, and to get clear of national prejudices, of which every country has its share. 13. To all these more essential improvements he must not forget to add the fashionable ornaments of life, such as are the languages and the bodily exercises most in vogue; neither would I have him think even dress itself beneath his notice.

A careful reading shows that this whole paragraph of 404 words develops Steele's concept of the ideal gentleman. The paragraph has unity; except for the excessive length, there would be no reason for dividing it. Fortunately it can (like most overlong paragraphs) be divided into shorter paragraphs, each developing a specific part of the general topic. Steele's long paragraph can be divided, without any rewriting, into three good paragraphs as follows:

FIRST PARAGRAPH (sentences 1–3) The method to be used in depicting the ideal gentleman and a general definition of him.

SECOND PARAGRAPH (sentences 4–7) The ideal gentleman's specific qualities of mind, heart, and manners.

THIRD PARAGRAPH (sentences 8–13) The education needed to develop these qualities.

If the long paragraph were thus divided into three, it would be much easier for the reader to comprehend. And each paragraph would be well unified, with good transitions from one to the other. Note especially the excellent transition to the third paragraph: "These amiable qualities are not easily obtained; neither are there many men that have a genius to excel this way."

31d

Master several different methods of paragraph development.

Analysis shows that good paragraphs may be developed by many methods and by innumerable combinations of methods. No one method, or combination of methods, is better than another except as it happens to fit the needs of a given paragraph. The experienced writer may be unaware of the method he is using. The inexperienced writer, however, can learn to develop his own paragraphs by studying the methods of professional writers.

(1) List specific details suggested by the topic sentence.

26 *My aunt was a tall, hard-featured lady, but by no means ill-looking.* There was an inflexibility in her face, in her voice, in her gait and carriage, amply sufficient to account for the effect she had made upon a gentle creature like my mother; but her features were rather handsome than otherwise, though unbending and austere. I particularly noticed that she had a very quick, bright eye. Her hair, which was gray, was arranged in two plain divisions, under what I believe would be called a mobcap; I mean a cap, much more common then than now, with sidepieces fastening under the chin. Her dress was of a lavender color, and perfectly neat, but scantily made, as if she desired to be as little encumbered as possible. I remember that I thought it, in form, more like a riding habit with the superfluous skirt cut off, than anything else. She wore at her side a gentleman's gold watch, if I might judge from its size and make, with an appropriate chain and seals; she had some linen at her throat not unlike a shirt collar, and things at her wrists like little shirt wristbands. —CHARLES DICKENS[19]

[Note that all the details have been carefully selected to contribute to the dominant impression of the stern but not ill-looking person that the author wishes to describe. Effective writers choose details with care, omit irrelevant details no matter how fascinating they may be in themselves.]

27 *My second great fortune was Lily Bess Campbell, professor of English literature at the University of California in Los Angeles.* She taught me to think exactly, to say the precise truth as nearly as I could perceive it. She taught me that there is vitality

[19] From *David Copperfield.*

in logic, that there is logic in humor and in beauty, that in humor the greater the truth the funnier, that in lyricism the more consistent and clear the more moving. She made me brief a Shelley ode as though it were a legal argument. She taught me that a sentence was organic with bones and sinews and for this reason had life, that the power of logic was a passionate power and that Euclid and Grammar were one. And for the first time I recognized Pattern, which is Law as well as Magic. —AGNES DE MILLE[20]

[The paragraph lists nine particulars in which Professor Campbell proved to be a "great fortune."]

28   When it was over and I escaped through the ropes, shaking, bleeding a little from the mouth, with rosin dust on my pants and a vicious throbbing in my head, *I knew all there was to know about being hit in the prize-ring.* It seems that I had gone to an expert for tuition. I knew the sensation of being stalked and pursued by a relentless, truculent professional destroyer whose trade and business it was to injure men. I saw the quick flash of the brown forearm that precedes the stunning shock as a bony, leather-bound fist lands on cheek or mouth. I learned more (partly from photographs of the lesson, viewed afterwards, one of which shows me ducked under a vicious left hook, an act of which I never had the slightest recollection) about instinctive ducking and blocking than I could have in ten years of looking at prizefights, and I learned, too, that as the soldier never hears the bullet that kills him, so does the fighter rarely, if ever, see the punch that tumbles blackness over him like a mantle, with a tearing rip as though the roof of his skull were exploding, and robs him of his senses.

—PAUL GALLICO[21]

[Details of this paragraph describe how the author learned what it is like to be a prizefighter. Note that in this paragraph and in paragraphs 26 and 27, the order of development is from the general to the particular.]

[20] From "The Valor of Teaching" by Agnes de Mille, *Atlantic Monthly,* June, 1955.
[21] From *Farewell to Sport* by Paul Gallico. Reprinted by permission of Alfred A. Knopf, Inc.

▶ EXERCISE 10   Supply specific details to develop one of the following topics:

1. The sergeant was stern without being cruel.
2. Our cook was in almost perpetual emotion.
3. The dean is an important administrative officer.
4. The modern farmer is a scientist.
5. The comedian looked as distressed as a freshman on registration day.
6. One teacher influenced my thinking.
7. It was a perfect day for a trip to the lake.
8. At that moment, I knew how it felt to have stage fright.
9. I was the first one to arrive after the accident.
10. It is exciting to travel by jet.

(2) Illustrate the topic sentence by an example or examples.

29   *The belief in punishment at a distance was strikingly illustrated by a report from South Africa last April.* It seems that the caning of offenders was being carried out in a magistrates' court located near the center of Cape Town. Sentences of up to ten cut were inflicted on malefactors, beginning with eight-year-old boys, in that particular jurisdiction. The matter became newsworthy when the public began to object to the practice. The objection, however, was not to the punishment itself but to the uncomfortable circumstance that it was administered in the business district of the city. One citizen complained, "We can clearly hear the swish and smack of the cane and the pleadings and screams of the people being beaten." It appears that this noise was upsetting women office workers. Not only the women were disturbed. One man said "that his conversations with important clients had been interrupted by the 'howling of somebody being thrashed.'" The problem was solved by police assurances that the beatings would thereafter be administered in the basement, where they would not disturb the public.   —JUDGE DAVID L. BAZELON[22]

[The topic sentence is developed by one striking example. Note that the example of the citizens' reactions to *nearby* punishment

[22] From "The Imperative to Punish" by David L. Bazelon, reprinted from the *Atlantic Monthly*, June, 1960. By permission of the author.

makes immediately clear what the author means by the rather abstract idea, "the belief in punishment at a distance." A good example is clearly related to the generalization it illustrates, and it makes that generalization easily understandable to the reader.]

30 *It is important to remember that, in strictness, there is no such thing as an uneducated man.* Take an extreme case. Suppose that an adult man, in the full vigor of his faculties, could be suddenly placed in the world, as Adam is said to have been, and then left to do as he best might. How long would he be left uneducated? Not five minutes. Nature would begin to teach him, through the eye, the ear, the touch, the properties of objects. Pain and pleasure would be at his elbow telling him to do this and avoid that; and by slow degrees the man would receive an education which, if narrow, would be thorough, real, and adequate to his circumstances, though there would be no extras and very few accomplishments. —THOMAS HENRY HUXLEY

[The topic sentence is developed by the one example, admittedly extreme, of a hypothetical modern Adam.]

▶ EXERCISE 11   Develop one of the following sentences by an example in the manner suggested by Huxley's paragraph: (1) No man is wholly fearless. (2) Even an illiterate man can be wise.

31 Disregarding the words and observing any considerable segment of economic behavior, *it is immediately apparent that activities are mixed, sometimes inextricably tangled.* The Tennessee Valley Authority, for instance, is owned by the federal government, but encourages new private enterprise thoughout the Valley, sells much power to private power companies, co-operates closely with state and local governments. Great corporations take on functions closely resembling governmental powers, as Peter Drucker has pointed out, while many private businesses are subsidized by governments—for example, trucks on the highways.
—STUART CHASE[23]

[The topic sentence is developed by several examples.]

[23] From *Power of Words*, copyright, 1953, 1954, by Stuart Chase. Reprinted by permission of Harcourt, Brace and Company, Inc.

32 *Perhaps the most extraordinary quality the Mo-hammedan religion developed in Jolo is its fanaticism.* For years, no Moro would attend school for fear of "invisible conversion" to Christianity. As recently as 1940 the students of one of the schools killed all their non-Moro teachers for no reason that the authorities were ever able to discern. And even today, some people of Jolo will not ride in a car, simply because Christians introduced automobiles to the island. It is also a problem for Moros to go to the hospital, because, according to their reasoning, if they died, a Christian would touch them, and this is not to be borne.

—FAUBION BOWERS[24]

[The topic sentence is developed by four instances or examples, each in a separate sentence.]

▶ EXERCISE 12   Select a suitable topic sentence and develop a paragraph; use several instances or examples.

(3) **Develop the topic by definition.**

33 *First, it is desirable to define the intellectuals.* They are all those who create, distribute and apply culture—the symbolic world of man, including art, science and religion. Within this group, three different levels can be set out. There is the hard core who are the creators of culture—authors, artists, philosophers, scholars, editors, some journalists. Second, there are those who distribute what others create—performers of various arts, most teachers, most reporters. Third, and the most peripheral group, are those who apply culture as part of their jobs—professionals such as physicians and lawyers.   —SEYMOUR MARTIN LIPSET[25]

[The topic sentence calls for a definition of *intellectuals;* the other sentences define and explain the word. A formal, or logical, definition such as Lipset uses, has two parts: first, the thing being defined is put into a *class* of similar things; then it

[24] From "The Land-Locked Pirate of the Pacific," *Harper's Magazine,* June, 1955.
[25] From "The Egghead Looks at Himself" by Seymour M. Lipset, reprinted from the New York *Times Magazine,* November 17, 1957. By permission of the author.

is differentiated from all other things in that class. Thus, *intellectuals* are defined as "those" men (*class*—i.e., mankind) "who create, distribute and apply culture" (*difference* from other kinds of men).]

34 *A guaranteed annual wage is money paid by an employer to people for all or some part of a year in which they are not making products.* The payments are part of the manufacturer's cost and hence part of the consumer's cost. If the manufacturer has ten employees but work for only eight, he must nevertheless recover in the price he gets for his product the payments he makes to his employees for hours they did not work, or he must go out of business. This is true of any employer, whether he has ten or ten thousand employees. —LELAND HAZARD[26]

[The topic sentence defines "guaranteed annual wage," and the remaining sentences serve to refine and clarify this definition.]

▶ EXERCISE 13   Select a suitable topic sentence and develop a paragraph by definition.

(4) Develop the topic by using classification.

35 There are three kinds of book owners. The first has all the standard sets and best-sellers—unread, untouched. (This deluded individual owns woodpulp and ink, not books.) The second has a great many books—a few of them read through, most of them dipped into, but all of them as clean and shiny as the day they were bought. (This person would probably like to make books his own, but is restrained by a false respect for their physical appearance.) The third has a few books or many—every one of them dog-eared and dilapidated, shaken and loosened by continual use, marked and scribbled in from front to back. (This man owns books.) —MORTIMER J. ADLER[27]

[26] From "Can We Afford a Guaranteed Wage?" by Leland Hazard, *Atlantic Monthly,* March, 1955.
[27] From "How to Mark a Book" by Mortimer J. Adler, reprinted from the *Saturday Review,* July 6, 1940. By permission of the publishers.

[Classification is like definition in that it develops an idea by putting things into classes. But it does not differentiate one member of a class from another; instead, it simply gives a complete or representative listing of the members of the class. Thus, Adler in the paragraph above classifies book owners into three main classes and lists each class.]

▶ EXERCISE 14   Use classification to develop one of the following topics:

1. I have two (or three, or four) reasons for choosing _____ as a profession.
2. I have known two (or three, or four) distinct types of _____.

(5) Develop the topic by using comparison or contrast.

36   To some of his contemporaries Socrates looked like a sophist. But *he distrusted and opposed the sophists wherever possible.* They toured the whole Greek world: Socrates stayed in Athens, talking to his fellow-citizens. They made carefully prepared continuous speeches; he only asked questions. They took rich fees for their teaching; he refused regular payment, living and dying poor. They were elegantly dressed, turned out like filmstars on a personal-appearance tour, with secretaries and personal servants and elaborate advertising. Socrates wore the workingman's clothes, bare feet and a smock; in fact, he had been a stonemason and carver by trade, and came from a working-class family. They spoke in specially prepared lecture-halls; he talked to people at street-corners and in gymnasium (like public baths and bathing beaches nowadays), where every afternoon the young men exercised, and the old men talked, while they all sun bathed. He fitted in so well there that he sometimes compared himself to the athletic coach, who does not run or wrestle, but teaches others how to run and wrestle better: Socrates said he trained people to think. Lastly, the sophists said they knew everything and were ready to explain it. Socrates said he knew nothing and was trying to find out.

—GILBERT HIGHET[28]

[28] From *The Art of Teaching* by Gilbert Highet. Copyright 1950 by Gilbert Highet. Reprinted by permission of Alfred A. Knopf, Inc.

[The first sentence is transitional, linking this paragraph with the author's foregoing one; the second sentence states the topic, which is developed by contrasting the sophists with Socrates. In making a comparison or contrast, a writer will often choose the things he wants to compare or contrast from the same class. Socrates and the sophists both belong to the class "philosopher-teachers." This common class provides the *basis* of the contrast. Thus the two kinds of philosophers can be contrasted not only in their methods and their personal habits but, most important, in the ideas or theories of knowledge they taught.]

37 *In all the countries of Europe I have visited there is a patent difference between metropolises and smaller towns.* In the provinces of France, or Austria, or Germany you notice the difference in every shop window, in every coffee house, in the universities themselves. When, for instance, you go from Paris to Lille or to Orleans or to Bordeaux the dresses, the books, the furniture you see in the windows will lag some months if not years behind those you were used to seeing in Paris. The hotels and restaurants will be more modest, uncomfortable, and rather shabby. Universities will lack the stimulating élan of the Sorbonne. *Nothing of this kind distinguishes Madison from, let us say, New York or Chicago.* Here you see just the same merchandise in the windows as in New York, the same neon lights, the same pictures in the same movie theaters, you read the same columns and comics in the local papers as in those of New York, and the university with its splendid installations, its rich library, its almost luxurious Students' Union certainly does not fall behind any university I saw in New York, though it is smaller. —PAUL SCHRECKER[29]

[The implied topic sentence, derived from the two italicized sentences, is: In Europe, but not in America, there is a patent difference between metropolises and smaller towns. European conditions (in four sentences following the first italicized sentence) are contrasted with American conditions (in one very long sentence following the second italicized sentence). Note that instances or examples are used to develop the separate parts of the contrast.]

[29] From "American Diary," *Harper's Magazine*, July, 1944.

▶ EXERCISE 15   Develop by contrast one of the following topics: (1) the service at a soda fountain and in a hotel dining room; (2) the dialogue of a motion picture and the dialogue of Shakespeare; (3) the architecture of the Washington Monument and of the Lincoln Memorial; (4) the relative effectiveness of radio and television.

38   *The living language is like a cowpath: it is the creation of the cows themselves, who, having created it, follow it or depart from it according to their whims or needs.* From daily use, the path undergoes change. A cow is under no obligation to stay in the narrow path she helped make, following the contour of the land, but she often profits by staying with it and she would be handicapped if she didn't know where it was and where it led to. Children obviously do not depend for communication on a knowledge of grammar; they rely on their ear, mostly, which is sharp and quick. But we have yet to see the child who hasn't profited from coming face to face with a relative pronoun at an early age, and from reading books, which follow the paths of centuries.

—E. B. WHITE[30]

[This paragraph compares the living language to a cowpath and the children who speak the language to the cows that use the path by pointing out similarities regarding creation, usage, change, and profitable knowledge and conformity. Note that, unlike the comparisons in paragraphs 35 and 36, the two things compared here are not members of the same class.]

Note that the last three paragraphs illustrate two different ways of making the contrast. In paragraphs 37 and 38 one side of the contrast is completely developed and then the other; in paragraph 36 both sides are contrasted in almost every sentence. Either way is good, and so is a combination of the two.

▶ EXERCISE 16   Develop one topic from Exercise 15 according to the organization used in paragraph 37 or 38.

[30] From the *New Yorker*, February 23, 1957. Reprinted by permission; Copr. © 1957, The New Yorker Magazine, Inc.

(6) **Develop the topic by showing cause or effect.**

39   Tragedy was a Greek creation because in Greece thought was free. Men were thinking more and more deeply about human life, and beginning to perceive more and more clearly that it was bound up with evil and that injustice was of the nature of things. And then, one day, this knowledge of something irremediably wrong in the world came to a poet with his poet's power to see beauty in the truth of human life, and the first tragedy was written. As the author of a most distinguished book on the subject says: "The spirit of inquiry meets the spirit of poetry and tragedy is born." Make it concrete: early Greece with her godlike heroes and hero-gods fighting far on the ringing plains of windy Troy; with her lyric world, where every common thing is touched with beauty —her twofold world of poetic creation. Then a new age dawns, not satisfied with beauty of song and story, an age that must try to know and to explain. And for the first time tragedy appears. A poet of surpassing magnitude, not content with the old sacred conventions, and of a soul great enough to bear new and intolerable truth—that is Aeschylus, the first writer of tragedy.

—EDITH HAMILTON[31]

[Hamilton here states that tragedy began when the ancient Greeks discovered, through free inquiry, that evil is an inevitable part of human life. This discovery is, then, the *cause* of the writing of tragedy. But before this cause could have an effect in the creation of tragic plays, a great poet had to come along— that was Aeschylus. A paragraph developed by causal analysis must not only raise the question *why* but answer it to the satisfaction of the reader. The cause or causes must satisfactorily explain the result. Has Hamilton done this?]

40   One might wonder why, after the Norman Conquest, French did not become the national language, replacing English entirely. The reason is that the Conquest was not a national migration, as the earlier Anglo-Saxon invasion had been. Great numbers of Normans came to England, but they came as rulers

[31] Reprinted from *The Greek Way* by Edith Hamilton. By permission of W. W. Norton & Company, Inc Copyright 1930, 1942 by W. W. Norton & Company, Inc.

and landlords. French became the language of the court, the language of the nobility, the language of polite society, the language of literature. But it did not replace English as the language of the people. There must always have been hundreds of towns and villages in which French was never heard except when visitors of high station passed through. —PAUL ROBERTS[32]

[The topic sentence raises the question why the Norman Conquest did not, as might have been expected, make England a French-speaking country. The topic sentence thus states an *effect* or *result* of the Conquest. The sentences that follow develop the topic by showing *causes* to account for the result.]

▶ EXERCISE 17 Notice how paragraphs 39 and 40 are developed by answering why the opening statement is true. In the same way develop a paragraph from one of the following topics:

1. Higher education has become more important than ever.
2. Our age is a dangerous one in which to live.

(7) Develop the topic by a combination of methods.

Many good paragraphs are developed not by any one specific method but by a combination of methods. Some good paragraphs almost defy analysis. The important consideration is not the specific method used but the adequacy of the development.

41 I wonder why American towns look so much alike that I sometimes mix them up in my memory. The reference to the standard influence of mass production whose agents are the traveling salesman, the mail-order houses, the five-and-ten cent stores, the chain stores, the movies, is not sufficient. If you stay two days in Bologna and in Ferrara, or in Arles and in Avignon, you will never mix them up in all your life. But it may well happen that after you spend two days in St. Louis and in Kansas City the

[32] From "A Brief History of English," reprinted from *Understanding English* by Paul Roberts. By permission of Harper & Brothers.

images of these towns soon merge into one. I think the real reason for this is that these towns have not yet had time enough to individualize and to crystallize visible local traditions of their own. Physiognomically speaking, children are much less differentiated from each other than grown people.   —PAUL SCHRECKER[33]

[Note how this effective paragraph combines both cause or effect and comparison or contrast.]

42 I have heard rumors of visitors who were disappointed. The same people will be disappointed at the Day of Judgment. In fact, the Grand Canyon is a sort of landscape Day of Judgment. It is not a show place, a beauty spot, but a revelation. The Colorado River, which is powerful, turbulent, and so thick with silt that it is like a saw, made it with the help of the erosive forces of rain, frost, and wind, and some strange geological accidents; and all these together have been hard at work on it for the last seven or eight million years. It is the largest of the eighteen canyons of the Colorado River, is over two hundred miles long, has an average width of twelve miles, and is a good mile deep. It is the world's supreme example of erosion. But this is not what it really is. It is, I repeat, a revelation. The Colorado River made it, but you feel when you are there that God gave the Colorado River its instructions. It is all Beethoven's nine symphonies in stone and magic light. Even to remember that it is still there lifts up the heart. If I were an American, I should make my remembrance of it the final test of men, art, and policies. I should ask myself: Is this good enough to exist in the same country as the Canyon? How would I feel about this man, this kind of art, these political measures, if I were near that Rim? Every member or officer of the Federal Government ought to remind himself, with triumphant pride, that he is on the staff of the Grand Canyon.   —J. B. PRIESTLEY[34]

▶ EXERCISE 18   Pick out the topic sentence in paragraph 42. Show how Priestley effectively develops his central idea. Does he use a specific method or combination of methods of development?

[33] From "American Diary," *Harper's Magazine*, July, 1944.
[34] From *Midnight on the Desert* by J. B. Priestley. By permission of the author.

43   After Colonel Carter was gone home I went to work on my new horse. The old one, the pony, I used only for business: to go to fires, to see my friends, run errands, and go hunting with my new shotgun. But the game that had all my attention was the breaking in of the colt, the beautiful cream-colored mare, who soon knew me—and my pockets. I carried sugar to reward her when she did right, and she discovered where I carried it; so did the pony, and when I was busy they would push their noses into my pockets, both of which were torn down a good deal of the time. But the colt learned. I taught her to run around a circle, turn and go the other way at a signal. My sisters helped me. I held the long rope and the whip (for signaling), while one of the girls led the colt; it was hard work for them, but they took it in turns. One would lead the colt round and round till I snapped the whip; then she would turn, turning the colt, till the colt did it all by herself. And she was very quick. She shook hands with each of her four feet. She let us run under her, back and forth. She was slow only to carry me. Following Colonel Carter's instructions, I began by laying my arm on a surcingle over her back. If she trembled, I drew it slowly off. When she could abide it, I tried buckling it, tighter and tighter. I laid over her, too, a blanket, folded at first, then open, and, at last, I slipped up on her myself, sat there a second, and as she trembled, slid off. My sisters held her for me, and when I could get up and sit there a moment or two, I tied her at a block, and we, my sisters and I, made a procession of mounting and dismounting. She soon got used to this and would let us slide off over her rump, but it was a long, long time before she would carry me.   —LINCOLN STEFFENS[35]

▶ EXERCISE 19   The topic sentence of paragraph 43— "But the game that had all my attention was the breaking in of the colt, etc."—is developed chiefly by giving details in time order. In like manner expand one of the following topics: (1) how I spent all my time training my hound; (2) how I shot my first deer; (3) how we won the football game; (4) how I got my first job; (5) how I cooked my first dinner.

[35] From *The Autobiography of Lincoln Steffens*, copyright, 1931 by Harcourt, Brace and Company, Inc.

▶ EXERCISE 20   Indicate an appropriate method of developing each of the following topic sentences:

1. The school is the servant of the individual, the family, and the community.
2. The guaranteed annual wage has aroused much controversy.
3. There is more than one reason why the college student should study English.
4. My roommate has helped me to understand myself.
5. The changing aspects of the seasons are as stimulating as they are restful.
6. As Tennyson once said, a lie that is half a truth is the blackest lie of all.
7. A circus has many mouths to feed.
8. Before talking about democracy we should at least say what democracy is not.
9. I no longer believe in fortune tellers.
10. Some men think our great cities are monuments of progress; others say they are symptoms of social disease.
11. You can solve most problems by taking a walk.
12. Intelligence means the ability to discriminate.
13. At college I have discovered two kinds of friends.
14. A self-reliant person must know his predominant weakness as well as his predominant strength.
15. Automation may revolutionize education.
16. The ability to think and the ability to write are closely allied.
17. There is a great deal of difference between a state college and a state university.
18. When the storm was over we all set to work in earnest.
19. My jalopy reminds me of a frumpy old woman.
20. I had two reasons for failing chemistry in high school.

▶ EXERCISE 21   Select a topic sentence and develop a paragraph by one or more of the methods described in **31d**.

Planning and Writing the Whole Composition

32
Arrange and express your ideas effectively.

The four units of composition, in an ascending order, are (1) the word—Sections **19-22,** (2) the sentence—Sections **23-30,** (3) the paragraph—Section **31,** and (4) the whole composition—Section **32.** Words make up the sentence, sentences make up the paragraph, and paragraphs make up the whole composition.

A paragraph is usually a series of sentences developing one topic, such as "Advertisements of facial soap are deceptive." A composition is usually a series of paragraphs developing several topics which are closely related, such as "Advertisements of (1) facial soap, (2) breakfast cereals, and (3) filter-tip cigarettes are deceptive." Just as a unified paragraph has a stated or implied topic to which each sentence contributes, a unified composition has a central idea to which each paragraph contributes. Therefore, many of the techniques used to write paragraphs (*e.g.*, developing a central idea, arranging supporting details logically and effectively, making appropriate transitions) are applicable to the composition as a whole. See Section **31.**

In fact. sometimes the major difference between a paragraph and a composition is merely a matter of scale. For example, the topic sentence of paragraph 1 on page 321 could easily be converted to the central idea of a composition. The three points made within paragraph 1 could then be topic sentences for separate paragraphs. Of course, more specific details would be necessary to develop each paragraph adequately; an introductory and a concluding paragraph might also be added.

32a

Choose an appropriate subject and limit it properly.

Be sure to select a topic that will enable you to say something interesting about what you know well. Limit the topic you choose so that you can develop it adequately, specifically.

A subject is appropriate:

1. If it appeals to you, or if you can develop an interest in it as you work on it.
2. If it is acceptable to the intended reader.

A subject is properly limited:

1. If you know enough about it or can learn enough in a reasonable period. (Subjects that require extensive reading should be reserved for the library paper. See Section 33.)
2. If the topic is not too broad to treat in the time or space at your command. "Amateur Photography" might be a satisfactory title for a paper of several thousand words; but if you must limit yourself to several hundred words, you will do better with "Developing a Film" or "The Growth of My Interest in Photography."

Let us suppose that you have chosen (or have been assigned) "Sports" as a general subject for a paper of five hundred words. Obviously, you cannot cover everything to be said about sports in five hundred words. You must therefore find a more limited topic. You may be particularly interested in one sport, but "Football" or "Baseball" is still too broad for your short paper. Therefore you should concentrate on a narrow phase of the sport chosen, such as "The Importance of Fumbles in Saturday's Game" or "Characteristics of a Good Shortstop."

PURPOSE

Before making a final decision regarding the specific topic, you should consider your purpose in writing the composition. If your purpose is to inform the reader, either "The Importance of Fumbles in Saturday's Game" or "Characteristics of a Good Shortstop" would be appropriate. If, however, your primary aim is to describe your feelings as you watched a particularly heart-breaking defeat, you might want to title your theme "A Cold Day at Memorial Stadium." On the other hand, you might decide that you want to argue about the merits of watching football as compared with watching baseball. You might then write a theme on the topic "Football or Baseball as a Spectator Sport" or "I Would Rather Watch Football than Baseball." Finally, you might decide to write a narrative account of the most exciting football game you have ever seen. Then your topic might be "A Game I Will Never Forget—Texas 20, Baylor 19."

Each of the purposes you might select corresponds to one of the four main types of writing as they are conventionally classified in rhetoric—exposition or explanation (to inform), description, argument (or persuasion), and narration. *Exposition* is the most common kind of non-fiction writing and the kind most frequently written by college students. *Argument* is similar to exposition but written with the intention of convincing rather than simply explaining. In *narration,* events are presented in a time sequence, and in *description* a sensory impression of an object or feeling is conveyed. (See paragraph 5, Section **31.**) Very seldom is description written independently. Usually it is only part of a composition in which one of the other types dominates. In fact, few compositions are a single form of discourse. Most are mixtures in which one form predominates. Thus, a paper on "How to Drive a Car" would be primarily exposition but would also contain bits of description (perhaps of the steering mechanism) and narration (perhaps an anecdote about the author's first drive).

Whatever form of discourse a paper may take, it does not fall into order by chance. *Order is the result of careful planning.*

CENTRAL IDEA

After deciding upon your purpose, you will find it helpful to set down, in a single sentence, the central or controlling idea for your paper. If the purpose is to inform, the sentence may read, "A good shortstop thinks and acts quickly." This thesis statement helps to limit the subject and especially helps determine the items to be included in the outline. In fact, if in the beginning you can set down a central idea containing logically arranged main points (see Example 1 below), you will already have the main headings of your outline. If you do not give the main points in your central idea (see Examples 2 through 5 below), you may later wish to reword it in order to show its close relationship to the items in your outline. In dealing with some subjects, you may need to list your ideas and then find and consider more evidence before you can decide upon an appropriate central idea. If not determined in the process of limiting the subject, the central idea should be written out before the outline is completed and then used to test the contents of the outline.

EXAMPLES

1. *Purpose:* To inform by pointing out ways to appraise a used car [Exposition]

   Title: How to Buy a Good Used Car

   Central Idea: Before selecting a used car, a wise buyer will carefully inspect the car himself, talk to the former owner of it, and engage a good mechanic to examine its motor.

2. *Purpose:* To convince the reader of a need for change [Argument]
   Title: Why Have Final Examinations?
   Central Idea: Final examinations should be abolished.

3. *Purpose:* To describe Rushville and its surroundings [Description]
   Title: Rushville: A Beautiful City in the Mountains
   Central Idea: Rushville is a beautiful city in the mountains.

4. *Purpose:* To tell a story about a childhood experience [Narration]
   Title: I Will Never Play Post Office Again!
   Central Idea: Playing "postmaster," my brother once shocked my friends and me by wiring a group of old post office boxes.

5. *Purpose:* To describe Old Tony and show that he is a colorful individual [Exposition and Description]
   Title: Old Tony
   Central Idea: Old Tony is the most colorful individual that I know.

Each of the suggestions listed below is a suitable subject for a student paper. Some of the suggestions, as worded, may provide the exact title you need for your paper. In all likelihood, however, you will wish to limit the subject to the scope of your experience and to sharpen the wording to suit your purpose. (For the proper capitalization of titles, see 9c.)

Suggestions for Written Work

HOME AND THE INDIVIDUAL

1. My town
2. Being an elder brother (*or* elder sister, only child, etc.)
3. My favorite author (*or* book, poem, magazine, newspaper, radio program, television program, etc.)
4. My hobby and why I like it (hiking; photography; collecting stamps, old glass, coins, books, furniture, etc.)
5. Learning to swim (*or* play tennis, ride horseback, sail a boat, ride a bicycle, skate, play the saxophone, etc.)
6. How to choose a second car for the family.

7. Color schemes (*or* draperies, period furniture, etc.) in interior decorating
8. Milk (meat, vegetables, etc.) in the diet
9. Changes in men's (women's) clothing
10. Peacetime draft and its effect on the individual

SCHOOL AND COLLEGE

1. Differences between school and college
2. Freshman Week
3. College slang
4. Earning one's way
5. My first field trip
6. The course I find most practical (*or* difficult, interesting, etc.)
7. The student union
8. Campus politics
9. Why I should (*or* should not) join a fraternity (*or* sorority)
10. My room at college
11. The writing laboratory
12. Using a microscope
13. Are examinations fair?
14. The honor system
15. How to be a cheer leader
16. What makes school spirit?
17. Why I am going to college
18. Duties of the quarterback (*or* halfback, fullback, etc.)
19. What is sportsmanship?
20. Life in a dormitory (*or* fraternity house, sorority house, etc.)

HISTORY, ECONOMICS, AND SOCIOLOGY

1. What do our taxes buy?
2. Is television getting better or worse?
3. Recessions
4. The State of Israel
5. The Monroe Doctrine today
6. Our Foreign Aid Program
7. The guaranteed annual wage
8. The Iron Curtain
9. Status symbols
10. Socialized medicine
11. Today's teen-agers
12. The National Park Service
13. Reforestation
14. Causes of juvenile delinquency
15. Living in a housing development
16. Television advertising
17. The parole system
18. Unemployment insurance
19. Sharecroppers
20. The right to strike (*or* compulsory arbitration)

SCIENCE AND MEDICINE

1. Atomic submarines
2. Wild plants and their uses in medicine
3. The prevention of forest fires
4. Vitamins from plants
5. Color television
6. Chemical warfare on insects (*or* DDT, etc.)
7. Yeasts and vitamins
8. Migration of wild ducks and geese
9. Blood plasma
10. Beneficial bacteria
11. Synthetic diamonds
12. Nylon (*or* acrilan, dacron, etc.)
13. Amateur photography
14. The Salk vaccine
15. What is food allergy?
16. Penicillin (*or* streptomycin, aureomycin, sulfathiazole, etc.)
17. Space flight
18. Guided missiles
19. Uses of uranium
20. Plastic surgery

FARM AND MACHINE

1. Soil erosion
2. How to grow tomatoes (*or* asparagus, strawberries, celery, dahlias, mushrooms, chrysanthemums, etc.)
3. Wild life on the farm
4. The apple, from tree to consumer
5. Sports cars
6. Good seeds make good crops
7. Judging cattle
8. Making a tobacco bed
9. Curing tobacco
10. The work of the 4-H Club (*or* home demonstration work, etc.)
11. Frozen foods
12. Newsprint from Southern pine
13. Soilless farming
14. Air conditioning every home
15. A practical "do-it-yourself" project
16. "Don't be a dish washer. Buy one!"
17. Mining coal (*or* lead, copper, zinc, etc.)
18. Building a boat (*or* desk, dog house, etc.)
19. The most wonderful machine I know
20. Advantages of living on a farm (*or* in the city, in a small town)
21. Operating a tractor (*or* any other machine used on the farm)
22. How to eliminate the wheat (*or* cotton, corn, etc,) surplus

▶ EXERCISE 1 After selecting five subjects from the preceding "Suggestions for Written Work," decide how it may be necessary to limit each one and what your purpose would be in writing a composition on each topic. Then write (1) your purpose, (2) an appropriate title, and (3) the central idea for each subject that you choose. (You may find it helpful to refer to the examples on pages 361–62.)

32b

Develop a working plan or an outline before writing a composition. See also 33c.

Although a formal outline may not be required for every paper you write, learning to make and use a good outline is important to inexperienced writers because it is a working plan that can make the actual writing of a composition easier.

The outline is the blueprint of the composition. Just as the carpenter or the engineer follows his blueprint implicitly in order to avoid costly structural blunders, so the writer—especially the student writer—follows his outline carefully so that he may arrange his ideas effectively.

But blueprints can be changed and improved, and so can outlines. The writer should make the outline his helpful tool; he should not become its slave. He should keep the outline a growing, developing plan which he will not hesitate to change at any stage of his composition whenever he hits upon a way to improve it. He will naturally try to perfect his outline before he starts to write the paper, but the actual writing will almost certainly suggest a few desirable changes in the arrangement of details.

The first step in the preparation of an outline is the jotting down of ideas on the topic. Keeping the purpose of the composition firmly in mind, the student should not hesitate to jot down a long list of ideas; and he should jot them down rapidly, without much concern for the proper order. When he begins to classify his ideas, he will find it easy to reject needless ones; he may find also that he needs to supplement his knowledge by further observation or reading.

Suppose, for example, a student has chosen to write on the subject "Books I Have Read." He first limits the subject to autobiographies. Then he limits it further by deciding upon his purpose: to inform his reader about the types of autobiographies he has read. Next, he selects a tentative title: "Types of Autobiographies." Finally, he writes out a tentative central idea and jots down a list of items closely related to the thesis statement.

LIST OF IDEAS FOR A COMPOSITION

ON AUTOBIOGRAPHIES

Tentative Central Idea: Autobiographies reveal significant facts about the authors' experiences.

Types of Autobiographies	*What They Reveal*
adventure stories	actions
success stories	achievements
journals like Pepys's *Diary*	contemporary life
travel books	explorations, sights
collections of letters	problems, attitudes
religious accounts	temptations
so-called war records	decisions, battles
disguised autobiographies	emotional conflicts
reports of events	personality

The next step in making an outline is the grouping of the listed items under a few main headings. After some thought, the writer will see that if he uses each of the nine types of autobiographies (listed in the first column above) as a main heading, the development of each would prove to be too unwieldy for a short paper. Therefore he may prefer to group these types further as subheadings under more general headings that will classify all autobiographies according to what they reveal about the authors' experiences; he could thus show that any autobiography could be appropriately entitled "What I Saw," "What I Felt," or "What I Did," and he could illustrate each type by representative examples. Then he would list these main headings in a logical order (see **31b** and **32e**):

I. Autobiographies that could be issued under the title "What I Did"
II. Autobiographies that could be called "What I Saw"
III. Autobiographies that could be entitled "What I Felt"

After more thought, the writer may limit his subject further by omitting some of the items listed in the first column—*e.g.*, journals like Pepys's *Diary*, collections of letters, and disguised autobiographies. The logical arrangement of the remaining items as miscellaneous details (with further additions during the writing of the paper) under the three main headings gives the outline as it appears under **32c** below. The writer's purpose thus is to *inform* (exposition), and he decides to develop his central idea chiefly by the method of classification—see **31d(4)**—with exemplification as a subordinate method—see **31d(2)**. All the other methods of development described in Section **31** are equally adaptable to the development of the whole essay.

Only one other decision in planning the composition remains: whether or not to include introductory and concluding paragraphs. See **32g(2)**. If these paragraphs are desirable or deemed necessary, the writer should add to his plan an explanation of each. In a topic or a sentence outline, these statements need not be numbered. See **32c**.

Once the writer has thought his subject through, he may wish to select a more appropriate or more interesting title. He may also change the wording of his tentative central idea.

32c
Use an outline of the type specified by your instructor.

The types of outlines most commonly used are (1) the topic outline, (2) the sentence outline, and (3) the paragraph outline. Many persons prefer the sentence outline because the use of complete sentences forces the writer to express himself with greater clarity. Topic outlines and sentence outlines have the same parts and the same groupings; they differ only in the fullness of expression. In the paragraph outline no effort is made to classify the material into major headings and subheadings: the topic of each paragraph is simply listed in the order in which it is to come. Paragraph outlines are especially helpful in writing short papers. Topic or sentence outlines may be adapted to papers of any length.

Topic Outline:

THE FACE IN THE MIRROR

CENTRAL IDEA   Since the three types of autobiographies mirror their authors' experiences, any autobiography can be appropriately entitled "What I Saw," "What I Did," or "What I Felt."

INTRODUCTION: An interesting autobiography—one of three possible kinds—inside of every person if he would tell the whole story of his life

I. Autobiographies that could be issued under the title "What I Did"
   A. Books by self-made men like Franklin and Cobbett
   B. *The Second World War* by Churchill

II. Autobiographies that could be called "What I Saw"
   A. Books like *Kon-Tiki*
   B. *Travels in Arabia Deserta* by Doughty
   C. Some descriptions of wars
      1. *Recollections of Rifleman Harris*
      2. Documents concerning the Civil War

III. Autobiographies that could be entitled "What I Felt"
  A. Books about failure, disaster, regeneration
  B. Descriptions of the process of growing up
    1. Edward Gibbon's autobiography
    2. Self-studies of Mill, Spencer, and Adams
  C. Records of religious struggles and spiritual victories
    1. *Confessions* of St. Augustine
    2. Journals of John Bunyan
    3. Writings of George Fox
  D. Many reports of contemporary events
    1. Reminiscences of Cellini, Rousseau, and Boswell
    2. Works of Yeats and Gide

CONCLUSION: Difficulty in classifying autobiographies because the most interesting give something of all three kinds of experience.

Sentence Outline:

THE FACE IN THE MIRROR

CENTRAL IDEA   Since the three types of autobiographies mirror their authors' experiences, any autobiography can be appropriately entitled "What I Saw," "What I Did," or "What I Felt."

INTRODUCTION: An interesting autobiography—one of three possible kinds—is inside of every person if he would tell the whole story of his life.

  I. The first group of autobiographies could be issued under the title "What I Did."
  A. Self-made men like Franklin and Cobbett have written books of this type.
  B. Churchill told about what he did in *The Second World War.*

 II. The second group of autobiographies might be called "What I Saw."
  A. Books like *Kon-Tiki* place emphasis upon the authors' observations.
  B. *Travels in Arabia Deserta* by Doughty is probably the greatest autobiography of this type.
  C. Some documents about war describe what the authors saw.

      1. *Recollections of Rifleman Harris* gives scenes from the Napoleonic Wars.

      2. Other books describe scenes of the Civil War.

III. The third group of autobiographies could be entitled "What I Felt."

    A. Among these are books about failure, disaster, and regeneration.

    B. Other books of inner adventure describe the process of growing up.

      1. One example is Gibbon's autobiography.

      2. More famous examples are the self-studies of Mill, Spencer, and Adams.

    C. Some autobiographies mirror the inner struggles and spiritual victories of religious authors.

      1. One example is St. Augustine's *Confessions.*

      2. Another example is John Bunyan's journals.

      3. Still another example is George Fox's writings.

    D. Many autobiographies show how contemporary events affect the personalities of authors.

      1. Such are the reminiscences of Cellini, Rousseau, and Boswell.

      2. Such also are the works of Yeats and Gide.

CONCLUSION: It is difficult to classify types of autobiographies because the most interesting give us something of all three kinds of experience.

Paragraph Outline:

THE FACE IN THE MIRROR

CENTRAL IDEA Since the three types of autobiographies mirror their authors' experiences, any autobiography can be appropriately entitled "What I Saw," "What I Did," or "What I Felt."

1. An interesting autobiography is inside of every person if he would tell the whole story of his life.

2. There are three kinds of autobiography.

3. The first group could be issued under the title "What I Did."

4. Churchill's *The Second World War* is an autobiographical record describing what the author did.

5. The second type of autobiography might be called "What I Saw."
6. The third kind of autobiography describes "What I Felt."
7. It is difficult to make divisions between types of autobiographies because the most interesting give us something of all three kinds of experience.

32d

Make sure that the outline covers the subject, that it treats of everything promised in the title.

An adequate outline is essential to a successful composition. The major headings (I, II, III, etc.) must be sufficient in number and in scope to satisfy the expectation aroused by the title. And each of these major headings must, in turn, be covered by its subheads just as the title is covered by the major headings. These subheads, however, should not be unduly detailed.

TITLES NOT ADEQUATELY COVERED BY MAJOR HEADINGS:

Geology of the United States
  I. States east of the Mississippi
 II. Texas

History of the United States
  I. Period before 1800
 II. Period from 1800 till 1860

TITLES PROPERLY COVERED:

Geology of the United States
  I. States east of the Mississippi
 II. States west of the Mississippi

History of the United States
   I. Period before 1800
  II. Period from 1800 till 1860
 III. Period since 1860

It would also be proper to leave the main headings unchanged and to alter the titles to agree, thus: "Geology of Texas and the States East of the Mississippi" and "History of the United States before the Civil War." In the same way the student can revise the title of his paper, thus limiting it further, if he finds that his original topic cannot be covered adequately in the allotted space.

32e

Make sure that the parts of the outline are logically arranged.

Logical arrangement is second in importance only to adequacy. If the outline is disorganized and ineffective, the paper that follows it will also be disorganized and ineffective. (See also **31b**.)

(1) Group related ideas.

Although you may begin your outline by hastily jotting down as many ideas on the topic as possible, without regard to order, you should later bring related ideas together, grouping them under major headings. Compare the first list of ideas on "The Face in the Mirror" (page 366) with the groupings in the finished outline (**32c**).

(2) Arrange the parts in a natural, logical order.

The problem of arrangement within the paper as a whole is much the same as that within each separate paragraph. (See pages 328–32.) The nature of the subject will suggest an appropriate arrangement, such as time order, space order, or order of climax.

EXAMPLES

Order of climax:

Subject: End of the drought in Texas

   I. Rains soak the countryside.
  II. Texans rejoice.
 III. Headlines all over the nation announce end of the drought.
 IV. Rains steal attention from the most significant world affairs.

Time order:

Subject: Process of riveting

   I. Preparation of rivets
  II. Passing of red-hot rivets
 III. Securing the rivets in place

▶ EXERCISE 2   First make a list of three, four, or five main points closely related to one of the following subjects; then arrange the items in a natural, logical order. (In parentheses are suggestions for appropriate arrangements.)

1. Ways to start an argument (order of climax)
2. An amusing practical joke (time order)
3. Redecorating a three-room apartment (space order—see page 329)
4. A successful experiment (time order)
5. The joys of being a freshman in college (order of climax)

(3) Do not allow headings to overlap.

Overlapping often occurs when a writer attempts a division according to more than one principle.

OVERLAPPING HEADINGS (three types of arrangement mixed):

> History of the United States
>
> I. Period before 1800   [Time]
> II. The South   [Space]
> III. Negroes   [Group]

DIVISION ACCORDING TO A SINGLE PRINCIPLE OF ARRANGEMENT (time, space, or group):

History of the United States

Time	*Space*	*Group*
I. Period before 1800	I. The North	I. Indians
II. Period from 1800 till 1860	II. The South	II. Original settlers
	III. The West	III. Negroes
III. Period since 1860		IV. Recent Immigrants

(4) Do not co-ordinate any heading that should be subordinated. Do not subordinate any heading that should be co-ordinated.

WRONG   History of the United States before the Civil War

> I. Period before 1800
>   A. Period from 1800 till 1860
> II. The War of 1812
> III. The Monroe Doctrine

RIGHT   History of the United States before the Civil War
                    I. Period before 1800
                   II. Period from 1800 till 1860
                        A. The War of 1812
                        B. The Monroe Doctrine

(5) Do not allow single headings or subheadings to stand anywhere in the outline.

Headings and subheads stand for divisions, and a division denotes at least two parts. Therefore, each outline, to be logical, should have at least two main headings, I and II. If it has a subheading marked A, it should also have a B; if it has a 1, it should also have a 2.

ILLOGICAL   History of the United States
                        I. Period before 1800

If the history continues after 1800 the outline should indicate it by another major heading. Otherwise the title should read, "History of the United States before 1800."

32f

Check the outline for the formal details of (1) notation and indention and (2) parallel structure.

(1) In the outline use consistently one system of notation, and indent headings to indicate degrees of subordination.

Any intelligible system of notation is acceptable. The one used for the complete sentence outline and the topical outline in **32c** is in very common use and may well be adopted. This system, it will be noted, is as follows:

I. . . . .   [Used for major headings]
  A. . . . .   [Used for subheadings of the first
  B. . . . .   degree]
    1. . . . .   [Used for subheadings of the second
    2. . . . .   degree]

Seldom will a short outline (or even a longer one) need subordination beyond the first or second degree. If it does, it may use "a," "b," "c," etc., for the third degree and (1), (2), (3), etc., for the fourth degree.

The indention, as well as the notation, should indicate the degree of subordination. Major headings (I, II, III, etc.) should be indented equally, subheadings of the first degree (A, B, C, etc.) should be indented more, and subheads of the second degree (1, 2, 3, etc.) should be indented still more. If a heading or subheading runs beyond the end of the line, it is given "hanging indention," as in the sentence outline above (**32c**).

(2) **Give parallel structure to parallel parts of the outline to make clearer the co-ordination of the parts.** (See the full discussion of parallel structure under Section **26**.)

FAULTY PARALLELISM:

I. Authors' actions in autobiographies
   [adjective—noun—prepositional phrase]
   A. Books describing self-made men like Franklin and Cobbett
      [noun—participial phrase with prepositional phrase]
   B. Churchill describes his actions in *The Second World War*.
      [sentence]
II. Autobiographies that could be called "What I Saw"
   [noun—adjective clause]

PARALLEL STRUCTURE:

I. Autobiographies that could be issued under the title "What I Did"
   [noun—adjective clause]
   A. Books by self-made men like Franklin and Cobbett
      [noun—prepositional phrases]
   B. *The Second World War* by Churchill
      [noun (a title)—prepositional phrase]
II. Autobiographies that could be called "What I Saw"
   [noun—adjective clause]

The major headings (I, II, III, etc.) should be expressed in parallel structure, as should each group of subheads. But it is unnecessary to strive for parallel structure between different groups of subheads; for example, between A, B, C under I and A, B, C under II. Parallel structure is no problem in the complete sentence outline, for parallelism is insured by the requirement of complete sentences.

▶ EXERCISE 3   Make an outline (of the type specified by your instructor) on one of the subjects you used for Exercise 1. Then check your outline with the principles set forth in **32d-f.**

32g

Write the paper from the outline.

Once you have checked your outline to make sure that it covers the subject (see **32d**), is logically arranged (**32e**), and has proper notation, indention, and parallel structure (**32f**), you are ready to write the paper. You simply write a series of effective paragraphs, with good transitions between them (see **31b(6)**), to cover all items in the outline, taking up each item in the order in which it comes in the outline. The actual writing of the paper may very well suggest a better arrangement for some of the details.

(1) **The paragraphs in relation to the outline.** Although the paragraphs must develop the headings (including the subheadings) of the outline in the exact order in which they come in the outline, there is no rule regarding the number of these headings a paragraph may cover. In a general way, however, the writer is limited by the need to make each paragraph a unit and to keep it from being unduly long or short. Let us notice, for example, how the seven paragraphs of "The Face in the Mirror" (see pages 377–80) are related to the topic outline (see pages 368–69):

Paragraphs	Relation to outline
1 and 2	Introduction
3	I and the subheading A
4	Subheading B (special treatment requires more words than for A)
5	II and all subheadings
6	III and all subheadings
7	Conclusion

Since each paragraph in the body of a composition (see paragraphs 3 through 6 above) should be easily identified with a main heading or subheading in the outline, the writer may wish to revise his outline to make it agree with his organization into paragraphs.

▶ EXERCISE 4 Carefully read the following essay so that you can intelligently participate in a class discussion of the (1) selection and limitation of the subject, (2) purpose of the writer, (3) choice of the title, (4) development of the central idea, (5) arrangement of main points, (6) transitions between ideas, and (7) relationship of the division into paragraphs to the topic outline on pages 368–69.

THE FACE IN THE MIRROR[1]

Every man and every woman has one book inside him or her. Some have more, but everybody has at least one—a volume of autobiography. We have all been talked almost to death by bores who attached themselves to us in a club car or a ship's smoking room and insisted on giving us a play-by-play account of their marital troubles or their complete medical history. I once met one who carried a set of his own x-rays. Yet even these people might be interesting if they could tell the whole truth. They are boring not because they talk about themselves but because they talk about only one aspect of themselves, that phase of their lives which fascinates and worries them personally. If they were really to tell us everything, we should listen with amazement.

[1] Abridged from *Talents and Geniuses*, copyright 1957 by Gilbert Highet. Reprinted by permission of Oxford University Press, Inc.

(2)   Apparently there are three kinds of autobiography: three different ways of telling the story of one's life. (We can leave out journals like Pepys's *Diary*, which was not meant to be published, and collections of letters and disguised autobiographies, which so many modern novels are.)

(3)   The first group could all be issued under the same title. They could all be called "What I Did." They are essentially success stories. In them, a man who has achieved something of wide importance explains how he did it, what were the obstacles in his way, how they were overcome, and what was the effect on the world. Self-made men often write such books—or have such books written for them. There is a splendid one by Ben Franklin and an equally good one by his English opposite number, William Cobbett: these are optimistic works, a good tonic for anyone who despairs of solving his own problems.

(4)   Sir Winston Churchill's six-volume work *The Second World War* is really an autobiographical record. He himself says it is "the story as I knew and experienced it as Prime Minister and Minister of Defence of Great Britain." Therefore it cannot be called anything like a complete history of the war. For example, Churchill tells the story of one of the crucial events of the war, one of the crucial events of this century—the reduction of Japan to impotence and surrender by intensive bombardment culminating in what he calls the "casting" of two atomic bombs—in only eight pages, while a greater amount of wordage is devoted to a reprint of the broadcast which he made to British listeners on VE day.

(5)   So much for the first type of autobiography: "What I Did." The second type might be called "What I Saw." Here the emphasis is not on the achievements of the narrator but rather on the strange sights he saw and the strange experiences through which he lived. Most good books of exploration are like this. Both the book *Kon-Tiki* and the film were absorbingly interesting, not because the author was an unusual man but because he could describe to us some unique adventures. We shall never cross New Guinea on foot or spend a whole year alone with two companions on the Arctic ice or climb Mount Everest; therefore we are delighted when a man who has done such a thing can tell us about it clearly—and modestly. The greatest of all such books in the English language is probably Doughty's *Travels in Arabia Deserta*. Some good adventure autobiographies have been written by ordinary soldiers

and sailors. Many of our finest descriptions of the Napoleonic wars come from such books as the *Recollections of Rifleman Harris,* and there are similar documents from the American Civil War.

⑥   Then there is a third kind of autobiography. It does not describe "What I Did" or "What I Saw" but "What I Felt," "What I Endured." These are the books of inner adventure. In them there is achievement, yes, but it is a struggle and a victory within the spirit. In them there are dangerous explorations and the discovery of unknown worlds, but the explorer is making his way through the jungles of the soul. Such are the books of failure, disaster, and regeneration which are now so popular: for example, Lillian Roth's *I'll Cry Tomorrow,* which tells how a woman wrecked her life with drink and then rebuilt it. Such also are the books which describe one of the most dangerous of all adventures: the process of growing up. My own favorite among them is Edward Gibbon's autobiography, partly because it is unconsciously funny. More famous perhaps are the self-studies of John Stuart Mill, Herbert Spencer, and Henry Adams—all of which seem to me excruciatingly pompous and dull. The famous records of religious suffering and conversion could all be subtitled "What I Felt": the *Confessions* of St. Augustine, the journals of John Bunyan and of the first Quaker, George Fox. And many of the most famous autobiographers have concentrated on reporting the events which happened during their lifetime, not as objective facts but simply as occurrences which impinged upon their own personalities: in books like the reminiscences of Benvenuto Cellini, of Rousseau, of Boswell, Yeats, and André Gide, we see the world as in an elaborate distorting mirror.

⑦   "What I Did," "What I Saw," "What I Felt"—really, it is difficult to make a sharp division between these types of autobiographical writing. The emphasis in one book is more toward reporting of external happenings, in another toward self-analysis, but a man can scarcely describe what he did without also letting us know what he felt and saw. Even the most egoistic of men, like St. Augustine and James Boswell, do from time to time give us valuable information about their outer as well as their inner worlds. The most interesting of these books give us something of all three kinds of experience. For a time, while we read them, it is possible to enjoy one of the rarest artistic pleasures—complete escape: escape into another sphere of action and perception.

From that escape we return—with what relief!—to the real center
of the universe, which is our own self.

▶ EXERCISE 5   After making an outline, write a paper on
one of the following topics (or any other topic assigned by
your instructor): (1) types of detective stories, (2) kinds of
bores, (3) the heroes of TV Westerns, (4) what language
habits reveal about a speaker, (5) what dogs (or any other
pets) reveal about their owners, (6) the best reasons for
going to college.

(2) Effective beginnings and endings.

Although formal introductions and conclusions are often
not necessary for short papers, every composition should
have an effective beginning and ending.

BEGINNINGS   There are two ways to begin a composition
effectively. One way is to begin with a sentence which
not only arouses the reader's interest but also starts the
development of the topic by discussing the first main
point in the outline. For an example of this type of beginning, see the first library paper in 33e(4). The second way
is to begin with a formal introduction (often only one
paragraph). This arouses the reader's interest and introduces the central idea of the paper but does not start
the development of the topic. Sometimes the limitations
of the subject are defined in a formal introduction. See
the first two paragraphs of "The Face in the Mirror" in
Exercise 4 on page 377. The choice of the type of beginning depends upon the nature of the topic and the length
of the composition.

Whichever method you use, remember that an effective beginning gains the reader's interest. One of the
easiest and best ways to gain interest is to use specific
facts and details instead of dull generalizations. See 20a(2)
and 31d. Compare the effectiveness of the introductions
on the next page.

Topic: A football game in the Rose Bowl

GENERAL

When football teams play an important bowl game, lots of fans are very enthusiastic supporters of the home-town team. I especially noticed this fact when I recently saw a game in the Rose Bowl.

SPECIFIC

There are two American cities that genuflect to no one in their uncontrollable—one could even say undying—affection for the home-town football team. When citizens of these two cities, Seattle and Minneapolis, assembled for a contest between their Washington Huskies and their Minnesota Gophers on the green grass of Pasadena, sensible natives took shelter. The less sensible—97,000 of them—were at the Arroyo Seco, where the Rose Bowl sits, and everyone but the ushers appeared to be related to a player on one or the other team. In its long history, the Rose Bowl had never been shaken by such passion from the stands.[2]

Another way to arouse interest is to refer to some common experience (such as shyness on a first date, an encounter with an eccentric door-to-door salesman, a clumsy slip of the tongue on an important occasion, the joy of winning a game or a special honor) which the reader will probably associate with himself; see the introduction to "Carousel— A New Experience" on page 382. A third way to interest the reader is to start with a striking fact; see the beginning of "The French Horn" in 33e(4). Still another method is to begin with an interesting incident or anecdote that is closely related to the topic:

Title: The Elusive Dr. Szilard

At a party in a university community a few weeks ago the guests amused themselves by drawing up a list of men who have played unique roles in recent history. They finally agreed upon five who had done things which could not have been accomplished, in their times, by anybody else. The first four are familiar to every-

[2] From "They Ran All the Way: The Wildest Rose," reprinted from *Sports Illustrated*, January 9, 1961. By permission of the publishers.

body—Lincoln, Gandhi, Hitler, and Churchill. But the fifth might puzzle even many well-informed people. It was Leo Szilard.[3]

An effective beginning introduces a subject and is therefore directly related to it. As you read the following paragraph (written by a student), notice the repetition of the key words of the title: *Carousel, new, experience.* In the last sentence the controlling idea of the composition is given. Such an introduction is closely related to the topic and contributes to the unity of the whole composition.

Title: Carousel—A New Experience

All of us enjoy wearing a new pair of shoes, eating a dish we have not had before, seeing a movie with an unusual plot, or touring in a new section of the country; in other words, we like experiences which are novel, different. I happen to be one of those people who enjoy discovering an unfamiliar poem by a famous poet, reading a good book, or attending a choral or band concert I like new and different cultural outlets, and a few weeks ago my English assignment brought me face to face with just such an experience: Carousel, theater-in-the-round. The play which 1 attended was an Irish drama by Paul Vincent Carroll, entitled *Shadow and Substance*, and I should like to use it as the vehicle in my description of Carousel itself—the interior of the theater, the actors, the techniques used.

Caution: Do not write aimless, dull introductions. If you have difficulty writing an interesting and pertinent introductory paragraph which contributes to the effectiveness of your whole composition, then begin with an immediate discussion of your first main point.

EXAMPLE

Title: Characteristics of a Nonconformist

One of the distinguishing characteristics of a nonconformist is his lack of respect for established authority. For example, . .

[3] From "The Elusive Dr. Szilard" by Alice Kimball, reprinted from *Harper's Magazine*, July, 1960. By permission of *Harper's Magazine*.

▶ EXERCISE 6   Evaluate the effectiveness of the following beginnings of student papers.

1. *Title:* A Description of My Home Town

It is early morning. A light drizzle falls upon the gray cobblestones, and you see two lace-shawled women hurrying to the Cathedral. The trolley-cars begin to clatter down the broad island of Canal Street, and the city begins to awake. This is a day in my city. This is New Orleans.

Soon the sun peeks through the misty heavens, and the city begins to erupt into a myriad of noises. . . .

2. *Title:* Justice in *The Unvanquished*

Justice is a word with many applications and definitions. This point is well illustrated in *The Unvanquished,* a novel of Civil War times by William Faulkner. Justice, as practiced by Faulkner's characters, takes on many forms; indeed, the meaning of the word is warped to suit any occasion which may arise. Applications of justice may range all the way from mouth soaping to murder; many different situations call for different forms of justice.

Loosh, the old Negro slave, felt that he was justified in tearing down Bayard's and Ringo's model of the city of Vicksburg. . . .

ENDINGS   A composition should end; it should not merely stop. Two ways to end a composition effectively are (1) to stress the final point of the main discussion by using an emphatic last sentence and (2) to write a strong concluding paragraph. Often a concluding paragraph clinches, restates, or stresses the importance of the central idea or thesis of the composition. See the concluding paragraph of "The Face in the Mirror," pages 379–80. When the body of a composition describes an experiment or presents evidence, the conclusion often presents a discovery or a theory. A conclusion may also present a brief summary, a pertinent question, a suggestion or challenge, or a solution to a problem.

SUMMARY (ending of an article giving reasons for the growing popularity of FM radio programs)

FM, in short, is prospering in direct ratio as it provides adults with a refuge from the blaring Children's Hour of the AM juke boxes and from the vacuity of most TV.

QUESTION (ending of an essay describing the dangers of modern chemical, biological, and radiological warfare)

The question that cannot be avoided is whether any nation, even in its own defense, has the right to destroy half of the rest of the world.

SUGGESTION (ending of an article discussing the interest of consumers in deceptive packaging which conceals rises in prices)

Efforts at industry self-government directed toward higher ethical standards are, of course, laudable and welcome. But consumers probably would do well to continue to hope, and to urge, that all existing Governmental agencies which exercise regulatory powers in this area—including the FTC, the FDA, certain divisions of the Department of Agriculture, and the Treasury's alcohol-control agency—will, in the future, act with more vigor and with a greater awareness of consumer needs.[4]

SOLUTION TO A PROBLEM (ending of an essay explaining the problem of American doctors who are barred from hospitals)

What will help to solve the complicated and disturbing problem, he [John G. Steinle, management consultant to hospitals] says, is a greater public awareness of the role of the hospital as a community institution and a willingness on the part of the public to become involved in the management of its community affairs. Such a force of informed public opinion can right more wrongs than any laws devised.[5]

Caution: Do not devote too much space to introductions and conclusions. A short paper often has only one paragraph for a beginning or an ending; frequently one sen-

[4] From *Consumer Reports*, January, 1961. By permission of Consumers Union, Mount Vernon, New York, a non-profit organization.
[5] From "Why Hospitals Lock Out Doctors," reprinted from *Look*, January 17, 1961. By permission of *Look*.

tence for each is adequate. Remember that the bulk of your composition should be the development of the central idea, the discussion of the main headings and the subheadings in the outline.

▶ EXERCISE 7 In a magazine recommended by your instructor, find and copy a good conclusion to an article. Be prepared to explain why the conclusion is effective and how it is related to the central idea of the article.

▶ EXERCISE 8 Giving special attention to the beginning and ending, write a composition based on the outline you prepared for Exercise 3.

▶ EXERCISE 9 Carefully observe the errors marked on the outline which follows. If you do not understand the nature of an error, look up the rule with the corresponding number in this handbook. Also read the revised outline on page 386 and observe how the errors are corrected.

OUTLINE

Important: Make either a sentence or a topic outline. Study 32c.

The Moods of the Sea

2 - See 32a.

<u>Central</u> <u>Idea</u>: The moods of the sea

and my reaction.

32 a (3)

32 f (2)

I. I love the sea for its calmness.

A. Its placid behavior.

B. Happily plays games with

boats.

22- Your reaction?   II.   Uncontrollable fury of the sea.

A.   Strikes the land.

B.   Tosses and sometimes smashes boats.

20- Relation to main heading?   C.   Finally becomes calm again.

REVISED OUTLINE

The Moods of the Sea

<u>Central Idea</u>:   I love the sea for its calmness but hate it for its uncontrollable fury.

I.   I love the sea for its calmness.

     A.   It is beautiful when it gently raps the beach.

     B.   It happily plays games with boats.

II.   I hate the sea for its uncontrollable fury.

     A.   It angrily strikes the land.

     B.   It tosses and sometimes smashes boats.

     C.   Its fury finally exhausts itself.

▶ EXERCISE 10   Revise the composition you wrote for Exercise 5, using the Check List for Revision (**8d(1)**).

Library Paper

33

Learn how to use the library as you prepare a library paper.

The library is a storehouse of knowledge on which you must draw heavily throughout your college course. You can learn how to use the library efficiently, and also continue to develop your skill in writing, by preparing a library paper (sometimes called a research, reference, or term paper).

Instead of first learning how to use the library and then writing the paper, you will find it more interesting and more efficient to do the two together. In fact, one never learns much about the library until he begins to use it. Therefore you may wish to select and limit your subject (**33a**) at once and to prepare the paper step by step, getting knowledge about the library as you can apply it to your paper: first while preparing the bibliography (**33b**); then while developing an outline (**33c**) and taking notes (**33d**); and finally while using the outline, bibliography, and notes to write a properly documented paper (**33e**).

33a

Select and limit the subject. (Follow the general suggestions given in **32a**.)

Let us suppose that you are interested in the general field of music and have limited your subject to the orchestra.

But since this is still a subject broad enough for a book, you decide to limit yourself further to one of the many instruments in the orchestra, selecting the one in which you have a special interest—the French horn—and investigating its development. Or you may decide upon a subject related to literature, specifically Russian literature, and more specifically recent Russian literature. But this subject is still much too broad, and you restrict it further to one distinguished writer, Boris Pasternak. You are then reminded of a significant event in Pasternak's career, an event sufficiently limited for a library paper of two or three thousand words: Pasternak and the Nobel Prize. If your working up of a preliminary bibliography (**33b**) indicates that adequate source materials are available in the library, you may well conclude that either the development of the French horn or Pasternak's involvement with the Nobel Prize would be a satisfactory topic for your library paper.

REPORT OR THESIS   But you may not yet know what your purpose will be in writing the paper. Do you wish simply to collect and organize the facts about the development of the French horn, or do you wish to *prove* that it developed in spite of certain handicaps? If it is the former, you will be writing a *report* and will concentrate on "development"; if it is the latter, you will have a *thesis* to prove and will emphasize the "obstacles" the French horn had to overcome. Although either purpose should enable you to write an effective paper, the purpose you select will influence your collecting of facts and should therefore be determined as soon as possible.

▶ EXERCISE 1   List three general fields in which you have some interest. Then by process of limitation derive three topics (1) which are suitable for library papers of two or three thousand words each and (2) in which you have a special interest. The subject headings and the cross references in the card catalog or the *Readers' Guide* (see **33b** below) may suggest subjects and possible limitations of them. Determine, if possible, whether each topic lends itself to development as a *report* or a *thesis*.

33b

Prepare a bibliography in acceptable form (and learn your way about the library).

The bibliography lists sources of information—such as books, pamphlets, and articles—from which you will draw the material for your paper. Use (1) the card catalog, (2) indexes to periodicals, and (3) reference books (as explained on the following pages) to make a preliminary bibliography by writing down the most promising titles you can find. Copy each title on a separate card (usually 3 × 5 inches) in the form shown below in **33b(4).** You can keep these cards in alphabetical order until you complete your paper, adding useful titles as you find them and discarding those that prove useless. The final bibliography to be copied at the end of your paper will most often include only those works that help in the writing—usually those cited in the footnotes.

(1) The Card Catalog.

The card catalog is the index to the whole library. It lists all books and all bound magazines, whether they are housed in the stacks, on the open shelves of the reference room, or in any other part of the building. In many libraries one general card catalog lists all books owned by the university and indicates whether the book is kept in the general library or with some special collection in another building.

Usually the card catalog consists of cards 3 × 5 inches in size, arranged alphabetically in drawers. These may be "author" cards, "title" cards, or "subject" cards; for in most libraries each book is listed—in its proper alphabetical place—once according to its author, again according to its title, and yet again according to its subject or subjects. Let us take, for example, *Thesaurus of Orchestral Devices*, by Gardner Read. The student writing on the French horn might have found this book in his examination of the catalog cards under the subject, "Musical instruments." Or he might have run across the title in another book. He can determine whether his library has the book by looking under the name of the author—Read, Gardner. But if he does not know the author's given name, he may save time by looking for the book under the title—*Thesaurus of Orchestral Devices*. The typewritten call number, usually in the upper left-hand corner, shows exactly where the book is shelved and must be written out on a "call slip" when the book is requested for use. The cards are furnished by the Library of Congress as a convenience for libraries throughout the country. Let us note what printed information is given on these carefully prepared cards.

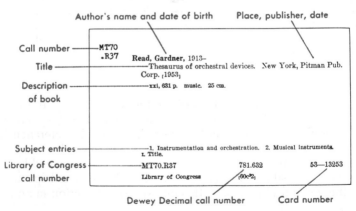

The illustration above is for the "author" card, filed in the card catalog under *R*. The "title" card is identical except for the title typewritten at the top (Thesaurus of orchestral devices), filed under *T*. The two "subject" cards are also identical except that each is headed by its subject typewritten in red and filed under *I* and *M* respectively.

Most libraries use call numbers from either the Library of Congress system or the Dewey Decimal system. The Library of Congress has the following main classes:

A	General Works	M	Music
B	Philosophy, Religion	N	Fine Arts
C	History	P	Language and Literature
D	Foreign History	Q	Science
E, F	American History	R	Medicine
G	Geography, Anthropology	S	Agriculture
H	Social Sciences	T	Technology
J	Political Science	U	Military Science
K	Law	V	Naval Science
L	Education	Z	Library Science, Bibliography

The Dewey Decimal system has the following main classes:

000	General Works	500	Natural Science
100	Philosophy	600	Useful Arts
200	Religion	700	Fine Arts
300	Sociology	800	Literature
400	Philology	900	History

A student working on a library paper will probably begin by consulting the subject cards. Since a book may be listed under any one of various subjects, he should not be discouraged if he fails to find all he wants under the first subject consulted. He should look, next, under related subjects. Works not listed under "Agriculture" may appear under "Farming," or "Gardening," or "Soils." Especially helpful are the cards giving cross references to other subjects under which the reader should look. Under "Agriculture," for example, might appear a card reading "Agriculture, *see also* Agronomy." Works not listed under "Vitamins" but nevertheless important to that subject might appear under "Nutrition," or "Foods," or "Diet." Works not listed under "French horn" or "Horn" may be found under "Musical instruments," "Wind instruments," or "Instrumentation and orchestration." Even so general a subject as "Music" might list books that treat of the French horn.

THE ORDER OF THE CARDS

It is not enough, especially in a large library, to know that the cards are arranged alphabetically. Hundreds of cards may be listed under a single heading such as "England," "Lincoln," or "Washington." The reader who knows the principles of arrangement will save much time in finding what he wants.

Cards for subjects. Cards on a single subject are arranged alphabetically according to the name of the author, which appears on the line immediately below the subject heading. Subdivisions of most subjects are arranged alphabetically.

EXAMPLE   Michigan
           Michigan—Agriculture
           Michigan—Biography
           Michigan—Constitutional convention
           Michigan—University

But subdivisions of history are arranged chronologically.

EXAMPLE   Mexico—History—Conquest, 1519–1540
           Mexico—History—Spanish colony, 1540–1810
           Mexico—History—Wars of Independence, 1810–1821
           Mexico—History—European intervention, 1861–1867

Names or titles beginning with abbreviations; numbers. Abbreviations and numbers are filed as if they were spelled out. Instead of *Mc* look for *Mac;* instead of *Dr.* look for *Doctor;* instead of *St.* look for *Saint;* etc. Look for 2 under *Two* and for 4 under *Four.*

"Short before long." In the catalog a short word followed by other words always comes before a longer word of

which the short word is a part. *Post office* comes before *Postage.*

EXAMPLE   Post, Post office, Postage, Postal

(1) Person, (2) place, (3) title. The order is person, place, title.

EXAMPLE   Lincoln, Abraham   [Person]
Lincoln, Nebraska   [Place]
Lincoln and Seward, by Gideon Welles   [Title]

(1) Books by a person, (2) books about a person. Books written by a person come first; books written about a person follow. Various editions of an author's work are listed chronologically with collections first and single works second in alphabetical order.

EXAMPLE   Shakespeare, William.   Works
Shakespeare, William.   Hamlet
Shakespeare, William.   Macbeth
Shakespeare, William.   A life of William Shakespeare, by Sidney Lee

(1) Saints, (2) popes, (3) kings, (4) others. Saints, popes, and kings are listed in this order by their first names, followed by the surnames of other persons. Kings are listed by countries.

EXAMPLE   John, Saint.
John XXIII, Pope.
John, King of England.
John, Augustus.

▶ EXERCISE 2   Make a rough floor plan of your library (or a part of it) and locate on the plan (1) the card catalog, (2) the delivery desk, (3) the stacks, and (4) the reference room. Write out five or more of the subject headings under which the card catalog lists books of interest to you in the preparation of your library paper. How many of these were brought to your attention by a cross reference ("*see also*") card?

▶ EXERCISE 3   Write a bibliography card for a promising book on the subject of your paper. Use a 3 × 5 card and follow the exact form shown on page 404, including the library call number. How many subject listings are recommended for this book by the printed Library of Congress card? Make out two additional bibliography cards for other promising books on your subject that you can find listed in the card catalog. (Note that the subject listings or "entries" are given near the bottom of the printed library card. See the specimen card on page 390, listing two subjects.)

(2) **Indexes to Periodicals.**

The titles of magazines, newspapers, and other periodical publications are listed in the card catalog, but not the articles contained in periodicals. For these the reader must go to periodical indexes, which do for articles in periodicals what the card catalog does for books in the library. Articles are listed by subject, sometimes also by author or title. Subjects such as "French horn," "Wind instruments," or "Music," with the many cross references, can be followed through just as in the card catalog. The chief indexes are mentioned below, with the years covered by each.

Note: Magazines are usually issued weekly, biweekly, monthly, or quarterly; newspapers, daily or weekly. For the convenience of those who wish to consult the recent issues, magazines are often kept for a few months or possibly a year on open shelves or racks; then they are bound into volumes, each of which commonly includes the issues of six months or a year. These bound volumes may be kept on the open shelves in the reference room, in a special periodical room, or in the stacks. The general card catalog lists all periodicals in the library and often indicates where each may be consulted. But a more convenient list of periodicals is often kept in the reference room or periodical room, or at the circulation desk.

INDEXES TO PERIODICALS

GENERAL

Poole's Index. 1802–1906. (Subject index only)
Nineteenth Century Readers' Guide. 1890–1899. (Author, subject)
Readers' Guide. 1900—. (Author, title, subject)
Book Review Digest. 1905—. (Author, title, subject)
International Index. 1907—. (Author, subject)
New York Times Index. 1913—. (A useful guide for finding the
    dates of important events which can then be looked up in all
    other newspapers)

SPECIAL

Agricultural Index. 1916—. (Subject)
Art Index. 1929—. (Author, subject)
Bibliographic Index. 1937—. (Subject)
Biography Index. 1946—. (Subject)
Catholic Periodical Index. 1930—. (Subject)
Dramatic Index. 1909—. (Subject)
Education Index. 1929—. (Author, subject)
Engineering Index. 1884—. (Subject)
Index Medicus. 1879–1926; *Quarterly Cumulative Index Medicus.*
    1927—. (Author, subject)
Index to Legal Periodicals. 1908—. (Author, subject)
Industrial Arts Index. 1913–1957. Succeeded by *Applied Science
    and Technology Index.* 1958—; *Business Periodicals Index.*
    1958—. (Subject)
Music Index. 1949—. (Subject)
Psychological Index. 1894–1936. (Author, subject)
Public Affairs Information Service. 1915—. (Subject)
Technical Book Review Index. 1917–1929; 1935—.

[See also the various abstracts, such as *Biological Abstracts,*
1926—, *Chemical Abstracts,* 1907—, and *Psychological Abstracts,* 1927—.]

These indexes are compiled as soon as possible after the
periodicals appear. The *Readers' Guide* (an index to over
one hundred magazines of general interest) is only a few
weeks behind the appearance of the articles. From time
to time the issues of the *Readers' Guide* indexes covering

single months or short periods of a few months are combined into longer units, and finally into a volume covering more than a year. The earlier volumes cover as many as five years, as will be seen from the following list.

READERS' GUIDE

I	1900–1904	XII	July, '39—June, '41
II	1905–1909	XIII	July, '41—June, '43
III	1910–1914	XIV	July, '43—April, '45
IV	1915–1918	XV	May, '45—April, '47
V	1919–1921	XVI	May, '47—April, '49
VI	1922–1924	XVII	May, '49—March, '51
VII	1925–1928	XVIII	April, '51—March, '53
VIII	1929—June, '32	XIX	April, '53—Feb., '55
IX	July, '32—June, '35	XX	March, '55—Feb., '57
X	July, '35—June, '37	XXI	March, '57—Feb., '59
XI	July, '37—June, '39	XXII	March, '59—Feb., '61

A reader wishing to find all references to a given subject listed by the *Readers' Guide* would have to look through each of the larger volumes and the smaller ones covering the most recent months or month. Usually he is concerned only with articles that have appeared during a certain period, and he looks accordingly in the volumes covering that period.

▶ EXERCISE 4   On the rough floor plan made for Exercise 2 locate the *Readers' Guide* and the other indexes to periodicals that give promise of being helpful in the preparation of your library paper. Choose two volumes from the *Readers' Guide* that might contain articles on your subject. How many articles do you find in each volume? (Specify each volume examined.) Write bibliography cards for the two most promising articles you can find in the *Readers' Guide,* using a separate 3 × 5 card for each article and following the exact form given in **33b(4)** below. Note that the abbreviated form used by the periodical indexes is not the standard bibliographical form.

▶ EXERCISE 5   List three other periodical indexes in which you can find articles on your subject and write a bibliography card on a promising article from each. Use a separate 3 × 5 card for each article and follow exactly the recommended bibliographical form (not the abbreviated form of the periodical indexes).

(3) Reference Books.

Dictionaries, encyclopedias, atlases, and other books especially helpful for reference are usually kept on the open shelves of the reference room, where students may use them directly without the trouble of having them brought from the stacks. Each of these books is listed in the card catalog, and the call number will often aid in finding the book. The student should learn the general location of the chief classes of reference books in order that he may turn to them without loss of time. For a detailed list of such books, with a short description of each, he should consult Constance M. Winchell's *Guide to Reference Books* (Seventh Edition, supplements 1950–52). Since many reference books, especially some of the encyclopedias, are kept up to date by frequent revisions, the student should cite the last copyright date of the edition he is using. A few of the more important reference books are listed below (with abbreviated entries).

GENERAL DICTIONARIES (UNABRIDGED)

Century Dictionary and Cyclopedia. 12 vols. 1911. 3 vols. 1927–1933.
Dictionary of American English. 4 vols. 1936–1944.
New Standard Dictionary. 1947, 1952.
Oxford English Dictionary. 12 vols. and supplement. 1933. Originally issued as *A New English Dictionary.* 10 vols. and supplement. 1888–1933.
Webster's New International Dictionary, Second ed., 1934.
Webster's Third New International Dictionary, 1961.

SPECIAL DICTIONARIES

Allen, F. S. *Allen's Synonyms and Antonyms.* 1938.
Crabb, George. *Crabb's English Synonyms.* 1945.
Fowler, H. W. *Dictionary of Modern English Usage.* 1926.
Horwill, H. W. *Dictionary of Modern American Usage.* 1935.
Lewis, Norman. *The New Roget's Thesaurus.* 1961.
Nicholson, Margaret. *A Dictionary of American-English Usage.*
    1957. (Based on Fowler)
Partridge, Eric. *Dictionary of Slang and Unconventional English.*
    1949.
Roget's International Thesaurus. 1946, 1960.
Webster's Dictionary of Synonyms. 1942.
Wentworth, Harold. *American Dialect Dictionary.* 1944.
Wright, Joseph. *English Dialect Dictionary.* 6 vols. 1898–1905.

GENERAL ENCYCLOPEDIAS

Collier's Encyclopedia. 20 vols.
Columbia Encyclopedia. 1950, 1953.
Encyclopedia Americana. 30 vols.
Encyclopædia Britannica. 24 vols.

SPECIAL ENCYCLOPEDIAS

Adams, J. T. *Dictionary of American History.* 6 vols. 1942.
Bailey, L. H. *Cyclopedia of American Agriculture.* 4 vols. 1907–
    1909.
Bryan's Dictionary of Painters and Engravers. 5 vols. 1903–1905.
Catholic Encyclopedia. 17 vols. 1907–1922. New edition, 1936—.
Encyclopaedia of the Social Sciences. 15 vols. 1930–1935.
Encyclopedia of World Art. 1959—.
Grove's Dictionary of Music and Musicians. 9 vols. 1954.
Harris, Chester W. *Encyclopedia of Educational Research.* 1960.
Hastings, James. *Dictionary of the Bible.* 5 vols. 1898–1904.
———. *Encyclopaedia of Religion and Ethics.* 13 vols. 1908–1927.
Jewish Encyclopedia. 12 vols. 1925.
McGraw-Hill Encyclopedia of Science and Technology. 15 vols.
    1960.
McLaughlin, A. C., and A. B. Hart. *Cyclopedia of American Gov-
    ernment.* 3 vols. 1914. Reprint, 1949.

Monroe, Paul. *Cyclopedia of Education.* 5 vols. 1911–1913.
Monroe, W. S. *Encyclopedia of Educational Research.* 1950.
Munn, Glenn G. *Encyclopedia of Banking and Finance.* 1949.
New Schaff-Herzog Encyclopedia of Religious Knowledge. 13 vols.
    1908–1912.
New Standard Encyclopedia of Art. 2 vols. in 1. 1939.
Thompson, O. *International Encyclopedia of Music and Musicians.*
    1956.
Thorpe's Dictionary of Applied Chemistry. 12 vols. 1937–1956.
Universal Jewish Encyclopedia. 10 vols. 1939–1943.
Van Nostrand's Scientific Encyclopedia. 1958.
Worldmark Encyclopedia of the Nations. 1960.

ATLASES AND GAZETTEERS

Collier's New World Atlas and Gazetteer. 1953.
Columbia Lippincott Gazetteer of the World. 1952.
Encyclopædia Britannica World Atlas. 1962.
Hammond's Ambassador World Atlas. 1954.
Rand-McNally Commercial Atlas. 1962.
Times (London) *Atlas of the World.* 5 vols. 1955—
Webster's Geographical Dictionary. 1959.

YEARBOOKS—CURRENT EVENTS

Americana Annual. 1923—.
Annual Register. 1758—.
Britannica Book of the Year. 1938—.
Economic Almanac. 1940—.
Information Please Almanac. 1947—.
New International Year Book. 1907—.
Statesman's Year-Book. 1864—.
Statistical Abstract of the United States. 1878—.
Whitaker's Almanack. 1869—.
World Almanac. 1868—.

BIOGRAPHY

Current Biography. 1940—.
Dictionary of American Biography. 20 vols. and index. 1928–1943.
    Supplements to date.

Dictionary of National Biography. (British.) 22 vols. 1908–1909. Indexes and supplements to date.

International Who's Who. 1935—.

Kunitz, S. J., and Howard Haycraft. *American Authors, 1600–1900.* 1938.

———. *British Authors of the Nineteenth Century.* 1936.

———. *Twentieth Century Authors.* 1942. Supplement, 1955.

———. *British Authors before 1800.* 1952.

Webster's Biographical Dictionary. 1943, 1956.

Who's Who. 1848—.

Who's Who in America. 1899—.

LITERATURE—MYTHOLOGY

Apperson, G. L. *English Proverbs and Proverbial Phrases.* 1929

Baker, E. A. *Guide to the Best Fiction.* 1932.

Barnhart, Clarence L. *The New Century Handbook of English Literature.* 1956.

Bartlett's Familiar Quotations. 1955.

Bateson, F. W. *Cambridge Bibliography of English Literature.* 5 vols. 1941–1957.

Benét, William Rose. *The Reader's Encyclopedia.* 1955.

Brewer's Dictionary of Phrase and Fable. 1953.

Cambridge History of American Literature. 4 vols. 1917–1921.

Cambridge History of English Literature. 15 vols. 1907–1927.

English Association. *Year's Work in English Studies.* 1920—.

Fiction Catalog. 1941. Seventh ed., 1960.

Frazer, Sir J. G. *The Golden Bough.* 12 vols. 1907–1915.

Gayley, C. M. *Classic Myths in English Literature and in Art.* 1939.

Granger, Edith. *Index to Poetry and Recitations.* Fourth ed., 1953.

Harper's Dictionary of Classical Literature and Antiquities. 1897.

Hart, James D. *Oxford Companion to American Literature.* 1956.

Harvey, Sir Paul. *Oxford Companion to Classical Literature.* 1937.

———. *Oxford Companion to English Literature.* 1946.

Millett, Fred B. *Contemporary American Authors.* 1940.

———, J. M. Manly, and Edith Rickert. *Contemporary British Literature.* 1935.

Modern Humanities Research Association. *Annual Bibliography of English Language and Literature.* 1920—.

Mythology of All Races. 13 vols. 1916–1932.

Oxford Classical Dictionary. 1949.
Sears, Minnie Earl, and Marian Shaw. *Essay and General Literature Index.* 1900—.
Short Story Index. 1953. Supplements.
Spiller, Robert E., and others. *Literary History of the United States.* 3 vols. 1956. (Helpful bibliographies)
Stevenson, B. E. *Home Book of Quotations.* 1956.
Thrall, Hibbard, and Holman. *A Handbook to Literature.* 1960.

▶ EXERCISE 6   Draw a floor plan of the reference room of your library (or use the plan drawn for Exercise 2 if it is adequate) and indicate the location of the most important books of reference. Locate, for example, the (1) unabridged dictionaries, (2) general encyclopedias, (3) atlases, and (4) the *Dictionary of National Biography* or some other collection of short biographies. (Include other reference books mentioned above that give promise of helping with your library paper.)

▶ EXERCISE 7   Which of the general encyclopedias has the most useful article (and short bibliography) on your subject? Make a bibliography card for this article, following the exact form given in 33b(4) below. Make a second bibliography card for a useful article in one of the special encyclopedias.

▶ EXERCISE 8   Make a bibliography card for a promising article in each of two other reference works.

(4) Bibliographical Form.

The student should put each item of his bibliography on a separate card (3 × 5 or 4 × 6 inches in size) so that he can readily drop or add a card and can arrange the list alphabetically without copying. He should write in ink and follow *exactly* and consistently the bibliographical form he is directed to use. The form illustrated by the models below (and by the footnote forms on pages 412–

15) is based on the revised *Style Sheet* of the Modern Language Association (MLA). Note that the author's name, when it is given, always comes first; otherwise the title.

MODEL BIBLIOGRAPHICAL ENTRIES

BOOKS

Anderson, Virgil A. *Training the Speaking Voice.* New York: Oxford University Press, 1942.

Duverger, Maurice. *Political Parties.* Translated from the French by Barbara and Robert North. New York: John Wiley & Sons, Inc., 1954. [A translation][1]

Hervey, George F., and Jack Hems. *Freshwater Tropical Aquarium Fishes.* London: Batchworth Press, 1952. [Two authors]

Johnson, R. U., and C. C. Buel, editors. *Battles and Leaders of the Civil War.* 4 volumes. New York: The Century Company, 1887–88. [Edited work]

McConnell, F. J., and others. *The Creative Intelligence and Modern Life.* Boulder: The University of Colorado Press, 1928. (University of Colorado Semicentennial Series, 1877–1927. Vol. V.) [A book by more than two authors; also a book in a series]

Prescott, William Hickling. *History of the Reign of Philip the Second, King of Spain.* Edited by John Foster Kirk. 3 volumes. Philadelphia: J. B. Lippincott & Company, 1871. [Author and editor]

Scott, Sir Harold. *Scotland Yard.* New York: Random House, 1955.

[1] Note that this bracketed comment and the others below are not a part of the bibliographical entries, which fall into three units separated by periods: (1) the author's name; (2) the title; (3) the facts of publication—place, publisher, date (sometimes found only on the copyright page). Another common bibliographical form uses commas between all parts, thus:

Anderson, Virgil A., *Training the Speaking Voice,* New York, Oxford University Press, 1942.

Menard, Henry W., "Fractures in the Pacific Floor," *Scientific American,* CXCIII (July, 1955), 36–41.

Curti, Merle. "Intellectuals and Other People." *American Historical Review*, LX (January, 1955), 259–82.

Menard, Henry W. "Fractures in the Pacific Floor." *Scientific American*, CXCIII (July, 1955), 36–41.

Salisbury, Harrison E. "Farm Goals Cited by Soviet Official." New York *Times*, August 24, 1955, pp. 1 ff. [The *p.* or *pp.* (for *page* or *pages*) are not used when the volume number in Roman numerals precedes, as in the two items above.]

"Will the Credit Medicine Be Enough?" *Business Week* (August 13, 1955), pp. 26–28.

ENCYCLOPEDIAS

"Jackson, Andrew,' *Encyclopædia Britannica*, 1954, XII, 851 853.

Lee, Edwin A. "Vocational Education." *Encyclopedia Americana*, 1950, XXVIII, 160–61. [A signed article]

BULLETINS AND PAMPHLETS

Standards of Practice for Radio Broadcasters of the United States of America. Washington: The National Association of Radio and Television Broadcasters, 1954.

Velvetbean Caterpillar, The. Dept. of Agriculture, Bureau of Entomology and Plant Quarantine Leaflet No. 348. Washington: Government Printing Office, 1953.

UNPUBLISHED DISSERTATION

Blair, Carolyn L. "Browning as Critic." Ph.D. dissertation, University of Tennessee, 1961.

The models given above, with hanging indention, show the proper form for the entries in the final bibliography, which is to be written out and submitted as a part of the library paper. On the separate bibliography cards, the same form may be used; or the author, title, and facts of publication may be written on separate lines as in the following specimen. (The library call number in the lower left-hand corner will save the trouble of looking in the card catalog again when the book is needed. See page 404.)

Scott, Sir Harold.
Scotland Yard.
New York: Random House, 1955.

HV
8198
L753
1955

The form of the bibliographical models given above (referred to as MLA style) is commonly used by books and periodicals in languages and social sciences. Scientific periodicals tend to use boldface Arabic numerals for the volume number and to place the date at the end. Indexes to periodicals employ a compact form, but one not commonly used in books or periodicals and consequently not suitable as a model. The card catalog is also unsuitable as a guide, since it capitalizes only the first word and the proper names in book titles and publication data.

Whatever bibliographical form a writer adopts, he should give due heed to the three divisions of each entry: the author's name (if it is given), the title, and the facts of publication. He should take great pains to be consistent, each time using commas, periods, italics (underlining), and quotation marks exactly as they are called for by his model. This model will usually be suggested by the periodical, the organization, or the department for which the paper is being written. If the instructor does not specify a form, the student may adopt the commonly used form illustrated above.

▶ EXERCISE 9   Prepare a preliminary bibliography on the topic selected for your library paper by adding, to the twelve cards already made for Exercises 3–8, six cards for the most promising references (books, bulletins, articles in periodicals or reference books) you can find. (Often you will find helpful bibliographies in the books that you consult, especially at the end of articles in encyclopedias and other reference works.) Then arrange the eighteen cards in alphabetical order.

33c
Prepare the outline.

[Follow the general directions given under **32b-f.** But the outline for the library paper will need even more change and development than the outline for the ordinary exposition. You must write down at least a few tentative headings to guide your first note-taking; then the extensive reading and note-taking required to find material for the paper will show many ways to develop the headings into a complete outline.]

After completing a preliminary bibliography and a minimum of general reading on his subject (an encyclopedia article and parts of one or two other works may suffice), the student writing on the French horn or on Boris Pasternak will make a preliminary outline that will give direction to his investigation. This tentative outline will enable him to discard irrelevant material from his bibliography and to begin spotting valuable passages on which he will want to take notes. There is nothing but frustration in store for anyone who attempts to take notes without first knowing what he is looking for.

The student should be careful, however, not to become a slave to his preliminary outline. For although the outline will direct his reading, his reading will almost certainly suggest ways in which the outline may be improved. No outline should be regarded as complete until the research paper has been finished. As the student takes notes, he will probably revise his original outline frequently, adding subheads to it, changing subheads to major headings, perhaps dropping some headings entirely. After some general reading, he might make an outline such as one of the following:

First Preliminary Outlines

THE FRENCH HORN

   I. History of the horn
      A. Early horns
      B. Modern horns
  II. Characteristics of the French horn
 III. Musical scores featuring the French horn
 IV. Noted players of the French horn—Dennis Brain, etc.
  V. The French horn in the twentieth century

BORIS PASTERNAK

   I. Early life of Pasternak
      A. Childhood
      B. Writings
  II. *Doctor Zhivago* and the Nobel Prize
 III. Death of Pasternak

With such a rough and incomplete outline as a guide, the student is ready to begin his note-taking (see **33d** below). While reading and taking notes he will write into his preliminary outline each desirable addition or change as it occurs to him. The student writing on the French horn will soon drop Topic III, "Musical scores," on discovering that it is too technical for his paper; and he may decide to omit IV, "Noted players," on the grounds that he can write a better paper by limiting himself to "The French Horn: Its Development and Use." At this point, if he has not been able to do so before, he can state in a single sentence the central or controlling ideas of his paper.

After a few days his developing outline might look somewhat as follows:

Second Preliminary Outline

THE FRENCH HORN: ITS DEVELOPMENT AND USE

CENTRAL IDEA   The French horn has evolved from a humble
origin and has won a secure place in modern orchestras.

    I. Origin and development of the instrument
        A. Early horns
            1. Roman
            2. Saxon
        B. Seventeenth- and eighteenth-century horns
        C. Nineteenth-century horns
   II. Characteristics of the instrument
        A. Dimensions
        B. Quality of tone
  III. The French horn in orchestras
        A. Seventeenth century
        B. Eighteenth century
        C. Nineteenth century
        D. Twentieth century

The student writing on Boris Pasternak might soon find
his chief interest in the international repercussions of the
Nobel award, write out the central idea, and begin selecting
his material accordingly. He would then revise Topic I of
the preliminary outline to serve as an introduction to the
body of his paper, which would be covered by the new
Topics II–VI as they appear in the finished outline (see
pages 429–30).

33d

Take notes (after evaluating the sources).

In taking notes, the student should learn how to find
and evaluate useful passages with a minimum of time and

effort. Seldom will a whole book, or even a whole article, be of use as subject matter for any given research paper. To find what is needed for his paper, the student must turn to many books and articles, rejecting most of them altogether and using from others only a section here and there. He cannot take the time to read each book carefully. He must use the table of contents of the book and its index, and he must learn to scan the pages rapidly until he finds the passages he needs.

One important consideration always is the reliability of the source. Does the author seem to know his subject? Does he have an official position that implies competence? Do others speak of him as an authority? Is he prejudiced? Is the work recent enough to give the information needed? Is the edition being used the latest one available? The student should use his best judgment to determine the most dependable sources for his paper. He can often find in the *Book Review Digest* convenient summaries of critical opinion on a book in his bibliography.

▶ EXERCISE 10   Consult the *Book Review Digest* for critical opinion on the three most promising books in your list. How many reviews do you find for each book? (Check the year when the book was published and also one or two years following.) Do the reviews indicate that all three of the books are reliable sources for your paper? Does any one seem more reliable, or more useful to you, than the others? Write out your answers in a brief note to be read or submitted when called for.

The common and best way to take notes is on cards or paper sheets of uniform size, usually 3 × 5 or 4 × 6 inches. (Often the smaller card is used for bibliography and the larger for notes.) Each card should contain a single note with a heading keyed to a significant word in the outline—not to the notation (IA, II, IIIC, etc.), which is especially subject to change. If the paper is to use the customary footnotes, each card must also show the source of the note, the exact page or pages.

The student preparing a library paper on the French horn might find the following passage and write from it the note given below.

In *Saxon* times horns were used by the huntsmen and in battle, and carried by the peaceful traveler as well, to make known his presence. An ancient law stated that "if a man come from afar or a stranger go out of the highway, and he neither shout or blow a horn, he is to be accounted a thief, either to be slain or to be redeemed." [2]

Early horns - Saxon
   The early Saxons used horns in the hunt, in battle, and in traveling. According to ancient law, any stranger or anyone off the highway was required to cry out or sound his horn to insure himself against being "accounted a thief either to be slain or to be redeemed."
Edgerly, p. 263.

This note is an abbreviation or précis of the source, expressed by the student in his own phraseology except for the last eleven words, which he wishes to quote. He may use this note in his paper (see Note 8, page 423) just as here written or he may revise it as he writes the paper.

Quotations. Very seldom should a student write a note that is merely a quotation. Too many quotations in the library paper suggest a lack of mastery of the subject.

[2] Beatrice Edgerly, *From the Hunter's Bow* (New York, 1942), p. 263.

And besides, the more a student quotes, the less practice he gets in composition. A quotation must be a very telling and important one before a student is justified in using it in his paper. Occasionally, however, a student will discover such a passage. When he does, he should take down the passage verbatim—that is, write every word, every capital letter, every mark of punctuation exactly as in the original. Then he should enclose the quoted passage in quotation marks. When a note-taker quotes, he should quote accurately. When he is not quoting, he should use his own phraseology, getting entirely away from that of the original.

Plagiarism. Any failure to acknowledge borrowed material is a serious offense called plagiarism. If a borrowed idea is expressed in the student's phraseology, an acknowledgment of the source is sufficient. If it is in the phraseology of the source, it should be put in quotation marks and also acknowledged. Usually any conscious quotation (except well-known or proverbial passages) of three or four connected words or more should be placed in quotation marks. In a library paper, acknowledgments are made in footnotes.

▶ EXERCISE 11   Use the third paragraph of the library paper on Pasternak at the end of this section to write a short note of fewer than forty words. [Be careful to avoid the sentence patterns of the source. Write two or three effective sentences to express the gist of the paragraph.]

▶ EXERCISE 12   Use the same paragraph to write a longer note, perhaps three-fourths the length of the source. [Avoid entirely the sentence patterns of the source. Include more details than the shorter note of Exercise 11 permitted. Make the sentences as effective as you can.]

▶ EXERCISE 13   Make a paraphrase of the first paragraph of the library paper. [Avoid entirely the sentence patterns of the source. A paraphrase is approximately the same length as the source and should be expressed in equally effective sentences.]

▶ EXERCISE 14   Read carefully the paragraph by Harlow Shapley reprinted on pages 335–36. First write, in a single sentence, the central idea of the paragraph. Then write a note half as long as the paragraph. Finally write a note approximately as long as your source. [Avoid entirely the sentence patterns of the source. Choose your words carefully. Give variety to your sentences.]

33e

Use the outline, the bibliography, and the notes to write the library paper. (Follow the general suggestions given under 32g.)

After the outline has been made as complete as possible and after a number of notes have been taken on every major section of the outline and every subsection, the student is ready to begin writing. He will arrange his notes in the order of the outline and then use them as the basis of his paper, section by section. Naturally he will have to expand some parts, to cut others; and especially will he need to provide transitional sentences and even transitional paragraphs. He must write the material in the best way he can—in his own style, in his own words.

(1) Footnotes and Footnote Forms. Since the student gets his material for the library paper largely from others, he should, of course, give proper credit. To do so, he uses footnotes numbered consecutively throughout the paper and placed at the bottoms of the pages (or in one list at the end of the paper, if so directed). The number needed will vary with the paper. Every quotation must have its footnote, and so must all the chief facts and opinions drawn from others. Usually from two to six footnotes per

page will be needed for proper documentation of the average library paper.

In the model forms that follow, note that the first footnote reference to a source is similar to, but not identical with, the bibliographical entry.

Moorehead, Alan. The White Nile. New York: Harper &

   Brothers, 1960.   [Bibliographical entry]

¹Alan Moorehead, The White Nile (New York, 1960),

p. 351.   [First footnote reference]

The footnote has the normal paragraph indention (not the hanging indention used to make each entry stand out in a bibliography); the author's name comes in normal order with surname last (since the name is not to be alphabetized as in the bibliography); a comma replaces the period between author's name and title, and the facts of publication are put in parentheses without the publisher's name; and the exact page of the source is given.

MODEL FOOTNOTES—FIRST REFERENCES

BOOKS

[1] Virgil A. Anderson, *Training the Speaking Voice* (New York, 1942), p. 11.

[2] Maurice Duverger, *Political Parties*, trans. from the French by Barbara and Robert North (New York, 1954), p. 114. [A translation]

[3] George F. Hervey and Jack Hems, *Freshwater Tropical Aquarium Fishes* (London, 1952), p. 44. [Two authors]

[4] R. U. Johnson and C. C. Buel, eds., *Battles and Leaders of the Civil War* (New York, 1887–88), I, 9. [Edited work; also a work in several volumes]

[5] General James Longstreet, "Our March Against Pope," in *Battles and Leaders of the Civil War*, ed. R. U. Johnson and C. C. Buel (New York, 1887–88), II, 516. [Contributing author in an edited work]

6 F. J. McConnell and others, *The Creative Intelligence and Modern Life,* University of Colorado Semicentennial Series, V (Boulder, Colo., 1928), pp. 29–30. [A book by more than two authors; also a book in a series]

7 William Hickling Prescott, *History of the Reign of Philip the Second, King of Spain,* ed. John Foster Kirk (Philadelphia, 1871), III, 87.

8 Sir Harold Scott, *Scotland Yard* (New York, 1955), p. 101.

MAGAZINES AND NEWSPAPERS

9 Merle Curti, "Intellectuals and Other People," *American Historical Review,* LX (January, 1955), 279–80.

10 Henry W. Menard, "Fractures in the Pacific Floor," *Scientific American,* CXCIII (July, 1955), 36.

11 Harrison E. Salisbury, "Farm Goals Cited by Soviet Official," New York *Times,* August 24, 1955, p. 1. [A signed news story]

12 Louisville *Times,* June 4, 1938, p. 16. [An unsigned news story]

13 "Will the Credit Medicine Be Enough?" *Business Week* (August 13, 1955), pp. 26–27. [An unsigned magazine article]

ENCYCLOPEDIAS

14 "Jackson, Andrew," *Encyclopædia Britannica,* 1954, XII, 853. [An unsigned encyclopedia article. The title here is given as "Jackson, Andrew" because it is found listed alphabetically under *J* and not under *A* in the encyclopedia.]

15 Edwin A. Lee, "Vocational Education," *Encyclopedia Americana,* 1950, XXVIII, 160. [A signed encyclopedia article. Note the variant spellings: *Encyclopædia* for the *Britannica; Encyclopedia* for the *Americana.*]

BULLETINS AND PAMPHLETS

16 *Standards of Practice for Radio Broadcasters of the United States of America* (Washington, 1954), p. 18.

17 *The Velvetbean Caterpillar,* Department of Agriculture, Bureau of Entomology and Plant Quarantine Leaflet No. 348 (Washington, 1953), p. 3.

UNPUBLISHED DISSERTATION

¹⁸ Carolyn L. Blair, "Browning as Critic" (Ph.D. dissertation, University of Tennessee, 1961), p. 186.

MODEL FOOTNOTES—SECOND REFERENCES

The second (or later) footnote references below follow the order of the works cited in the Model Footnotes—First References.

BOOKS

¹⁹ Anderson, p. 11. ²⁰ Duverger, pp. 113–14.
[It is permissible to place extremely short footnotes two, and even three, on a line, so long as there is no appearance of overcrowding.]

²¹ Hervey and Hems, p. 41. ²² Johnson and Buel, I, 5.

²³ Longstreet, II, 515. ²⁴ McConnell and others, p. 28.

²⁵ Prescott, III, 125.

²⁶ *Ibid.* [Same work, same volume, and same page as in footnote immediately preceding]

²⁷ *Ibid.*, II, 94–95. [Same work (Prescott's), but a different volume]

²⁸ *Ibid.*, p. 95. [Same work, same volume, but only one page this time]

²⁹ *Ibid.*, III, 125. [Same work, but back to a volume not cited in the *immediately* preceding footnote]

³⁰ Scott, p. 133.

³¹ Prescott, III, 127. [An *ibid.* here would refer to Scott's work, not Prescott's.]

³² Scott, p. 133.

MAGAZINES AND NEWSPAPERS

³³ Curti, p. 279. ³⁴ Menard, p. 39. ³⁵ Salisbury, p. 1.

³⁶ Salisbury, "Farm Goals Cited by Soviet Official," p. 1. [This is the form that would have to be used if Salisbury had furnished more than one of the sources included in your bibliography.]

³⁷ Harrison E. Salisbury, p. 1. [This is the form that would

have to be used if another author also named Salisbury were included in your bibliography.]

38 Louisville *Times*, p. 16. [Proper if only one article from this newspaper is used. If more than one are used, the secondary form is the same as the primary. See footnote 12.]

39 "Will the Credit Medicine Be Enough?" p. 27.

ENCYCLOPEDIAS

40 "Jackson, Andrew," pp. 851–52. [It is possible that a research paper may use articles with identical titles from several different encyclopedias. In that case, the proper secondary footnote form would be as follows (footnote 41).]

41 "Jackson, Andrew," *Encyclopædia Britannica*, pp. 851–52. [The year of publication and the volume number are cited in your primary footnote and need not be repeated here.]

42 Lee, p. 160.

BULLETINS AND PAMPHLETS

43 *Standards of Practice for Radio Broadcasters of the United States of America*, p. 17.

44 *The Velvetbean Caterpillar*, p. 3.

UNPUBLISHED DISSERTATION

45 Blair, p. 220.

Abbreviations. Some abbreviations used in footnotes are as follows (those from Latin usually written in italics):

c. or *ca.* (*circa*)	about (*ca.* 1550)
cf. (*confer*)	compare [The English *see* is more common.]
ch., chs.	chapter, chapters
ed.	edited by, edition, editor
f., ff.	and the following page, pages
ibid. (*ibidem*)	in the same place
l., ll.	line, lines
loc. cit. (*loco citato*)	in the place cited
MS., ms., MSS., mss.	manuscript, manuscripts
n.d.	no date given

n.p.	no place (of publication)
op. cit. (opere citato)	in the work cited
p., pp.	page, pages
passim	here and there
rev.	revised
tr., trans.	translated by
vol., vols.	volume, volumes

(2) Final Outline and Paper. After the student has written the first draft of his paper on the French horn or Boris Pasternak, complete with footnotes, he will read it over carefully, correcting all errors in spelling, mechanics, and grammar, and making sure that the arrangement is logical and that the writing is as clear, concise, and pleasing in style as he can possibly make it. He will probably rewrite some sentences, strike out others, and add still others. His outline, which has developed steadily throughout the note-taking and the first draft of the paper, should now be in its final form. It has served primarily, of course, as a guide to the writing of the paper; but it will also serve, if copied in its final stage, as a guide to the contents of the paper.

With his first draft corrected and revised, and with his outline put in its final form, the student will write the final draft of his paper. He will use a typewriter if possible; if not, he will use pen and ink, taking pains to write legibly and neatly.

(3) Final Bibliography. We have already noticed that the student assembles a preliminary bibliography early in his research. As he pursues his investigation, he eliminates some items and adds others. Not until he has completed his paper can he know the items that should make up his final bibliography. Now, with his writing completed, he may look through his footnotes. Every book or article appearing even once in a footnote belongs in his bibliography. His instructor may ask him to include everything that he has examined, whether he has actually used it in his writing or not. In that case his bibliography may have, instead of a dozen items, as many as fifty or a hundred. But, on the whole, the best practice is to include only items which have actually been used. Once the student has determined the items that should be included, he can easily arrange the bibliography cards and copy them, either in one alphabetical list or in a list classified according to the instructor's directions.

The completed library paper consists of four units (illustrated by the complete library paper on pages 428–46):

1. Title page, giving title, author's name, instructor's name, and course number, and also date of writing.
2. Outline, serving as the table of contents (numbered with small Roman numerals if it occupies more than one page).
3. Text of the paper, with footnotes.
4. Bibliography, on a separate page or pages numbered with the text (with Arabic numerals).

Students are often asked to submit, along with the completed paper, the materials used in the preparation of the paper: (1) one of the preliminary outlines, (2) the notes, on cards, (3) the rough draft of the paper, with footnotes, and (4) the bibliography, on cards.

(4) **Sample Library Papers.** In the preceding part of this section you have observed how students have prepared, step by step, library papers on the French horn and on Boris Pasternak. The complete paper on the French horn (printed in part on pages 418–27) consists of twenty-seven paragraphs covering the three major divisions of the outline in thirteen, four, and ten paragraphs respectively. The paper on Pasternak (given in full on pages 428–46) develops the six major headings of the outline in fourteen paragraphs distributed thus:

I. Paragraphs 1, 2	IV. Paragraphs 8, 9
II. Paragraphs 3, 4, 5	V. Paragraphs 10, 11
III. Paragraphs 6, 7	VI. Paragraphs 12, 13, 14

The French Horn: Its Development and Use

By Jack Howard Wilson

English 113, Section 36

Professor Stewart

May 9, 1955

OUTLINE

<u>Central Idea</u>: The French horn has evolved from a humble origin and has won a secure place in modern orchestras.

   I. Origin and development of the instrument

    A. Early horns

       1. Shells and animal horns

       2. Biblical horns

       3. Roman <u>cornua</u>

       4. Saxon and medieval horns

    B. Innovations of the seventeenth and eighteenth centuries

    C. The valve horn of the nineteenth century

  II. Characteristics of the instrument

    A. Dimensions of the instrument

    B. Quality of tone

    C. Difficulties of performance

III. Use of the instrument in orchestras

    A. Seventeenth century

    B. Eighteenth century

C. Nineteenth century

    1. Beethoven and his contemporaries

    2. Brahms

    3. Tchaikovsky

D. Twentieth century

The ancestors of the modern French horn may be traced back to the earliest days of man, when conch shells picked up from the seashore were used for horns.[1] Other primitive horns were made from the horns of cattle, oxen, and deer. These instruments of prehistoric times—which could sound but one or two rough, indefinite tones[2]—may be classified properly as noisemakers, for the sounds they made were not musical.

One of these early horns, the Hebrew ram's horn or <u>shophar</u>, is still used in Jewish temple rites. This very pure-sounding horn is mentioned in the Bible over one hundred times. The priests blew on the shophar when the walls of Jericho tumbled down.[3] Another forerunner of the French horn found in the Bible is the cornet mentioned by Daniel as the first instrument in King Nebuchadnezzar's orchestra. "Cornet" is the rendering in the King James Version, but the Revised Standard

---

[1]Beatrice Edgerly, <u>From the Hunter's Bow</u> (New York, 1942), p. 4.

[2]"Horns," <u>Encyclopaedia Britannica</u>, 1954, XI, 750.

[3]Edgerly, p. 144.

Version is probably more accurate in the translation
"horn," since the Oriental orchestras of those days
probably began playing with a call or flourish from the
horn. The other instruments followed, each playing individually.[4]

(3)   The ancient Romans were using brass horns as early
as the first century B. C.[5] These <u>cornua</u> (the Latin
word for "horns") were of three types: (1) the <u>tuba</u>,
a straight trumpet; (2) the J-shaped <u>lituus</u> carried by
horse soldiers; and (3) the <u>buccina</u>, a curved brass horn
that wound around the player's body.[6] These horns were
not used as musical instruments, but they were excellent
for sounding fanfares.[7]

(4)   The early Saxons used horns in the hunt, in battle
and in traveling. According to ancient law any stranger

---

[4]Curt Sachs, <u>The History of Musical Instruments</u>
(New York, 1940), pp. 83-85.

[5]Cecil Forsyth, <u>Orchestration</u> (New York, 1947),
p. 68.

[6]Edgerly, pp. 135-136

[7]"Horns," XI, 750.

or anyone off the highway was required to cry out or to sound his horn to insure himself against being "accounted a thief, either to be slain or to be redeemed."[8]

The nobles of the Middle Ages had little to do but fight and hunt. At first they used animal horns (as in Saxon England) to signal their soldiers and hunting companions. Later they discovered that they could get more and clearer tones from a brass horn. The hunting horn that was developed for them was a marked improvement over the animal horn, but it was still very simple. It was a circular tube carried with the arm through the coil and the weight on the shoulder.

---

[8]Edgerly, p. 263.

[Paragraphs 6–25 are omitted here.]

(26)   The repertoires of our modern symphony orchestras consist largely of eighteenth- and nineteenth-century music. There are generally in any symphony orchestra five or six versatile horn players who can play melody, accompaniment, or sustaining harmony equally well. In the popular-music or dance band, the French horn is usually in the background and rarely gets a chance to solo. Exceptions to this practice are made by the bands of Hugo Winterhalter and Mitch Miller, which quite often feature the French horn. Leroy Anderson, composer of semi-classical music, favors the French horn in his compositions. Almost any high school band has two French horn players, but four is a more usual number, and five or six horns are not uncommon. The number of horns in college bands, as in high school bands, depends on the size of the organization. While the horn is of little value in a marching band, it is virtually indispensable to a concert band.

(27)   The French horn has made remarkable advances since its conch-shell beginning. It has become a respected

member of most musical organizations. Because of its unique tonal quality, it is used as a solo instrument for special effects. And it makes a very pleasing contribution to any band or orchestra, whatever part it plays. We wonder how the many musicians who have contributed in earlier centuries to the development and use of the French horn would feel if they could see and hear it in its modern form. They would be surprised, no doubt, but the surprise would be a pleasant one.

BIBLIOGRAPHY

Andrews, George W., editor. Musical Instruments, IV,
in The American History and Encyclopedia of Music,
W. L. Hubbard, editor-in-chief. 10 volumes. New
York: Irving Squire, 1908.

Berlioz, Hector. A Treatise upon Modern Instrumentatio
and Orchestration. Translated from the French by
Mary Cowden Clarke. London: Novello and Company,
1858.

Edgerly, Beatrice. From the Hunter's Bow. New York:
G. P. Putnam's Sons, 1942.

Elson, Arthur. Orchestral Instruments and Their Use.
Boston: The Page Company, 1922.

Forsyth, Cecil. Orchestration. New York: The Mac-
millan Company, 1947.

Geiringer, Karl. Musical Instruments. New York: Oxford University Press, 1945.

"Horns." Encyclopaedia Britannica, 1954, XI, 749-750.

Huneker, James Gibbons. Mezzotints in Modern Music.
New York: Charles Scribner's Sons, 1905.

Mason, Daniel Gregory. The Orchestral Instruments and
What They Do. New York: H. W. Gray Company, 1909

Niemann, Walter. Brahms. Translated from the German
by Catherine Alison Phillips. New York: Alfred
A. Knopf, 1941.

Piston, Walter. Orchestration. New York: W. W. Norton & Company, 1955.

Read, Gardner. Thesaurus of Orchestral Devices. New
York: Pitman Publishing Corporation, 1953.

19

Sachs, Curt. <u>The History of Musical Instruments</u>. New York: W. W. Norton & Company, 1940.

Schlesinger, Kathleen. "Horns." <u>Encyclopaedia Britannica</u>, 1911, XIII, 697-706.

Terry, Charles Sanford. <u>Bach's Orchestra</u>. London: Oxford University Press, 1932.

"Young Man with a Horn." <u>Time</u>, LXII (July 6, 1953), 38-39.

Boris Pasternak and the Nobel Prize

By Ruth Alane Gresky

English 113, Section 12

Professor Lyles

February 23, 1961

<u>OUTLINE</u>

<u>Central Idea</u>: The awarding of the 1958 Nobel Prize

in Literature to Boris Pasternak profoundly af-

fected the author's reputation, both at home and

abroad, and started a controversy between Russia

and the Western world.

  I. Pasternak's life prior to the composition of <u>Doctor</u>

      <u>Zhivago</u>

      A. Parentage

      B. Education

      C. Writings: poetry and translations

 II. <u>Doctor</u> <u>Zhivago</u>

      A. Suppression in Russia

      B. Publication in Italy

      C. Interpretations of the theme

III. Possible reasons for the Nobel award

      A. Literary

      B. Political

 IV. Reactions to the award

      A. In Russia

      B. In the West

V. Pasternak's personal involvement

    A. His reasons for refusing the award

    B. His persecution and response

VI. Aftermath

    A. Pasternak's undying spirit

    B. Russia's continuing reaction

(1)   Were it not for the effect of <u>Doctor Zhivago</u> on the cold war, few Americans would ever have heard of its author, Nobel Prize winner Boris Leonidovich Pasternak, who was when the novel was published one of the greatest living poets.[1] Poet-novelist Pasternak was born in Moscow on February 10, 1890, the eldest son of painter Leonid Pasternak and Rosa Isodornovna Pasternak, nee Kaufman, a former concert pianist.[2] His mother, aided by private tutors, gave the boy his preschool education. Pasternak entered a Moscow secondary school in 1901, and in 1913 he graduated from Moscow University, having spent the summer of 1912 studying Kantian philosophy under Hermann Cohen at Marburg University. During this time the young man's principal interest shifted from music to law to philosophy and ultimately to poetry.[3]

---

[1] Ernest J. Simmons, "Boris Pasternak," <u>Nation</u>, CXC (June 11, 1960), 503.

[2] "Boris Pasternak," in Boris Pasternak, <u>I Remember</u>, trans. from the Russian by David Magarshack (New York, 1959), pp. 4, 180.

[3] Pasternak, <u>I Remember</u>, pp. 33, 177-78.

2

②   His first book of poems, <u>A Twin in the Clouds</u>,
published in 1914, was followed by numerous other poems
and books of verse, in addition to a few short stories,
an autobiography (<u>Safe Conduct</u>), a novel in verse (<u>Spek-
torsky</u>), and translations of the Russian Georgian poets.[4] These early original poems, which emphasized the
fate of the individual, were criticized in Soviet reviews for their abstractness.[5] The Russian public, however, liked them so much that in later years devotees
circulated Pasternak poems in typewritten form and often memorized even unpublished, forbidden ones.[6] To escape the repeated attacks on his individualism, the poet
turned for his livelihood almost entirely to translations, the only works of which his reviewers approved.[7]

---

[4]<u>Ibid</u>., pp. 178-79.

[5]"Pasternak, Boris Leonidovich," <u>Collier's Ency-
clopedia</u>, 1959, XV, 467.

[6]"Farewell: A Poet's Land," <u>Life</u>, XLVIII (June 13,
1960), 86A-86B.

[7]"Pasternak, Boris Leonidovich," <u>Biographic
Directory of the U.S.S.R.</u> (New York, 1958), pp. 476-77.

After 1932 he seems to have centered most of his efforts on Shakespeare and Goethe.[8]

⟨3⟩   After years of translating other writers' poems
and plays into Russian, Pasternak gave to the Western
World in 1958 the novel <u>Doctor Zhivago</u>, his first original work published since <u>The Death of a Sapper</u> in 1943.
He himself referred to the later controversial book as
"my chief and most important work, the only one I am
not ashamed of and for which I can answer with the utmost confidence."[9] To his great disappointment the
book, when submitted to Russian publishers in 1954,
was rejected. Max Hayward, a co-translator of <u>Doctor
Zhivago</u>, believes "that the original decision not to
publish the novel was to a large extent based on personal animosities." He says that the Secretary of the
Union of Writers, Alexei Surkov, openly hated Pasternak
and could easily have been offended by several passages

----

[8]Pasternak, <u>I Remember</u>, p. 179.

[9]<u>Ibid</u>., pp. 15, 121-22.

in the book, particularly those making unfavorable references to name-dropping officials.[10] At any rate, it
is unlikely that Doctor Zhivago was suppressed for pure-
ly political reasons, because the Literary Gazette published the full text of a letter by the editors of Novy
Mir giving the reasons for rejection of the novel, and
this letter quoted almost all of the passages that were
believed to be the cause for not publishing the book.
Furthermore, the poet's attack on Stalin, which at one
time would have been an understandable source of irri-
tation, could hardly be considered strong in view of
Khrushchev's revelations about Stalin. Besides, Pasternak had offered to revise or remove entirely any
passages that were found offensive.[11]

(4)   Unable to find in his own country an outlet for
his pride and joy, the disconsolate author gave the manu
script to the representative of an Italian publisher

---

[10] Max Hayward, "Zhivago's Suppression--A New
Theory," Library Journal, LXXXIV (May 15, 1959), 1563.

[11] Ibid., p. 1562.

who had expressed sincere interest in what he considered a literary masterpiece. Although at the request of Soviet authorities pro-Communist publisher Giangiacomo Feltrinelli returned the original manuscript to Russia for ostensible revision, the Italian translation was printed and issued in Milan. Feltrinelli, who had been somewhat disillusioned by the Hungarian Revolution in 1956, made his final break with Communism shortly after the book went to press in 1957. [12] Translations in seventeen other languages, excluding Russian, soon followed this first edition.[13]

⑤   Many thousand non-Russian people have bought and read Pasternak's novel and are almost uniform in their opinion that the book is of exceptional literary quality. Disagreement arises, however, in interpretation

---

[12]E. Lyons, "The Book the Kremlin Is Afraid to Let the Russians Read," Reader's Digest, LXXIV (February, 1959), 62; "Doctor Zhivago," in Boris Pasternak, Doctor Zhivago, trans. from the Russian by Max Hayward and Manya Harari (New York, 1958), flap of book jacket.

[13]"Pasternak's Way," Time, LXXII (November 3, 1958), 24.

of the theme. Some people feel that <u>Doctor Zhivago</u> is a portrayal of the physical and spiritual misery of Pasternak's world[14]--that the story emphasizes the author's lack of "faith in current practices of social betterment in Russia."[15] Others argue that greater evidence is given of the novelist's unwavering faith in the goodness of man and in man's unceasing quest for the highest good. This second group of critics firmly believes that despite Pasternak's objectivity in describing Russia, Russians, and events in Russian history during the period from 1903 to 1945,[16] the theme is predominantly hopeful, even religious.[17]

(6)   Dissent regarding the nature of <u>Doctor Zhivago</u>'s theme has occasionally reached the point of outright

---

[14]"Prize to Pasternak," <u>New Republic</u>, CXXXIX (November 3, 1958), 5.

[15]Harrison E. Salisbury, "The Triumph of Boris Pasternak," <u>Saturday Review</u>, XLI (November 8, 1958), 22

[16]Lyons, pp. 59-62.

[17]Irving Howe, "Of Freedom and Contemplation," <u>New Republic</u>, CXXXIX (September 8, 1958), 20.

vehemence; yet there are probably few readers who would disagree with the statement of critic Irving Howe and the author himself that the novel was Pasternak's greatest literary work.

(1)   Members of the Nobel committee were far from disagreeing, for on October 23, 1958, they awarded the Nobel Prize for Literature and the accompanying prize money ($41,420) to Boris Leonidovich Pasternak. Upon hearing the news, the novelist sent the committee a six-word cable written in English: "Immensely thankful, touched, proud, astonished, abashed."[18] Possibly the committee was rather abashed, too, when their motives in awarding the Prize to Pasternak were questioned. Although the exceptional quality of Doctor Zhivago may well have been enough to warrant the award, many people felt that the timing, at least, was determined by politics.[19] The Russians loudly declared this to be true, and with

---

[18]Lyons, p. 58; "Pasternak's Way," p. 24.

[19]"Prize to Pasternak," p. 5.

some cause. Few of the author's other works were known
outside the Soviet Union, and the Prize had never before
been given on the merits of a single novel.[20]

⑧   The award undeniably increased tensions in the
cold war, and Soviet leaders apparently felt that the
Swedes intended that it do so.[21] Whether or not the
publication of <u>Doctor Zhivago</u> had caused personal controversy between Pasternak and Union of Writers Secretary Surkov, its translation into other languages made
it an affair of state, and the award now turned it
into a national crisis. Russian prestige was at stake,
and Pasternak's "quiet old Russian scorn," as revealed
in the novel, was harder for the Communists to deal
with than an open attack from a foreign power.[22] They
felt that prompt and vigorous action was needed. Frus-

---

[20] Hugh Massingham, "Award to Pasternak Was
Irresponsible," <u>New Republic</u>, CXXXIX (December 15,
1958), 8-9.

[21] "More Honors for Pasternak," <u>Nation</u>, CLXXXVII
(November 8, 1958), 330.

[22] Hayward, p. 1563; "The Nature of Pasternak's
Protest," <u>Life</u>, XLV (November 3, 1958), 34.

trated officials expelled the poet from the Soviet writers' union, stripped him of the title Soviet Writer, and asserted that he had betrayed the Bolshevik Revolution and provided his country's enemies with a useful weapon.[23] Russian author Ilya Ehrenburg, however, felt that Pasternak and his book were really victims in this cold war battle. He said that Western publishers, desirous of making books by Russian writers look like attacks on the Soviet way of life, were more concerned about the need to appear anti-Communist than about their obligation to literature.[24]

⑨ Although some Western journalists felt that the awarding of the Nobel Prize to Pasternak would help the West convey to the Russian people the fact that it wants to meet them on terms of friendship and understanding rather than warfare, others were too anxious about the

---

[23] "Pasternak, Boris Leonidovich," Collier's Encyclopedia, pp. 467-68.

[24] Norman Cousins and Ilya Ehrenburg, eds., "Readers and Writers in Russia," Saturday Review, XLII (October 3, 1959), 17.

author's safety to foresee any favorable outcome of the incident.[25] This latter group feared that the Soviets would murder Pasternak or send him to a concentration camp. The novelist himself said at the time, "I am an old man; the worst which could happen to me would be death."[26]

⑩   Shortly thereafter Pasternak was given the choice of either rejecting the award or being exiled from his homeland. Commenting that leaving his native country would be like dying for him, he refused the Nobel Prize.[27] Patricia Blake, correspondent for _Life_ magazine, feels that Pasternak's main reason for asking Khrushchev not to exile him was his concern for his long-time friend Olga Ivinskaya and her daughter Irina. Olga had been questioned frequently by secret police and had been imprisoned once as a direct result

---

[25]"Prize to Pasternak," pp. 5-6.

[26]"Pasternak's Way," p. 24.

[27]"Pasternak, Boris Leonidovich,' _Collier's Encyclopedia_, p. 468.

of her friendship with the poet. He undoubtedly real-ized that her aid in editing and typing the manuscript of Doctor Zhivago placed her in even greater danger than before.[28] Another journalist suggests the pos-sibility that Pasternak may have refused in order to put his government on the spot by emphasizing the con-trast between his plight and the security of the group of Russian scientists also chosen to receive Nobel Prizes. His stated reason for declining was "the meaning the award had been given in the community to which he belonged."[29]

Even after he refused the Prize, Pasternak was attacked in Russia, for the publicity about the award made it impossible for the Kremlin to keep Doctor Zhivago's existence a secret from the Russian people any longer. To avoid scandal within the Soviet Union, Russian leaders were forced to declare publicly that

---

[28]Patricia Blake, "Russian Revenge on a Poet's Love," Life, L (January 27, 1961), 65-66.

[29]"More Honors for Pasternak," p. 330.

the award was an insult and the book a disgrace.[30]
The novelist was still being persecuted when Anthony
Brown of the London _Daily Mail_ published a poem that
he felt shed some light on Pasternak's attitude toward
the events that followed his being awarded the Nobel
Prize. The poem was included in a manuscript collection entrusted to Brown by the poet for delivery to
Jacqueline de Proyart, curator of the Tolstoy Museum
in Paris. When the poem appeared, Pasternak declared
that its publication was a betrayal of a trust and that
the poem had been written "in a black pessimistic mood"
that had passed. The _Daily Mail_ retorted that Pasternak had known his poem would be published, and therefore they had felt justified in printing it.

                    Nobel Prize

    I am lost like a beast in an enclosure;
    Somewhere are people, freedom and light.
    Behind me is the noise of pursuit,
    And there is no way out.

    Dark forest by the shore of the pond,
    The trunk of a fallen fir tree

    ————————————
    [30]Lyons, p. 59.

Cuts off my way.
It is all the same to me, come what may.

What offense have I committed?
Am I a murderer or a villain?
I who forced the whole world to weep
Over the beauty of my land.

Now almost in my coffin,
I believe the time will come
When the spirit of good will conquer
Wickedness and infamy.[31]

Whatever Pasternak's mood in writing the poem, its prophecy was soon fulfilled. Pasternak died at home in Peredelkino, a writers' colony, on May 30, 1960.[32]

Although the official Soviet press withheld for two days the news of Pasternak's death, and then gave it only brief coverage in an obscure newspaper, Literature and Life, over one thousand mourners arrived at Peredelkino for the poet's funeral.[33] At four o'clock

---

[31]"Lost Like a Beast," Time, LXXIII (February 23, 1959), 32.

[32]Pasternak, I Remember, p. 4.

[33]"Sad Day, a Snub," Newsweek, LV (June 13, 1960), 48.

in the afternoon, six pallbearers carried the open coffin half a mile to the graveyard of the Orthodox Church of the Transfiguration, where Boris Pasternak was laid to rest--[34] that is, where his physical being was laid to rest. His restless spirit, still searching for the highest good, pervades the pages of Doctor Zhivago and bears a message for the Western World.

(14)   Only a short time ago, the Communists showed signs that they were still fighting the influence of the novel. An article in the newspaper Soviet Culture discussed the problem of Russian writers who deviate from the line of Communist doctrine, suggesting that the Soviets may be considering the posthumous rehabilitation of Pasternak.[35] Perhaps one day the Soviet people may be able to read Doctor Zhivago, a masterpiece of twentieth-century literature made known to the free world by the cold war.

---

[34]"Death of a Man," pp. 27-28.

[35]"The World Today," Knoxville News-Sentinel, February 3, 1961, p. 9.

BIBLIOGRAPHY

Blake, Patricia. "Russian Revenge on a Poet's Love."
Life, L (January 27, 1961), 65-66.

Cousins, Norman, and Ilya Ehrenburg, editors. "Readers
and Writers in Russia." _Saturday Review_, XLII
(October 3, 1959), 15-17.

"Death of a Man." _Time_, LXXV (June 13, 1960), 27-28.

"Farewell: A Poet's Land." _Life_, XLVIII (June 13,
1960), 86-86B.

Hayward, Max. "Zhivago's Suppression--A New Theory."
Library Journal, LXXXIV (May 15, 1959), 1562-63.

Howe, Irving. "Of Freedom and Contemplation." _New
Republic_, CXXXIX (September 8, 1958), 16-20.

"Lost Like a Beast." _Time_, LXXIII (February 23, 1959),
32.

Lyons, E. "The Book the Kremlin Is Afraid to Let the
Russians Read." _Reader's Digest_, LXXIV (February, 1959), 58-64.

Massingham, Hugh. "Award to Pasternak Was Irresponsible." _New Republic_, CXXXIX (December 15,
1958), 8-9.

"More Honors for Pasternak." _Nation_, CLXXXVII (November 8, 1958), 330.

"The Nature of Pasternak's Protest." _Life_, XLV (November 3, 1958), 34.

Pasternak, Boris. _Doctor Zhivago_. Translated from
the Russian by Max Hayward and Manya Harari.
New York: Pantheon Books, Incorporated. 1958.

Pasternak, Boris. I Remember. Translated from the
     Russian by David Magarshack. New York:
     Meridian Books, Incorporated, 1959.

"Pasternak, Boris Leonidovich." Biographic Directory of
     the U.S.S.R. New York: Scarecrow Press,
     Incorporated, 1958

"Pasternak, Boris Leonidovich." Collier's Encyclopedia
     1959, XV, 467-68.

"Pasternak's Way." Time, LXXII (November 3, 1958), 24.

"Prize to Pasternak." New Republic, CXXXIX (November 3
     1958), 5-6.

"Sad Day, a Snub." Newsweek, LV (June 13, 1960), 48-49

Salisbury, Harrison E. "The Triumph of Boris Pasternak
     Saturday Review, XLI (November 8, 1958), 22.

Simmons, Ernest J. "Boris Pasternak." Nation, CXC
     (June 11, 1960), 503.

"The World Today." Knoxville News-Sentinel, February 3
     1961, p. 9.

Letters

34

Letters should follow the forms prescribed by usage.

Many college graduates will find letter-writing a major part of their life's work. All the principles of good writing set forth in this handbook apply to letters and should be used by the student whenever he is called on to write letters.

Business letters are preferably typewritten on one side only of sheets 8½ × 11 inches in size. These sheets are folded either (1) once horizontally and twice in the other direction to fit an envelope about 3½ × 6½ inches in size or (2) twice horizontally to fit an envelope about 4 × 10 inches in size.

Personal letters and social notes are commonly written by hand on note paper—a four-page sheet to be folded once horizontally for insertion in a matching envelope; or on club paper—a sheet about 7¼ × 11 inches, to be folded twice horizontally to fit a matching envelope 3¾ × 7½ inches. Both sides of the sheets may be used.

34a

Business letters should follow prescribed usage with respect to the six essential parts:

(1) Heading.
(2) Inside address.
(3) Salutation (or greeting).
(4) Body of the letter.
(5) Complimentary close.
(6) Signature.

MODEL BUSINESS LETTER

(1) {
1288 Catawba Street
Columbia 2, Missouri
May 3, 1961

(2) {
Mr. J. W. Rice
Editor of the Rushville <u>News</u>
122 East Market Street
Rushville, Missouri

(3) Dear Mr. Rice:

(4) {

Mr. Erskine Freeman, of your City Room, has mentioned to me your regular practice of employing two student reporters every summer. I am now majoring in journalism at the University of Missouri, and I should like, therefore, to apply for one of those positions for this next summer.

By the end of this college year I shall have completed three quarters of the university program in journalism. Included in this work are two courses in reporting and one in copyreading. Before I began my college work, I had served four years as sports editor of my high school newspaper, where I learned some of the fundamentals of page make-up. Last year I was awarded the Missouri Press Association Scholarship for journalism.

I have permission to refer you to my employer of the last three summers:

> Mr. George Armour
> Armour Drug Store
> Rushville, Missouri

and to the professors under whom I have taken courses in journalism:

> Dr. James D. Turner
> Professor of Journalism
> University of Missouri
> Columbia, Missouri

> Dr. John M. Cain
> Assistant Professor Journalism
> University of Missouri
> Columbia, Missouri

I shall be in Rushville after June 6 and should appreciate an opportunity to call at your office for an interview at your convenience.

(5) Very truly yours,

(6) {
Donald Burke
Donald Burke

(1) The heading must give the full address of the writer and the date of the letter.

The heading is blocked as in the model.

BLOCKED | 860 Fremont Street | [End punctuation is regu-
| Bessemer, Alabama | larly omitted with the
| February 3, 1962 | blocked heading.]

If there is a letterhead (which supplies the address), the date may be written either under the letterhead or flush with the right margin.

(2) The inside address (identical with the address to appear on the envelope) must give the name and the full address of the person to whom the letter is written.

The inside address must be consistent in form with the heading. The inside address is typed flush with the left margin about four spaces lower than the heading.

(3) The salutation (or greeting) should be consistent with the tone of the letter, the first line of the inside address, and the complimentary close.

The salutation is written flush with the left margin two spaces below the inside address and is followed by a colon. The following salutations are used:

FOR MEN	FOR WOMEN
Dear Sir:	Dear Madam:
Dear Mr. Smith:	Dear Mrs. Smith:
Gentlemen:	Ladies:

Note: The masculine salutation is used to address an organization (Gentlemen) or an individual (Dear Sir) whose name the writer does not know.

In some instances a business letter is addressed to a company or a department of a company but marked for the attention of a particular person. In such letters, the "attention line" is placed two lines above the salutation, thus:

Attention Mr. L. W. Jones

Gentlemen:

[Note that no *"of"* is used after *attention.*]

For the proper form of salutation in letters to government officials, ecclesiastical dignitaries, etc., see *Webster's New International Dictionary,* Second Edition, pp. 3012–14; *Webster's Third New International Dictionary,* pp. 51–54; *The American College Dictionary,* Text Edition, p. xxxiii; *Webster's New World Dictionary,* pp. 1717–19.

In salutations and addresses, abbreviations are generally disapproved except for *Mr.* (plural, *Messrs.*), *Mrs.* (plural, *Mmes.*), and *Dr.*

MODEL ADDRESSED ENVELOPE

Donald Burke
1288 Catawba Street
Columbia 2, Missouri

        Mr. J. W. Rice
        Editor of the Rushville <u>News</u>
        122 East Market Street
        Rushville, Missouri

(4) The body of the letter should follow the principles of good writing.

Typewritten business letters are usually single-spaced, with double spacing between paragraphs. All paragraphs

(1) should begin flush with the left-hand margin, as in the model business letter on page 448, or (2) should be indented equally (usually five spaces). The subject matter should be well organized and paragraphed, but the paragraphs will frequently be shorter than in ordinary writing. The style should be clear and direct. Indirect, abbreviated, or outdated phrasing should be avoided.

INDIRECT	Your kind favor . . . Your esteemed favor . . .
BETTER	Your letter . . .
INDIRECT	I beg to inform you that we have . . . I beg to send . . . Permit us to report that we now supply . . . I wish to apply . . .
BETTER	We have . . . I send . . . We now supply . . . I apply . . .
ABBREVIATED	Hope to have . . . Enclose check for six dollars.
BETTER	We hope to have . . . I enclose a check for six dollars.
OUTDATED	Yours of the 5th instant . . . Hoping to receive . . . Wishing you success . . . Trusting you will be pleased . . .
BETTER	Your letter of May 5 . . . We hope to receive . . . We wish you success . . . I trust you will be pleased . . .

Note: If the letter goes over to a second page, the sender's address (whether on letterhead or a typed heading) should not be repeated. The name (surname only) of the recipient, the page number, and the date should be given, arranged either across the top of the page or at the upper left margin, thus:

Mr. Rice   -2-   May 3, 1961

or:

Mr. Rice

Page 2

May 3, 1961

(5) The complimentary close should be consistent with the tone of the letter and with the salutation.

Ordinary business letters addressed to strangers beginning with the usual *Dear Sir,* etc., should close with *Yours truly, Yours very truly,* or *Very truly yours.* Professional letters, or business letters addressed to an individual with such an opening as *Dear Mr. White,* may well close with the more friendly *Yours sincerely, Sincerely yours, Sincerely, Faithfully yours,* or *Cordially yours.*

(6) The signature should be written by hand directly below the complimentary close.

If the writer's name does not appear in the letterhead, it may be typed just below the signature. Ordinarily, neither professional titles nor degrees should be used with the signature, but the writer's official capacity may be indicated:

WRONG   James M. Smith, LL.D.

PERMISSIBLE   James M. Smith
               President

A married woman should sign her own name (*Mary Hughes Black,* not *Mrs. John K. Black*). In business letters her status is indicated by the use of parentheses as follows:

CORRECT   Mary Hughes Black
           (Mrs. John K. Black)

CORRECT   (Mrs.) Mary Hughes Black

34b

Personal letters and informal social notes follow in general the form of business letters.

Friendly letters usually omit the inside address. If it is included, it may be placed either at the beginning flush with the right margin or at the end of the letter flush with the left margin.

The salutation is usually followed by a comma instead of the more formal colon. As in the business letter, the salutation should be in keeping with the complimentary close and with the tone of the letter. A letter beginning with *Dear Mr. Brown* may close with *Sincerely yours, Yours sincerely,* or *Cordially yours.* A more familiar salutation and complimentary close may be justified by the intimacy of the correspondents.

The body of the letter will vary greatly with the occasion and with the personality of the writer. An easy, informal style is best.

34c

Formal social notes—announcements, invitations, answers to invitations—follow very definite conventions.

For the rare occasions when formal notes are required, engraving or handwriting (not typing) is the rule. Formal notes are always written in the third person. They have no inside address, no salutation, no complimentary close, and no signature. The writer's street address and the month and the date may be placed below at the left. Every word (except the street number and the abbreviations *Mr., Mrs.,* and *Dr.*) is spelled out in full. Acceptances and regrets follow the form of the invitation closely, repeating the hour and the date to insure understanding. The verb used in the reply is always in the present tense.

EXERCISES ON LETTERS

▶ EXERCISE 1   Write the following business letters:

1. Request the circulation manager of your newspaper to send your paper to a new address.
2. Ask the manager of a New York hotel to reserve a room for you.
3. Call the attention of your representative in the city government to some needed repairs in a street near your home.
4. Apply for a position that you are competent to fill. Be sure to include the following: (a) a brief description of the job desired—be specific; (b) your qualifications, including age, schooling, and experience; (c) at least three references—people who know you well and are able to evaluate your ability; (d) a request for an interview. See the model business letter on page 448.
5. Explain to your employer why you must resign your position at the end of the year.
6. Recommend to your employer (to fill the position you must resign) a young man or woman with whom you have worked.
7. Request permission of a former employer to use his name as a reference in applying for a new position.

▶ EXERCISE 2   Write the following personal letters:

1. Invite a friend to spend a weekend in your home.
2. Accept an invitation to spend a weekend with a friend.
3. Answer a friend's inquiry about the course in dramatics (or chemical engineering, astronomy, political science, etc.) in your college.
4. Congratulate a friend in another college on his election to some class office (or on any other honor).
5. Introduce a friend to one of your former classmates who lives in a distant city.

Grammatical Terms

35

Consult the following list as needed for explanations of grammatical terms.

Absolute phrase. A phrase that is grammatically independent but closely related in meaning to the rest of the sentence. A rather formal construction not often found in informal writing. A **nominative absolute** consists of a noun or a pronoun followed by a participle.

> *The game having ended,* the crowd went home.

See also **12d(3)**.

Abstract noun. See **Noun**.

Active voice. See **Voice**.

Adjective. A part of speech used to modify (*i.e.*, describe or limit) a noun or noun substitute.

> *Descriptive adjectives:*
> *blue* sky, *good* will, *American* citizen, *waving* flag, *elaborate* preparations
>
> *Limiting adjectives:*
> *my* book, *its* nest, *his* car, *their* homes (possessive)
> *this* idea, *that* one, *these* men, *those* nets (demonstrative)
> *Whose* cap? *Which* one? *What* dress? (interrogative)
> the boy *whose* dog had died (relative)
> *some* money, *more* effort, *several* others, *many* freshmen (indefinite)
> *one* pear, *three* plums, *first* robin, *third* base, *twentieth* anniversary (numerical)

See also Section **4, Adjectives and Adverbs.**

Adjective clause. A subordinate clause used as an adjective.

The man *who is honest* will succeed.

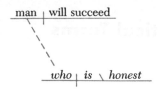

[The clause, equivalent to the adjective *honest,* modifies the noun *man.*]

Adverb. A part of speech used to modify a word (or word group) other than a noun or pronoun. An adverb may qualify or limit a verb, an adjective, another adverb, or even a whole clause. An adverb often indicates time ("are *now* going"), place ("stayed *there*"), manner ("acting *quickly*"), or degree ("*very* eager").

Stand *here.* [*Here* modifies the verb *stand.*]
Stand beside the *very* old clock. [*Very* modifies the adjective *old.*]
Stand *very* quietly. [*Very* modifies the adverb *quietly,* which modifies the verb *stand.*]
Certainly you may be seated. [*Certainly* modifies the main clause.]

    See also Section **4, Adjectives and Adverbs.**

Adverb clause. A subordinate clause used as an adverb.

    I shall leave the house *after she comes.*

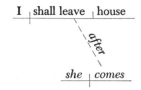

[The adverb clause *after she comes* modifies the verb *shall leave* and indicates time. Adverb clauses may also indicate place, manner, cause, purpose, condition, concession, comparison, or result.]

Agreement. The correspondence in form of one word with another (for example, a verb with its subject or a pronoun with its antecedent) to indicate person and number. See Section **6**, **Agreement.**

Antecedent. The name given to a word or group of words to which a pronoun refers.

> This is the *man who* came to the house. [*Man* is the antecedent of the relative pronoun *who*.]
>
> When *John* and *Mary* came, *they* told us the facts in the case. [*John* and *Mary* are the antecedents of the personal pronoun *they*.]

Appositive. A noun or noun substitute set beside another noun or noun substitute and identifying or explaining it.

> Dr. Smith, our *dentist,* is visiting England, his native *country.* [*Dentist* is in apposition with *Dr. Smith,* and *country* is in apposition with *England.*] See also **12d(2).**

Article. The definite article *the* and the indefinite articles *a* and *an* are usually classed as adjectives. They indicate that a noun or noun substitute is to follow.

Auxiliary. A word that is used to form various tenses of verbs. *Have, may, can, be, shall, will, must, should,* and *do* are common auxiliaries.

> I *shall* go.
> He *was* sent away.
> He *has been* promoted.

See also Section **7.**

Case. The inflectional form of a noun (*man's*) or pronoun (*he, his, him*) to show such relations as subject (subjective or nominative case—*he*), possession (possessive case—*man's, his*), or object (objective case—*him*). See also **Inflection** and Section **5, Case.**

Clause. A group of words that contains a verb and its subject and is used as a part of a sentence. A clause may be main (independent, principal) or subordinate (dependent).

> (1) A main (independent, principal) clause can stand by itself as a simple sentence.
>
> *The moon rose* and *the stars came out.* [Two main clauses, either of which can stand by itself as a simple sentence]
>
> (2) A subordinate (dependent) clause cannot stand alone. It is used as a noun, an adjective, or an adverb.

That he will run for office is doubtful. [Noun clause: a subordinate clause used as subject of the sentence]

Collective noun. See **Noun.**

Colloquial. Appropriate for conversation and informal writing rather than for formal writing.

Common noun. See **Noun.**

Comparison. The change in the form of an adjective or adverb to indicate degrees of superiority in quality, quantity, or manner. There are three degrees: positive, comparative, and superlative.

EXAMPLES	*Positive*	*Comparative*	*Superlative*
	good	better	best
	high	higher	highest
	quickly	more quickly	most quickly

See also **Inflection.**

Complement. A word or words used to complete the sense of the verb, the subject, or the object. The complement may be an object, a predicate noun, or a predicate adjective.

OBJECTS

John gave the *boy* a *book*. [*Book* is the direct object; *boy* is the indirect object.]

PREDICATE NOUNS

Samuel was a good *child*. [The predicate noun *child*, referring to the subject *Samuel*, is also called the **predicate complement**, the **subjective complement**, or the **predicate nominative**.]

He called the man a *hero*. [*Man* is the direct object. The noun *hero*, referring to *man*, is called the **objective complement** or the **predicate objective**.]

PREDICATE ADJECTIVES

The boy is *obedient*. [The predicate adjective *obedient*, referring to the subject *boy*, is also called the **subjective complement** or the **predicate complement**.]

Jack colored the egg *blue*. [*Egg* is the direct object. The predicate adjective *blue*, referring to *egg*, is also called the **objective complement** or the **predicate objective**.]

Complete predicate. See **Predicate.**

Complete subject. See **Subject.**

Complex sentence. See **Sentence**.

Compound sentence. See **Sentence**.

Compound-complex sentence. See **Sentence**.

Concrete noun. See **Noun**.

Conjugation. A grouping of verb forms to indicate tense, voice, mood, number, and person. See the conjugation of the irregular verb *to see* in Section **7**. See also **Inflection**.

Conjunction. A part of speech (often called a function word) used to connect words, phrases, or clauses. There are two kinds, co-ordinating conjunctions and subordinating conjunctions.

> (1) **Co-ordinating conjunctions** connect words, phrases, and clauses of equal rank: *and, but, or, nor, for,* and sometimes *so* and *yet*.

> (2) **Subordinating conjunctions** connect subordinate clauses with main clauses: *if, although, since, in order that, as, because, unless, after, before, until, when, whenever, where, while, wherever,* etc.

Conjunctive adverb. An adverb which can also be used to connect or relate main clauses: *however, therefore, nevertheless, hence, then, besides, moreover, thus, otherwise, consequently, accordingly,* etc.

Construction. See **Syntax**.

Co-ordinate, co-ordinating. Of equal rank. For example, two nouns, two infinitives, or two main clauses.

Copula (Copulative verb). See **Linking verb**.

Declension. See **Inflection**.

Demonstrative adjective. See **Adjective**.

Demonstrative pronoun. See **Pronoun**.

Dependent clause See **Clause**.

Descriptive adjective. See **Adjective**.

Diagraming. An arrangement of words on lines to show relationships within the sentence. Various forms are used. Any form is serviceable if it helps the student to understand the sentence. A diagram is only a means to an end, not an end in itself. One form of diagraming in common use is illustrated on page 460.

The very feeble woman carefully placed the cakes on the shelf

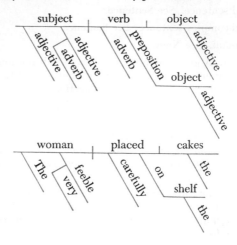

To decide was difficult.

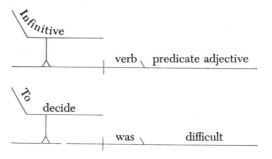

See other diagrams under **Adjective clause, Adverb clause, Noun clause, Sentence,** and especially in Section **1, Sentence Sense.**

Direct address (Nominative of address, vocative). A noun or pronoun used parenthetically to direct a speech to a definite person

I hope, *Mary,* that you will go. *Mary,* close the door.

Direct object. See **Object.**

Direct quotation. The exact oral or written words of others.

> *Direct quotation:* John asked, "Why don't you join us, Martha?"

> *Indirect quotation:* John asked Martha why she didn't join the group.

See also **16a.**

Ellipsis (Elliptical expression). An expression in which words are omitted but which is nonetheless clear because the omitted words can be readily supplied.

> Mary is prettier than Helen (is pretty).
> Whenever (it is) possible, you should take exercise.

For the ellipsis mark in quoted passages, see **17a(3).**

Expletive. *It* or *there* used merely as an introductory word or filler.

> *It* is true that he is not coming.
> *There* were few men present.

Finite verb. A verb or verb form that makes a complete assertion and may thus serve as a predicate. "The sun *rose*." "The sun *is rising.*" Infinitives, participles, and gerunds are **verbals,** not finite verbs.

Form change. See **Inflection.**

Gerund. See **Verbals.**

Gerund phrase. See **Phrase.**

Idiom. An expression in good use that is peculiar to a language. (Idioms sometimes violate established rules of grammar, but are nevertheless sanctioned by usage.)

> I have known him for *many a year.*
> I am *not myself* today.

Imperative. See **Mood.**

Indefinite pronoun. See **Pronoun.**

Independent clause (Main clause, principal clause). See **Clause.**

Independent element. Any word or group of words that has no grammatical connection with the rest of the sentence.

> DIRECT ADDRESS   I hope, *William,* that you can go.
> INTERPOLATION   The whole family, *we hope,* will come.

ABSOLUTE EXPRESSION *Darkness having come,* he slipped away.

INTERJECTION *Ah,* this is the sport I enjoy.

Indicative. See **Mood.**

Indirect object. See **Object.**

Indirect quotation. See **Direct quotation.**

Infinitive. See **Verbals.**

Infinitive phrase. See **Phrase.**

Inflection. A change in the form of a word to show a change in meaning or in grammatical relationship to some other word or group of words. The inflection of nouns and pronouns is called **declension;** the inflection of verbs, **conjugation;** that of adjectives and adverbs, **comparison.**

> **Inflections of verbs** (indicating tense, person, mood)
> look, looking, looks, looked
> drink, drinking, drinks, drank, drunk
> know, knowing, knows, knew, known
> be, being, am, is, are, was, were, been

> **Inflections of nouns** (indicating number, case)
> dog, dogs; dog's, dogs'
> child, children; child's, children's

> **Inflections of pronouns** (indicating case, person, number)
> I, me, my, mine   we, us, our, ours
> who, whom, whose   someone, someone's
> *This* is old. *These* are old. *That* is older than *those.*

> **Inflections of modifiers** (indicating comparison, number)
> fast, faster, fastest   bad, worse, worst
> attractive, more attractive, most attractive
> *this* letter, *these* letters, *that* letter, *those* letters

Intensive pronoun. See **Pronoun.**

Interjection. A part of speech expressing emotion and having no grammatical relation with other words in the sentence.

> *Oh,* I can hardly believe it.
> *Whew!* That was a narrow escape.

Interrogative pronoun. See **Pronoun.**

Intransitive. See **Verb.**

Irregular verb. See **Strong verb.**

Limiting adjective. See **Adjective.**

Linking verb. A verb used to express the relationship between the subject and the predicate noun or predicate adjective. The chief linking verbs are *be, become, seem, appear,* and verbs pertaining to the senses.

He *is* brave.   I *feel* bad.   Fred *became* a lawyer.

Main clause (Independent clause, principal clause). See **Clause.**

Modifier. Any word or group of words that describes or qualifies another word or group of words. See **Modify.**

Modify. To describe or qualify the meaning of a word or group of words.

A very old man hobbled *slowly along the road.* [A and *old* modify *man; very* modifies *old; slowly* and *along the road* modify *hobbled;* the modifies *road.*]

See also **Inflection** and Sections **1d** and **4.**

Mood (Mode). The form of the verb that is used to indicate the manner in which the action or state is conceived. English has indicative, imperative, and subjunctive moods. See Section **7.**

The **indicative mood** states a fact or asks a question.

You *have* a good mind.   *Have* you any ideas?
Mother *is* here.   *Is* Mother here?

The **imperative mood** gives a command, makes a request, or gives directions.

Be careful.   *Watch* your step, please.
Take the next street on the right.

The **subjunctive mood** expresses a doubt, a condition contrary to fact, a wish or regret, a concession, a supposition.

I wish that Mother *were* here.
If I *had* my way, you would not go.

Nominative. Equivalent to **subjective.** See **Case.**

Nominative absolute. See **Absolute phrase.**

Nominative of address. See **Direct address.**

Nonrestrictive modifier. A nonessential modifier. A parenthetical phrase or clause which does not identify the person or thing modified. See **12d.**

The airplane, *now being manufactured in large numbers,* is of immense commercial value. [Phrase]

The airplane, *which is now being manufactured in large numbers,* is of immense commercial value. [Clause]

See also **Restrictive modifier.**

Noun. A part of speech (the name of a person, place, thing, quality, or action: *Mary, America, apples, courage, departure*) that usually changes form to make the possessive case and the plural, as in *man, man's, men.* See also **Inflection.**

Nouns are used as:

(1) SUBJECTS OF VERBS: The *dog* barked.

(2) OBJECTS OF VERBS, VERBALS, OR PREPOSITIONS: He opened the *door* to let the *dog* into the *house.*

(3) PREDICATE NOUNS: She was his *secretary.*

(4) APPOSITIVES: Mr. Brown, our *neighbor,* is sick.

(5) NOMINATIVES OF ADDRESS: *Mary,* will you help us?

(6) PREDICATE OBJECTIVES (OBJECTIVE COMPLEMENTS): He called the man a *traitor.*

Nouns are classified as:

(1) COMMON or PROPER.

A **common noun** is the name applied to any one of a class of persons, places, or things: *man, woman, city, state, chair, bed.*

A **proper noun** is the name applied to a specific individual, place, or thing: *Henry Ford, Jane Addams, New Orleans, Texas,* the *Parthenon,* the *Washington Monument.*

(2) COLLECTIVE.

A **collective noun** is a name applied to a group: *band, flock, jury, army.* See **6a(7)** and **6b(3).**

(3) CONCRETE or ABSTRACT.

A **concrete noun** names something that can be perceived by one or more of the senses: *water, trees, man, river.*

An **abstract noun** names a quality or general idea: *love, ambition, hate, pity.*

Noun clause. A subordinate clause used as a noun. It may be used as subject, direct object, appositive, predicate nominative, object of a preposition.

Whoever comes will be welcome. [Subject]

I hope *that he will recover.* [Object of the verb]

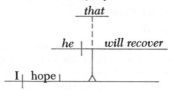

The hope *that he might win* upheld him. [Appositive]
This is *what I asked for.* [Predicate nominative]
I shall spend the money for *whatever seems best.* [Object of the preposition *for*]

Noun substitute. A pronoun or any group of words (especially a gerund phrase, an infinitive phrase, or a noun clause) functioning as a noun. See also **Substantive.**

Number. The change in the form of a word (*e.g.*, noun, pronoun, etc.) to designate one (*singular*) or more than one (*plural*). See also **Inflection** and Section **6.**

Object. A noun or pronoun (or a phrase or clause used as a noun) that follows and completes the meaning of a transitive verb or follows a preposition.

Direct object. Any noun (or its equivalent) that answers the question *What?* or *Whom?* after a transitive verb. Direct objects ordinarily receive, or in some way are affected by, the action of the verb.

He raked *leaves.* [Noun]
He knows *what we need.* [Noun clause]

Indirect object. Any noun (or its equivalent) that is indirectly affected by the action of the verb and that states to whom or for whom something is done.

He gave *me* an apple. [*Apple* is the direct object, *me* the indirect object, of the verb *gave.* It is usually possible to substitute for the indirect object a prepositional phrase with *to* or *for.*]

Object of a preposition. Any noun (or its equivalent) following a preposition. See **Preposition.**

He walked into the house. [*House* is the object of the preposition *into.*]

Objective complement. See **Complement.**

Participial phrase. See **Phrase.**

Participle. See **Verbals.**

Parts of speech. The eight classes into which most grammarians group words according to their form changes and/or their uses in the sentence: *verb, noun, pronoun, adjective, adverb, conjunction, preposition,* and *interjection.* Each of these is discussed separately in this section. It is important to note that *part of speech* is determined by function. The same word is often used as several different parts of speech. See **1c.**

Passive voice. See **Voice.**

Person. Changes in the form of verbs and pronouns which indicate whether a person is speaking (first person), is spoken to (second person), or is spoken about (third person).

FIRST PERSON   *I* see the boy.
SECOND PERSON   Can *you* see the boy?
THIRD PERSON   *He* sees the boy.

Personal pronoun. See **Pronoun.**

Phrase. A group of related words which lacks subject and verb and is used as a single part of speech.

   Prepositional phrase:
     The man *with red hair* is my brother. [Adjective]
     My brother lives *in the city.* [Adverb]

   Participial phrase:
     The door *leading to the porch* is open. [Adjective]

   Gerund phrase:
     Reckless driving along the highways is responsible for many wrecks. [Noun substitute]

   Infinitive phrase:
     To err is human. [Noun substitute]

   Verb phrase:
     He *has been employed* for a year. [Verb]

   See also **Verb, Verbals,** and **1c** and **1d.**

Predicate. The part of the sentence comprising what is said about the subject. The **complete predicate** consists of the verb (the **simple predicate**) along with its complements and modifiers.

He *runs* through the house. [*Runs* is the simple predicate; *runs through the house* is the complete predicate.]

Predicate adjective, predicate complement, predicate nominative, predicate noun, predicate objective. See **Complement.**

Preposition. A part of speech (often called a function word) that is used to show the relation of a noun or noun-equivalent to some other word in the sentence.

The telephone is *in* the hall. [The preposition *in* shows the relationship of the noun *hall* to the verb *is.*]

Across, after, at, before, between, by, for, from, in, of, on, over, to, under, with, up, and *near* are commonly used prepositions.

See also **1c.**

Prepositional phrase. See **Phrase.**

Principal clause (Main clause, independent clause). See **Clause.**

Principal parts. The forms of any verb from which the various tenses are derived: (1) present stem (infinitive), (2) past tense, and (3) past participle.

EXAMPLES	see	saw	seen
	take	took	taken
	love	loved	loved

See also Section **7.**

Progressive verb. A form of the verb (ending in -*ing* and following a part of the auxiliary *be*) used to express continuous action or state of being.

Sally *was singing* a cowboy ballad.
I *have been playing* tennis all afternoon.

See also Section **7.**

Pronoun. A part of speech used instead of a noun.

Personal pronouns: *I, you, he, she,* etc. See the declension under Section **5, Case.**

Interrogative pronouns: *who, which, what*
Who is he?

Relative pronouns: *who, which, that*
He *who* steals my purse steals trash.

Demonstrative pronouns: *this, that, these, those*
This is more useful than *that.*

Indefinite pronouns: *each, either, any, anyone, some, someone, one, no one, few, all, everyone,* etc.

Reciprocal pronouns: *each other, one another.*

Reflexive pronouns: *myself, yourself, himself,* etc.
  I blamed *myself.*

Intensive pronouns: *myself, yourself, himself,* etc.
  I *myself* will go.

See also **Inflection.**

Proper adjective. An adjective formed from a proper noun, as *Spanish* from *Spain.*

Proper noun. See **Noun.**

Quotation. See **Direct quotation.**

Reciprocal pronoun. See **Pronoun.**

Reflexive pronoun. See **Pronoun.**

Regular verb. See **Weak verb.**

Relative pronoun. See **Pronoun.**

Restrictive modifier. An essential modifier. A phrase or clause which identifies the word modified and which therefore cannot be omitted without changing the essential meaning of the sentence.

  Any girl *who talks incessantly* is a bore.

See also **Nonrestrictive modifier.**

Sentence. A unit of expression that may stand alone. A grammatically complete sentence contains at least a verb (predicate) and its subject (one or the other sometimes implied), with or without modifiers. (For the incomplete sentence see pages 34–35.) Sentences are classified structurally as (1) simple, (2) compound, (3) complex, or (4) compound-complex.

(1) **Simple sentence.** A sentence containing but one main clause and no subordinate clauses.

Five basic patterns of the simple sentence:

  1. SUBJECT—VERB.
     Birds are singing happily.
     The *horses were led* to the water
  2. SUBJECT—VERB—DIRECT OBJECT.
     I forgot my *assignment.*

3. SUBJECT—VERB—INDIRECT OBJECT—DIRECT OBJECT.
   She mailed me a birthday *gift.*
4. SUBJECT—LINKING VERB—PREDICATE ADJECTIVE.
   Recently *she appears* very *unhappy.*
5. SUBJECT—LINKING VERB—PREDICATE NOUN.
   She may be a famous *actress* someday.

Simple sentences may have compound subjects, verbs, objects, etc.

Birds and bats swoop and fly.

(2) **Compound sentence.** A sentence containing two or more main clauses but no subordinate clauses.

The moon rose and the stars twinkled.

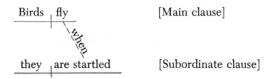

(3) **Complex sentence.** A sentence containing one main clause and one or more subordinate clauses.

Birds fly when they are startled.

(4) **Compound-complex sentence.** A sentence containing two or more main clauses and one or more subordinate clauses.

Engines roared overhead and a bomb fell where we had stood.

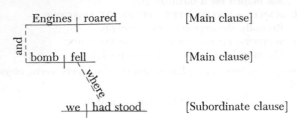

Engines | roared	[Main clause]
bomb | fell	[Main clause]
we | had stood	[Subordinate clause]

Simple predicate. See **Predicate.**

Simple sentence. See **Sentence.**

Simple subject. See **Subject.**

Strong verb (Irregular verb). A verb that forms its principal parts in various ways *other than* by the addition of *-ed, -d,* or *-t.* See also **Inflection** and Section **7.**

EXAMPLES
Vowel changes: swim, swam, swum
Addition of -en: beat, beat, beaten
No change: set, set, set

Subject. The person or thing (in a sentence or a clause) about which an assertion is made. The subject and the words associated with it make up the **complete subject.**

The *dog* at the front of the house barked at the car. [*Dog* is the **simple subject;** *the dog at the front of the house* is the complete subject.]

Subjective. See **Case.**

Subjective complement. See **Complement.**

Subjunctive. See **Mood.**

Subordinate clause. A dependent clause. See **Clause.**

Substantive. Any word or group of words used as a noun. Substantives may be nouns, pronouns, phrases (especially gerund or infinitive phrases), or noun clauses.

Syntax (Construction). Sentence structure. The grammatical functions of words, phrases, clauses.

Tense. Change in the form of the verb to indicate time. See **Inflection** and Section 7.

Transitive. See **Verb.**

Verb. A part of speech that is used to assert action or being and that changes form to indicate time, person, mood. See **Inflection** and Section 7.

> **Transitive verb.** A verb either passive in form (see **Voice**) or with a direct object to complete its meaning. See **Object.**
>
> The boy *sold* his bicycle.
>
> **Intransitive verb.** A verb not having an object and not passive in form. See **Voice.**
>
> I *was* in New York last Christmas.
> She *has been waiting* patiently for hours.

Verb phrase. See **Phrase.**

Verbals. Words derived from verbs but used as nouns or adjectives (or sometimes as adverbs). The three verbals are gerunds, participles, infinitives.

> The **gerund** is used only as a noun and always ends in *-ing.* It may be used as subject ("*Swimming* is fun"), as object of a verb ("I enjoy *swimming*"), as object of a preposition ("By *swimming* he reached shore"), as a predicate noun ("My chief recreation is *swimming*"), or as an appositive ("My chief recreation, *swimming,* is healthful"). The gerund, like a noun, may be modified by an adjective: "*Skillful* swimming saved his life." The gerund shows its verbal origin by its ability to take an object ("Swimming a choppy *stream* can be dangerous") or to be modified by an adverb ("By swimming *rapidly,* he escaped").

> The **participle** is used only as an adjective. Since the present participle ends in *-ing,* it can be distinguished from the gerund only by its use in the sentence.
>
> *Swimming* is fun. [Gerund—a noun, subject of the verb *is*]
> A *swimming* suit is needed. [Participle—an adjective modifying the noun *suit*]

Participles: the *rising* sun, a *concealed* weapon, a *lost* cause, a *broken* bone, a bone *broken* by a fall, a *worn* coat, a coat *worn* by a beggar. [Note the varying endings of the past participle— *-ed, -t, -en*—and the internal shift in *worn* (from *wear*).]

The **infinitive** is used chiefly as a noun, less frequently as an adjective or an adverb. It is made up of *to* plus a verb, but after certain verbs this *to* may be omitted: "He helped (*to*) *make* the kite." "He dared not (*to*) *go* away."

USED AS A NOUN

To walk was a pleasure. [Subject]

He began *to open the box*. [Object of verb]

Her wish was *to see him leave*. [Predicate noun]

I will do anything except (*to*) *wash* dishes. [Object of preposition]

USED AS AN ADJECTIVE

I have work *to do*. [*To do* modifies the noun *work*.]

USED AS AN ADVERB

He enlisted *to become an aviator*. [The infinitive modifies the verb *enlisted*.]

The infinitive shows its verbal origin by its ability to take a subject ("I asked *him* to go"), to take an object ("I wanted to pay *him*"), or to be modified by an adverb ("I asked him to drive *slowly*"). Note that the subject of the infinitive is in the objective case.

Vocative. See **Direct address.**

Voice. Distinction in the form of a verb to indicate whether the subject acts (**active voice**) or is acted upon (**passive voice**). See the conjugation of the verb on pp. 75–77.

Weak verb (Regular verb). Any verb that forms its principal parts by adding *-ed*, *-d*, or *-t* to the infinitive: *love, loved, loved; sweep, swept, swept.*

Index

[Numbers in **boldface** refer to rules; other numbers refer to pages. A colon is used after each boldface number to indicate that the following pages refer to the rule or the part of the rule concerned. An *ex* indicates that appropriate drill exercises are included. An *n* indicates reference to a footnote.]

a

A, an, **19i**: 211

A half a, for *a half*, **19i**: 220

Abbreviations, **11**: 110–113 *ex*
capitalization of, **9a**: 97–99
Christian names, **11e**: 111
contractions, with apostrophe, **15c**: 149
from Latin, in italics, 415
in footnotes, 112, 415–16
misused in letters, 451
names of organizations, 111
names of states, months, days of week, **11b**: 111
parts of proper names, **11c**: 111
period after, **17a**: 158–59
titles, **11a**: 110
verified in dictionary, 112
volume, chapter, page, **11d**: 111
when permissible, 112
with dates or numerals, 112

Absolute phrase
commas with, **12d**: 131
defined, 455

Abstract and general words, **20a**: 236–38 *ex*

Abstract noun, defined, 464

Accent, shown in the dictionary, 190

Accept, except, **19i**: 211

Accordingly, as a conjunctive adverb, 140

Accusative case. *See* Objective case.

Acknowledgment of borrowed material, in footnotes, 410

Active voice
defined, 472
for emphasis, **29d**: 309–10 *ex*

Ad, for *advertisement*, **19i**: 212

Address of a letter, 447–50
consistency, 449
inside address, 449
model addressed envelope, 450
one of six essential parts, 449
punctuation of, 449
shown in model letter, 448

Adjective clause
defined, 19, 455–56
diagramed, 456
position of, for coherence, **25a**: 280
restrictive or nonrestrictive, punctuation of, **12d**: 125–28 *ex*

Adjectives, **4**: 46–52 *ex*
adverbs identical with, 47
after linking verbs, **4b**: 48–49 *ex*
among parts of speech, 9
comparative form, **4c**: 49–50
co-ordinate or in series, commas with, **12c**: 122–24 *ex*
defined, 46, 455
descriptive, 455
diagramed, 10, 47, 460

b

e

f

g

Semicolon (*Cont.*)
position of, with quotation marks, **16e:** 155–56 *ex*
to set off elements containing commas, **14b:** 141
used only between co-ordinate parts, **14c:** 142
with conjunctive adverbs, **14a:** 140
with co-ordinating conjunctions, **14a:** 141
Sensory verbs, adjectives after, **4b:** 48–49 *ex*
Sentence, defined, 22, 468
Sentence coherence. *See* Coherence in the sentence.
Sentence completeness, test for, 29–30
Sentence fragment, **2:** 28–36 *ex*
Sentence outline, **32c:** 369–70
Sentence patterns, for parts of the simple sentence
adjective, 48, 49
adverb, 49
auxiliary (linking) verb, 7, 11, 48, 58, 316, 469
complement, 58, 316
expletive, 7
object (direct), 7, 49, 316, 468, 469
object (indirect), 7, 469
predicate adjective, 11, 469
predicate noun, 469
subject, 7, 11, 48, 49, 58, 315, 316, 468, 469
verb, 7, 49, 315, 316, 468, 469
Sentence patterns, for punctuation
comma, 20, 21, 38, 117, 120, 121, 140
semicolon, 38, 139, 140
Sentence patterns, for variety, 315–16
Sentence patterns, of complex sentences, 20, 21, 120, 121
Sentence patterns, of compound sentences
with conjunctive adverb, 140
with co-ordinating conjunction, 38, 117
with transitional phrase, 140

without connective, 139
"Sentence sense," **1:** 1–27 *ex*
Sentence unity. *See* Unity in the sentence.
Sentences
and sentences, **24b:** 274–75 *ex*
balanced, for emphasis, **29g:** 311 *ex*
beginnings of, for variety, **30b:** 315–17 *ex*
capitalization of, **9e:** 101–02 *ex*
choppy, **24a:** 272–73 *ex*
classified and defined, 22–23, 468–69
climax in, for emphasis, **29c:** 308–09 *ex*
coherence between, **31b:** 328–37 *ex*
coherence in, **25:** 278–85 *ex*
comma splice or fused sentence, **3:** 37–45 *ex*
completeness, test for, 29–30
complex
defined, 23, 469
diagramed, 469
compound
defined, 22, 469
diagramed, 469
compound-complex, defined and diagramed, 23, 469–70
declarative, to be varied, **30e:** 318
diagramed, 7, 469–70
effective, **23–30:** 260–319 *ex*
elliptical, not fragments, 34
emphasis in, **29:** 305–13 *ex*
exclamatory, for variety, **30e:** 318
fragmentary (incomplete), **2:** 28–36 *ex*
fused, or run-together, **3:** 37–45 *ex*
grammar of, **1:** 1–27 *ex*
imperative, for variety, **30e:** 318
incomplete, for special effects, **2:** 34–35
interrogative, for variety, **30e:** 318
length of, for variety, **30a:** 315
logic in, **23d:** 266–70 *ex*
loose and periodic, **29b:** 307–08 *ex*
misplaced parts, **25a:** 278–81 *ex*
mixed and obscure, 264–66 *ex*

3
D 4
E 5
F 6
G 7
H 8
I 9
J 0
K 1